LETTS GUIDE TO
CACTI
of the
WORLD
BRIAN M. LAMB

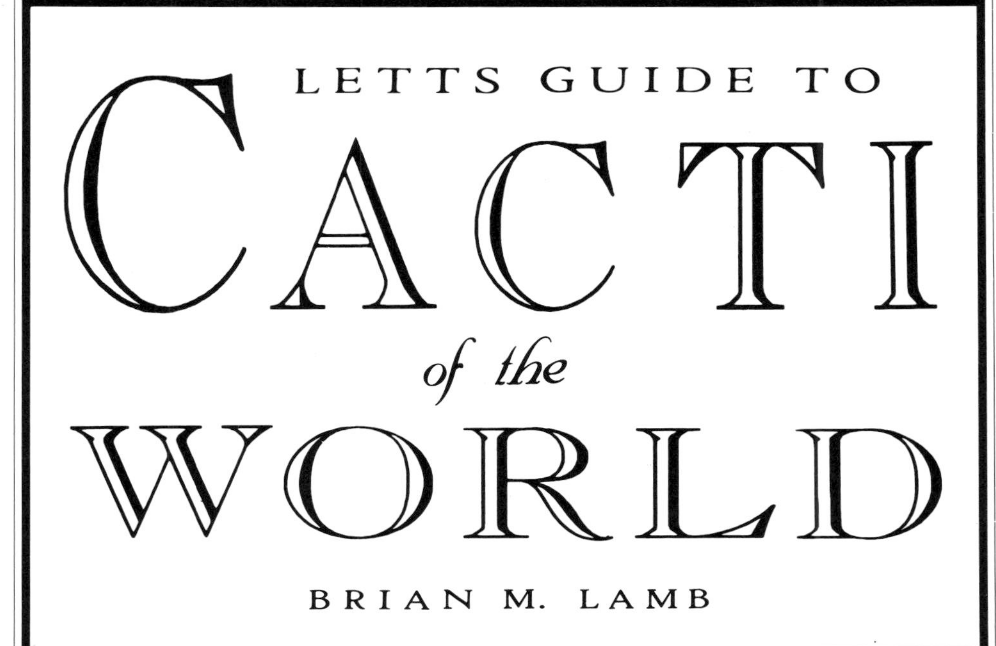
LETTS GUIDE TO
CACTI
of the
WORLD
BRIAN M. LAMB

CHARLES LETTS
Letts
FOUNDED 1796

First published in the United Kingdom in 1991
by Charles Letts & Co Ltd
Diary House, Borough Road,
London SE1 1DW
England

by arrangement with CollinsAngus&Robertson
Publishers Pty Limited (ACN 009 913 517)
A division of HarperCollinsPublishers
Unit 4, Eden Park Industrial Estate
31 Waterloo Road
North Ryde
New South Wales 2113
Australia

British Library Cataloguing in Publication Data:
Lamb, Brian
Letts guide to cacti of the world.
1. Cacti. Cultivation
I. Title
63593347

ISBN 1-85238-121-3

'Letts' is a registered trademark of Charles Letts (Scotland) Ltd

Cover photograph: Andre Martin
Typeset in Garamond Light by Midland Typesetters, Australia
Printed in Hong Kong

Contents

ACKNOWLEDGMENTS

I would like to thank the following friends who have assisted me in different ways over a period of many years.

Alan & Betty Blackburn (Tucṣon, Arizona)
John & Beryl Donald (Worthing, England)
Ed & Betty Gay (Tarzana, California)
Don & Eloise Johnson (Corpus Christi, Texas)
Gordon Rowley (Reading, England)
Roy & Ina White (London, England)

I would also like to express my gratitude to fellow members of the International Organisation of Succulents, directors of botanical gardens and superintendents and rangers of national parks. In particular, I would like to thank the rangers at Saguaro National Monument, Organ Pipe Cactus National Monument and Big Bird National Park, in the United States.

My special thanks to Professor Wilhelm Barthlott, Bonn, Germany, and Professor Werner Rauh, Heidelberg, Germany, for their assistance over many years.

Finally, I thank my wife Sally for coping with me and my large collection of plants for nearly 30 years and for doing hours of proofreading.

PHOTOGRAPHY

The majority of photographs were taken by Brian Lamb in habitat and at 'The Exotic Collection', Worthing, Sussex, England (which was moved with the author to the south of Spain in 1987), using Leicaflex equipment and either Kodachrome or Fujichrome film.

Professor W. Barthlott pages 158, 192, 194 (TR, TL).

PREFACE

Although many books have been written about cacti, most of the cultural information has been for greenhouse or conservatory culture. Few people realise that these plants come from a tremendous environmental range in nature, whereby they can be used for landscaping under equally varied conditions. Cacti come in a wide variety of shapes and sizes, often possessing beautifully coloured flowers that can vary from almost microscopic to as much as 25 cm (10 in) in diameter. This alone attracts enthusiasts to the hobby, but unfortunately they are sometimes told that they do not have available the ideal conditions in which to grow them.

Today, however, it is possible for anyone to grow some of these plants, provided they select the correct ones. Because of their range of conditions in habitat, from jungle to desert or from near the sea to the tops of mountain ranges where they can be covered with snow, there are species available to suit all sorts of artificial habitats. It is possible to control the environment more easily in a greenhouse or conservatory, even to different minimum or maximum temperature levels, degree of atmospheric humidity, and so on. There are, however, cacti that can be grown in gardens in temperate climates where heavy frost and snow occurs, provided sufficient drainage is given. A wide range of species can also be grown indoors, some in sunny situations, others in partial shade. Equipment is available in the form of different types of lighting so that virtually any species could be grown in a cellar, without the need for any natural lighting.

In more tropical parts of the world, people have realised that cacti are ideally suited for landscaping; once established many can be left to their own devices, as they do not need a continuous supply of water for their survival. The house building explosion in many drier parts of the world is in some cases outstripping water supplies, so these plants have come into their own, being far more tolerant of the vagaries of the weather than many other kinds used previously. A cacti garden can easily reduce your water consumption by half.

Although a real interest in collecting these plants started in England more than a century ago, today there can be few countries in the world where there are not collectors. At least ten countries possess societies which regularly publish magazines on a monthly or quarterly basis, and there are numerous other countries where clubs exist, often as a section of a much larger horticultural society. This interest is just a small part of the 'leisure business', which continues to grow as so many more people have time on their hands as a result of fewer hours being worked today.

The illustrations will show you the variation and beauty that exists within this field of plant life. This book will also show you that the majority of species are very easy to grow and propagate, even if your main aim is to use them for decorative purposes indoors, on your patio as tub grown specimens, or for landscaping.

My intention is that this book is not only very informative but also easy to read and well illustrated, so that it suits a wide range of readers, including many who have not yet grown any of these beautiful and fascinating plants.

Rhipsalidopsis rosea

Abbreviations

Lt — Latin

Gk — Greek

fa. — Form/forma: subdivision of a variety, which in taxonomical terms is the smallest degree of differentiation to qualify for a name.

sp. — Species

syn. — Synonym: indicates an older name that applies to the same species.

var. — Variety: subdivision of a species.

X — Natural native hybrid cross: indicates the name given to the resultant plant, or is used to link the names of the two parents.

PRONUNCIATION SYMBOLS

´ — the accentuated pause position

¯ — a longer sounding of the vowel

˘ — a short sounding of the vowel

· — a very short sounding of the vowel

¨ — an exceedingly short sounding of the vowel

There is a prescribed ruling in Latin on where the accent falls. It falls on the next to last syllable, if the accentuation is 'long' and if a word consists of only two syllables. In other cases the accentuation is on the preceding syllable.

Climate Key

CLIMATE	MINIMUM TEMPERATURE	MAXIMUM TEMPERATURE
Tropical	15° C (59° F)	43.5° C (110° F)
Low Elevation (Mediterranean)	5° C (40° F)	35° C (95° F)
Medium Elevation	-5° C (23° F)	38° C (100° F)
High Elevation	-20° C (0° F)	32.5° C (90° F)

This key lists average minimum and maximum temperatures, but it is important to remember that a few cacti are to be found where temperatures can drop much lower — this will be in regions where atmospheric humidity is virtually zero.

It is not uncommon in medium elevation climates that are inland for temperatures in summer to reach 49° C (120° F) or more. Habitats such as these will have an annual rainfall of only 12.5 cm (5 in).

The great majority of cacti are able to cope with extremes of temperature, provided the below freezing temperatures occur when rainfall is very low, or preferably none at all.

Medium Elevation includes up to 1500 m (4700 ft). High Elevation covers above 1500 m (4700 ft).

INTRODUCTION

Generally speaking, people tend to think that if a plant has spines it must be a cactus. There are in fact cacti such as *Astrophytum asterias*, or species of *Lophophora* that possess no spines at all, but they still belong within the family CACTACEAE. Also, there are other succulent plants with spines or thorns but that does not make them a cactus. With the exception of *Pereskia* species, cacti flowers are sessile, often tubular, and the petals form spirally. There is a gradual change usually from petal to sepal, and to scaly bracts. The fruit (berry) is formed from an inferior ovary, which usually has areoles and often spines.

Cacti vary tremendously, ranging from miniatures no larger than a fingernail, such as *Blossfeldia* (page 45), to giant branched trees with swollen succulent stems that can reach 24 m (80 ft) in height, such as *Pachycereus grandis*. The well-known *Carnegiea gigantea* (page 2) from Arizona is equally impressive, but does not grow quite so tall. There are also a few thin stemmed cacti that bear small leaves, for example *Pereskia* and *Pereskiopsis*. The spines which occur on most cacti arise from a felted areole, which is common to all cacti. The variability in the amount of fleshy storage tissue depends on the environment in which they live. Some stems may be covered with a waxy coating, which reflects light and heat and thus reduces the water loss from the plant (that is, transpiration). Some of the *Copiapoa* species from Chile, and the various forms of *Astrophytum myriostigma*, protect themselves from the sun in a very similar manner. The density of the spine covering in many cacti can be such that the body of the plant is virtually obscured, thus transpiration is slowed considerably, as the stomata (the pore from which water is transpired) is well protected from the sun. There are some habitats where rain rarely falls, but mist condenses on the spines and the resulting water drops off to be picked up by the roots near the surface of the soil. In contrast, the very green stemmed clambering cacti, such as the epiphytic kinds from jungle areas, obtain sufficient natural shade and therefore do not need these extreme protective measures.

Many of you will have come across the term 'xerophyte' and cacti, quite correctly, belong under this heading. There are many xerophytes that grow in the same regions as cacti, in the form of small plants, shrubs and trees. These xerophytic plants, over a long period of time, have evolved to cope with the arid conditions. For example, *Selaginella lepidophylla* (pictured with the cactus *Epithelantha bokei*—see page 2) under drought conditions virtually rolls up into a tight rosette. Within 24 hours of rain falling it opens out again. Other desert shrubs and trees have reduced their water loss by having leaves with a very reduced surface area, often needle-like in appearance. In other cases, they have quite normal leaves, however they are produced very rapidly after rain has fallen and with the return of dry

Echinocereus melanocentrus

Pachycereus grandis *A specimen close to a height of 24 m (80 ft) in Mexico.*

Epithelantha bokei *A plant that started life due to the shade given to it as a seedling by* Selaginella lepidophylla *(Resurrection Plant) in Texas.*

Carnegiea gigantea *A young plant in the shade of a Palo Verde tree in Arizona.*

conditions the leaves soon drop off and the plant remains virtually dormant until wetter conditions return. For example, *Pereskias* will also drop their leaves.

Interestingly there are many cacti which owe their survival to other xerophytic trees and shrubs. In the Chihuahuan desert the seeds of a number of the smaller growing cacti may germinate and grow initially in the shade of the *Selaginella* (Resurrection Plant). The Saguaro cactus (*Carnegiea gigantea*) of Arizona invariably starts life beneath the Palo Verde tree. As with the *Selaginella lepidophylla*, the seeds of *Carnegiea gigantea* germinate in the shade and succeed. For their first few years they need the shade protection of the Palo Verde tree. Eventually, the roots of the Saguaro spread out beyond those of the protecting tree and starve it of water, such that it dies. It is not uncommon in Arizona to come across a Saguaro amidst a dead Palo Verde tree, which in time will disintegrate and disappear, leaving this wonderful cactus to perhaps grow to 10 to 13 m (30 to 40 ft). There are many cacti that permanently grow beneath other xerophytic trees and shrubs, or even beneath another much larger growing cactus. The photograph (page 3) of *Melocactus macracanthus* in habitat in Curacao illustrates how one of the globular growing cactus plants may permanently grow in a partially shaded position.

The first cactus came to Europe in the 16th century. It was a plant which is now known as *M. communis*. In 1753, Carl von Linné (Linnaeus) erected the genus *Cactus*, and called the plant *Cactus melocactus*. At the same time some 21 other species were included under *Cactus*. This generic name is no longer used because of the confusion it caused, particularly today when there are so many genera, let alone 2000 or more species, all within the family CACTACEAE. Backeberg in 1962 considered there were over 230 different genera, whereas David Hunt in 1967 reduced it to 84. As

Melocactus macracanthus *A mature plant beneath a xerophytic bush in Curacao.*

Melocactus macracanthus *A mature plant growing amongst grass in Curacao.*

one of 26 IOS members involved with cactus nomenclature at the 1989 inter-Congress meeting in Palermo, Sicily, further adjustments will be made. In the end, we shall possibly recommend that a figure somewhere between the two is acceptable.

Cacti are natives of the New World basically, with species to be found as far north as Alberta in Canada, to as far south as Patagonia in South America. The only exceptions are a few epiphytic species of *Rhipsalis* that occur in East Africa and Madagascar, which were possibly taken there by migrating birds and have evolved still further. In the last 400 years or so, some cacti have escaped from cultivation, and are now a common sight in Australia, South Africa and around the Mediterranean region. The climate has suited them well, perhaps too well in some parts of Australia where certain *Opuntia* species (Prickly Pear) have become a nuisance. To many people, because they are part of the general landscape, they are thought to be native plants.

I have endeavoured in this book to include about two-thirds of the accepted genera, plus a special reference to those other generic names that some or all of the species from a certain genus have been transferred to at varying times. This will help you find the correct species you are looking for. It is very easy to blame the horticultural firm you are buying your plants from for incorrect naming. At the present time the nomenclature of the family CACTACEAE is in a rather confused state. However, with a few exceptions, the generic naming system put forward by Britton and Rose in 1919, in their four volume monograph *Cactacae*, is still the best system to follow as a basis.

As far as common names are concerned, only a very small number of species have one that would be recognised around the world. I have included some common names in connection with the North American species, but even many of these would not be known by cacti enthusiasts in Europe and elsewhere.

Parts of a Cactus

Cacti come in many sizes, from miniatures to giant trees 24 m (80 ft) or so in height. However, with the exception of *Pereskia* and its close relatives, which have normal leaves and spines and a somewhat more basic flower and fruit structure, all the other genera are very similar. These other genera are virtually without leaves in the normal form, instead the photosynthesis process takes place in green fleshy stems. These are usually of a ribbed or tubercled structure (sometimes spirally arranged), usually bearing felted areoles from which the spines (if present) appear. In the case of the epiphytic cacti, which come from humid jungle conditions, the green stems are flat or winged, invariably without spines and sometimes with aerial roots.

It is from the areoles that spines, new branches and flowers appear. There are exceptions, such as *Echinocerei*, whose flower buds burst through the body wall near an areole, and *Mammillarias* and *Coryphanthas*, where the flower buds come from an axil position between the tubercles, or a groove from the areole on the tubercle.

Cacti flowers are sessile, the only exception being *Pereskia*, which has stalks. Cacti flowers are basically tubular and are spirally formed, whereby the petals gradually change to sepals and on to bracts. They have an inferior ovary, with areoles and often spines. The stamens within the flower are also spirally arranged from one or more levels within the flower tube, surrounding a central style, which in some genera has very pronounced lobes. The flowers are mostly actinomorphic (radially symmetrical), but some are zygomorphic in varying degrees.

The fruits are usually a juicy berry, but in some genera it is a dry capsule, from which the seeds escape either from a basal pore or because the capsule has split open irregularly.

A Cactus Flower Based on Opuntia

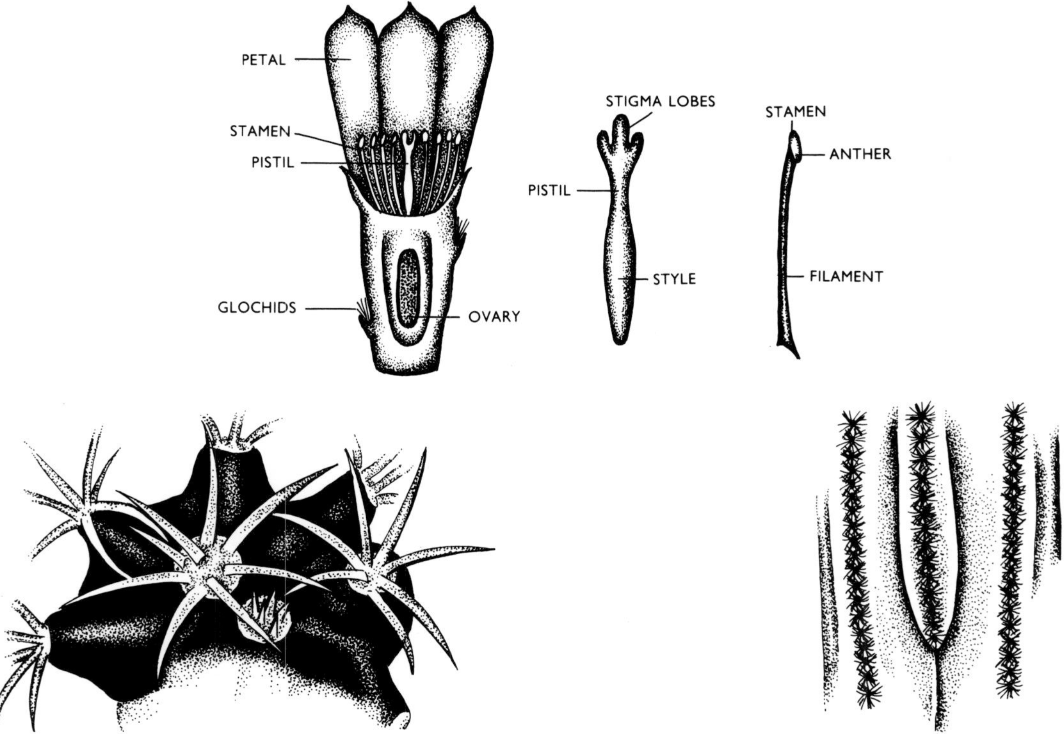

Young plant of Ferocactus recurvus *showing its tubercled structure, which as it approaches maturity will change to a ribbed formation. Note the felted or woolly areoles and that it has radial spines and one central.*

Section of a stem of Carnegiea gigantea *showing the ribbed structure, and how as the stem expands another rib forms.*

Typical actinomorphic flower of Echinocereus pectinatus *var.* rigidissimus *with the stamens closely surrounding the central style.*

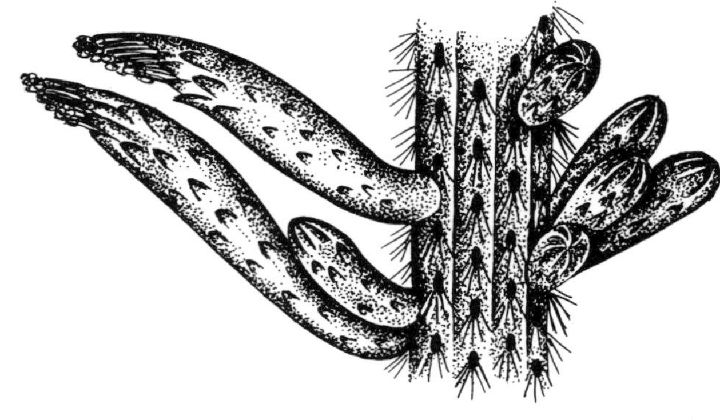

The oblique or somewhat zygomorphic flower of a Cleistocactus *species, where the flower opens just enough for the style, surrounded by the stamens, to protrude.*

The spiral arrangement of the flowers on this Mammillaria *matches the spiral arrangement of the tubercles.*

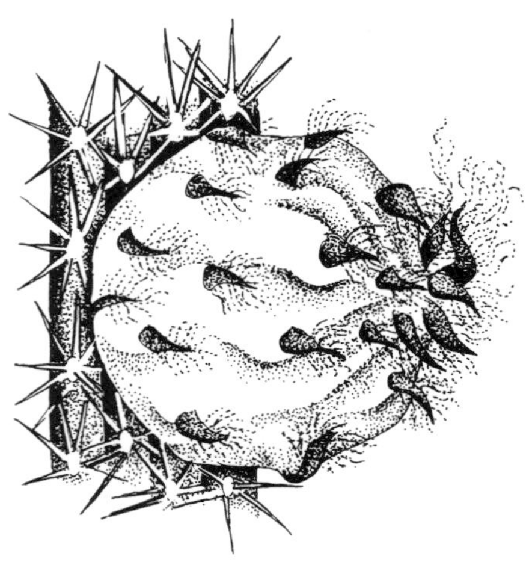

The fruit of Harrisia simpsonii. *Note the presence of hairs from the areole positions on the fruit. It is very fleshy within and likely to contain a few hundred seeds.*

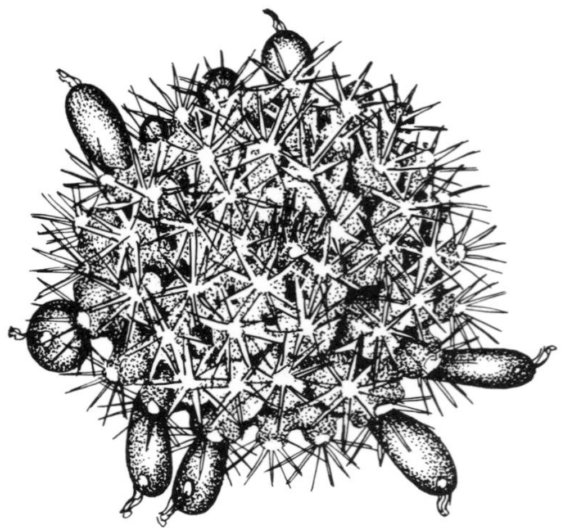

Mammillaria mammillaris *with a few small fruit, which are typical for this genus. Unlike the* Harrisia, *one of these fruits may only contain twenty or thirty tiny seeds.*

Unlike most cacti, Pereskia bleo *is thin stemmed, small leaved and does not have sessile, tubular and spirally formed petals.*

CLASSIFICATION OF CACTI

CACTACEAE

A modification of the classification system used in *The Illustrated Encyclopaedia of Succulents* by Gordon Rowley.

***Pereskia* Group:** Plants with leaves but no glochids. The black seeds are without an aril (an outer covering or appendage attached to the stalk of the ovule).
Genera: *Maihuenia, Pereskia*

***Opuntia* Group:** Plants with small or minute leaves, and glochids. Seeds winged or with an aril.
Genera: *Opuntia, Pereskiopsis, Pterocactus, Quiabentia, Tacinga*

***Cereus* Group:** Plants without leaves or glochids, and have black or brown seeds. Plants usually columnar, ribbed and usually possessing plenty of spines. Exterior of the base of flower tube is either naked or with spines.
Genera: *Armatocereus, Arrojadoa, Bergerocactus, Brachycereus, Browningia, Calymmanthium, Carnegiea, Cephalocereus, Cereus, Corryocactus, Dendrocereus, Echinocereus, Erdisia, Escontria, Eulychnia, Harrisia, Jasminocereus, Lemaireocereus, Lophocereus, Machaerocereus, Micranthocereus, Monvillea, Myrtillocactus, Neoraimondia, Nyctocereus, Pachycereus, Peniocereus, Pilosocereus, Rathbunia, Stetsonia, Wilcoxia*

***Echinopsis* Group:** Same as the *Cereus* Group, except plants can be dwarf and exterior of the flower tube usually hairy, or may possess narrow scales.
Genera: *Acanthocalycium, Arequipa, Arthrocereus, Borzicactus, Cephalocleistocactus, Chamaecereus, Cleistocactus, Denmoza, Echinopsis, Espostoa, Haageocereus, Hildewintera, Lobivia, Matucana, Mila, Oreocereus, Oroya, Rebutia, Sulcorebutia, Thrixanthocereus, Weberbauerocereus, Weingartia*

***Hylocereus* Group:** As for *Cereus* Group, but plants are epiphytic, often with aerial roots, and ribbed. Spines often rather weak or completely absent.
Genera: *Aporocactus, Cryptocereus, Deamia, Disocactus, Epiphyllum, Heliocereus, Hylocereus, Mediocactus, Nopalxochia, Pfeiffera, Rhipsalidopsis, Rhipsalis, Schlumbergera, Selenicereus, Weberocereus, Wittia, Zygocactus*

***Neoporteria* Group:** Plants usually dwarf, globular to short, cylindrical and ribbed. Base of flower tube somewhat woolly, with spines further up.
Genera: *Austrocactus, Blossfeldia, Eriosyce, Frailea, Neoporteria, Notocactus, Parodia, Uebelmannia, Wigginsia*

***Melocactus* Group:** Same as the *Neoporteria* Group, with base of flower tube either naked or woolly, but without any spines further up. Flowers borne on a terminal cephalium, except *Buiningia* where it is lateral.
Genera: *Buiningia, Discocactus, Melocactus*

***Echinocactus* Group:** As for *Melocactus* Group, except flowers appear from the centre but without a cephalium.
Genera: *Ancistrocactus, Ariocarpus, Astrophytum, Aztekium, Cochemiea, Coloradoa, Copiapoa, Coryphantha, Dolichothele, Echinocactus, Echinomastus, Echinofossulocactus, Encephalocarpus, Epithelantha, Escobaria, Ferocactus, Gymnocalycium, Hamatocactus, Homalocephala, Islaya, Leuchtenbergia, Lophophora, Mamillopsis, Mammillaria, Neobesseya, Neogomesia, Neolloydia, Ortegocactus, Pediocactus, Pelecyphora, Sclerocactus, Solisia, Strombocactus, Thelocactus, Toumeya, Utahia*

Habitat

Cacti have evolved and adapted themselves to a very wide range of habitats, whereas the usual misconception is that they are only to be found in deserts. The generally accepted definition of a desert is a place where the average annual rainfall is no more than 25 cm (10 in). Under this definition only a very small percentage of cacti grow in true deserts. By far the majority of species grow in habitats where they receive on average at least twice that amount of rain per year. Some types of cacti grow in even wetter habitats, in particular many of the epiphytic species that grow in tropical evergreen forests where the atmospheric humidity is invariably high.

Although I have referred to an average rainfall, there are some species that grow under true desert conditions and obtain moisture purely from coastal fogs. This moisture is deposited on the spines and then drops off around the plants where their roots pick it up. Such species tend to be very shallow rooted, but these roots may radiate out over many metres (yards). It is likely that the moisture they receive equates around 2.5–5 cm (1–2 in) per year.

Few of the very succulent cacti can tolerate an excess of moisture around the neck of the plant and the roots. So as a result, if they are to be found on fairly level ground the soil will be very porous. A wide variety of cacti are to be found on mountain slopes amongst rocks, often growing out of rock fissures where many other plants could never survive. Sometimes they are to be found growing in gullies where the leaves from other xerophytic bushes and trees have collected over the years.

Another misconception is that all cacti like full sun conditions. Only a limited number of cacti can cope with conditions where daytime temperatures are regularly around 50° C (over 120° F). Even those species that can cope with these conditions in maturity have started life in partial shade. As you will have observed from the illustrations accompanying the 'Introduction', cacti often seek the shade of other cacti, or grow beneath bushes or trees and amongst grass.

Cacti habitats range from coastal to inland areas, from sea level to altitudes approaching 4000 m (over 12 000 ft), and from as far north as Alberta in Canada to as far south as Tierra del Fuego in Patagonia. At these extremities of North and South America, as well as at high altitudes, some cacti have adapted to cope with severe cold, as well as snow. A few species that are to be found by the sea growing in sand only perhaps a metre (yard) or so above sea level, can obviously cope with salt. I have observed *Pachycereus pringlei* growing very close to the sea in Mexico, by the Gulf of California. This does not mean that this species is a true halophytic (salt-loving) plant as with genera such as *Batis* and *Salicornia*. However, I have observed *Opuntia dillenii** clumps growing happily near salt pans, north of Cadiz in south-western Spain. The white salt was literally solid around these specimens but they were growing well and flowering freely.

* *Opuntia dillenii* originates from the West Indies but has gone wild in the Canary Islands and in a few parts of southern Spain.

Pollination and Reproduction

The flowers of virtually all cacti are normally hermaphrodite, which means that they possess both male (stamens) and female (carpels) organs. The receptive part of the female organ is the stigma, which is the tip of the pistil, and it is this area that receives the pollen in order for fertilisation to occur, which will then result in the seeds eventually forming. The normally fine powdery pollen comes from the anthers on top of the filaments, which together make up the stamens.

In nature, with cacti this transference of pollen is generally carried out accidentally by many differing kinds of insects, which have been attracted to the flowers in search of nectar or even the pollen itself. The pollen usually gets on to the bodies of the insects which they then take to another flower, some of which will, again by accident, get on to the stigma. Some genera ensure that the pollen gets on to the insects by having very sensitive filaments, which when touched close towards the stigma. Usually 5 to 10 minutes later the stamens return to their normal position. Genera where this occurs includes *Opuntia* and *Wigginsia*, to name but two. On a hot day this movement of the stamens can be quite rapid; you can observe this by inserting your finger for a moment amongst the stamens of an *Opuntia* flower.

Some of the larger flowers attract birds or even bats. Birds usually come for the nectar, whereas the bats will come for the nectar and the stamens themselves. These night-flying creatures are attracted by the scent of night-flowering species of cacti. There are some genera within the family CACTACEAE that have cleistogamous flowers — in these cases fertilisation can take place without the flowers ever opening. The genus *Frailea* is one of the best known for this; most species that have cleistogamous flowers produce an abundance of fruit as a result.

Artificial transference of pollen to the stigma of a flower is very easy to do, by means of a small artist's paint brush. With large flowers a larger brush can be used. The success of your artificial pollination will depend on the genera and species. Some species can be fertilised by pollen transfer within the same flower, whereas others have to be from different flowers, or more often than not, between flowers fertilised from different plants. If pollen gets wet it is usually spoiled, so if you are watering overhead, as one should, avoid getting water into an open flower. Once pollination has taken place most cacti flowers will start to close earlier than they would have done if this had not happened.

In other respects, the fertilisation follows the same pattern as other flowering plants, whereby the fertilised ovary develops seeds. The fruits (berries) are very variable in size and structure, as you will gather when you read the descriptions for each genus. Some are dry fruits when ripe, which is when the seeds run out; whereas others are very fleshy when ripe and attract birds or other creatures. Birds are usually after the flesh, so the seeds pass through their digestive system and can be scattered far and wide. In contrast, other creatures that feed on the fruit, such as rodents, are after the flesh and the seeds, so a far smaller proportion of seeds survive. Most *Ferocacti* produce a large quantity of fruit each year, each containing perhaps a few hundred seeds, but if one per cent escape being eaten by the rodents the species has done well.

PROPAGATION

SEED RAISING

You will find if you read a variety of books on this subject numerous methods being suggested, each being supposedly the *only* satisfactory method, for raising cacti from seed. There are in fact numerous methods that can be used provided certain simple precautions are taken.

As a general rule most enthusiasts new to this hobby start off with a general mixed packet of seeds, and believe it or not it is far more difficult to get a high percentage of success with such a packet. Usually the mixtures that are sold contain not only vigorous tall growing kinds, but also miniature slow growing ones. So often I have heard from new enthusiasts when they were visiting 'The Exotic Collection' the statement 'I am no good at growing cactus from seed', or 'It is a waste of time and money for me to grow cacti from seed.' Assuming these mixed seeds have been given sufficient warmth and about the correct amount of water they will germinate quite well, particularly the vigorous ones. These will by their nature need more water than the miniatures alongside them, which soon disappear through rotting caused by too much water. This leaves new enthusiasts with only a few identical looking columnar *Cerei* for all their efforts.

Hopefully, if this has happened to you, you will persevere and have another attempt at growing cacti from seed. Cacti seeds as a general rule, with only a few exceptions such as *Frailea*, remain viable for many years provided they have been kept cool, dry and have not been attacked by any tiny insects, which could have eaten away the interiors. In nature often many years pass before the ideal conditions come along one spring for them to germinate, so they mostly develop a hard coating to their seeds to remain viable. So no matter when you bought the seeds they will still germinate.

The basic requirements needed to raise the majority of cacti from seed are as follows:

1. Correct warmth — The night temperature should not fall far below 18.3°–21.1°C (65°–70°F), but the daytime temperature may often reach 32.2° C (90°F).
2. Correct moisture — Once the seeds have been sown, and they have had a very thorough soaking, they require to be kept just moist, but not soaking wet, and they must not be allowed to dry out completely, even for an hour.
3. Correct shading — Seeds and young seedlings must be shaded from direct sunlight, yet not in complete darkness once seedlings begin to appear.
4. A free air circulation around the seedlings at all times — A circulation of air around the seed pans, but not with cooling draughts, is important. This condition favours cacti but is not very favourable to disease, fungus, or moss. (Reference is made on page 12 to seed raising without any air circulation, including the advantages and disadvantages of such a method.)
5. A suitable seed-raising mixture — A seed-raising mixture made from very fine dusty leaf mould or peat, plus gritty sand, provided it is thoroughly sterilised, is ideal for most species of 'cacti'.

You must remember that with the smaller growing cacti the seedlings remain very small for the first 6 months, and with some species they remain small for as long as 18 months. Because of this it is imperative that not only must the seed-raising containers be thoroughly sterilised, but also the seed-raising mixture and anything else that is used. If you were to get moss spores germinating along with the cacti seeds they would soon strangle and swamp the tiny cacti seedlings. For the average amateur the seed-raising mixture can be sterilised in a loosely sealed tin in your oven, as long as it has been steam sterilised for about one hour. There are available in the United Kingdom and some other countries small greenhouse heaters operated by natural gas, to which you can attach a proper steam sterilising unit, whereby everything will be sterilised once the steam has been passing through the container for 10 minutes or so. In the same way it is advisable to use either boiled water or properly distilled water for your seed sowing and after care. This will again reduce the chances of other organisms causing harm. Periodically during the after care period a soluble fungicide can be added to the water as well.

Today with plastics in such general use it is an easy matter to obtain small plastic pots plus trays capable of withstanding boiling water. If they have been used before they can be first washed in hot soapy water, after which they can be treated with boiling water. The other simple requirements are cottonwool, small plastic labels and a pair of spade-ended metal tweezers. The slower growing cacti and other succulent plants do not require a seed-raising mixture that contains much nourishment. I favour a very poor mixture that drains well rather than one containing too much humus, which can quickly become green on top if it stays moist too long. There are available in many countries ready-mixed seed-raising soils on sale but in most cases it needs more grit added to it for the best results. Often they are stated to be already sterilised but it does no harm to do it again.

For almost 50 years a mixture of about ten per cent dusty humus and 90 per cent grit (per volume) was used in 'The Exotic Collection' as the seed-raising mixture. This has proved so successful that many thousands of enthusiasts have also found it to be an ideal medium. To obtain the correct ingredients use a household sieve as used in the kitchen for flour. Sift some dry leaf mould or peat, keeping that which has passed through the sieve. As regards the grit or coarse sand, this presents more of a problem not only within one's own country but also from country to country. If you can obtain a well-washed sand that has a variable grain size, dry it completely and then sieve it with your flour sieve. This time you will be keeping for use the part which remains in the sieve. If you cannot obtain a suitable sand an alternative is to use the smallest grit that is used in small aquariums for tropical fish. This is usually well washed and should serve the job admirably, although it will be more expensive. In addition to using the grit or sieved coarse sand with the dusty humus, you will need some grit kept separately (also sterilised) for top dressing each seed pan after the seeds have been sown.

Follow the step by step illustrations for the actual process of filling the seed containers and sowing the seeds.

Once the seeds are sown each container should be allowed to completely soak up a mild solution of fungicide.*

* The fungicide which I use is CHINOSOL (Potassium hydroxyquinoline sulphate). There are many kinds available suitable for seed-raising purposes, if the above is unavailable.

1. *Start with a clean bench with all the equipment — clean pots, trays, tweezers, cottonwool, labels, sterilised soil mixture, sterilised grit, sterilised sand, a fungicide, and the packets of seeds.*

   Write out your seed label. A small amount of cottonwool is spread out in the base of the pot or seed container.

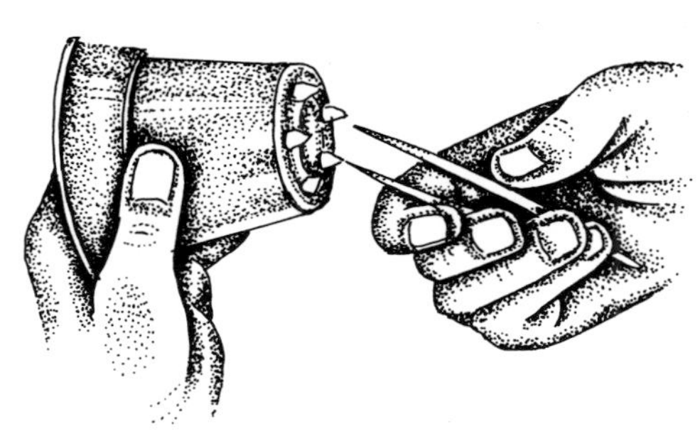

2. *This cottonwool is now pulled a short distance through the drainage holes, by using your tweezers. The cottonwool will then act as a wick to soak up water and fungicide. You then put in a thin layer of moist sterilised sand on top of the cottonwool. (See illustration No. 7.)*

3. *The pot is then filled with moist sterilised soil mixture, firmed down. Insert the seed label.*

4. *The seeds are now scattered as evenly as possible on to the surface of the sterilised soil mixture. Then carefully scatter some dry grit very thinly on to the seeds and soil mixture.*

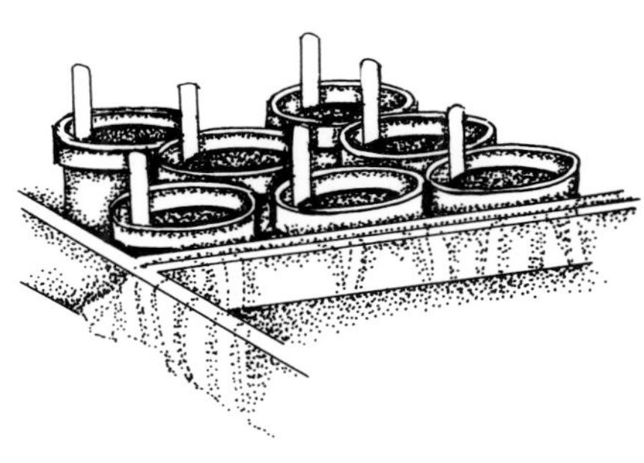

5. *Trays containing diluted fungicide solution.*

6. *Tray filled with pots of non-germinated seeds.*

7. *A demonstration pot with a section of the side removed to show the different layers. At the bottom — the thin layer of sterilised moist sand. In the middle — the sterilised seed soil mixture. On top — the thin layer of dry sterilised grit.*

This should prevent any damping-off problems. You then transfer them into another tray that has a thin film of the same mild solution. The containers should then be covered with a few layers of paper an inch or so above the top of the containers. The bottom of the containers should be kept warm by using either electric soil heating cables or the bottom of an electric propagator. You may have a suitable 'airing cupboard' which would be ideal up to the germination stage. From then on they require a little light, but still good shade overhead, and some warmth at the bottom of the containers.

During the pre-visible germination stage the seed containers must never dry out, not even for a few hours. If they do dry out at the critical stage when the root tip is emerging from the seed they will quickly die. This is a common cause of failure often interpreted by the average amateur as 'nil germination'. Assuming your seeds have germinated it is important to make sure for the first few months that the seedlings do not dry out completely, but they must not be soggy either. If this happens the smaller kinds may well rot.

You will find that some seedlings develop faster than others, particularly the easier growing columnar kinds. These can be pricked on within a few months. However, with the very tiny ones do not be in a hurry to disturb them and move them on into a somewhat richer compost. You may feel that things are not happening fast enough but please be patient, it will be worth it. Some species of *Parodia* are initially very slow from seed and may need to be left in the seed container for 15 to 18 months before being pricked out. Even if some of your seedlings stay in the seed container for a year or more they will need some shade throughout that period, except perhaps during very dull weather in the worst of the winter months. By this time they will still need some warmth, so a little water can be given to them at intervals.

In warmer more tropical climates the sealed seed-raising system has many advantages. With this method, once the seeds have been sown and the container watered with a dilute fungicide, each container is sealed into a polythene bag and placed in a warm and well shaded position. The seedlings can be expected to germinate in the normal way without any further watering being necessary. This is a distinct advantage in a hot climate where the soil can dry out very quickly. But it is imperative that the container, seed mixture, etc, have been thoroughly sterilised because in a sealed moist environment, fungi and mosses can form rapidly and quickly ruin the entire operation. After a period of a month or so the bags can be opened if they need a little additional moisture. This also changes the air within. Use distilled water with a little fungicide dissolved in it.

Whether the sealed or unsealed method has been used the after care is the same. Seedlings are moved into a compost containing a greater degree of nourishment. With the slower growing kinds the soil must not be too rich, otherwise young plants can still rot. If the soil stays too moist for too long this will also cause them to rot. If seedlings or young plants become infected with any pests care must be taken as to the type of insecticide used. Do not use a systemic type as the chemicals are absorbed into the sap of the plant. It is safer to use a contact type. Be very careful to use it at the correct concentration. Mature plants can sometimes survive an over-strength solution but young ones are less likely to.

(a) *Polythene lifted to one side, showing the commercial method of seed raising on a large scale in Holland.*

(b) *Seedlings of* Mammillaria esseriana *when 3 weeks old.*

(c) *Seedlings of* Mammillaria esseriana *when 8 weeks old.*

(d) *Seedlings of* Mammillaria esseriana *when 15 months old.*

(e) *Seedlings of* Echinocactus grusonii *when 15 months old.*

(f) *A greenhouse full of young cacti, 2–3 years old.*

CUTTINGS

In addition to the enjoyment obtained by actually raising your own plants from seed, most gardeners like to propagate their plants by taking cuttings. Initially, with this particular hobby, this method often comes before seed raising.

The majority of cacti are very easy to root from cuttings, requiring no sophisticated equipment. Certainly in the United Kingdom *Echinopsis multiplex* hybrids, various *Opuntia*, and sundry *Epiphyllum* or *Zygocacti* (Christmas Cacti) are amongst the first plants to be found in an amateur's collection. All of them are very easy to propagate vegetatively, so I will use these as our main examples.

The tools of the trade are a sharp knife, a razor blade, a small pair of secateurs and a pair of tweezers for handling anything of a spiny nature. The ideal time for taking cuttings is during the spring and summer months, and even in early autumn (fall), but never during the winter in temperate climates. For those in warmer parts of the world it is usually possible to successfully sow seeds or root cuttings at any time of the year.

Most *Echinopsis* cluster quite freely, and the offsets are usually detached very easily without using a knife. It is not uncommon for these offsets to already possess a few roots, even if they were not in contact with the soil. The most important difference between these and ordinary garden plants is that the cutting should not be immediately planted and watered. If you do this, you run a very serious risk of the cutting rotting within a few days. Because of the fleshy succulent nature of these plants, cuttings should be left in a warm dry place for a few days, so that the freshly cut area can be allowed to callus. However, they should not be left in direct sun. The length of time you leave cuttings to dry will usually depend on the surface area of the cut. In the case of an *Echinopsis* offset three or four days will be enough, although you will not lose it if you leave it considerably longer. Most *Opuntia* cuttings, even when taken at the joint positions, will have a broader cut area, so that a drying period of 10 to 14 days is advisable. In contrast, *Zygocacti* and related genera are far less succulent, so cuttings of these could dry up if left on the bench too long. Knowing the correct drying period will only come with experience, but fortunately the majority of these plants will survive a too lengthy drying period far better than they will a too short one.

If possible all cuttings should be taken at narrow joint positions. This shortens the drying period and many species will root more rapidly than if the cut had been taken at a broad stem section. In 'The Exotic Collection' it was sometimes necessary to prune plants before they went through the roof of the greenhouse, so a joint position cannot always be chosen. However, in most cases these cuttings could still be rooted, but the drying period can be from 10 to 20 days or more. If the weather is dull and cool

VEGETATIVE PROPAGATION

(a) *Demonstration of the best position for taking cuttings, which is the joint position where the cut will be narrow. In actual fact many cacti, including an* Opuntia *like this one, will root even when cut at the widest point. However, there are some species that are difficult to root, in which case it is essential to cut at the correct point. It also means that the cut area callouses much quicker, so it is a good idea to get into the correct habits.*

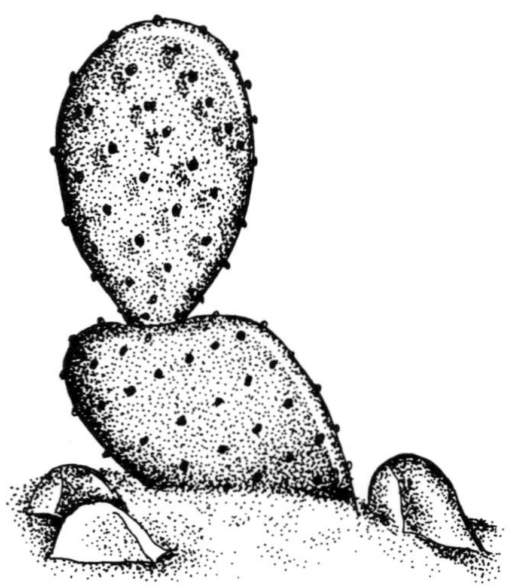

(b) *An example of an unfertilised* Opuntia *fruit, which had dropped off a plant in my garden. It has rooted, and started to produce a normal flat pad. This can happen to most types of* Opuntia, *not just the cylindrical stemmed ones which can produce a continuous chain of fruits.*

a longer period of drying is always safer. Where this is necessary, cuttings will tend to bend gradually at their tips. In such cases the cuttings should be turned 180 degrees every few days so that a nice straight cutting can be planted at the end of the drying period. In warmer climates the recommended drying period can usually be halved.

Notocactus ottonis produces offsets from below ground, around the original main head. If you wish to break up a clump of this sort it is necessary to first knock the plant out of its pot. You then carefully knock off or scrape away the soil from around the bases of the offsets until you find the narrow neck position between them and the parent plant. You can then cut them away from the parent plant, pulling each off along with the roots, which each offset will already have. This type of plant division should be done when the soil is dry. This is very important so that not only the offsets but also the parent plant do not start to rot through moist soil coming into contact with the freshly cut areas. After the offsets have been removed it is advisable to leave them and the parent plant on the greenhouse bench in a warm and shaded position for a few days, to allow the cut areas to callus. Offsets that already possess roots can be potted on into a normal potting soil and lightly watered.

So far, I have only referred to the actual taking of cuttings, nothing about the medium into which the calloused cuttings should be planted. In actual fact, the cuttings of many of the easy-to-grow plants that most beginners possess could be successfully rooted in any ordinary cactus compost. I would much prefer, however, to get you into good habits by planting all cuttings into gritty sand, vermiculite, or loamalite (perlite). Gritty sand, provided it is well washed, suits the majority of species very well.

For rooting cuttings you do not need any nourishment value in the rooting medium. The sand can be in clay or plastic pots, sufficiently deep for the cuttings to be firmed into it, so that they do not topple over once they are watered from above.

As with seed raising, bottom heat will speed the process of root formation, but it is really only important with the more difficult and rarer plants.

Most species will root up well in an ordinary greenhouse or conservatory, or even on a sunny windowsill. In the home, central heating radiators below windowsills will give just the right amount of bottom warmth to aid rooting. In a greenhouse or sunny conservatory they should be under lightly shaded glass, otherwise some cuttings may shrivel too much before sufficient roots have formed. In the same way, the use of rooting hormones is not really necessary for the majority of species you will be dealing with at first. Once cuttings have rooted and even started to visibly grow, they can be potted on into a normal cactus compost.

In the past it used to be common practice to dip the cut area of freshly taken cuttings into 'Flowers of Sulphur' and to also brush this on to the part of the parent plant from which the cutting had been removed. During warm dry weather this is not really necessary as the cut area soon forms a callus, thus preventing an infection entering. If you are forced to take cuttings in early spring or very late in autumn (fall), the above procedure can be followed.

GRAFTING

Although people are quite happy to buy fruit trees or rose bushes and many other shrubs as grafted specimens, there is a tendency for many people to frown upon or dislike cacti that have been grafted. Admittedly in some cases it is very obvious that a cactus has been grafted, such that it looks rather unnatural, but grafting does have many uses.

In cooler climates such as in the United Kingdom and northern Europe, where there is high atmospheric humidity during the cold winter months, there is always the danger of losing certain cacti through rotting. The plants may have been kept completely dry yet they may still rot; this particularly applies to tightly clumping plants such as the cristate forms of *Mammillaria wildii* and *M. zeilmanniana*. You may have successfully kept a plant for many years without any problems and then disaster strikes. This is an instance where it can pay to have a spare plant as a grafted specimen. A grafted plant is not in contact with the soil, and is usually in a more elevated position with better air circulation around it. As a result it will safely survive a cold and wet winter even though it is growing in the same greenhouse or conservatory.

It has become a common sight in supermarkets and garden centres to see a red-coloured cactus grafted on to a triangular stock. This is in fact a completely variegated (possessing no chlorophyll) cactus that can only survive by being grafted on to another cactus. There are a number of different colour forms of the variegated *Gymnocalycium mihanovichii* var. *friedrichiae*, but usually a species of *Hylocereus* has been used as the grafting stock. There are also completely variegated forms of other plants, some of which are yellow in colour, but again they have to be grafted in order to survive. In these instances it is impossible to grow them on their own roots, so you have no other options left open to you.

The 'Rat's Tail' cactus or *Aporocactus flagelliformis* (see page 36) can be grown on its own roots, but there is a tendency for stems to become too thin or die off at the tip, particularly when it is grown in a hanging basket.

This is an instance where very robust and floriferous plants can be grown using a rooted *Opuntia* pad as the grafting stock. In this case one uses the V graft system plus a strong cactus spine as the means of holding the scion (the shoot used to form the graft) in place, in this case a 2.5 cm (1 in) piece of *Aporocactus*.

Although a lot of plants can be grown to flowering size in 2 or 3 years, there are other species which can take at least 10 or 20 years to reach maturity, sometimes even longer. Grafting can speed this process, and from experiments I have carried out over many years' study in 'The Exotic Collection' I have achieved seven years' growth in one year by using a suitable stock plant. In most cases it is possible to remove the quickly obtained 'mature' specimen from the stock plant, and then put it back on its own roots. Having cut it away cleanly from the stock plant, it is treated as a normal cutting with the appropriate drying period, before attempting to root it. The only exceptions to the rule are some of the cephalium-bearing cacti such as *Melocactus* and *Disocactus*. I have not had any success in putting these back on their own roots if I have allowed it to start to form a cephalium, before cutting it off the stock plant.

Commercially, grafting has many uses because plants can be grown much more quickly. Plants that branch naturally on their own roots can produce 50 or perhaps 100 offsets per year, of a size which can be rooted and sold within a few more months. The same plant will continue to do this year after year provided a strong stock has been used, such as a species of *Cereus* or *Trichocereus*. Visitors to 'The Exotic Collection' have been able to observe many such grafts, of which I have used *Cereus* stock that were already 0.6–1.3 m (2–4 ft) high. These have produced spectacular results as can be seen by the photographs above.

For the amateur with his small collection it is not necessary to use large pieces of stock — very good results can be obtained by using surplus *Opuntia* pads or *Echinopsis* offsets that have been rooted. Alternatively, buy in some seed of sundry species of *Cereus* and *Trichocereus* and grow them to about two years of age, before using them as grafting stock. I have deliberately refrained from mentioning the use of *Myrtillocactus* or *Hylocereus* stock as these genera are temperature sensitive in cooler climates. For those of you who live in more tropical parts of the world they can be ideal, as they are readily available and grow very quickly. Those genera prefer a minimum temperature of 50° F (10° C), otherwise they can develop orange spots and quickly rot off. In these days of energy conservation it is better to recommend kinds which are quite happy at 40° F (5° C) or even lower, provided one can obtain equally good results.

The actual process of grafting is not unduly difficult provided a little care is taken. It does not require any expensive equipment beyond a sharp knife and/or razor blade. The flat graft method is probably the easiest one to try, and assuming the scion and stock are of fairly similar diameter, the task is very simple.

For a successful graft to take place you require the vascular tissue of the scion to join with the vascular tissue of the stock plant. The inner tissue of these plants is considerably softer than the exterior epidermis, so it is necessary for a little of the epidermis of both scion and stock to be trimmed off at an angle as shown in the accompanying illustrations (page 17). The softer inner tissue of a plant will shrink more than the tougher epidermis, so the trimming off will ensure that the epidermis of the scion and the epidermis of the stock do not meet. If they did meet you run the risk of the softer internal tissue being pushed apart, whereby the vascular tissues are unable to join and the graft will fail.

If the scion is of a smaller diameter than the stock it should be placed on one side of the stock, so that the central vascular tissue of the scion will meet part of the vascular ring of the larger diameter stock plant. Having don this, it is imperative that the two are held firmly togethe Cactus spines will usually prevent the scion slipping sideways but you may need to weight the scion down on to the stock. If you are using seedling *Cereus* stock or *Echinopsis* offsets for the simple flat grafting system, a wire hoop pressed into the soil will usually suffice, or rubber bands as shown in the accompanying illustrations (page 17). If you are grafting on to a tall stock plant, I have found that soft string with weights on each end is very satisfactory.

Rebutia muscula on *Cereus* stock

Lobivia famatimensis on *Cereus* stock

Uebelmannias on *Echinopsis* stock

Step by Step Grafting

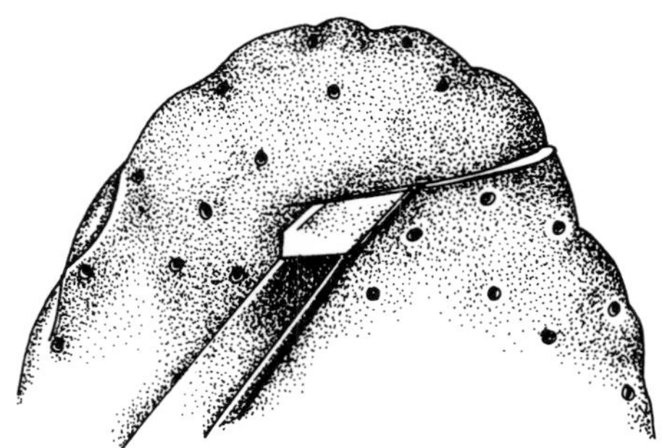

USING AN OPUNTIA *PAD*

(a) *Cutting the top off a fairly spineless pad of* Opuntia ficus-indica.

(b) *Cutting away the epidermis at an angle of the stock plant. (The same is done to the scion, before putting it onto the* Opuntia*).*

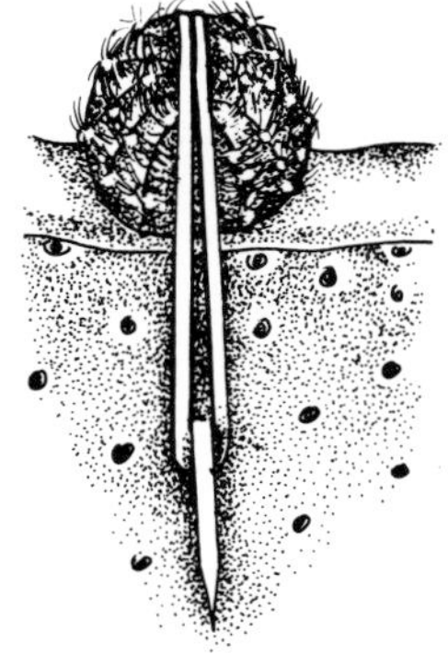

(c) *One toothpick is inserted through the* Opuntia *pad. The scion is then placed in position and held in place by a rubber band, which is placed over the scion and hooked on to each end of the toothpick. If there is a tendency for the scion to slide around, this can be prevented by pinning it to the* Opuntia *stock with one or more cactus spines.*

USING A TRICHOCEREUS *PLANT*

(a) *Top of* Trichocereus *having cut the tip off.*

(b) *Top of* Trichocereus *having cut the epidermis away at an angle.*

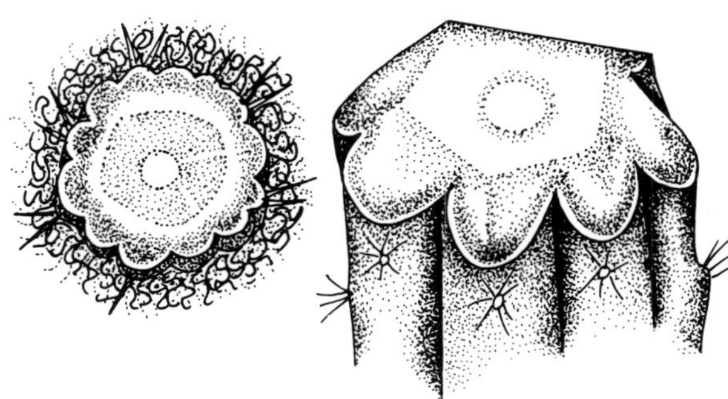

(c) *Base of scion (left), and top of* Trichocereus *showing that the epidermis has been cut away from both. Note the vascular ring of the* Trichocereus.

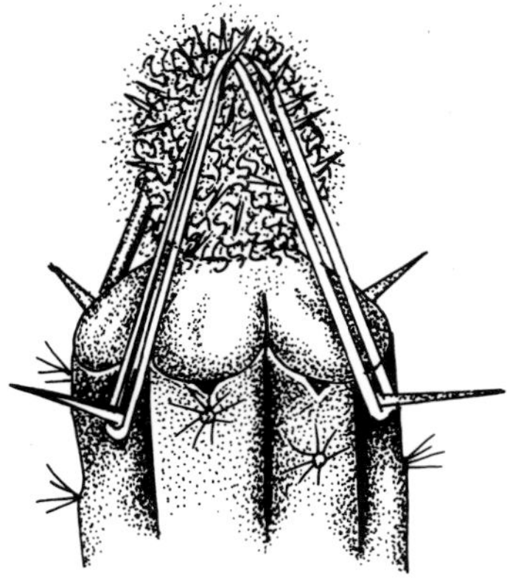

(d) *Scion in place, slightly to one side, to ensure that it is over part of the vascular ring.*

Provided you apply sufficient pressure so that the scion does not move, the success of your graft is almost ensured.

Once this is done the grafted plant should be placed in a warm but shaded position; alternatively, fold a piece of newspaper in half, so that it can sit on top of the scion, whereby the sun's rays do not strike the joining area between scion and stock. This should stay in place for about two weeks, during which time the stock plant should not be watered overhead.

Once the two weeks have elapsed the paper cover and the weighting system can be removed and if all has gone to plan, the scion will be showing signs of new growth within a few days. If you have used a cactus spine to help keep the scion in place it can be left where it is, as it will soon disappear amidst the rapidly expanding graft. Some people have recommended the use of rubber bands for holding a graft in place. If the weather is hot these can sometimes break, thus releasing the all important downward pressure of the scion on to the stock.

The V graft system is very suitable for grafting slim stems as the chisel shaped base to the scion wedges into the V, which has been cut out of the stock plant. In this case one or two cactus spines will usually hold it in place. The shading procedure is again very important, as is watering around the plant rather than over the top.

The thin flat stems of *Zygocacti* and *Schlumbergera* species can also be grafted using *Opuntia* pads as the stock plants. These are too thin for the flat or V grafting systems. With *Opuntia* pads you can again achieve the linking of the fascular tissue by making a slot with a razor blade, downwards at an angle from just above an areole position. Having very carefully trimmed the epidermis off one or both sides of the base of a *Zygocactus* or *Schlumbergera* stem, this can be slipped into the incision and held in place by a cactus spine.

Once your graft has taken and is growing, it is only necessary to water it for rapid growth to take place. This watering can be done from above in the same way as one normally waters plants. Some stocks may produce their own offsets. They should be removed as fast as they appear, otherwise they will take over and your graft will eventually fail. If it is possible to use stock such as *Cereus peruvianus*, *C. jamacaru*, *C. caesius*, etc, do so, as these tend to offset far less.

(a) Sulcorebutia kruegeri *(x .25) — This photograph was taken four years after one small head 2.5 x 1.25 cm (1 x 0.5 in) had been grafted on to a 1.3 m (4 ft) high stem of* Cereus variabilis. *This type of grafting can quickly speed the commercial production of many rare species of cacti, and thus aid their conservation.*

(b) Lobivia famatimensis *(form) (x ·5) — This photograph was taken in May 1984, three years after it was grafted, when it was also 2.5 x 1.25 cm (1 x 0.5 in). The original head has grown tremendously and has only produced two offsets. In 1983 it produced nearly 100 large brilliant crimson flowers, each about 6.25 cm (2.5 in) across. When this photograph was taken, exactly 150 flower buds were counted, plus an additional head starting to form. I have had similar successes with certain of the rarer larger flowered* Mammillaria, *which means a lot more seed has been produced, yet another way in which grafting aids conservation.*

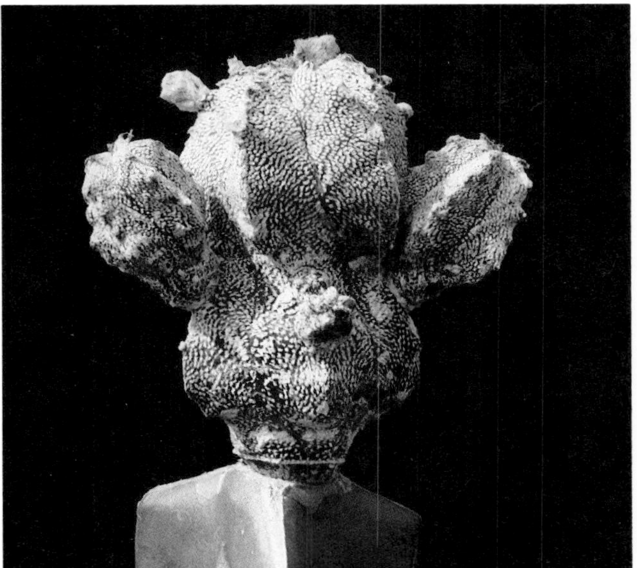

(c) Astrophytum myriostigma *(form) (x 1.5) — This photograph shows the type of three-sided grafting stock (*Hylocereus*) so often seen in florists and garden centres. It is a rather short-lived stock, and is very temperature sensitive, requiring a minimum temperature in excess of 50°F (10°C). If the temperature goes too low, the* Hylocereus *stock can develop orange spots and invariably dies. Most of these grafted cacti have been imported from Japan or Europe, where hundreds of thousands are prepared each year.*

(d) Arrojadoa eriocaulis *(x 1.75) — As with the previously illustrated grafts, the flat graft method has been used, but the scion has been cut on the angle and then pinned to the stock plant. The reason for this is that the small piece of* Arrojadoa *is rather slender, such that if it had been grafted in the same manner as illustrations (a) to (f) page 17, it might not have joined properly. The alternative method would have been to use the V shaped or chisel shaped method as shown in the next illustration.*

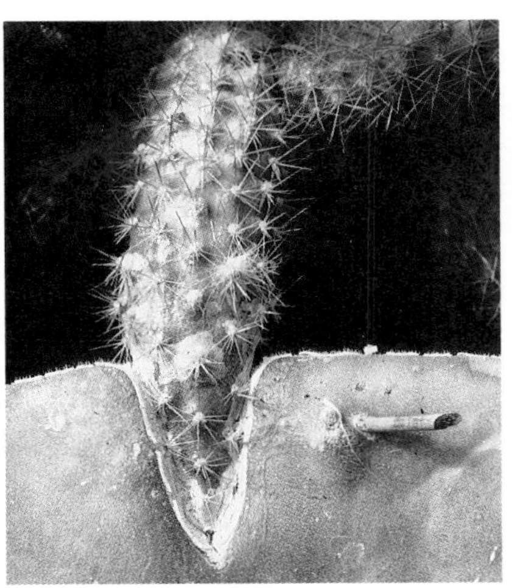

(e) Aporocactus flagelliformis *(x 2) — When you are grafting slender stemmed or flat stemmed cacti,* Opuntia *stock is ideal. In this instance the top has been cut off an* Opuntia *pad, and then a V shaped cut has been made into it. The scion (in this case a piece of* Aporocactus*) has been cut in a chisel shaped manner at its base, and inserted into the V shaped incision. It has been fixed in place with a cactus spine, sometimes two may be needed. It is essential that the scion fits very tightly into the V shaped incision.*

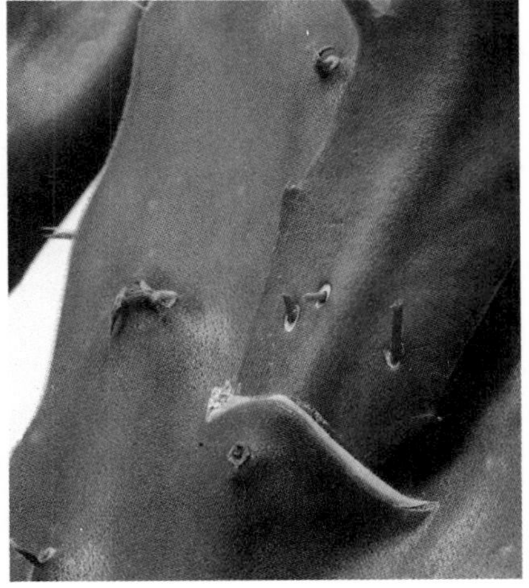

(f, g) Zygocactus truncatus *(x 0.5) —* Zygocacti *and some other epiphytic cacti have quite thin flat stems, almost like leaves. Again using* Opuntia *stock these can be grafted by grafting on to the side of the pad by making an incision just above an areole position. The small piece of* Zygocactus *is inserted into this, having carefully removed the epidermis on one or both sides near the base, so that the soft tissue will join with that of the* Opuntia*. It is held in position with a cactus spine. This type of graft is a little more difficult, and one tends to get a lower percentage success rate. However, the results within a few weeks can be quite spectacular, as can be seen by the second illustration.*

Cultivation

SOIL REQUIREMENTS

The majority of cacti will grow fairly successfully in a wide range of soils provided the soil is not of a type that will clog or harden when dry. In habitat, it is possible to find the same species growing in very different soils and at widely differing altitudes. Therefore it is not surprising that the soil in which a species grows at a high altitude differs from that at sea level. Many cacti are very adaptable, whereby the high altitude form of a certain species is growing in a very well drained soil because it has to be able to survive perhaps much higher rainfall and freezing conditions during the winter months. In contrast, the low altitude form never has to endure frosts, enjoys much higher temperatures and possibly receives much less rain. Under these circumstances, it can grow in a soil that does not lose its moisture content so rapidly. This same point is applicable in cultivation when one is using either clay or plastic pots, or actually growing plants under free root-run conditions, as in a rockery.

In general, it is true to say that the majority of cacti will grow very well in a soil that contains humus. **Leaf mould** in its many forms is available in most countries. Generally, a soil mixture made up of equal parts by volume of a well-rotted leaf mould and well-washed coarse or gritty sand will be suitable for most of your plants. There is sufficient natural nourishment in such a mixture for at least two or three years, perhaps more. This will be dependent on the growth rate of the plants, and how quickly they use up all the natural ingredients from the leaf mould.

In the United Kingdom leaf mould is rarely available at garden centres and nurseries. Instead, a variety of types of peat are to be found, the **sedge peat** type being most suited for cacti. If peat moss is used in a compost it is perfectly satisfactory for plants that do not have a lengthy dry resting period during the winter. Many amateurs have made the mistake of using it for their cacti, and have run into problems in the early spring when they started to water their plants again. They have found that the root ball would not absorb the water very well. There is no harm in using peat moss in your soil mixture for epiphytic cacti, such as *Epiphyllum*, *Rhipsalis*, *Rhipsalidopsis* and *Zygocacti*, as these plants need some water throughout the year. In other words, the root ball never gets really dry and it is for this reason that if you cannot obtain leaf mould locally, try to obtain sedge peat. It is usually very dark brown or almost black in colour, and when used in a soil mixture for cacti you will have no problems when it comes to watering, following a dry period of a few months. When it has been used in a soil mixture in about the same proportions as previously recommended for leaf mould, you need to add to it bone meal, gypsum and superphosphate for added nourishment.

Instead of doing this, you can use **liquid fertilisers**, but they must be used very carefully. It is far too easy with a liquid fertiliser to give a plant too much, which may cause the plant to become lank or even to physically split some species of cacti or, at the very least, cause the soil to become sour. It is also possible to purchase various granular slow acting fertilisers, whereby a small amount dissolves each time you water. A German company, 'Gardena', has produced a wide range of gardening equipment, including special watering equipment. These take special fertiliser blocks, which gradually dissolve as you water.

The type of coarse **sand** or grit that is to be added to the humus can vary considerably according to where you live. The main requirement of the coarse sand is that it is of a well washed type, otherwise it may contain impurities that will cause the soil mixture to set very hard when dry, or even to cake on the top of the pots, causing an impervious layer. River sand is always a fairly safe bet, but pit and sea sand can be used, provided they have been well washed free of all impurities. If you are in doubt about this point, you can usually obtain a very good coarse sand from a shop that supplies all the needs for tropical fish enthusiasts. However, you are likely to pay rather a high price for your sand. If you are still in doubt about which one to use, contact your local Parks and Gardens department for your own town or city. They are usually very helpful, and will point you in the right direction.

I have so far studiously ignored any reference to **garden loam** as part of the cactus soil mixture. This has been quite deliberate, as so often one sees references in books and magazines to use so much 'good garden loam'. A good garden loam is one which does not set too hard after rain, in other words it naturally contains the correct proportions of sand, humus etc., and little or no clay. If you think you have the right type of loam, you can obviously reduce the cost of making up your cactus soil.

A good cactus soil can be made up as follows:

1 part loam
1 part sand — Per volume
1 part leaf mould

To this can be added the following, easily obtainable ingredients, mainly for the true cacti, in the proportions given:

To 4.5 litres (1 gallon) mixture of loam, sand and leaf mould, add:

4 heaped teaspoons of Bone Meal
3 heaped teaspoons of Gypsum
1 heaped teaspoon of Superphosphate

In climates where frosts are unknown and the average annual rainfall is less than 40 cm (16 in), it is possible to reduce the sand content in the above recommended cactus soil mixture. Even so, one still has to be careful, because it is possible that the major part of that rainfall will come at one time. In the south of Spain, the average annual rainfall normal ranges between 25 to 45 cm (10 to 18 in), also most of the rain falls in November and February. One of the rockeries below our villa here, was constructed using a mixture of one part loam, two parts sand, and one part peat, to ensure good drainage. This was very fortunate, as the latter part of 1989 produced exceedingly freak weather conditions, whereby we ended up with over 125 cm (50 in) of rain! Because I had used such a porous soil mixture, knowing that many slow growing rarities were going into that rockery, I only had a few losses.

When you are considering an outdoor rockery, you must take into account your local weather conditions, particularly when the rains come. If your higher rainfall is during the summer, drainage is less of a problem.

I have also refrained from mentioning the **pH** of the soil, as this can frighten the amateur away from a wonderful hobby. When one considers my comments earlier on regarding the very different soils in which the same species are to be found in habitat, much too much has been written on this point with cacti. There are instances in other fields of horticulture where the correct pH of the soil for certain genera is very important. This is certainly not necessary with the vast majority of cacti.

Finally today, in the plastic bag world that we live in, it is usually possible to buy ready mixed soils for 'House Plants', 'Cacti' etc., but I do feel that sometimes they are not always a good buy. It will certainly be more expensive than mixing your own and you will not always find consistent quality with many of these products. If you try out such a product, and your plants succeed, all well and good. It may be safer to just try the ready mixed soil with a few of your plants, rather than repotting all of them at one time. See how they respond over a period of at least three months, before repotting your entire collection.

WHAT TO GROW THEM IN

Plastic **pots** have certainly taken over from clay, and for the new enthusiast this does not matter, as most of the plants he or she will be growing in the first few years will be easy growing kinds, which are less likely to be lost through over-watering. As this hobby takes hold of you, you will naturally want to obtain some of the more difficult and much slower growing species. This is when I consider clay pots are virtually essential if you live in a country such as the United Kingdom where the weather is so changeable. If you must grow all of your plants in matching plastic pots, you will have to use a much more porous soil mixture for these slowing kinds, genera such as *Ariocarpus, Epithelantha, Pelecyphora, Strombocactus.* For those of you in more tropical parts of the world, plastic pots have their advantages over clay because they hold the moisture longer. The main disadvantage is that they become brittle with age, and in hot countries that may be in a couple of years or so. Even in an English greenhouse temperatures can top 38°C (100°F) and as a result plastic pots do not always last much longer. Some plastic pots are better than others, particularly those that are thicker and heavier. I did use some large plastic tubs that were 5 mm (¼ in) thick, and they had not become brittle after ten years of use in and outside the greenhouses in the United Kingdom.

A plastic pot usually has a number of small holes in its bottom, so you only need to put a small amount of shingle in it, before filling it with soil mixture. Clay pots usually have one much larger hole, so it will need crocking with small pieces of broken clay flower-pot. You may if you wish add some shingle on top of this, before adding the soil.

It is not advisable to use containers without drainage holes, as any watering will have to be done very carefully. Requirements are listed in the chapter 'Caring for Cacti in the Home' (page 24).

Pot grown plants make life very easy for you if you exhibit your plants at shows, but there are many enthusiasts who just enjoy growing plants and have no wish to exhibit them. A **rockery** in a **greenhouse** can be made to look very attractive. Much the same applies in warmer climates, where you can design your cacti garden outside.

A rockery can be either built at waist level on to a strong greenhouse staging, or at floor level. In 'The Exotic Collection' at Worthing there were a number of such beds. The raised ones had been built on 5 cm (1 in) thick floor boarding, covered with two layers of good quality roofing felt with a surrounding wall of rock-faced concrete blocks. These had side drainage positions at intervals of about every 1 m (3 ft). The soil depth within was about 15 cm (6 in) at the sides and 20 cm (8 in) in the middle.

The soil mixture used in these raised rockery beds was about 45% per volume of sedge peat to 55% of gritty sand with a slow acting fertiliser mixture that incorporated bone meal, gypsum and superphosphate. The bed was top-dressed with an almost white shingle, which I also used around our potted plants. This ensured good drainage around the necks of the plants and also it meant that they could be watered at fairly high pressure provided a moderately fine rose was used. This often surprised many people but it helped to keep the plants clean, and the shingle prevented the plants, particularly white and nice golden spined ones, from becoming stained with brown from the peat. A shallow depth bed of this sort is ideal for a wide range of species, particularly most of the globular kinds. It is not a good idea to put together plants with totally different growth rates.

The floor beds are ideal for the taller growing species, which usually have stronger root systems. This means that you can economise with the soil mixture, by using some of your garden loam, assuming it is suitable. In colder parts frost can extend into the soil of a greenhouse, so before preparing the soil it is advisable to put in an insulation division. This can be done very cheaply using 2.5 cm (1 in), or even better 5 cm (2 in), thick polystyrene sheeting. To be really effective it should be sealed into plastic sacks so that it remains dry. These should be slotted into the soil vertically just inside the exterior wall or footings of your greenhouse. Ideally they should be put in to a depth of about 65 cm (2 ft). You can then prepare your soil as per the mixture of loam, peat and sand described on page 20. No doubt you will be wondering if this soil insulation will be necessary if the floor bed layout is going to be down the middle of your greenhouse. This will largely depend on the severity of the weather in your country. I did experience such a problem during the winter of 1962/63 in a greenhouse which had a width of 8 m (25 ft). Despite a greenhouse minimum air temperature of 8°C (45°F) the soil temperature in the middle of the greenhouses went below freezing point. That occurred in a large greenhouse, so it is still advisable to take this precaution in most smaller ones. The cost of doing this is very small compared with losing plants that you have carefully nurtured for many years.

GREENHOUSE DESIGN FOR COLD AND HOT CLIMATES

Today there are a vast array of greenhouses that can be purchased, from wooden ones of very traditional design to metal kinds, including circular ones, and others using plastics. If you are contemplating the wooden type, ideally you should choose one made from red cedar but the price will be considerably higher than those made from a softer type of wood. However, present day wood preservatives can be very effective. It is possible to purchase either the materials or a wooden greenhouse in kit form, where the timber has been specially pressure treated. In the United Kingdom I had a number of the more traditional type of greenhouse, most of them rebuilt around 1950 using soft wood that had been treated with Cuprinol (a copper based preservative). Every few years the exterior timbers were treated with the same substance. A red cedar greenhouse should last a lifetime, but it all comes down to how much you are prepared to pay. Wooden greenhouses have the advantage of being easier to alter when it comes to new shelving etc.

Metal greenhouses are usually made of an aluminium alloy and require no maintenance, although in seaside areas problems can occur with the alloy being affected by the salt air. If the glass (which is usually fitted with patent clips) is rather tight it is not unknown for it to crack. They do tend to be a little colder than wooden ones, and of course the metal work in winter can also be covered with condensation in the same way as the glass. Compared with a wooden greenhouse the framing is very slim, so you get maximum light entering the greenhouse.

Reinforced plastic framed greenhouses are becoming available. They are based on the same system that has been used for a number of years for the double glazing of houses. The designs are much the same, the framing is bulkier than metal but the framework does not become covered with condensation as happens with metal greenhouses.

It is also possible to use various forms of corrugated plastic for greenhouse roofing. These corrugated sheets can be screwed to a relatively light-weight wooden frame. Your greenhouse will be virtually maintenance free if you use corrugated plastic roofing. Many of the true desert cacti require very high light intensity, particularly in maturity. This type of plastic allows a much higher degree of ultraviolet light penetration, compared to glass. I had two greenhouses that were entirely roofed with corrugated plastic. These proved to be very successful, whereby shy-flowering species were blooming profusely. Many of the larger growing *Echinocacti* and *Ferocacti* developed much longer and stronger spines than they ever did under glass, even though the glass was not shaded at all in summer. However, the plastic had to be shaded a little more than even ordinary glass if the plants within the greenhouse were normally types that enjoyed some shade in habitat. Plants can scorch more easily under it but overall it does make the greenhouse virtually maintenance free as no wood is exposed to the weather.

There are many viewpoints on greenhouse ventilation, as to whether ventilators should be on the roof or on the side. Most greenhouses that are purchased in kit form have roof ventilators but this is a matter for personal choice. The main problem can be that as the greenhouse gets older they can become a source of leaks. If you are building the greenhouse to your own design I suggest that you fit the ventilators on the sides where they can be equally effective. Much has been written over the years regarding the siting of a greenhouse — north to south or east to west. It is usually suggested that north to south is best, however I think it is a matter of choice.

Energy conservation is another factor to consider when deciding on the type of greenhouse to purchase as it is possible to obtain types which are already double or triple glazed. Because your greenhouse is intended for cacti this type of greenhouse is not ideal as there will be too much loss of light, particularly ultraviolet light. However, if you live in an area where sub-zero temperatures are quite common you have no option but to permanently double or triple glaze your greenhouse. It does mean that as the growing season approaches you will need to supplement the light intensity by means of GRO-LUX tubes. In northern parts of the United States many enthusiasts do not do this — instead they move their plants outside for the summer months. In much of the United Kingdom permanent double glazing is not necessary but a temporary form can be put up for the winter months, using either polythene sheeting or bubble plastic. If you use gas or paraffin heating it is imperative that you allow some air to get into the greenhouse, otherwise you will have combustion problems and heaters might go out on a cold night. If your greenhouse is electrically heated the temporary double glazing can be virtually everywhere.

In very hot climates a normal type of greenhouse would have to be shaded very heavily, also cooling extractor fans would be needed, otherwise your plants could literally boil! I have seen in other parts of the world metal greenhouses that have cold water running over the exterior of the glass in order to keep the temperature low enough in summer. For example, in Arizona temperatures can be very high in summer, but cool in winter, but with a low degree of atmospheric humidity. The plants require overhead protection from the sun in summer and maximum ventilation. This can be done by removing at least one side of the greenhouse for the hottest months.

Another material that is used in hot climates is corrugated fibreglass sheeting as a roofing material. This already has built-in shading potential, but it is capable of withstanding the light and heat for a number of years before it starts to break down. It will largely depend on where you live, but even fibreglass may need replacing after ten years usage. Most plastics as yet are incapable of enduring the ultraviolet intensity of the tropics. Corrugated fibreglass is the type of roofing I have used for my greenhouse in southern Spain, and barring very large hailstones it is much stronger. In a hot climate a high greenhouse is preferable, that is one over 3.5 m (11 ft) in height. It is also important to locate your greenhouse in a position where it is shaded from the late afternoon sun, otherwise fans and perhaps water cooling may be necessary. I have managed to keep my greenhouse in southern Spain shaded from the late afternoon sun by locating the greenhouse below the parapet of the swimming pool, facing south-east. It is on a sloping site and is also on two levels inside. It virtually opens up in summer by means of the high sliding aluminium framed doors, as well as normal doors on the upper level and sliding ventilators at each end. In this way I have avoided the need for extractor fans or any other methods of cooling, even though we can get shade temperatures outside exceeding 38°C (100°F) from late June to early September.

Some parts of the world can endure very severe hailstorms, where the hailstones will break glass, even fibreglass, because of their size. This problem can usually be prevented by small gauge wire netting being fitted very tightly about 5 cm (2 in) or so above your greenhouse. During June 1984 some of my greenhouses in the United Kingdom were wrecked by a freak hailstorm, but golf ball size hailstones are exceptionally rare in the United Kingdom.

Internal view of the seedling propagation greenhouse at 'The Exotic Collection', Worthing, which was roofed with corrugated plastic sheets.

Internal view of greenhouse in Fife, Scotland, which is permanently double glazed.

CARING FOR CACTI IN THE HOME

Not all cacti including other succulents are suited for indoor culture, particularly if you are going to rely on natural lighting and not boost it artificially. Straight away you will realise from what you have read in this book already, that the true desert species will be less suited to this sort of environment because heat and light intensity will be much less than its natural habitat. If you have a room that is almost all glass on its south side, vice versa if you live in the southern hemisphere, a wider variety of plants can be grown successfully as the conditions will be approaching that of a conservatory or greenhouse.

Temperature and Humidity

In addition to the amount of light available and how some species will succeed where others fail, the same applies when it comes to temperature and humidity in the home. Today many more houses are centrally heated whereby the humidity level is lower. This has adversely affected many of the non-succulent plants which were previously grown indoors. Most cacti thrive in conditions where the level of humidity is low. This is one of the reasons why more and more people have these plants indoors, they last so much longer even when treated rather badly.

The only type of cacti which prefer a more moist atmosphere are the epiphytic species, that is the Christmas Cactus (*Zygocactus truncatus*), Easter Cactus (*Schlumbergera gaertneri*) and those often referred to as *Phyllocacti* (*Epiphyllum* and *Epiphyllum* hybrids). However even these kinds will adapt to a certain extent to a drier atmosphere. The effects of this drier atmosphere can be further altered by standing the pots on special moisture holding granules.

In a centrally heated home the main snag to it is that for some of the smaller, free flowering globular cacti it can be a little too warm during the winter months, particularly at night. Many of the genera will flower better after a cool but dry winter resting period. In a home of this kind many of the plants would be looking very shrivelled and unhealthy if left dry for perhaps five months with a minimum temperature not much below 21°C (70°F). If your windows are single glazed and the curtains are in front of the sill, the temperature during the evening and night will be considerably lower than that of the rest of the room. Even so, this higher minimum winter temperature can adversely affect the flowering qualities of some species more than others. It does not mean that you will not get any flowers at all, but they will be produced in rather smaller numbers. So try to stop watering these plants for at least a few weeks during the coldest part of the winter, but this must not be done to the extent whereby the plants shrivel unduly.

Some of the cacti from low level equatorial regions where frosts never occur thrive in centrally heated homes because they can be kept growing throughout the year. They can be grown more easily than in the average greenhouse in a climate such as northern Europe, North America, Tasmania, or the South Island of New Zealand.

Choice of Genera as Regards Their Lighting Requirements

There are very few cacti which can be grown for any length of time in a shady spot indoors, particularly during the spring to autumn (fall) growing season. If you do put them in such a spot, it will be essential to minimise the watering so that very little growth occurs. The growth that does occur will be etiolated, that is the stems will get very thin and the spine length and strength will be much reduced. All plants when they are grown on a windowsill should be turned through 180° at least every week. This means that each side of the plant will receive an approximately equal amount of light during the year. This is particularly important with the taller growing plants.

Many of the plants sold in shops and supermarkets are not really the ideal species to buy because they are the kinds which can be grown quickly to a certain size and sold. Although the 'Prickly Pear' types are popular (*Opuntias* always seem popular, particularly with newcomers to the hobby because of their unusual branching habit), few of them can be expected to flower indoors. The same also applies to such genera as *Cereus, Cephalocereus, Lophocereus, Myrtillocactus, Pachycereus* and *Trichocereus.* Most of these plants are easily grown either from seed or cuttings, but the majority are unlikely to flower before they reach 2–4 m (6–12 ft). In other words to see them in maturity, you will need a rather large windowsill!

In contrast there are many small growing globular species of cacti that will grow really well on a sunny windowsill, and they will flower regularly each year. The genus which I consider to be the best is *Rebutia,* as in nature these plants often grow amongst grass; they come from fairly high up in South America, so they are not used to exceptionally high summer temperatures. The flower buds appear from around the base of each head in the spring, and you can virtually have any colour except blue. They can be grown very easily from seed, sometimes flowering in their second year, but virtually always in their third. Within a very few years most species start to branch, such that clusters of 20 or 30 heads are not at all uncommon. On a big clump you can expect to get 100 or so flowers at least each spring, over a period of three or four weeks.

Other small growing and mostly globular cacti that can be expected to do well on a sunny windowsill are to be found amongst the following genera: *Chamaecereus, Coryphantha, Echinopsis, Echinocereus* (not the pectinate spined species), *Hamatocactus, Lobivia, Mammillaria,*

Melocactus, Notocactus and *Parodia.* There are many species within the above genera which can be expected to bloom on a sunny windowsill.

The genera listed will be a good base on to which you can build up a collection of plants for the home. Having obtained some of them and succeeded with them, there is nothing wrong with experimenting further with other genera as there are many thousands of species to choose from. Probably the biggest problem for many of you will be in obtaining correctly named plants. At the very least you can take this book and perhaps one of my others, *The Pocket Encyclopaedia of Cacti in Colour* (Blandford Press, United Kingdom, 1969), with you when you next go out to purchase some species for the home.

Differing Watering Requirements

In many ways watering your plants indoors is probably easier than in the greenhouse or conservatory, as they can be inspected and watered individually. I have quite deliberately avoided mentioning watering in any detail until now, as the same rules apply indoors as they do in the greenhouse. In the home, plants tend to be watered either from the bottom by putting the water into the saucer in which they stand, or by pouring it onto the soil around the neck of the plant. Ideally plants should always be watered overhead; this helps to keep the plants clean from dust and reduces the risk of attack from pests. In the greenhouse this is easy to do using either a watering can with a fine rose on it, or the garden hose. I would certainly advise those of you who grow your plants indoors to either put them in the bath, or outside if you have a garden or a balcony and periodically douse them overhead with water. This should be done every four to six weeks during the spring to autumn (fall) period.

One of the commonest questions to be asked is 'How often should I water my cacti?' This is almost an impossible question to answer as the soils used by growers can differ a lot, the soil in clay pots dries out quicker than in plastic ones, and then it depends on the temperature of the environment. There are gadgets which can be pushed into the soil and they show you on a scale how much water is left in the soil. They work very well when new, but once the probe corrodes a little they can then become very inaccurate. Personally I always suggest that you look at the underside of the pot, and also probe the soil to the depth of about 2–3 cm (about 1 in) and if it is dry, water is required. You will soon find that you will know when they need it, rather than having to probe the soil in each pot. In warm weather the majority of kinds can usually be safely watered even if they have not completely dried out. More care does have to be taken if plastic pots are being used, as the soil dries out much more slowly.

In the home today it is possible to use self-watering pots for plants, where the reservoir needs refilling about every two to three weeks. This does not mean that you should not water them overhead. Many cactus gardens can be seen for sale, also many amateurs make up their own using bowls containing no drainage positions. Ideally you need an inspection position so that you avoid over-watering. This can be done very easily if you are making up the garden yourself, by first having a good layer of shingle or other drainage material on to which is placed a short glass or plastic tube about 2.5 cm (1 in) across. (See diagram below). This will enable you to inspect the drainage layer to see that it is completely dry before watering the plants. If the plants are over-watered it does not take long for the soil to become sour, which will mean that repotting will have to be done very quickly, otherwise the plants will quickly suffer.

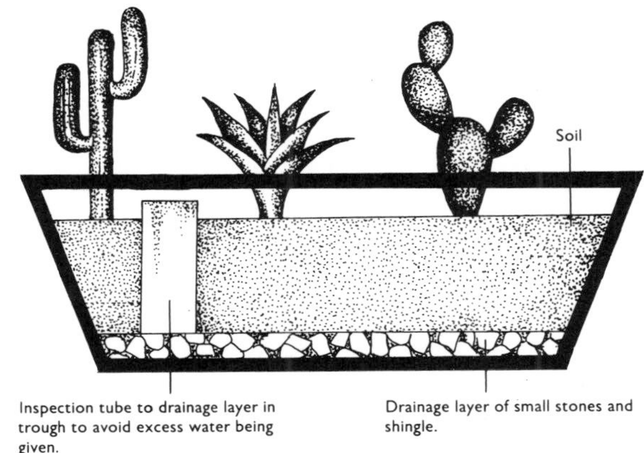

In bowl gardens as with mixed beds of cacti in a greenhouse, watering can be made more difficult if plants of mixed growth rates have been put together. So often I see in stores and garden centres cactus gardens containing the wrong mixture of plants. They look very fine at the time, but in three or four months' time, some of the cacti will probably have rotted through over-watering, whilst one or two of the quick growing other succulents have taken the bowl garden over.

The quality of water differs considerably from place to place, particularly in regards to its hardness. As a general rule one uses tapwater, but if sediment appears on the soil after watering I would suggest that you consult your local government department for their advice. Rainwater is perfectly satisfactory, but having been stored in a garden water-butt or tank it is invariably far dirtier than tapwater, even though it will be soft water.

Treatment of Pests Indoors

I am not at all happy about the safety angle of using insecticides on one's plants indoors, particularly the modern day systemic types, as they remain active for quite a few weeks. If you have a garden, balcony, or a flat-roof it is possible to still use them by moving your plants outside, putting a temporary plastic or glass cover over them, and seeing that they are shaded from any direct sunshine once the plants have been drenched with insecticide. My personal view is that they should remain there until they have been watered once or twice more. Most insecticides have had rather unpleasant pungent smells added to them, and these tend to make themselves known again when you next water the plants normally.

On page 195 I have referred to the use of rather more simple methods of getting rid of small insect pests, that is using surgical spirit or household liquid soap. If plants have developed root mealy bug and you do not wish to use an insecticide, the only real answer is to knock the plants out of their pots, get rid of most of the soil, and then wash the roots in soapy water. Then allow the roots to dry for a few days, before repotting into new clean soil.

Culture by Artificial Light Only

To many of you such an idea may seem impossible, particularly with the true desert cacti which require a high light intensity. Few species present any great problems, in fact the more densely spined they are, the more perfect they can be grown by this method. Oddly enough the less densely spined species of *Rebutia* are amongst the few which do not adapt so well, and yet they can be grown and flowered on the average sunny windowsill.

My first sight of cacti being grown beneath tubular fluorescent lights was back in 1970, in the Chicago area. In this case, because of the severe winter conditions in that part of the world, heating a greenhouse sufficiently is almost impossible, at the least exceedingly expensive. So they put over one room of their home to their plants, using tubular fluorescent GRO-LUX tubes suspended over tables, plus a large three tiered trolley which has tubes above each shelf. This is a very compact method of doing it, ideal for the smaller globular cacti. Ready made trolleys of this sort are available in the United States, but so far I have not seen them for sale yet anywhere in Europe, or in the United Kindgom. In fact this type of culture has been commonplace in the United States and Canada for many years now, such that a great deal of study has been going on for all sorts of plants.

I have seen the collections of many of the subscribers to 'The Exotic Collection' monthly colour magazine, during various lecture tours I have made to the United States over the last 20 years. In so many cases the use of fluorescent tubes for growing plants has been apparent even if it was only for seed raising and bringing on young seedlings.

There are a number of makes of fluorescent tubes suitable for horticultural use, so it is easy to obtain most of the suitable equipment. They are usually available in 0.6–1.3 m (2–4 ft) lengths, and they can be obtained with accompanying reflectors, which normally house two tubes, some three. They are usually 20 watt or 40 watt tubes, so in comparison to ordinary 100 or 150 watt light bulbs in the home, the running costs are considerably reduced. In more recent years improvements have been made by the manufacturers, whereby you can obtain wide spectrum tubes which give even better results, compared with those made ten years ago or more.

If you have a cellar or a room that can be devoted to plants, this is basically what you have to do. Firstly install some benches or tables on which you have large metal or plastic trays; this is purely to avoid water going everywhere, particularly important if the room is upstairs. The reflectors which carry the tubes need to be suspended from the ceiling by an adjustable method, so that the actual tubes are between 35 and 40 cm (14–16 in) above the average height of the plants, assuming the plants are not too different in height, from one to the other. If you are attempting to grow much taller types of plants by this method, it would be better to group them together, whereby the lights will be on a shorter suspension length of cord or chain. Ideally the lights want to be connected to a time clock, so that they switch on and off automatically. Assuming you have no natural light at all, you have to artificially not only give them the correct amount of light per day, but also produce an artificial winter period, when less light is made available. This is particularly important with some genera amongst the CACTACEAE, also they need to be cooler so that they can rest, otherwise they will not flower. With some of the other succulents, or certain cacti from more equatorial regions, that is *Melocacti*, this is not important. Quite honestly given sufficient warmth and light throughout the year, they will flower non-stop. Sixteen to eighteen hours of artificial light per day seems to give the best results during the spring, summer and autumn (fall), but reduce down to about 14 hours for the winter. This number of hours per day is more than they would normally receive in nature, but it does give good results.

Generally speaking with most of the really spiny cacti, growth rates are slower under lights, compared to culture in a greenhouse. The reason for this is not lack of light, but lack of heat during the artificial summer. In a greenhouse here temperatures on a sunny day often reach 44°C (110°F), sometimes even higher, but in a basement or in a spare room, even with the warmth off the tubes, the temperature rarely exceeds 32°C (85°F). So this will obviously slow the growth rate of the majority of the plants, but the biggest problem comes during the artificial winter when one wishes to keep the temperature down for certain genera. Most *Echinocerei* will not flower freely if they are not given a cool dry resting period for a few months. If your home is centrally heated, most of your cacti, with the exception of *Melocacti* and related kinds, will do better under the lights if the radiators are turned off in the room in question.

Even then you may well find that the room temperature will exceed 10°C (50°F) even at night. You may find that some ventilation will be necessary to try and keep the night temperature down to 8°C (45°F) or even a little lower. This is something you will have to experiment with over a period of a few weeks.

In addition to tubular fluorescent lights you can also obtain spot lamps which are suitable for horticultural use; these are also made by a number of manufacturers in different countries. This method allows for large specimen plants to be grown in a relatively dark environment in the home and the office, and yet grow remarkably well. These type of lamps are more expensive to run as they are much more powerful. Again some experimentation will have to be made as regards the power required, or whether you need two or three lamps for one large specimen.

Watering presents no great problem, but you will find that as excessively high temperatures do not occur, you will water less often. If you are growing some of the really slow growing cacti where normally extra sand and grit is advised in the compost, I would advise you to add even more, that is for *Ariocarpus* and related genera.

Finally you must remember that you cannot wait until the tubes pack up completely, because they do lose their power gradually. Tubes do need to be cleaned periodically with a damp cloth; this all helps to reduce the loss of light too. When your lights are new, and if you possess a photographic light meter, do take a reading off a fairly green plant, making a note of the distance at which you took the reading, and repeat this each month and record the readings. If your readings later on show a reduction of 20%, the time has come to renew your tubes.

CULTURE IN A COOL CLIMATE

Alpine (English) Garden

Many cacti are well suited for either temporary or permanent planting in the average English garden, or in countries where frost and snow is commonplace during the winter months. Some years will suit the plants better than others depending on whether they receive too much rain and too little sun. However there are many species that are not true desert dwellers and these are well suited for a garden during the frost-free months of the year.

In our garden back in the United Kingdom it had been common practice for some 35 years or so to actually plant out certain species of cacti into the ordinary ground amidst other plants and shrubs that you expect to see in an English garden. This usually means that the plants cannot be planted outside with a free root run until late April, when hopefully no further frosts are likely to occur. They will have to be repotted and returned to a greenhouse during early October, as frosts can be expected by the end of that month.

Most species of *Cerei, Trichocerei,* and *Opuntia* made ideal subjects for planting amidst fuchsias and the smaller growing conifers. Their bold appearance, particularly if they are branched specimens, can add a striking contrast to an otherwise English garden border. In early October when the plants were dug up, it was often necessary to trim the roots a little before potting them up. I then partially submerged the potted *Cerei, Opuntia* etc., in the soil, in the actual positions from whence they had come, until usually the end of October, occasionally even into early November. The repotted plants were kept watered if the weather was very dry, unless a lot of root trimming had been necessary in order to repot them. It does mean that your garden can still look very nice literally up to the day when the first real frost warning is given, when the plants are then rushed indoors.

It is possible to just plunge plants complete with their pots, but provided you select the correct genera free root-run conditions for a few months suits these types very well. I have myself made up slightly raised beds with a rock or rock-faced block surround into which these kinds have been placed, and then disguised the pots with shingle. Unless the summer is a moist one these plants with their pots submerged in shingle will still need watering regularly, and they will not grow so well as those that have a few months of free root run.

Alpine Rockery

It is possible to have a permanent planting of many species of cacti by selecting species that will cope with severe frosts and snow. In the United Kingdom the alternation between wet and cold in the winter can be more of a problem. Yet the same species will thrive much better in other countries that have a drier winter, even though temperatures are much lower than in the United Kingdom. There are many species of dwarf or somewhat low growing *Opuntia* from North America that are well suited for an alpine rockery, along with one or two *Echinocerei, Neobesseya* and *Coryphantha vivipara.* See page 29 for list of tested species that are well suited to an alpine rockery.

The main requirement for a hardy cactus rockery is good drainage and preferably a south or south-west facing sloping site. If you are going to build one yourself you will ideally require at least 15 cm (6 in) depth of rubble, rocks, or stones

General view of part of the hardy cactus rockery of 'The Exotic Collection', Worthing. In addition to Opuntias *certain other hardy succulents are also visible.*

at the bottom. The soil mixture has to be very poor, that is it has to contain a high percentage of shingle and grit. The cacti rockery I had in the United Kingdom had a soil mixture of about four to five parts per volume of shingle, grit and sand to one part humus, plus a little slow acting fertiliser. The top of the bed then needs about 2.5 cm (1 in) depth of shingle, in order to give good drainage around the neck of the plants.

Most of the *Opuntia* that I have listed on page 29 can be expected to flower profusely each summer even if the weather is not particularly warm. The accompanying photograph (page 29) of *Opuntia phaeacantha* depicts a 1 m (3 ft) diameter clump, which shows how one of the recommended species flowered outside on a rockery in the United Kingdom. In the late autumn (fall) or early winter the *Opuntia* pads should start to shrivel. It is this shrivelling that is so important for the plants to be able to survive the severe frosts. If the winter is very wet and alternates with severe frosts some of the species of *Opuntia* and genera such as *Coryphantha, Echinocereus, Neobesseya* and *Pediocactus* can rot. Under these circumstances a little overhead protection from the rain will usually prevent this happening. The species most likely to suffer in this way have been marked with an asterisk (*). Yet in habitat these species safely endure temperatures at times down to –18° C (0° F). With the exception of *Opuntia russellii*, these are all North American cacti and are safe to grow outside in a temperate climate. There are almost certainly other high altitude South American species which it would be worth experimenting with under identical cultural conditions.

Hardy Cacti

Coryphantha vivipara

Echinocereus baileyi (northerly form)
E. triglochidiatus (northerly form)
E. viridiflorus

Neobesseya missouriensis

Opuntia arenaria
*O. atrispina**
*O. ballii**
O. cantabrigiensis
*O. clavata**
O. compressa
O. compressa var. *allairei*
O. compressa var. *fusco-atra*
O. compressa var. *grandiflora*
O. compressa var. *humifusa*
O. compressa var. *macrorhiza*
O compressa var. *rafinesquei*
O compressa var. *stenochila*
O. cymochila
O. davisii
O. drummondii
O. engelmannii var. *linguiformis**
O. engelmannii var. *texana**
O. fragilis
*O. grahamii**
*O. hystricina**
O. hystricina var. *rubrispina*
O. hystricina var. *ursina**
O. imbricata
O. juniperina
*O. kleiniae**
O. leptocarpa
*O. leptocaulis**
*O. macrocentra**
O. phaeacantha
O. phaeacantha var. *brunnea**
O. phaeacantha var. *camanchica**
O. phaeacantha var. *tenuispina**
O. polyacantha
O. polyacantha var. *trichophora**
*O. plumbea**
O. pottsii
O. rhodantha
O. rhodantha var. *spinosior**
*O. russellii**
*O. schottii**
O. schweriniana
O. sphaerocarpa
*O. strigil**
O. tardospina

Pediocactus simpsonii

1.3 m (4 ft) diameter clump of Opuntia phaeacantha

CULTURE IN A TROPICAL CLIMATE

Landscaping with Cacti

Obviously the method of culture and the variety of plants that can be grown outside will depend on many factors, particularly the climate in your part of the world. If you live in a very hot arid climate there will be no limit to the variety of species that you can grow, although you will find it necessary to provide shade for some species. Epiphytic cacti will present more of a problem, as they also like more humidity. Landscaping with cacti in conjunction with other trees and shrubs, as well as other succulent plants, can provide areas where even some of the more robust epiphytic cacti can grow and flower. Obviously, when you are mixing totally different types of plant life, you have to select types which will succeed using the same soil, and similar cultural requirements. This can be achieved, producing natural shade (which many cacti need), and the right artistic effect. In contrast, if you live in a hot but moist climate it is likely that plants will have to be grown in raised beds to assist drainage. It may also be necessary to provide overhead protection from the rain for some species, either on a permanent basis or for a period of a month or so each year.

In the south-western part of the United States quite a wide variety of cacti and other succulent plants can be grown outside without any need for protection, but they have to be kinds that can cope with some frost. Frosts may occur here each winter, or occasionally in other seasons with temperatures dropping down to -4°C to -8°C (25°F–18°F) for a few hours. There are some places where temperatures can drop much lower, but invariably the atmospheric humidity is very low indeed, so many cacti can cope with it. Occasionally snow can fall, and sometimes this is accompanied by low temperatures for up to 48 hours, and then the growing points of even some of the native cacti can be damaged. If you are attempting to grow outside species which are less resistant to frost, this can often be successfully achieved by positioning them against the walls of your home or beneath hardy trees.

In Florida and along the Gulf Coast of Texas, the climate is generally very mild in winter, with temperatures up to 30°C (83°F), so plants need to be watered. However, the weather can change rapidly and temperatures drop to well below freezing, perhaps accompanied by quite heavy falls of snow. This only happens occasionally, as it did in 1983/84, and again during December 1989. A much wider range of plants has been successfully grown here for many years, compared with the south-western part of the United States. But from time to time gardens are devastated by one of these freezes, partly because plants which are less frost resistant are being cultivated, and these quickly succumb. But some of the more hardy species which safely survive

This artistically arranged cacti display was photographed at Ghost Lodge Ranch Motel in Tucson, Arizona. In addition to using large specimens of Echinocactus grusonii *there are Barrel Cacti, including* Ferocactus stainesii *var.* pilosus, Ferocactus covillei, *and sundry* Cerei *in the background.*

On of the author's rockeries in Spain, with the yellow flowered Dolichothele longimamma *at bottom left,* Arequipa leucotricha *at bottom right. The orange-brown flowered plant is an unusual colour form of* Neoporteria curvispina, *and at the rear three nice plants of* Astrophytum myriostigma *var.* coahuilenis.

south-western winters succumb as well, because they are being watered and are growing, so they are more sensitive. Back in the south-west those species would be dry and dormant.

Along the Mediterranean coast of France there are a number of world famous gardens, some of which have massive plantings of cacti and other succulent plants. The climate here is nothing like so hot in summer as the other places mentioned in this chapter, but to succeed with cacti, the problems are rather different. There are few problems during the spring to autumn (fall) period, beyond the fact that growth rates will vary more from year to year, compared with the south-western part of the United States or Florida. Summer temperatures can be more variable, and the growing season tends to be shorter. Rainfall tends to be greater here during the coolest months, so problems can arise from time to time when snow and frosts occur. The atmospheric humidity is much higher here in winter, and when temperatures suddenly drop to below freezing, plants are quickly damaged. There have been occasions at 'Jardin Exotique', one of the show places in the Principality of Monaco, when their large specimens of *Echinocactus grusonii* have been covered with snow, so the previous Director (Louis Vatrican) decided to have circular straw hats or disks made to protect them. If a frost warning came, these hats or disks were placed on certain species each night, to prevent damage being done to the centre of the plants. (Straw or hessian is much better for this purpose than plastic, as with the latter condensation collects on the underside, which might drop into the growing point and freeze.) In these particular gardens a lot has been learned about the hardiness of many cacti. The ordinary *Cerei* and many *Trichocerei* cope with frosts very well, as does *Pilosocereus polylophus*. Some huge specimens of this species have survived the occasional bad winter completely unscathed. 'Jardin Exotique' is built on a south facing cliff face, and it is because of the wonderful drainage on such a site that so many different species have been grown outside so successfully for so many years.

So, when you are planning to landscape your garden with cacti, do investigate in advance the climatic conditions for your area for the past ten or twenty years. In the main, it is the winter period which is most critical; whether it is cold and dry, or whether most of your rainfall occurs at that time of year. Once you have done that, you can decide if there already is sufficient natural drainage on the site, or whether special raised beds have to be built. When I was planning my garden in southern Spain, I learned from local records that the annual rainfall ranged from about 25–50 cm (10–20 in). Twenty-five cm (10 in) of rain per year is equivalent to the average rainfall in southern Arizona, or the northern Chihuahua and Sonora regions of Mexico, areas where a vast range of cacti originate from. When checking out the weather records for southern Spain, I discovered that most of this rain occurred from late autumn (fall) to early spring, with the heaviest amounts in November and February. Fortunately those winters with the coolest temperatures were also the driest ones, an important point for successfully cultivating a wide range of cacti in the open air. Generally speaking frosts are very rare on the southern side of the mountains which run along the south coast of Spain. Light frosts occur more regularly on the northern side, which limits the choice of cacti to use in landscaping. My garden is on the south side, has a drop of some 30 m (90 ft) from top to bottom, and looks out in a southerly direction to the Mediterranean. During a colder winter, temperatures here can occasionally fall to 2–5°C (35–40°C) for a few hours in the early morning. Because of these favourable conditions, I am able to grow a very wide range of cacti outside.

Because the rain does come at the cooler time of year, and because the rains can be very heavy, drainage was still important to my garden. As it slopes steeply, there is plenty of natural drainage, but as I wanted to grow some of the much slower growing species outside, I did construct a few raised rockeries, in which I used a very porous soil mixture. It consisted of two parts (by volume) of gritty sand, one part peat, and one part top-soil. The only disadvantage is that during the very hottest months, these rockeries need water two or three times per week, preferably given to them during the evening. As you can see by the accompanying illustrations, the plants are surrounded with small pieces of local rock. The main reason for this is that when heavy rains occur the plants can become discoloured by the soil mixture splashing over them. This particularly

Large white spined clusters of Mammillaria parkinsonii *in the foreground. The large golden yellow spined plants are* Echinocactus grusonii, *whilst in the background on the left are the white topped* Pilosocereus palmeri. *The tall, branched, erect growing plant on the right of the picture is* Lemaireocereus thurberi. Photographed at The Huntington Botanical Gardens.

Pilosocereus polylophus — *one of the finest columnar species for landscaping purposes.*

applies to cacti with pure white, or golden-yellow, hair or spines. The small rocks do serve other purposes, reducing weeds, and in very hot weather the roots of many of the shallow-rooted cacti seek moisture and coolness beneath them.

When I moved my collection of cacti from England to southern Spain in June (early summer here), I had an additional problem to contend with—the chance of plants being burned by the Mediterranean sun. This is something to remember, if you move your plants to a much hotter

Young specimens of Echinocactus grusonii, *along with white spined* Mammillaria, *contrasting with a bluish leaved Aloe and Agave (not cacti), backed by Oleander.*

Mammillaria *clusters and the arching stems of* Rathbunia.

location. The epidermis of cacti grown in greenhouses are considerably softer than that on plants grown out of doors. So some of my plants went into a well ventilated greenhouse with a corrugatd fibreglass roof, and the remainder went under two layers of green shade netting. This was reduced to one layer by mid-autumn (fall), and removed completely two months later.

This problem of plants being burned in hotter climates can also apply when plants are purchased and planted, or moved from one part of your garden to another. This applies to both young and mature plants. Young plants are likely to have been cultivated under partial shade, so they will need some protection in the first year. However, with mature cacti, it is imperative to replant them with the same side facing the sun, otherwise the plant body can burn. In severe cases, it could kill a plant, so do take these precautions.

Finally, when it comes to landscaping, you may purchase plants in different ways, containerised or freshly dug. Containerised plants from tubs and pots can be planted at almost any time of the year, except when heavy rainfall is imminent. Ideally in semi-desert areas, the autumn (fall) is best, but in areas where heavy rainfall occurs during the winter months, you must choose between early autumn (fall) and early spring. Under these conditions, containerised plants with undamaged root systems will grow very rapidly in the early autumn (fall). Freshly dug plants will be slower starting growing again, so spring is the ideal time for them.

Containerised plants are very easy to plant, as they only require a suitable hole, a little larger than the root ball. You can put a mixture of about equal parts gritty sand and peat in the bottom of the hole if you wish, as this will encourage the formation of new roots. Once you have filled in around the root ball with soil from the original hole, firm it down with your hand or shoe, before giving the plant a bucket of water. This should be sufficient to water the plant in—do not give any more until the soil has dried out for a few days around the plant.

Freshly dug plants will need to have their roots inspected for broken ones. Any broken roots should be cut off with secateurs or a sharp knife. The plant should then be put aside in a shady place for three to four days, so that those cuts can callous. Where there has been considerable root damage, planting is best done prior to the dry season, so watering can be better controlled. The hole for these plants should have a good layer at the bottom made up of equal parts of dry sand and peat, before planting is carried out. A little more of the same mix should be put in around the roots, before completing the job with soil removed from the original hole. Again, firm the soil down with a hand or shoe. If the surrounding soil is very dry, water the plant in with a bucket of water, otherwise leave any artificial watering for at least a month.

Finally, taller growing cacti (whether they were originally containerised or not) will need staking or surrounding with rocks to keep them steady. If the latter method is used, protect the base of the plant with corrugated cardboard, hessian, or foam. Even when staking plants, it is advisable to use these materials as cushioning. When you wire round the plant and fix it to the stake, put the wire through a small length of rubber hosepipe to protect the plant. When and if you remove these stakes will mainly depend on the species and exposure to wind. Some columnar kinds will become so well established in 12–18 months that stakes can be safely removed, but you will have to judge this for yourself. The materials I have recommended for protecting the plants are also ideal for use when handling some of the spiny species.

Cacti Genera

Epiphyllum X Conway's Giant

ACANTHOCALYCIUM

(ă-kăn'-thŏ-kăl-ĭs'-ĭ-ŭm)

Acanthocalycium contains 14 species. The generic name is derived from *acantha* (thorn or spine), and 'calyx' (the outer part of a flower ie where the sepals unite). The important identification feature of this genus is the spiny exterior of the ovary and scales on the tube of the flower. They are relatively small, straight ribbed plants, with either a globular or short cylindrical body, rarely exceeding 10 cm (4 in) in diameter and 8–20 ribs, according to the species. The areoles can be from less than 1 cm (0.4 in) to 2 cm (0.8 in) apart. These can bear 7–20 or more radial spines, and 1–3 centrals. The spines are usually stiffly subulate, some particularly so (as with *A. thionanthum*, see below), and can be 1–2.5 cm (0.4–1 in) in length. Their colour is equally variable from ash-grey, and golden brown to black.

NORTH AMERICA
NORTH PACIFIC OCEAN
NORTH ATLANTIC OCEAN
SOUTH PACIFIC OCEAN
SOUTH AMERICA
SOUTH ATLANTIC OCEAN

The funnel-shaped flowers are about 5 cm (2 in) in length and in diameter occasionally a little larger. Their colour can range from white and yellow, to pink and red. The fruits are globular, 1.5 cm (0.6 in) in diameter, very spiny and scaly, and usually the same colour as the spines on the plant.

Culture: *Acanthocalyciums* come from northern Argentina, and are usually found growing either among grass or beneath bushes on sloping ground, at altitudes of 500–3000 m (1640–9840 ft). They are generally easy plants to raise from seed, and can be expected to flower in 3 or 4 years (some species flower earlier). In winter they tolerate near freezing temperatures if kept dry, but in summer they do not like full sun.

Acanthocalycium thionanthum

Acanthocalycium thionanthum

Common Name: None.
Size: Height 15 cm (5 in).
Climate: High elevation.
Distribution: Northern Argentina.
Flowering Time: Summer.
Description: This is a globular species, although very old specimens can become taller than they are wide. The body is green, and the oval-shaped areoles have 8–10 radial spines and 1–4 centrals, all of which are ash-grey in colour. The spine length is 1–1.5 cm (0.4–0.6 in). The flowers are yellow, and just under 5 cm (2 in) in diameter. The fruit is globular, very spiny and scaly, and about 1.5 cm (0.6 in) in diameter.

Acanthocalycium thionanthum

APOROCACTUS

(ăp-ō-rō-kăk'-tŭs)

Aporocactus contains five species, and the generic name is derived from the Gk, meaning 'impenetrable cactus'. It is an epiphytic cactus, with long, slender, pendant spiny cylindrical stems, often bearing numerous aerial roots. The stems can be up to 2 m (6.5 ft) in length, but no more than 2.5 cm (1 in) in diameter, with 8–12 ribs. The areoles are set very close together, bearing 8–20 or more radial spines, and usually 3–4 centrals. These are all very short, fine, and golden or reddish-brown in colour.

The flowers appear in great profusion, are zygomorphic, and 7–10 cm (3–4 in) in length. Their colour can vary from pink or carmine to magenta. The fruits are small, spiny, globular and less than 1.25 cm (0.5 in) in diameter.

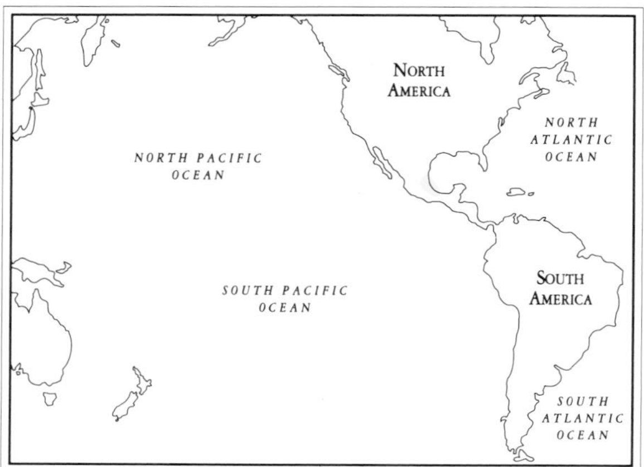

Culture: *Aporocacti* are native to central and southern Mexico and are to be found growing in well rotted humus in the forks of oak trees at altitudes above 2000 m (6560 ft). In cultivation they are easy plants to grow, provided they have a soil rich in humus, are not grown in full sun, and are given plenty of water during the hottest weather. They can be left dry during the winter months, provided they are kept fairly cool, otherwise they will need some water even at this time of year.

Aporocactus flagelliformis

Aporocactus flagelliformis

Common Name: Rat's Tail Cactus.
Size: Height 2 m (6.5 ft), width 30 cm (12 in).
Climate: Medium elevation.
Distribution: Central and northern Mexico.
Flowering Time: Spring.
Description: This is an epiphytic cactus with numerous spiny, cylindrical pendant stems, up to 2 m (6.5 ft) in length. The stems have 10–12 inconspicuous ribs, bearing small areoles closely set together. These have up to 12 fine radial spines, no more than 4 centrals and are usually golden brown in colour. The zygomorphic flowers can exceed 7.5 cm (3 in) in length, and are usually crimson in colour. The fruits are globular, spiny, and under 1.25 cm (0.5 in) in diameter.

Aporocactus flagelliformis

ARIOCARPUS

(ā'-rĭ-ō-kär'-pŭs)

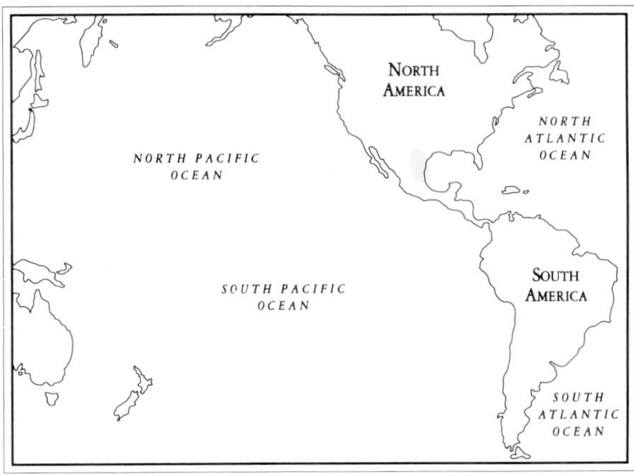

Ariocarpus contains eight species and a few varieties. The generic name is derived from the genus name *'Aria'* — the fruits of both species described below are similar. *Ariocarpus* are dwarf plants — a few exceedingly so, somewhat flat topped, single headed or clustering, and possess a very succulent carrot-like root structure. In the wild in most species only the top surface of the plant is above ground level. The diameter of a single head is 2.5–15 cm (1–6 in), but occasionally very old clumps can be two or three times as large as that. They are very hard, tubercled plants either with tubercles 5 cm (2 in) or more in length, as with *A. trigonus* (see page 38), or with flat knobbly tubercles often less than 1.25 cm (0.5 in) across which are also very woolly, as with *A. kotschoubeyanus* (see page 38). These tubercles are arranged spirally, have wool between them, and it is from this position that the flowers appear, a small distance from the centre of a head.

The funnel-shaped flowers are 2.5–5 cm (1–2 in) in diameter, and range in colour from white or cream, as with *A. trigonus*, to pink and carmine, as with *A. kotschoubeyanus*. The fruits are somewhat cylindrical, 1.25–2.5 cm (0.5–1 in) in length.

Culture: *Ariocarpus* are to be found in sandy and rocky positions, where there is good drainage, and come from northern Mexico and south-western United States. They are slow growing plants, and some species can live to a great age, of many hundreds of years. In cultivation they require a sandy compost, full sun, and should be watered freely during very hot weather and sparingly at other times. They can only be raised from seed and, with the exception of the miniature species such as *A. kotschoubeyanus*, it takes many years for plants to reach flowering size.

Ariocarpus kotschoubeyanus

Ariocarpus kotschoubeyanus

Common Name: Living Rock Cactus, although this name is usually used for *A. fissuratus*.
Size: Diameter up to 12.5 cm (5 in).
Climate: Medium elevation.
Distribution: Northern Mexico.
Flowering Time: Late autumn (fall) and early winter.
Description: Usually a single headed and very flat topped species, with numerous small tubercles, each with a furrow containing white wool on the top surface. The tubercles are no more than 0.7 cm (about 0.3 in) in height and in diameter. The light purple to magenta flowers are 3–5 cm (1.2–2 in) in diameter. The fruits are cylindrical, white and no more than 1.25 cm (0.5 in) in length.

Ariocarpus kotschoubeyanus

Ariocarpus trigonus in bud

Ariocarpus trigonus

Common Name: None.
Size: Diameter up to 20 cm (8 in).
Climate: Medium elevation.
Distribution: Northern Mexico.
Flowering Time: Late autum (fall) to early winter.
Description: It is usually a single headed and flat topped species with numerous tubercles, 3.5–5 cm (1.4–2 in) in length. These are slightly triangular in shape, and keeled below. The flowers are usually 5 cm (2 in) in diameter, and creamy-white to pale yellow. The elongated fruits are creamy-white, and about 2.5 cm (1 in) in length.

Ariocarpus trigonus

ARROJADOA

(ăr-rō-zhă'-dō-ă)

Arrojadoa contains about ten species and a few varieties. The generic name honours Dr Miguel Arrojado Lisboa of Brazil. The plants are mostly slender stemmed, erect or creeping, with stems up to 2 m (6.5 ft) in height, and 2–5 cm (0.8–2 in) in diameter. They do branch, but this usually occurs from the base of the plant. The green to dark green stems have 10–15 straight ribs, and the areoles are set quite close together. These can be oval or very elongated, bearing up to 12 radial spines and 8 centrals. In a few species it is very difficult to distinguish between the radials and the centrals. The fine radial spines can be 0.4–0.8 cm (0.1–0.2 in) in length, and the slightly stouter centrals can sometimes reach 1.5 cm (0.6 in) in length. In some species there is fine white hair interspersed with the radial spines. The spine colour can range from white with brown tips to dark brown or black.

The nocturnal flowers appear from an apical cephalium which consists of a mass of white wool and slender bristly spines, usually of a similar colour to the normal spines on the plant. The flowers are tubular in shape and 1–3 cm (0.4–1.2 in) in length, and 0.5–1 cm (0.2–0.4 in) in diameter. The flower colour ranges from pink to carmine. The fruits are globular, up to 1.5 cm (0.6 in) in diameter, pink or red when ripe, with the remains of the flowers still attached.

Culture: *Arrojadoas* are native to northern Brazil, where they may grow among rocks, or beneath other shrubs, which help to support their slender stems. They are easy to grow, free flowering plants, which can be propagated from seeds or cuttings. They like a soil containing some humus, and should be watered freely from spring to autumn (fall). In winter they should be left dry, with a minimum temperature of 10°C (50°F). But, as with some of the other cephalium-bearing cacti, in a warmer climate where temperatures do not drop very low in winter they can have some water, and will flower over a much longer period.

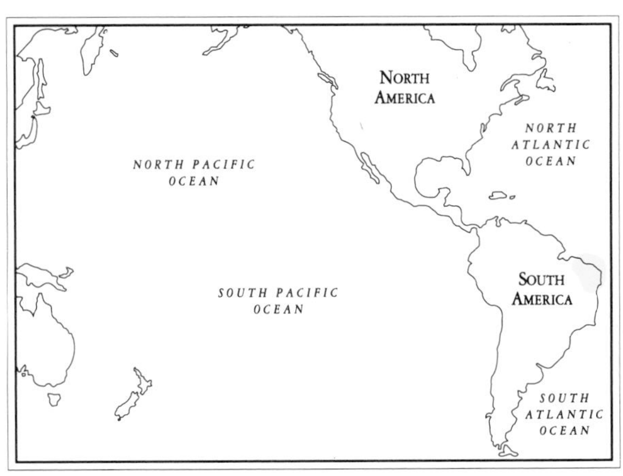

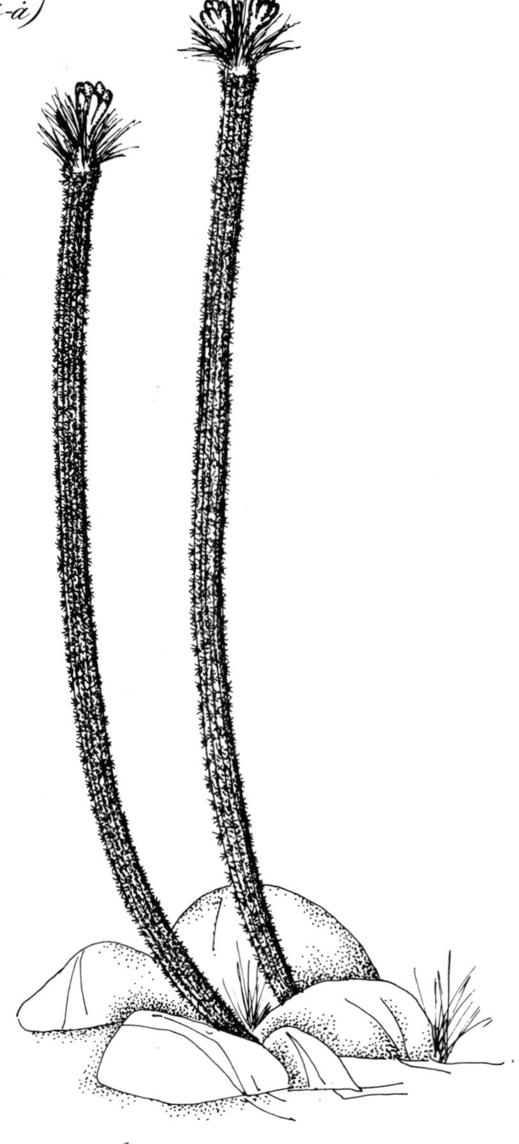

Arrojadoa penicillata

Arrojadoa pencillata

Arrojadoa penicillata

Common Name: None.
Size: Height 2 m (6 ft), width 2.5 cm (1 in).
Climate: Mediterranean.
Distribution: Northern Brazil.
Flowering Time: Late spring to late autumn (fall).
Description: This is a slender, green stemmed species. On old stems there are bristly tufts where new stems have grown through the cephalium position. The stems have up to 12 ribs, with small circular areoles containing a little white wool. These bear up to 12 radial spines, and up to 2 centrals. The radials are short and very fine, appressed, while the centrals are more rigid and can reach 3 cm (1.2 in) in length. The spines are off-white to brown. The tubular, bright pink, nocturnal flowers can be up to 1.25 cm (0.5 in) in length, and they appear from a cephalium containing a mass of white wool and reddish-brown bristly spines. The globular fruits are about 1 cm (0.4 in) in diameter.

Arrojadoa sp. *nova*

Arrojadoa sp. *nova* (aff. *A. rhodantha*)

Common Name: None.
Size: Stems up to 2 m (6 ft) in height, forming clumps up to 60 cm (2 ft) in diameter.
Climate: Tropical.
Distribution: Eastern Brazil.
Flowering Time: Early summer through to late autumn (fall).
Description: A much thicker stemmed species, erect or sprawling in habit, and branching mainly from the base. The dark green stems, as with most species, repeatedly grow through the cephalium, then form another one. The stems have from 10–14 ribs, and the areoles are set up to 1 cm (0.5 in) apart, bearing from 15–20 acicular spines, the longest being 2.5 cm (1 in), pale brown to reddish-brown in colour. The central and radial spines are not clearly defined. The tubular flowers which appear from the apical cephalium are 3 cm (1.4 in) long, and 1 cm (0.4 in) in diameter, orange-red in colour. The globular fruits are 1.5 cm (0.6 in) in diameter, purple when ripe.

Astrophytum

(ăs-trō-fī'-tŭm)

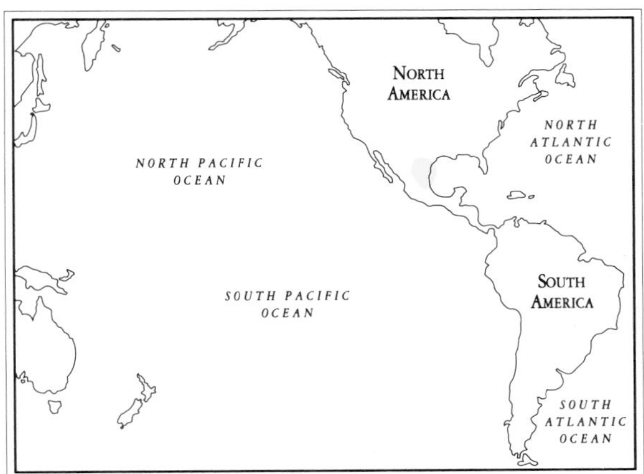

Astrophytum contains four species and a number of varieties. The genus name is derived from the Gk, meaning 'star-plant'. The plants are flattened, globular to cylindrical, with one species, *A. ornatum*, reaching 1 m (3 ft) in height. The plant body is either partially or completely covered with white, mealy, or flaky markings. The species illustrated clearly demonstrates this unusual surface (see below). The plants are hard bodied, with 5–9 ribs, bearing quite prominent woolly areoles, with spines set well apart. Certain species or varieties are completely spineless, while others may have stiff or flattened bristly spines. It is not possible to distinguish between the radials and the centrals. The spines are 3–10 cm (1.2–4 in) in length.

The funnel-shaped flowers appear from the centre of the plant, and 6–9 cm (2.4–3.6 in) in diameter. In colour they are in varying shades of yellow — some have yellow petals and orange-red centres. The fruits are globular and usually about 2.5 cm (1 in) across. The spineless species has a felted areole surface. The fruits of the spiny *Astrophytums* are covered with spines similar to those of the body of the plant. All the fruits split, or open up basally when ripe — depending on the species.

Culture: *Astrophytums* are from central, northern and north-western Mexico, and the habitat of one species, *A. asterias* (see page 42), extends into south-western United States. They are to be found at altitudes of up to 2100 m (6888 ft), growing in differing types of locations — among rocks, in sand and beneath other xerophytic bushes. In cultivation they are easily grown and freely flowering, preferring fairly cool conditions in winter. They have to be raised from seed, and depending upon the species, it can take 3–6 years to possess plants of flowering size.

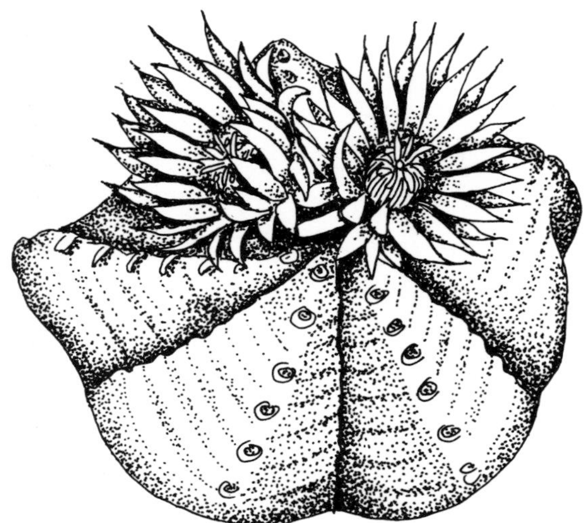

Astrophytum myriostigma var. *coahuilensis*

Astrophytum asterias

COMMON NAME: Sand Dollar Cactus.
SIZE: Width 12.5 cm (5 in).
CLIMATE: Medium elevation.
DISTRIBUTION: North and north-western Mexico and south-western United States.
FLOWERING TIME: Late spring to early autumn (fall).
DESCRIPTION: This species has a flattened globular habit, with usually 8 ribs, but can occasionally have as few as 6 or as many as 10 ribs. The green plant body is sparsely covered with the distinctive white, mealy, or flaky markings, and the woolly areoles are set well apart. The funnel-shaped flowers are yellow with orange-red centres and the globular, spineless fruits are about 2.5 cm (1 in) across and are greyish-red when ripe.

Astrophytum asterias

Astrophytum capricorne

COMMON NAME: None.
SIZE: Height 25 cm (10 in), width 12.5 cm (5 in).
CLIMATE: Medium elevation.
DISTRIBUTION: Central and northern Mexico.
FLOWERING TIME: Summer and early autumn (fall).
DESCRIPTION: Globular to short cylindrical habit. It usually has nine acutely formed ribs. The white mealy or flaky markings on the body are very variable as regards density with this species and its varieties. The areoles, which are well apart, bear up to about 10 spines. These are flattened and very flexible, ranging from grey to brown in colour, and are up to 7 cm (2.8 in) in length. The funnel-shaped flowers are yellow with a reddish centre. The fruits•are about 2.5 cm (1 in) across, have a flattened spiny covering, and are reddish when ripe.

Astrophytum capricorne

Astrophytum myriostigma var. *coahuilensis*

Astrophytum myriostigma var. *coahuilensis*

COMMON NAME: Bishop's Cap.
SIZE: Height 20 cm (8 in), width 10 cm (4 in).
CLIMATE: Medium elevation.
DISTRIBUTION: Central and northern Mexico.
FLOWERING TIME: Summer and early autumn (fall).
DESCRIPTION: This species has a globular to short cylindrical habit. It usually has 5 ribs, and the spineless areoles are moderately well apart. The body of the plant is very densely covered with white mealy or flaky markings. The flowers are funnel-shaped, up to 7 cm (2.8 in) in diameter, and yellow with a reddish centre around the stamens. The fruit is about 2.5 cm (1 in) across, and reddish when ripe.

AZTEKIUM

(ăs-tĕk'-ĭ-ŭm)

Aztekium is a monotypic genus (ie, it contains only one species), and the generic name honours the Aztek race. It is a flattened globular species, which clusters very slowly. Individual heads rarely exceed 5 cm (2 in) in diameter, and they have up to 11 ribs, which have a very creased appearance (as can be seen in the accompanying illustration). The body colour varies from pale green to greyish-green. The centre of the plant has plenty of white wool, and the areoles are very small, bearing up to three minute, weak spines.

The flowers are just under 1 cm (0.4 in) in diameter, with white petals and pinkish sepals. These are produced very freely even on plants which are no more than 1 cm (0.4 in) in diameter. The tiny berry-like fruits are pink, and when ripe they dry up, splitting irregularly, whereby the dust-like seeds are scattered in the white wool of the crown of the plant.

Culture: This rare and endangered species comes from central Mexico, where it is to be found growing on canyon walls in very arid areas. Offsets can be grafted, but even then the development is slow. Plants can be raised from seed, but great care has to be taken. Adult plants require a well drained soil mixture, and can only be watered fairly freely during the hottest months. In winter, plants should be left dry, but are safe at 5°C (40°F).

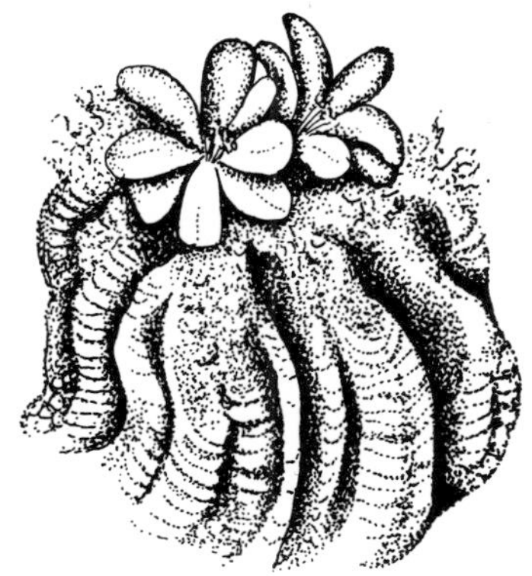

Aztekium ritteri

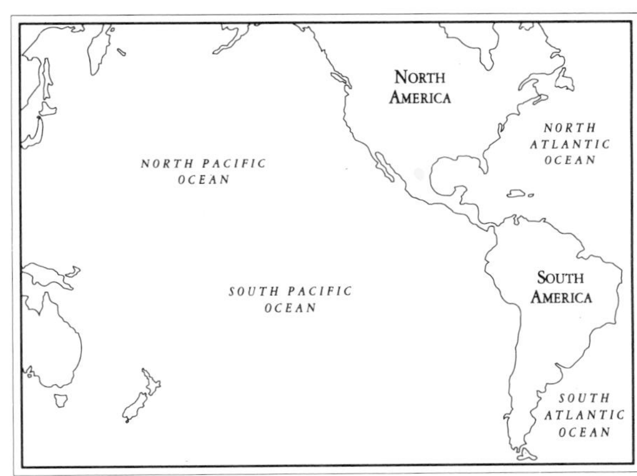

Aztekium ritteri

Aztekium ritteri

Common Name: None.
Size: Width 15 cm (6 in).
Climate: Medium elevation.
Distribution: As above.
Flowering Time: Summer.
Description: A flattened, globular species, which clusters very slowly. Individual heads rarely exceed 5 cm (2 in) in diameter, and they have up to 11 ribs, which have a very creased appearance. The plant's body colour varies from pale green to greyish-green, its centre has plenty of white wool, and the areoles are very small, bearing up to three minute, weak spines. The flowers are just under 1 cm (0.4 in) in diameter, with white petals and pinkish sepals. The tiny berry-like fruits are pink.

BERGEROCACTUS

(bĕr'-gĕr-ō-kăk'-tŭs)

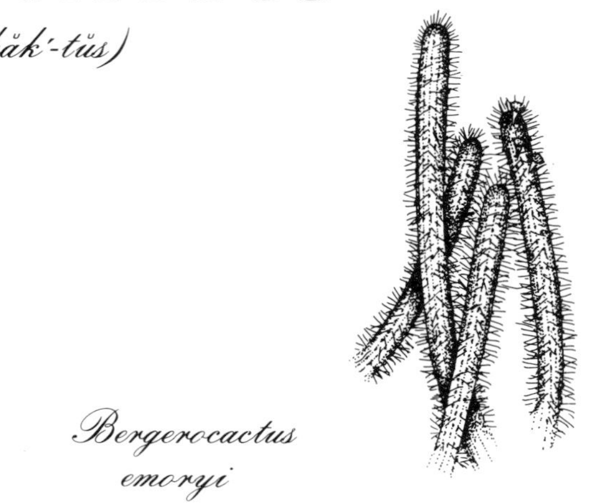

Bergerocactus emoryi

Bergerocactus is a monotypic genus, and the generic name is in honour of Alwin Berger. It is a slender, freely branching species, the stems rarely exceeding 1 m (3 ft) in height, but it grows into large colonies. The stems are usually less than 5 cm (2 in) in diameter, and they have up to 20 ribs. The areoles are set quite close together, and bear 20–30 acicular radial spines, and up to 3 centrals. They are 3–4 cm (1.25–1.6 in) in length, and yellow in colour blackening with age.

The flowers are 2 cm (0.8 in) in length and in diameter appearing from near the tops of the stems. They are funnel-shaped with a short tube, and yellow in colour. The exterior of the tube and the ovary is covered with felt and spines. The fruits are about 3 cm (1.25 in) across, and when ripe are completely dry.

Culture: *Bergerocactus* comes from coastal areas in north-western Mexico, the islands off Baja California, and the neighbouring coastline of the United States. The plant is easy to grow and can be raised from seed or propagated from cuttings. It appreciates plenty of water during the warmer months, and if left dry for too long in winter the stems can die back. In the resting period it will be unharmed if temperatures stay a few degrees above freezing point.

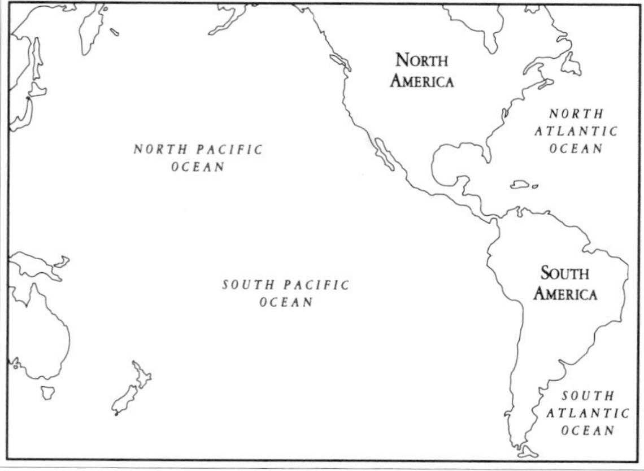

Bergerocactus emoryi

Common Name: None.
Size: Height 1 m (3 ft), width 4–6 m (13–16.5 ft).
Climate: Mediterranean.
Distribution: As above.
Flowering Time: Spring and early summer.
Description: As there is only one species, this information is found above.

Bergerocactus emoryi

BLOSSFELDIA

(blŏs'-fĕl'-dĭ-ă)

Blossfeldia contains only two species: *B. fechseri* and *B. liliputana* (although six species have been described, there is insufficient difference between four of these to designate them as separate species). The generic name honours H. Blossfeld, who discovered *B. liliputana*, the smallest cactus in the world. *Blossfeldias* are minute clustering plants, a single head rarely exceeding 1.5 cm (0.6 in) in diameter. When grown on their own roots, the top surface is fairly flat, but when grafted the top surface becomes more domed. The plants have quite a tuberous root system relative to their size. If part of this becomes exposed to the light, the plant promptly produces new heads from that area. In *B. liliputana*, these flat topped heads are usually a grey-green or bluish-green colour, and the clusters can reach 5–7.5 cm (2–3 in) in diameter. There is no visible rib or tubercle formation, although the tiny white areoles are spirally arranged. The plant body ranges in colour from a dark, often glossy green to a slightly bluish-green.

The white or creamy-white flowers rarely exceed 0.5 cm (0.2 in) in diameter. They appear from near the centre of each head. The fruits are minute, cream-white, and then reddish in the sun when ripe.

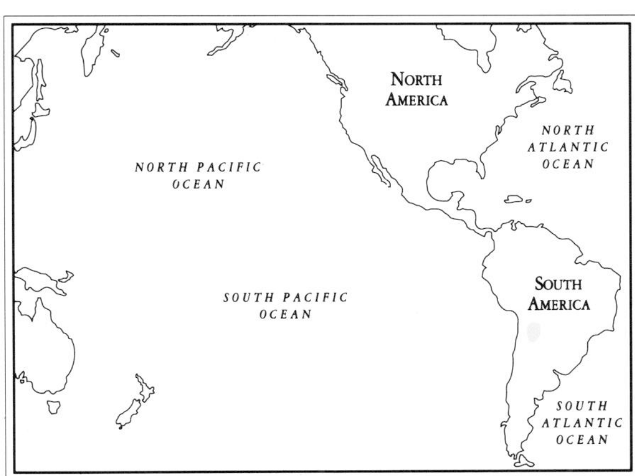

Culture: *Blossfeldias* are native mainly to Argentina, and just into Bolivia. They are not easy plants to raise from seed, because the seedlings are so small. This is why grafted specimens are invariably offered for sale. They require some shade and regular mist spraying during the hotter months. In winter they can be left dry, and will withstand cool conditions.

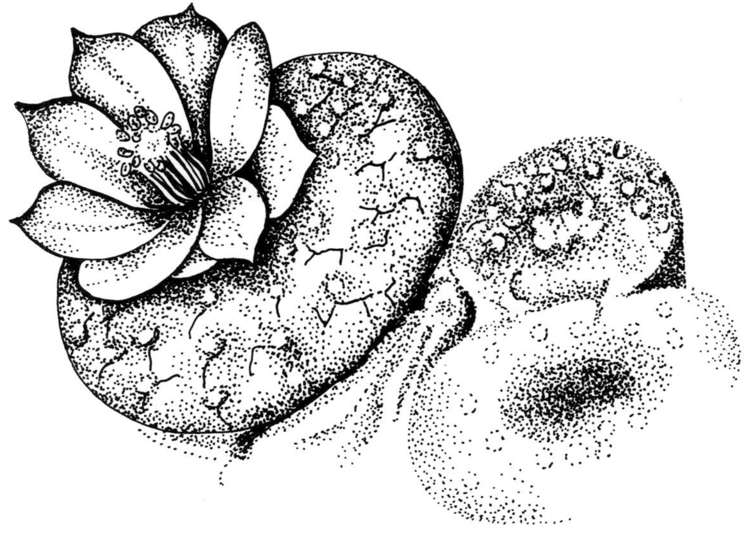

Blossfeldia liliputana

Blossfeldia fechseri

Common Name: None.
Size: Height 1.5 cm (0.6 in), width 7.5 cm (3 in).
Climate: High elevation.
Distribution: Argentina.
Flowering Time: Spring through to autumn (fall).
Description: A very freely clustering species, with single heads reaching 1.5 cm (0.6 in) in diameter. The flat topped heads are usually olive-green, and the minute white areoles are clearly in a spiral formation, but there are no spines. The flowers are white, but the outer sepals are prominently coloured in reddish-maroon. The tiny fruits are of the same reddish-maroon colour when ripe.

Blossfeldia fechseri

Blossfeldia liliputana

Blossfeldia liliputana

Common Name: None.
Size: Width 5-7.5 cm (2-3 in).
Climate: Medium elevation.
Distribution: Argentina and Bolivia.
Flowering Time: Spring to autumn (fall).
Description: This is a very freely clustering species; its single heads do not exceed 1 cm (0.4 in) in diameter, but clusters can reach 5-7.5 cm (2-3 in) across. The flat topped heads are usually a grey-green or bluish-green colour when grown on their own roots, but are rather greener when grafted. The minute spirally formed areoles are very white in colour, and there are no spines. The flowers are usually off-white or pale cream in colour. The tiny fruit is cream coloured, becoming slightly reddish in the sun when ripe.

Borzicactus

(bŏrt-sē-kăk'-tŭs)

*B*orzicactus contains ten species and a few varieties. The generic name honours Professor A. Borzi, who was director of the Botanical Gardens of Palermo, Sicily, in 1909. They are erect or semi-clambering plants, fairly free branching, with stems 1–2 m (3–6 ft) in length. They can be 2–8 cm (0.8–3.2 in) in diameter, with 8–16 rounded, straight ribs. The thicker stemmed species have quite a prominent V shaped notch below each areole position. The areoles are circular, with usually some white wool, and bear 8–15 or so radial spines and, when present, up to 3 or 4 centrals. The radials can be fine or bristly, are often appressed, sometimes minute, and up to 1 cm (0.4 in) in length. The centrals are straight, usually standing out from the stem, and 1–5 cm (0.4–2 in) in length. Both the centrals and the radials vary in colour from whitish, to brown and almost black.

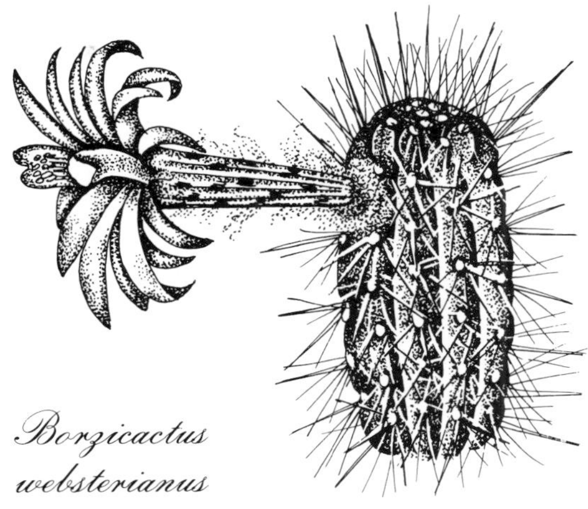

Borzicactus websterianus

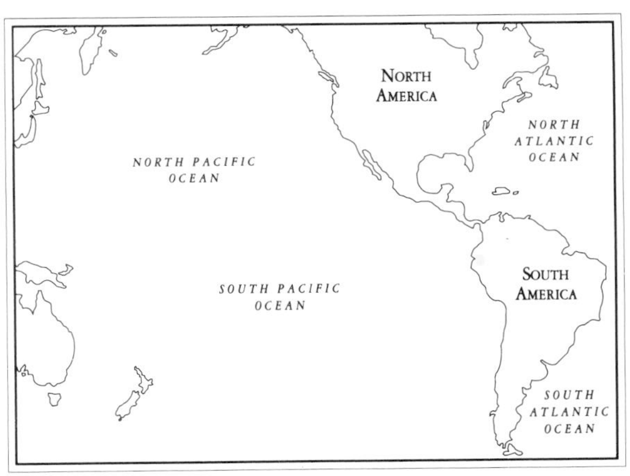

The flowers are tubular, but the petals do not open out completely. They are slightly zygomorphic (some species are more clearly zygomorphic), and can be 4–8 cm (1.6–3.2 in) in length. They appear in various shades of red or violet, with some off-white to brown hairs on the exterior of the tube. The fruits are spherical, 1–2 cm (0.4–0.8 in) in diameter, and green with white or brownish wool.

Culture: *Borzicacti* come from Bolivia, Ecuador and Peru, and *B. websterionus* (see below), for example, grows at an altitude of around 3000 m (9840 ft). They are all very easy to grow from seed or cuttings, and can be watered fairly freely from spring to autumn (fall). In winter most species need to be kept clear of frosts, and can be left fairly dry. They are very free flowering plants.

Borzicactus websterianus

Borzicactus websterianus

Common Name: None.
Size: Height 1–2 m (3–6 ft).
Climate: High elevation.
Distribution: Ecuador.
Flowering Time: Summer.
Description: This is a fairly erect, freely branching species, with green stems up to 1.5 m (5 ft) high and 6–10 cm (2.4–4 in) in diameter. The stems have about 14 straight ribs, with a V shaped notch below each areole. The areoles bear up to 20 radial spines and 4 centrals, varying from off-white to yellow in colour. The radials are finer, up to 1.5 cm (0.6 in) in length, whereas the slightly stouter centrals can reach 5 cm (2 in). The bright red flowers are 5–6 cm (2–2.4 in) in length. The spherical green fruits are 2 cm (0.8 in) in diameter, and densely covered with white wool.

BUININGIA

(bōi-nĭn'-gĭ-ă)

Buiningia contains just three species and two varieties. The generic name honours A. F. H. Buining, a well-known Dutch cactus enthusiast and collector. The plants are globular when young, but in age become columnar, and grow to just under 1 m (3 ft) in height. They offset from the base into fine clusters, and the dark green stems are 6–15 cm (2.4–6 in) or more in diameter, with 10–16 ribs. The areoles are either round or oval, and are found in notches along the ribs. Each areole can bear up to 15 radial spines, and up to 4 centrals. The radials can be curved or straight, 1.25–2.5 cm (0.5–1 in) and twice that or more in length, and usually stand out prominently from the stems. All of the spines range from golden yellow to reddish-brown in colour.

The special flowering zone, or cephalium, forms on the side of a stem, starting from near the top. The cephalium consists of a mass of whitish or yellowish wool, containing fine bristly spines of the same colour as the rest of the plant. The flowers are tubular, do not open very wide, and are not more than 2.5 cm (1 in) in length. They range in colour from greenish-yellow to purplish-magenta. The fruits are round or slightly elongated, and a bright shiny red colour when ripe. They are a little over 1.25 cm (0.5 in) in length and in diameter.

Culture: These plants were discovered in Brazil only within the last 25 years. They grow among rocks in pockets of quite rich soil, which often contains humus, and in association with orchids and bromeliads. They are easy plants to raise from seed and grow quite rapidly, but it can take 4 or 5 years for plants to reach maturity and start to flower. During the spring to autumn (fall) growing season they like a reasonable amount of water, but in winter at a minimum temperature of 10°C (50°F) should not be watered. If grown under much warmer winter conditions, some water can be provided.

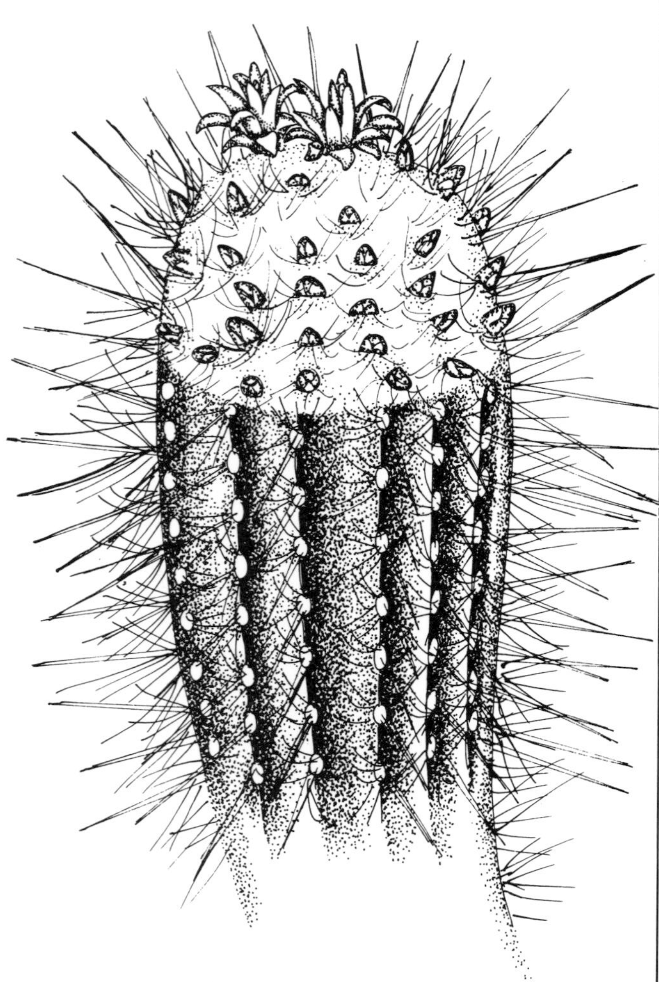

Buiningia purpurea

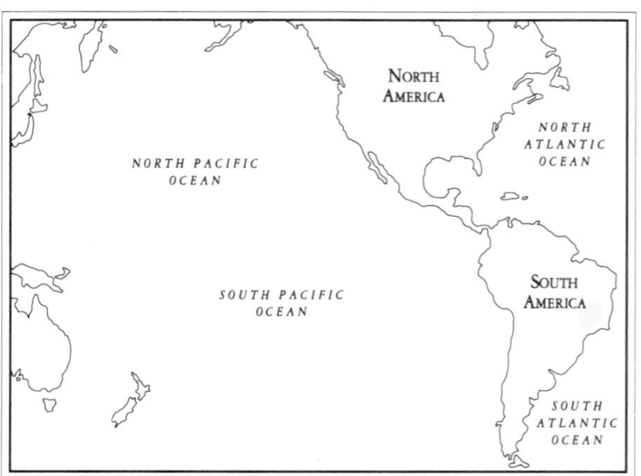

Buiningia brevicylindrica

Common Name: None.
Size: Height 30 cm (12 in), width 17.5 cm (7 in).
Climate: Medium elevation.
Distribution: Brazil.
Flowering Time: Spring to autumn (fall), but in warmer climates, all the year round.
Description: This species is initially solitary, later offsetting freely from the base. The fresh-green stems are somewhat conical and have up to 18 straight ribs. The slightly oblong areoles are set fairly closely together, and have whitish or yellowish wool. They bear up to seven radial spines and four centrals. The radials rarely exceed 2 cm (0.8 in) in length, and the centrals vary from 2.5-6 cm (1-2.4 in). All the spines are rather slender and flexible, and off-white to yellowish in colour. The cephalium is white, very woolly, and contains numerous yellow bristly spines. The tubular flowers can exceed 2.5 cm (1 in) in length, and are pale green. The fruits are spherical, about 1.5 cm (0.6 in) in diameter and are red when ripe.

Buiningia brevicylindrica

Buiningia purpurea

Buiningia purpurea

Common Name: None.
Size: Height 1 m (3 ft), width 20 cm (8 in).
Climate: Tropical.
Distribution: Brazil.
Flowering Time: Spring to autumn (fall), but in warmer climates all the year round.
Description: This is the most columnar species of the genus. Its stems are about 10 cm (4 in) in diameter, and it can grow close to 1 m (3 ft) in height. It does not usually start to offset at the base at an early age. The dark green stems have up to 13 straight ribs, and the round areoles contain short white or greyish wool. There are usually about 12 radial spines, up to 2.5 cm (1 in) in length, and up to 4 centrals, which can be up to 7.5 cm (3 in) in length. These are all reddish-brown in colour, becoming paler with age. The cephalium is white and very woolly, and contains many fine, bristly reddish-brown spines. The tubular purplish-magenta flowers slightly exceed 2.5 cm (1 in) in length. However, the nocturnal flowers are usually white although there are other varieties like the brightly coloured one opposite. Sometimes in slightly cooler weather the nocturnal flower will stay open for much of the following day. The fruits are usually described as being globular, but invariably those forming on my specimens are slightly elongated. They are bright red in colour when ripe.

CARNEGIEA

(kär-nā'-gē-à)

Carnegiea is a monotypic genus, and the generic name honours the philanthropist Andrew Carnegie. It is a columnar growing plant of fairly massive proportions, with specimens occasionally exceeding 12 m (40 ft) in height. In ideal conditions the plants start to branch after 20 or 30 years, and these branches do not normally appear from the base of the plant but form at a height of about 3 m (10 ft) from the ground. The basal trunk of the plant can be up to 60 cm (2 ft) in diameter, with up to 24 somewhat rounded ribs. The brown areoles are about 2.5 cm (1 in) apart, bear up to 20 radial spines and three to six stouter centrals. The centrals can be up to 6 cm (2.5 in) in length, and are whitish when new, but darken with age.

The nocturnal flowers appear from near the tops of the stems and are somewhat funnel-shaped, white, waxy, and up to 12 cm (5 in) in diameter. The fruits are egg-shaped, up to 7.5 cm (3 in) in length, scaly and green, becoming slightly red when ripe. When ripe, the fruit splits in a number of positions, and opens out almost like a flower, revealing the brilliant purplish-red interior flesh, into which the hard black seeds are embedded.

Culture: *Carnegiea* comes from south-western United States and the Sonoran desert, northern Mexico, where it grows at an elevation of up to 1300 m (4264 ft). It is the State flower of Arizona. It is an easy growing plant and can usually be raised from seed, but it cannot be termed a fast grower. If conditions are not ideal it can take up to 40–60 years or longer before it starts to branch. In cultivation it appreciates reasonable amounts of water during the warmer months, and if kept dry during the winter it can withstand light frosts.

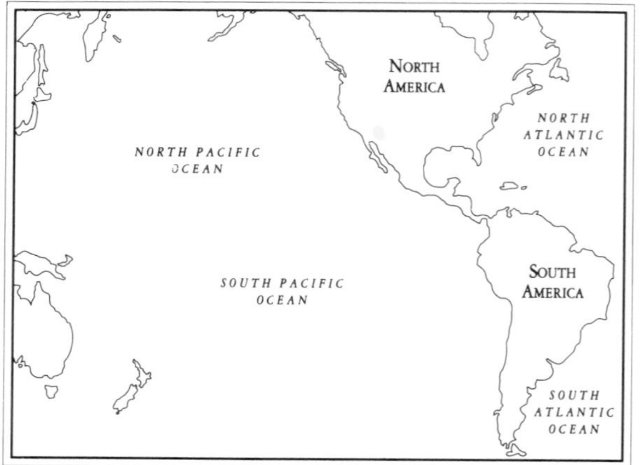

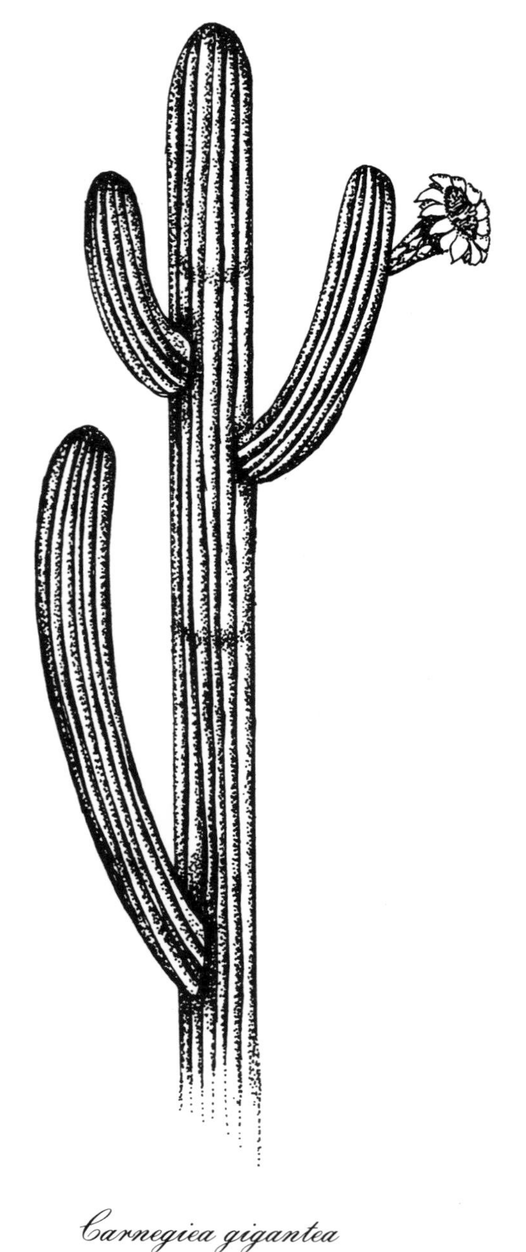

Carnegiea gigantea

Carnegiea gigantea fa. *cristata*

Carnegiea gigantea in flower

Carnegiea gigantea in flower

Carnegiea gigantea

Common Name: Saguaro (Spanish corruption of the Papago Indian word for 'the big cactus').
Size: Height 12 m (40 ft).
Climate: Medium elevation.
Distribution: See page 50.
Flowering Time: Spring and early summer.
Description: As there is only one species, this information is found in the genus text page 50.

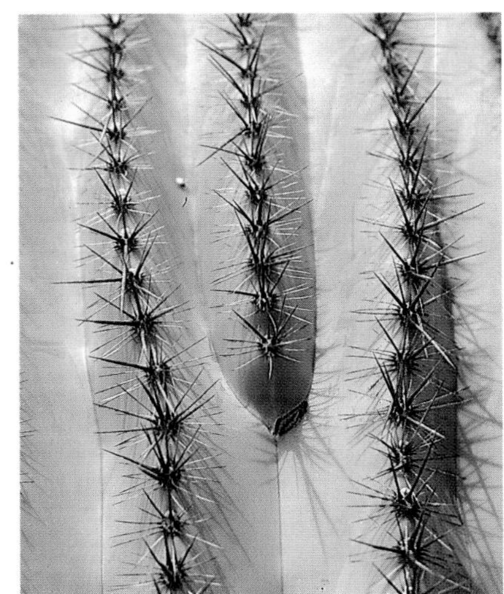

Carnegiea gigantea—ribbed structure of the stem

CEPHALOCEREUS

(sĕf´-ă-lō-se´-rē-ŭs)

Cephalocereus can now be termed a monotypic one (other species which were originally placed in this genus have been transferred elsewhere). The generic name is derived from the Gk and is in reference to the cephalium or 'head' from which the flowers appear. It is an erect growing, sparingly branching genus. The light green stems become grey with age, and have up to 30 low ribs. The closely set areoles bear up to 5 yellow to grey spines up to 4 cm (1.6 in) in length and numerous white or grey twisted coarse hairs. These are so dense they virtually mask the body colour.

The off-white to yellowish flowers are about 10 cm (4 in) in length and 7.5 cm (3 in) in diameter. These funnel-shaped flowers have pink tubes, 5 cm (2 in) in length. The flowers appear from a very dense, white hairy cephalium, which initially is on one side of the stem. As the plant ages the cephalium totally encircles the stem, and on an old specimen can be a few metres (yards) in length. The exterior of the base of the tube of the flower, and the ovary, are also hairy.

Culture: *Cephalocerei* are fairly easy to grow from seed, although in the first year or so they are easily killed by excess watering, and can be rooted from cuttings — even ones already possessing cephaliums, but this is not recommended as it has an adverse effect on the conservation of this magnificent plant. Once the plants are over 3 years of age, they can be watered freely during all hot weather, but care should be taken at other times. In winter the plants should be left dry, and protected from frosts.

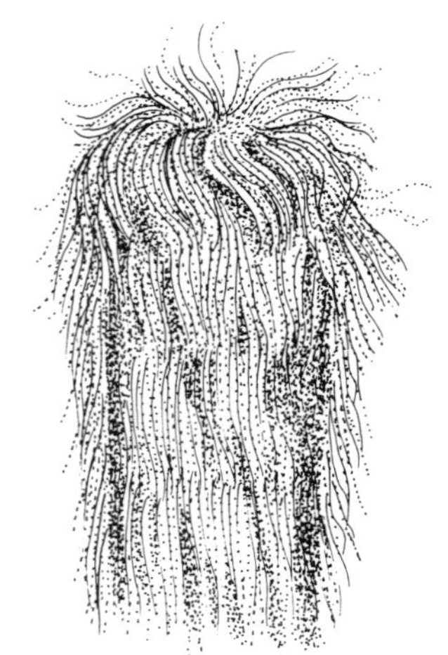

Cephalocereus senilis

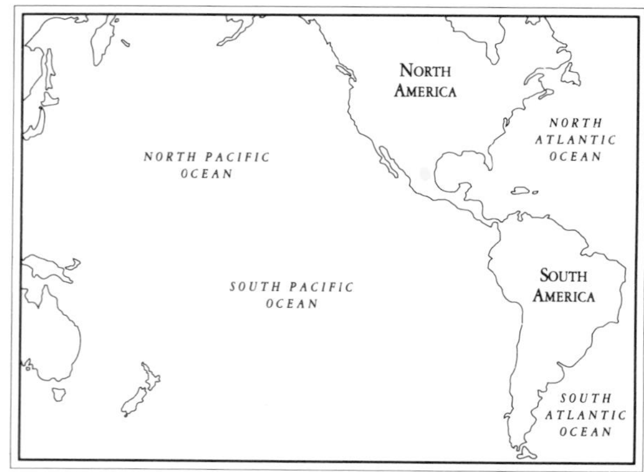

Cephalocereus senilis

Cephalocereus senilis

COMMON NAME: Old Man of Mexico.
SIZE: Height 15 m (49 ft).
CLIMATE: Medium elevation.
DISTRIBUTION: Central and eastern Mexico.
FLOWERING TIME: Summer.
DESCRIPTION: The fruits are globular, 5-7.5 cm (2-3 in) in diameter, red when ripe and have yellowish hair. As there is only one species, more detailed information is found above.

Cephalocleistocactus

(sĕf'-ă-lō-klīs-tō-kăk'-tŭs)

Cephalocleistocactus contains four species. The first part of the generic name refers to the appearance of long bristly and hair-like spines, similar to a cephalium, in the flowering area. The second part refers to the similarity of this genus to the genus *Cleistocactus*. The plants are erect, freely branching and slender stemmed with up to 17 ribs. The stems are 1–2 m (3–6.5 ft) high, and are usually 3–5 cm (1.25–2 in) in diameter. The small areoles are set quite close together and are brown when new, changing to white. They bear 30 or more radial spines and up to 5 centrals, and are 1–4 cm (0.4–1.6 in) in length. In some cases it is very difficult to distinguish between the radials and the centrals which can vary in colour from white or yellow to brown. The area from which most of the flowers appear, which is similar to a cephalium, has even longer spines of the same colour as the centrals and the radials.

The flowers are straight, slender and tubular, about 5 cm (2 in) in length, and range in colour from greenish-yellow, and yellow to red. They open only slightly at the tips. The fruits are usually less than 2.5 cm (1 in) in length, and possess short hairs and fine spines similar in colour to those on the stems.

Culture: *Cephalocleistocacti* come from Bolivia, and are exceedingly easy plants to grow from seed or cuttings. They like plenty of water during the warmer months, and have a long flowering period. In winter they can be left dry, and should be protected from frosts.

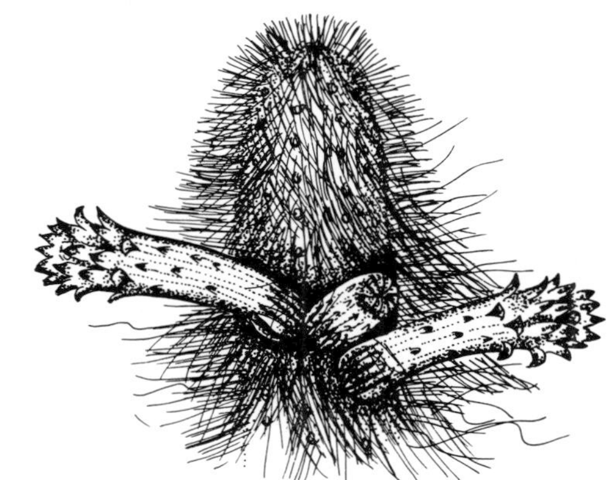

Cephalocleistocactus ritteri

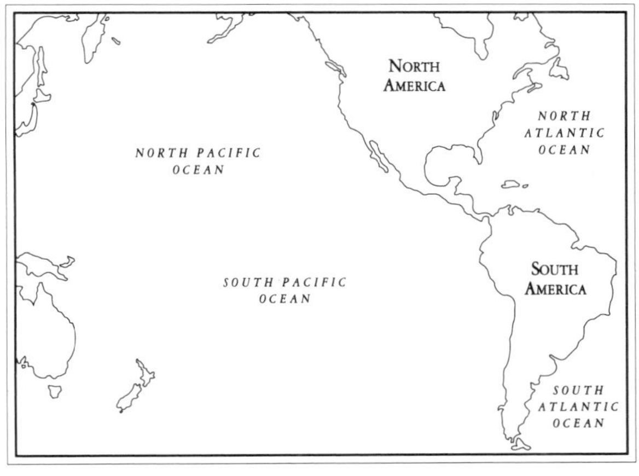

Cephalocleistocactus ritteri

Cephalocleistocactus ritteri

Common Name: None.
Size: Height 1.5 m (4.5 ft).
Climate: Medium elevation.
Distribution: Eastern Bolivia.
Flowering Time: Early summer to autumn (fall).
Description: This is an erect, slender stemmed species. It has 12–16 ribs, but the dense spination virtually obscures the closely set areoles. There are up to 30 or more fine radial spines and rarely more than 5 centrals, which are fractionally more robust than the radial spines. They are all about 1 cm (0.4 in) in length, and of a glassy white colour. Those which appear in the flowering region are more than twice that length, and often twisted. The tubular flowers are yellow with greenish tips. The fruits are about 2 cm (0.8 in) in length.

CEREUS

(sē'-rē-ŭs)

Cereus contains nearly 50 species, as well as many varieties. The generic name is derived from the Lat, meaning 'wax candle'. It is a very varied genus — from small shrubby species, to large columnar, freely branching species with stout trunks. The stem colour is quite varied — from green to powder blue. There are four to nine prominent ribs which have areoles generally set well apart. The radial and central spines, with few exceptions, are stout, acicular and up to 7.5 cm (3 in) in length (except in *C. peruvianus*, where the spines rarely exceed 3 cm (1.2 in). The spine colour ranges from off-white and yellowish-brown to almost black.

The nocturnal flowers are up to 30 cm (12 in) in length, and have long tubes. The exterior of the flower tube and ovary have scales set well apart, with glabrous axils. The petals are usually white, but the outer petals can have reddish-brown or greenish-brown median stripes. The fruits are globular to oblong, and green, yellow, or in various shades of red when ripe. The fruits of some species can reach 13 cm (5.2 in) in length, and up to 10 cm (4 in) in diameter.

Culture: *Cerei* have a wide distribution: from the West Indies, southwards to northern parts of South America, and on to Argentina and Brazil. Many species grow quite rapidly and can be cultivated from seeds or cuttings. They are ideal plants for enthusiasts new to the hobby as the majority will tolerate very varied cultural conditions and are difficult to overwater, and they also make ideal plants for landscaping in non-frosty areas. They are very free flowering, and the flowers are often sweetly scented. When the plants become too large the stems can easily be removed without any harm being done to the main part of the plant. In frost-free areas, most *Cerei* will tolerate winter rains, and a few species will withstand a few degrees of frost with impunity.

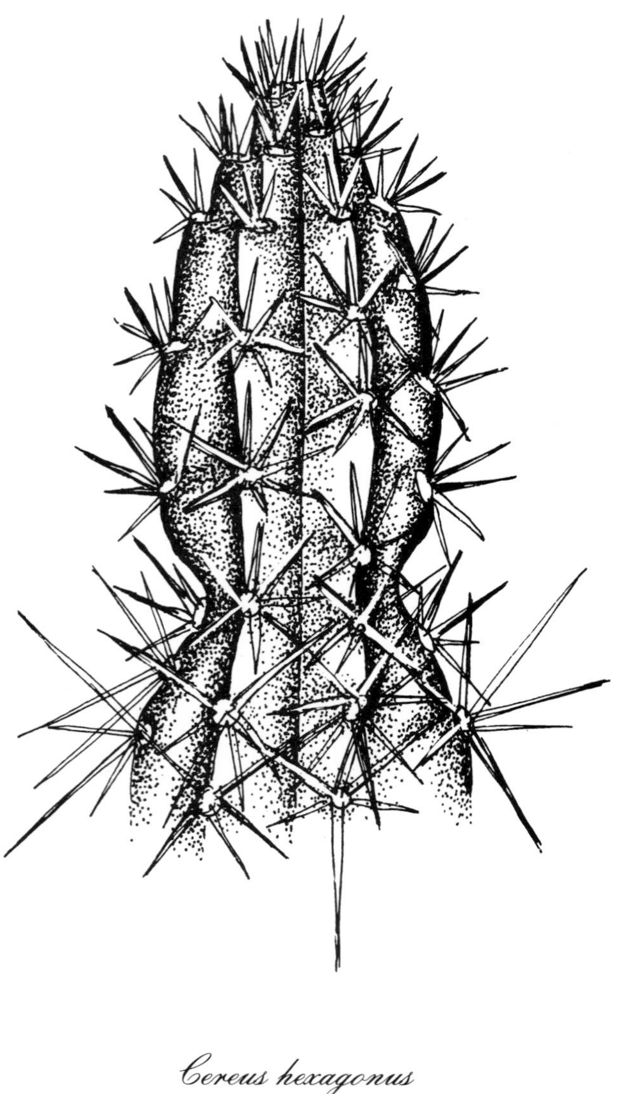

Cereus hexagonus

Cereus hexagonus

Cereus hexagonus

Common Name: Queen of the Night.
Size: Height 15 m (49 ft).
Climate: Tropical.
Distribution: Surinam, to northern Venezuela, and Tobago.
Flowering Time: Summer.
Description: This is a tree-like species and very freely branching. It has green to bluish-green stems, initially with 4 ribs when young, but later changing to 6 or 7 ribs. The areoles are small, set well apart, with up to 8 spines, which cannot be differentiated. On young plants the brown spines are very short, but with maturity they can exceed 6 cm (2.4 in) in length. The flowers are about 25 cm (10 in) in length and have white inner petals. The outer petals tend to be greenish-brown on the outside. The fruits are egg-shaped, up to 12.5 cm (5 in) in length and red when ripe.

Cereus peruvianus

Common Name: Queen of the Night.
Size: Height 16 m (52 ft).
Climate: Medium elevation.
Distribution: South-eastern areas of South America, but its original locality is unknown. The species was originally described by Linnaeus in 1753.
Flowering Time: Summer.
Description: This is another tree-like species and very freely branching. The variable green stems have 6–8 ribs. The branches are 10–20 cm (4–8 in) in diameter, and the areoles are small, set well apart, and bear up to 10 acicular, brown to black spines. These rarely exceed 3 cm (1.2 in) in length, and are often much less. The flowers are about 15 cm (6 in) in length, with white inner petals, and greenish-brown to reddish outer petals. The fruits are usually globular, rarely exceed 5 cm (2 in) in diameter and are orange to orange-red when ripe.

Cereus peruvianus

CHAMAECEREUS

(kăm-ē-sē'-rē-ŭs)

Chamaecereus is a monotypic genus. The generic name means *'cereus* on the ground'. It is a dwarf, freely clustering plant, with small cylindrical stems which are quite soft and very easily detached, particularly when the plants are dry. The light green stems are usually 5–7.5 cm (2–3 in) in length, but can grow to twice this length when cultivated in a greenhouse. They are 1.25–2.5 cm (0.5–1 in) in diameter, and have 6–9 ribs. The tiny areoles are set quite closely together and bear a few very short, weak whitish spines.

The flowers, which are produced in profusion, open wide, and are 4–5 cm (1.6–2 in) in length and in diameter — occasionally a little larger. The basal part of the tube of the flower and the ovary bear the same weak spines as the stems but have hairs. The flowers can be orange-red or a light yellow. The fruits are very small and pinkish-red when ripe.

Culture: This genus comes from the mountainous areas of northern Argentina. It is a very easy plant to grow from seed or cuttings. Small cuttings root very rapidly, and will cluster freely and produce numerous flowers within 12 months. It likes plenty of water from spring to autumn (fall). In winter it can be left dry, and it will withstand light frosts. In the growing period it is very prone to infections of red spider mite.

Chamaecereus silvestrii

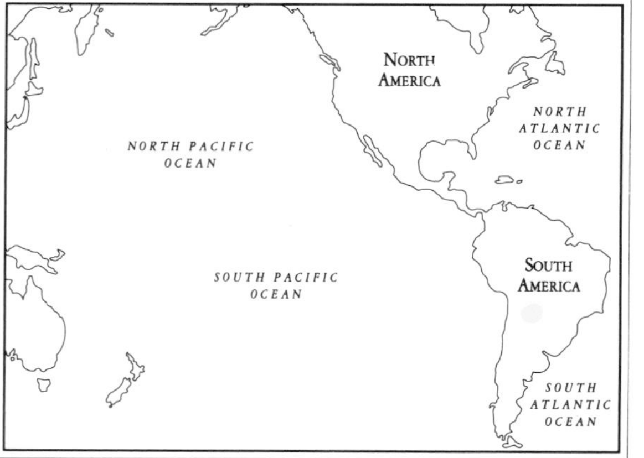

Chamaecereus silvestrii

COMMON NAME: Peanut cactus.
SIZE: Height 7.5 cm (3 in), width 30 cm (12 in).
CLIMATE: High elevation.
DISTRIBUTION: As above.
FLOWERING TIME: Late spring to early summer.
DESCRIPTION: As there is only one species, this information is found above.
NB: A number of wonderful hybrids have been produced by hybridising *Chamaecereus* with species of *Lobivia* (see page 197). They are very strong growers, and produce larger flowers over a longer period.

Chamaecereus silvestrii

CLEISTOCACTUS

(klīs-tō-kăk'-tŭs)

Cleistocactus has over 50 species and a number of varieties. The generic name is derived from the Gk meaning 'closed cactus' and is in reference to the fertilisation of the plant which can take place inside the unopened flower (ie it has cleistogamous flowers). They can be erect or sprawling, are slender stemmed, and branch quite freely. The erect growing species rarely exceed 2 m (6.5 ft) in height, whereas the sprawling ones, eg *C. dependens* (see page 58), can grow to 5 m (15 ft) or more in length. The stems are 2.5–6.25 cm (1–2.5 in) in diameter, with 8–25 ribs. In some species eg the very well-known *C. strausii* (see page 58), the rib structure is virtually obscured by the very fine dense spination. The areoles are usually set quite close together and are very small, but bear 8–30 or more radial spines, and up to 4 centrals. The radials are usually very fine, particularly in the species where there are 30 or more radials, and can be up to 1.25 cm (0.5 in) in length. The centrals are generally slightly stouter and longer.

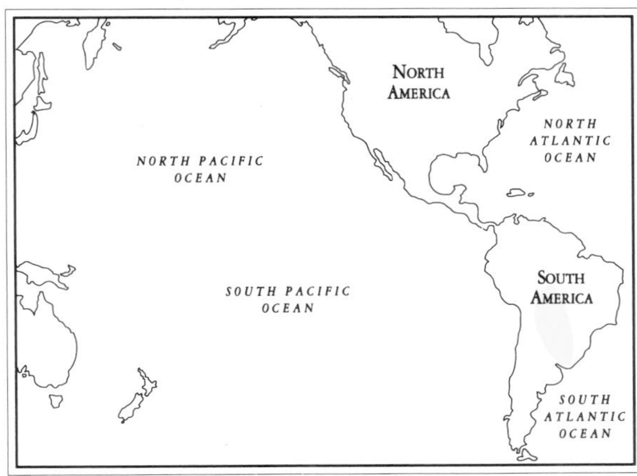

The flowers are tubular, open only slightly at the tips, but the tube can be straight or zygomorphic. In some species the flowers are very zygomorphic and are shaped like the spout of a coffee-pot. The exterior of the flower tube usually has some short hairs or short bristles forming from the bases of the sepals. In *C. strausii* the density of hairs on the tube is quite considerable. The flower colour can range from bright green or yellow, to various shades of red and purple. The fruits are globular, 1.25 cm (0.5 in) or less in diameter, and have a similar surface and colour to that of the exterior of the flower tube.

Culture: *Cleistocacti* come from central Peru, eastern Bolivia, northern Argentina, Paraguay and Uruguay. They are easily grown from seed or from cuttings, and are generally very free flowering — given plenty of water during all the warmer months they can produce an abundance of these unusual tubular-shaped flowers. In winter most species will withstand temperatures to within a few degrees of freezing point.

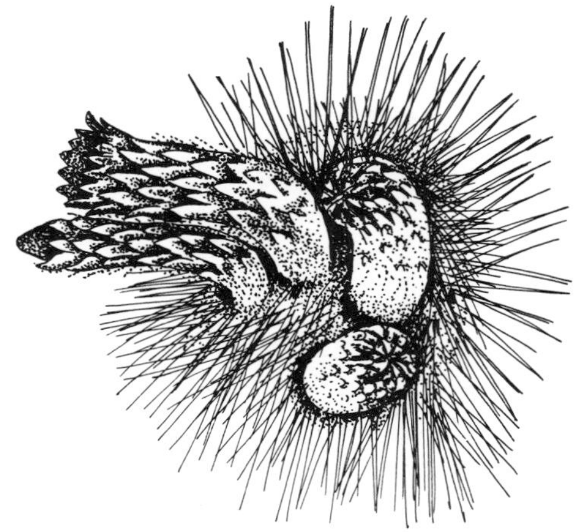

Cleistocactus jujuyensis

Cleistocactus jujuyensis

Cleistocactus dependens

Common Name: None.
Size: Length 5 m (15 ft).
Climate: Medium elevation.
Distribution: Bolivia.
Flowering Time: Late spring, to early summer.
Description: This is a somewhat clambering, long stemmed, freely branching species, with stems up to 3.5 cm (1.4 in) in diameter. It has up to 12 narrow ribs, and small greyish areoles bearing up to 12 radial spines and 3 or 4 centrals. The radials are minute, but the centrals usually exceed 1.25 cm (0.5 in) in length. All the spines are brownish or reddish-brown when young, but tend to grey with age. The flowers have quite a slender tube and are just under 5 cm (2 in) in length. The colour of the tube is variable, in varying shades of carmine-pink, but the petals are always greenish. The globular fruits are about 1.25 cm (0.5 in) in diameter and are dark red when ripe.

Cleistocactus dependens

Cleistocactus jujuyensis

Common Name: None.
Size: Height 1 m (3 ft), width 60 cm (2 ft).
Climate: High elevation.
Distribution: Argentina.
Flowering Time: Summer and early autumn (fall).
Description: This is an erect species which branches mainly from the base, and has stems up to about 1 m (3 ft) in height and 6 cm (2.4 in) in diameter, and up to 20 narrow ribs. The brownish or brownish-grey areoles bear up to 30 fine radial spines which are about 2.5 cm (1 in) in length. These tend to be whitish, whereas the 1–4 centrals are stouter, slightly longer and brown in colour. The flowers are about 4 cm (1.6 in) in length, pale pinkish along the tube, but have reddish to carmine petals. The fruits are about 0.7 cm (0.3 in) across, and reddish when ripe.

Cleistocactus strausii

Cleistocactus strausii

Common Name: None.
Size: Height 1–2 m (3–6.5 ft), width 60 cm (2 ft).
Climate: Medium elevation.
Distribution: Bolivia.
Flowering Time: Summer.
Description: This is an erect species which branches from the base, and has stems reaching 1–2 m (3–6.5 ft) in height, with a diameter of 6–8 cm (2.4–3.2 in). The green stems have about 25 ribs, and the white areoles are set very close together. They bear up to 40 hair-like radial spines, and up to 4 stronger centrals. The radial spines are white and appressed, and up to 1.5 cm (0.6 in) in length, whereas the centrals are yellowish and up to 2 cm (0.8 in) in length. The flowers are narrow and tubular, wine-red, and up to 9 cm (3.6 in) in length. The exterior of the tube has red and whitish hairs. The fruits are spherical, hairy like the tube, and red when ripe.

COLORADOA

(kŏ-lōr'-ă-dō-ă)

Coloradoa is a monotypic genus. The generic name is derived from the name Colorado, United States, where it was first discovered. It is normally globular and solitary, but clusters do occasionally occur (such as in the example illustrated). The body of the plant rarely exceeds 10 cm (4 in) in height, and a little less in diameter. As a young plant it is somewhat tubercled in appearance, but these gradually merge and up to 14 slightly spirally formed low ribs appear. It can have up to 10 curved radial spines, and sometimes 1 central, which stands out from the plant, but is more often than not absent. All of the spines rarely exceed 2 cm (0.8 in) in length, and are off-white to grey with darkish tips.

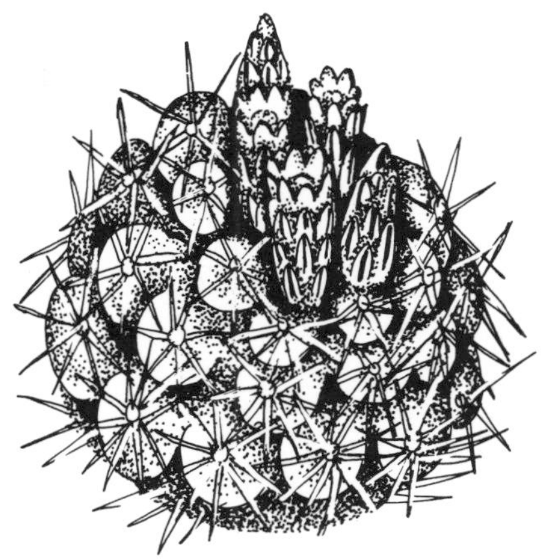

Coloradoa mesae-verde

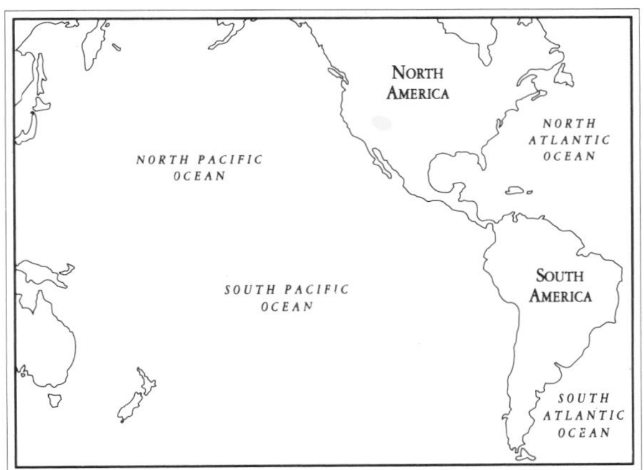

The flowers are about 3 cm (1.2 in) in length, and do not open wide. The petals are off-white to cream, with median stripes. The globular fruit is about 1.25 cm (0.5 in) across, and creamy-green when ripe.

Culture: It is a difficult plant to grow on its own roots, because in nature it grows in a powdery, but clay-like, soil. In nature it is to be found in only a few locations in south-western United States at altitudes close to 2000 m (6560 ft). However, it can be successfully grown — and will produce flowers in profusion — as a grafted plant.

Coloradoa mesae-verde

Coloradoa mesae-verde

COMMON NAME: Mesa Verde Cactus.
SIZE: Height 10 cm (4 in).
CLIMATE: High elevation.
DISTRIBUTION: Limited to a very small area in south-western United States,
FLOWERING TIME: Late spring to early summer.
DESCRIPTION: As there is only one species, this information is found above.

COPIAPOA

(kō'-pē-à-pō'-à)

Copiapoa This genus contains over 40 species and many varieties. The generic name is taken from the town of Copiapo in Chile. It is a very varied genus, from miniatures only a few centimetres (inches) across to others which exceed 1 m (3 ft) in height or cluster freely to form large mounds over 1 m (3 ft) in diameter. Some species possess a turnip-like root system. The plant body is very variable too, with 10–24 rounded or acute ribs, and it ranges in colour from green to chalky-blue and slate. The areoles are very pronounced, usually oval, and sometimes very large and woolly. The spine count is exceedingly variable, even on plants of the same species, and in some cases it is not possible to distinguish between the radials and the centrals. As a general rule there can be 1–12 radial spines, while there may be no centrals, or as many as 20. The smaller species tend to have fine spines, whereas the larger species have much stouter spines which may be straight or curved and can exceed 5 cm (2 in) in length. The colour range is equally varied from off-white, yellow, reddish-brown to black.

The flowers have a very short tube and appear from the normally woolly centre. They rarely exceed 3.5 cm (1.4 in) in diameter and often much less and are invariably in varying shades of yellow. The fruits are globular, fairly small, yellowish or grey in colour and split open when ripe.

Culture: *Copiapoas* are native to central and northern Chile, and are usually to be found in very arid areas. They are not unduly difficult to raise from seed, but the larger species are very slow growing. Only a few of the smaller clustering species can be propagated vegetatively, and even then the growth rate is fairly slow. However, the smaller species can be grown to flowering size within a few years. Most species require a well drained soil, plenty of sunshine, and can only be watered freely during the hottest weather. In winter, they should be kept dry, and most species can safely withstand temperatures close to freezing point. Where the atmospheric humidity is very low, as in their native habitat of central and northern Chile, many of these species cope with temperatures below freezing point.

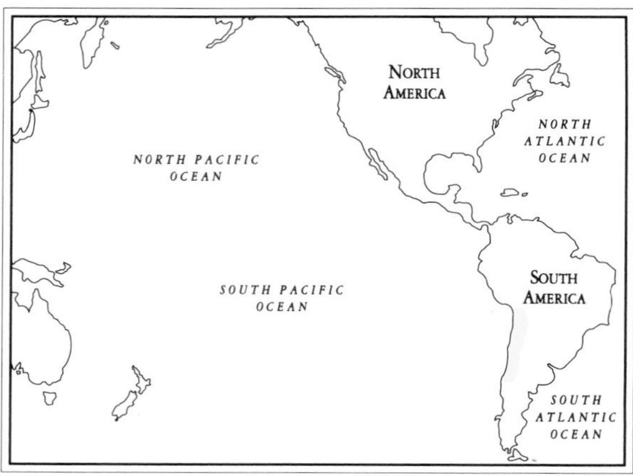

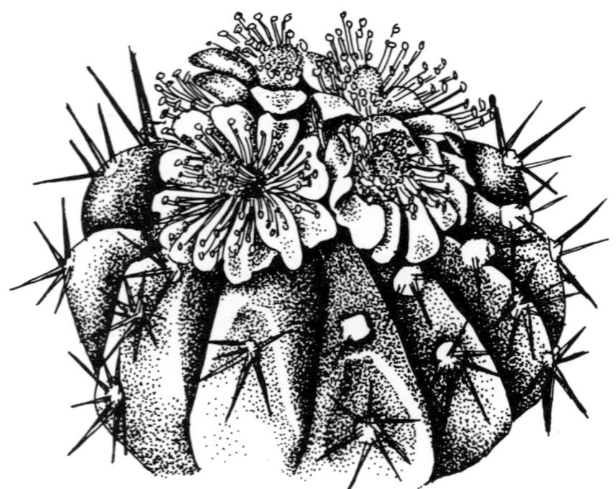

Copiapoa hypogaea

Copiapoa haseltoniana

Copiapoa haseltoniana

Common Name: None.
Size: Height 1 m (3 ft), width 2 m (6.5 ft).
Climate: Mediterranean.
Distribution: Northern Chile.
Flowering Time: Summer.
Description: This is a globular to short and cylindrical species which clusters in age and has a greyish-green or olive-green body. The apex of each head is full of yellowish-brown wool. Each head usually measures 20 cm (8 in) in diameter, with up to 20 straight, rounded ribs. The large oval areoles are full of wool, set well apart, and bear up to 9 or 10 radial spines, and sometimes 1 central. The longest of these radials can be 3 cm (1.2 in). The spines are yellowish in colour and sometimes possess darkish tips. The yellow flowers are about 3 cm (1.2 in) in diameter. The fruits are globular, about 1.25 cm (0.5 in) in diameter, and whitish when ripe.

Copiapoa hypogaea

Copiapoa hypogaea

Common Name: None.
Size: Width 15 cm (6 in).
Climate: Mediterranean.
Distribution: Central Chile.
Flowering Time: Summer.
Description: This is a somewhat flattened globular species which is sparingly branching, and has a brownish-grey to slate body, and rarely exceeds 5 cm (2 in) in diameter. It has up to 14 straight tuberculate ribs, and the areoles are set well apart for such a miniature species. These oval, slightly sunken areoles contain some white wool, and bear up to 6 radiating spines. The spines are usually under 0.5 cm (0.2 in) in length, and are grey in colour. The flowers are pale yellow, and about 3.5 cm (1.4 in) in diameter. The fruits are globular, rather small, and yellowish-grey when ripe.

CORRYOCACTUS

(kôr'-ē-ō-kăk'-tŭs)

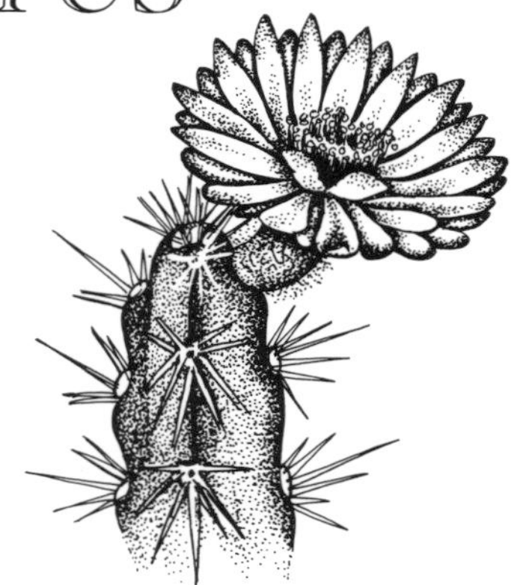

Corryocactus ayopayanus

Corryocactus contains some 15 species and a few varieties. The generic name honours T. A. Corry, who was the chief engineer of the Ferrocarril del Sur of Peru, and helped N. L. Britton and J. N. Rose in their exploration work. They are freely branching, shrubby, or tree-like plants up to 5 m (15 ft) in height. The branches are 3.5–10 cm (1.4–4 in) in diameter. The rib count is 4–12, and the areoles are prominent with 3–20 acicular or subulate spines. They range in length from as small as 0.5 cm (0.2 in) to as much as 25 cm (10 in) and their colour varies from off-white or yellow, to brown.

The flowers are bell-shaped, 2–7 cm (0.8–2.8 in) in diameter, and vary from yellow or orange to red. The fruits are usually spherical, spiny, and 3–10 cm (1.2–4 in) in diameter.

Culture: *Corryocacti* come from southern Peru and Bolivia, with some species being found at altitudes of 3300 m (10 824 ft). They are easy growing plants, whether they are raised from seed, or propagated from cuttings, can be watered freely from spring to autumn (fall), and are very tolerant as regards soil requirements. In winter they will take very cool conditions if kept dry, and the high altitude species will stand frosts.

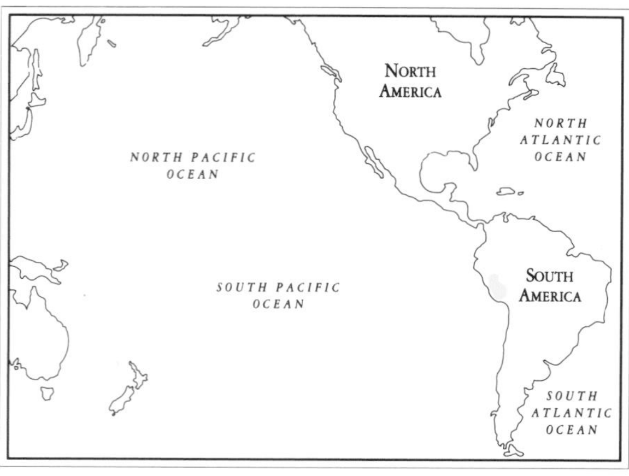

Corryocactus ayopayanus

Corryocactus ayopayanus

Common Name: None.
Size: Height 1.5 m (5 ft), width 60 cm (2 ft).
Climate: High elevation.
Distribution: Bolivia at altitudes of 3000 m (9840 ft).
Flowering Time: Summer.
Description: This is a freely branching species. The dark green stems are about 3.5 cm (1.4 in) in diameter, and have 4 or 5 ribs. The grey areoles are set well apart, and bear up to 13 spines 0.5–5 cm (0.2–2 in) in length. These are subulate, and white or yellowish in colour. The funnel-shaped flowers are 7 cm (2.8 in) in diameter, and salmon or orange-red in colour. The fruits are small — no more than 3 cm (1.2 in) in diameter — and covered with white or brown spines.

CORYPHANTHA

(kō-rĭ-făn'-thă)

Coryphantha contains some 70 species and varieties. The generic name comes from the Gk words for 'top' and 'flower', in reference to the flower position on the plants. The plants are quite variable, though not particularly large, and are globular to short and cylindrical, or even columnar, with stems 30 cm (12 in) high. They can be solitary or freely clustering and an old clump can have 50 or more heads, and be 65 cm (26 in) or more in diameter. Specimens of *C. recurvata* from southern Arizona have been found with 200 heads. The fairly prominent tubercles have a furrow for their entire length, and the areoles can be circular or oval, and bear up to 30 acicular spines. The majority of these are radials (with a possible 4 centrals), and rarely exceed 2.5 cm (1 in) in length. Occasionally one or two of the centrals can be slightly hooked.

The funnel-shaped flowers are 1.25–5 cm (0.5–2 in) in diameter, and in a wide range of colours, from yellow and orange to pink and magenta. Some species have petals with ciliate edges. The fruits are usually ovoid with the miniature species producing exceedingly small fruit, and other species producing fleshy fruit 5 cm (2 in) in length which, when ripe, can be green to various shades of red.

Culture: *Coryphanthas* have a very widespread distribution: from as far north as Alberta in Canada, throughout south-western United States, and into many parts of Mexico. They are also to be found from sea level to sometimes above 2000 m (over 6560 ft). *C. vivipara* has a very wide distribution, with the most northerly form in Alberta enduring very low temperatures and snow in winter. *Coryphanthas* in general can be found in grassland, or beneath trees.

With few exceptions they are very easy plants to cultivate and can be grown from seed. Most of the clustering types can be propagated by cuttings, which after their drying period root quite quickly in a sandy compost. It is not uncommon when dividing an old clump to find that most of the heads already have a few of their own roots. The plants appreciate a reasonable amount of water from spring to autumn (fall), and the softer bodied species prefer a lightly shaded position. In winter, if kept dry, most species will cope with temperatures approaching freezing point.

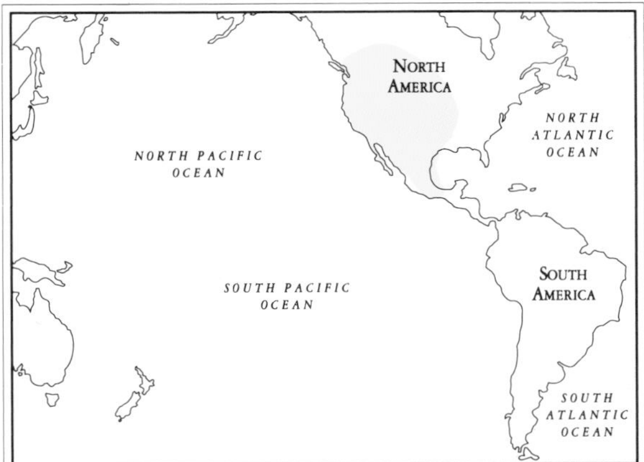

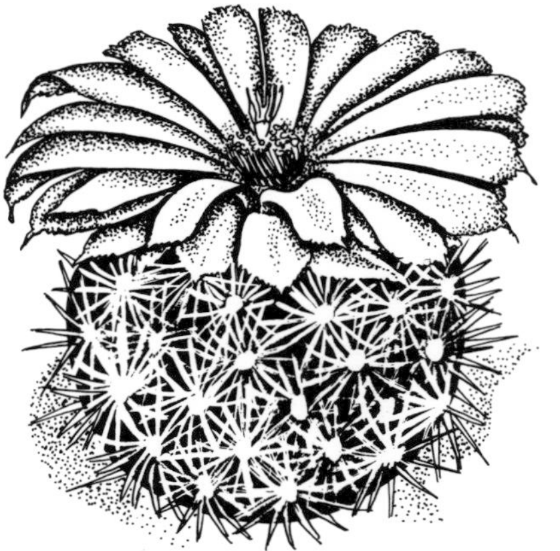

Coryphantha echinus

Coryphantha echinus

Coryphantha echinus

Common Name: Beehive cactus, but this is not a universally known name.
Size: Height 10 cm (4 in), width 7.5 cm (3 in).
Climate: Medium elevation.
Distribution: South-western United States and northern Mexico.
Flowering Time: Spring.
Description: The plants have a solitary, short, cylindrical habit, and a prominently tubercled body with 12-30 radial spines, which can be up to 1.25 cm (0.5 in) in length. There can be up to 3 or 4 centrals which are rather stout towards their bases and about 2.5 cm (1 in) in length. However, it is not uncommon for the centrals to be totally absent, which is why one plant was erroneously described as *C. pectinata*. The spination can be quite variable as can the flowers. They are about 5 cm (2 in) in diameter, and are in varying shades of yellow. The fruits are about 2.5 cm (1 in) in length, and are pale green when ripe.

Coryphantha hesteri

Common Name: None.
Size: Height 5-7.5 cm (2-3 in), width 30 cm (12 in).
Climate: Medium elevation.
Distribution: Only known from a small area in western Texas, United States.
Flowering Time: Spring to early summer.
Description: A miniature freely clustering species with spherical to egg-shaped pale green heads, 5-7.5 cm (2-3 in) in height. The diameter of an individual head rarely exceeds 5 cm (2 in). The tubercles are up to 1.25 cm (0.5 in) in length, and there are grooves on the upper surfaces from the areoles, almost to the axil positions. There is a little white wool in the base of these grooves nearest the newest tubercles. The areoles bear up to 20 whitish spreading radial spines, but there are no true centrals. The upper spines from each areole are stronger, and are from 1-1.25 cm (0.4-0.5 in) in length. The mauve to purplish flowers are 2.5-3.75 cm (1-1.5 in) in length and diameter. The fruits are spherical, very small, and greenish-brown when ripe.

Coryphantha minima

Coryphantha hesteri

Coryphantha minima

Common Name: None.
Size: Height 2-3 cm (0.8-1.2 in), width 5-6 cm (2-2.4 in).
Climate: Medium elevation.
Distribution: Only known from a small area in western Texas, United States.
Flowering Time: Spring to early summer.
Description: This is a solitary or sparingly clustering, miniature species with individual heads up to 3 cm (1.2 in) in height and up to 1.5 cm (0.6 in) in diameter. It can have up to 15 minute, fine radial spines, and usually 3 others which are about 0.6 cm (0.25 in) in length, and somewhat flattened. (As these do not come from the centre of the areole, they can hardly be referred to as central spines, in the true sense of the word.) The flowers are about 2.5 cm (1 in) in diameter, and usually rose-pink to rose-purple in colour. The outer petals have ciliate edges. The fruits are very small, and are grey-green when ripe.

Coryphantha sulcata

Common Name: Nipple Cactus.
Size: Height 7.5 cm (3 in), width 1 m (3 ft).
Climate: Low to medium elevation.
Distribution: South-western United States.
Flowering Time: Spring to early summer.
Description: A very freely clustering species, but individual heads rarely exceed 7.5 cm (3 in) in height and diameter. The fresh green body is quite prominently tubercled, and the slightly oval shaped white areoles bear up to 15 almost pectinate radial spines and up to three centrals, although these are sometimes absent. The radial spines are up to 1.5 cm (0.6 in) in length, and off-white to yellowish, but becoming brown or black with age. The centrals are about the same length, slightly stronger, stand out a little from the plant, and are of a similar colour. The flowers are funnel-shaped, up to 7.5 cm (3 in) in diameter, and vary in colour from a deep golden-yellow, to even greenish-yellow. The fruits are somewhat oblong, up to 2 cm (1.8 in) in length, and green when ripe.

Coryphantha vivipara var. *arizonica*

Coryphantha sulcata

Coryphantha vivipara var. *arizonica*

Common Name: Arizona Beehive.
Size: Height 25 cm (10 in), width 60 cm (24 in).
Climate: Medium to high elevation.
Distribution: South-western United States.
Flowering Time: Spring to early summer.
Description: A spherical, freely clustering species, with individual heads up to 10 cm (4 in) in height, each having a diameter of 6.25 cm (2.5 in). The dark green to bluish-green tubercled body is almost obscured by the dense white spination. The areoles bear up to 30 white, stiff radial spines, and up to eight, sometimes reddish, centrals. The radial and central spines range from 1.25–2.5 cm (0.5–1 in) in length. The flowers are in various shades of rose-pink, and are up to 5 cm (2 in) in diameter. The fruits are slightly egg-shaped, about 2 cm (0.8 in) in length, and green when ripe.

Coryphantha vivipara fa. *rosea*

Coryphantha vivipara fa. *rosea*

Common Name: Rose Beehive.
Size: Height 17.5 cm (7 in), width 7.5–12.5 cm (3–5 in).
Climate: High elevation.
Distribution: South-western United States.
Flowering Time: Early summer.
Description: Normally solitary, this species eventually has a cylindrical habit, with a green tubercled body which (with this variety) is just visible between the spines. The white circular areoles bear up to 16 spreading radial spines, and up to 12 centrals. The radial spines are about 1.5 cm (0.6 in) in length, fine and white, and the centrals are up to 2.5 cm (1 in) in length, off-white to pale pink with darker tips, and a little stouter. The flowers are up to 5 cm (2 in) in diameter, and rose to magenta coloured. The fruits are egg-shaped, up to 3 cm (1.2 in) in length, and are green at the base, but become reddish towards the top when ripe.

Denmoza

(dĕn-mō'-sa)

Denmoza contains just two species, and the generic name is derived as an anagram of Mendoza, a province in north-western Argentina. These plants are slow growing, and remain globular for many years, but do eventually grow into short columnar plants 0.5–1.5 m (1.5–5 ft) in height. Their diameter is 15–30 cm (6–12 in). The pale green to dark green bodies have 15–30 ribs, and the closely set areoles bear up to 30 spines 3–6 cm (1.2–2.4 in) in length. Usually a mixture of stout and bristly spines, they range in colour from reddish-brown to golden brown. On old plants the head is at an oblique angle, facing the sun.

The flowers are zygomorphic, up to 7.5 cm (3 in) in length, reddish in colour, with whitish hairs on the tube. The flower opens enough for the stigma and stamens to project from it. The fruits are spherical, about 2.5 cm (1 in) in diameter, pale green, sometimes tinged with red, and split open when ripe.

Culture: *Denmozas* come from north-western Argentina, but are not quick growing plants. However, they are easily raised from seed. The plants need to be about 15 cm (6 in) high before they start to flower regularly. They can be watered quite freely in hot weather during the spring to autumn (fall) period. In winter they should be kept dry and clear of frosts.

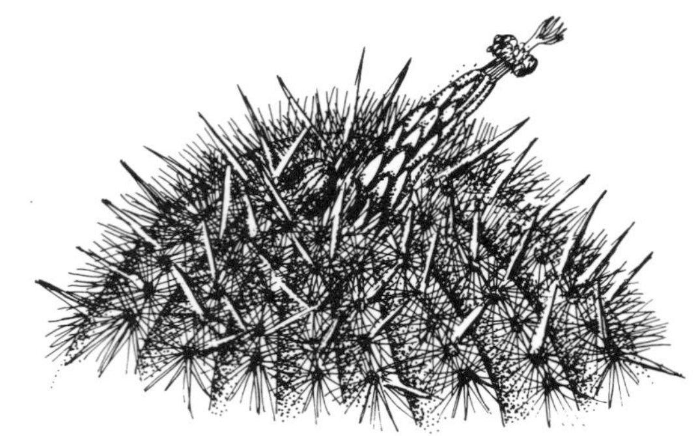

Denmoza erythrocephala

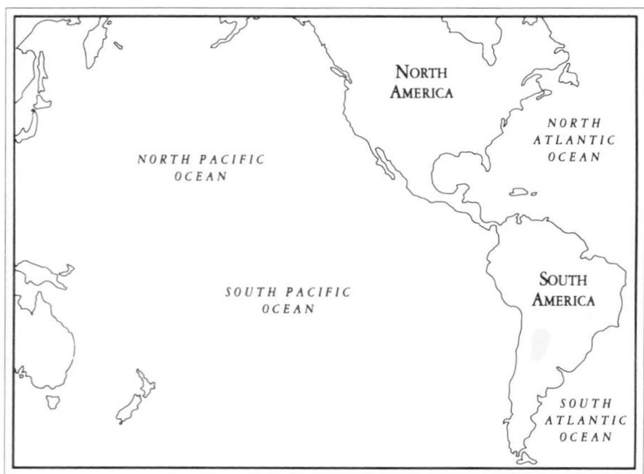

Denmoza erythrocephala

Denmoza erythrocephala

Common Name: None.
Size: Height 1.5 m (5 ft), width 30 cm (12 in).
Climate: Medium elevation.
Distribution: North-western Argentina.
Flowering Time: Summer.
Description: This is the larger species. The green body has 20–30 rounded ribs. In other respects the description is as given above.

Discocactus

(dĭs-kō-kăk'-tŭs)

Discocactus consisted of some 12 species about thirty years ago; today that figure has been trebled. However, in reality there are no more than 20 species. They are mostly low growing, flattened globular plants, which may be solitary, or branch with age. The body of the plant ranges in colour from pale green, to brownish-green and purplish-black. The rib count is 10–25, and the areoles are usually woolly and bear 5–20 radial spines and sometimes one central. In certain species the radials and centrals are virtually indistinguishable. The radials are generally appressed, often flattened, and up to 3 cm (1.2 in) in length. The centrals are generally longer, reaching 8 cm (3.2 in). The spine colour varies from off-white, yellowish, and brown to almost black.

The nocturnal white flowers are 5–10 cm (2–4 in) in height. They are funnel-shaped, have a very slender tube and appear very freely from a rather flat cephalium of wool and spines. The small berry-like fruits are white, cream or pink when ripe.

Culture: *Discocacti* come from Brazil, Bolivia and Paraguay. Old plants are not easy to keep alive if they are imported from their natural habitat, so it is better to obtain young cultivated plants, or to grow them from seed. They like a sandy–humus growing mixture, and warm humid conditions. In winter, they should be kept dry and no colder than 10°C (50°F). In hotter climates they can be given water during winter, and plenty of water during summer.

Discocactus horstii

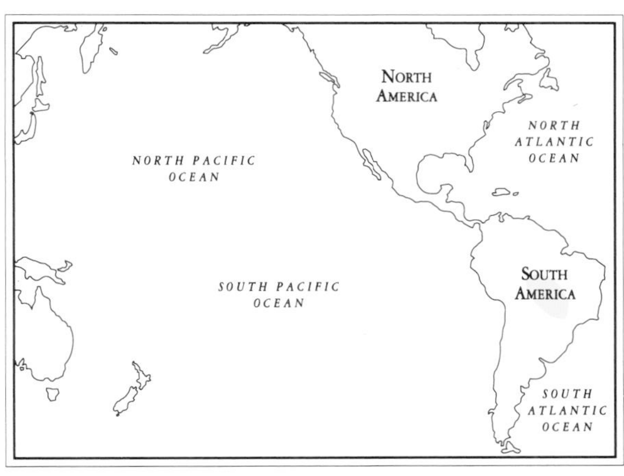

Discocactus horstii

Discocactus horstii

Common Name: None.
Size: Height 2 cm (0.8 in), width 6 cm (2.4 in).
Climate: Medium elevation.
Distribution: Central Brazil.
Flowering Time: Summer.
Description: This species was described in 1973. It has a very flattened globular habit. A mature plant can have up to 22 ribs, and the body colour ranges from brownish-green to almost purplish-black. The white felted areoles are set very close together and bear up to 10 very short pectinate spines. These have an unusual white powdery coating and black tips. The white nocturnal flowers are 6 cm (2.4 in) in length, and are produced very freely, even on plants no more than four or five years of age. The slender swollen tipped fruits can be up to 3 cm (1.2 in) in length and are naked and white when ripe.

DISOCACTUS

(dĭs-ō-kăk'-tŭs)

Disocactus contains about six species and a few varieties. The generic name is derived from the Gk, meaning 'double cactus', in reference to the plants' floral structure. They are bushy, epiphytic plants, and usually branch from the base. The green shoots are narrow at the base, up to 25 cm (10 in) in length, and 3-5 cm (1.2-2 in) in width. The shoots are slightly notched between the areole positions.

The slender tubular flowers are in varying shades of red or purple, 5-9 cm (2-3.6 in) in length, and possess relatively narrow petals. The fruits are globular, small, red or white when ripe, and are completely glabrous.

Culture: *Disocacti* are native to Honduras and Guatemala in central America. Being epiphytic plants, they need a soil rich in humus, and some shade and plenty of overhead watering to provide humidity during the hottest weather. In winter some water is still required, but a minimum temperature of 10°C (50°F) is advisable, otherwise the shoots can develop unsightly orange blotches (as do the shoots of *Hylocerei*, see page 105). They are easy plants to grow from seed or cuttings, and are very freely flowering.

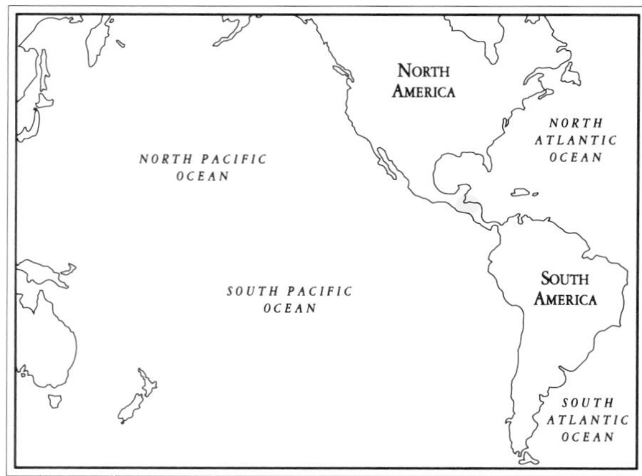

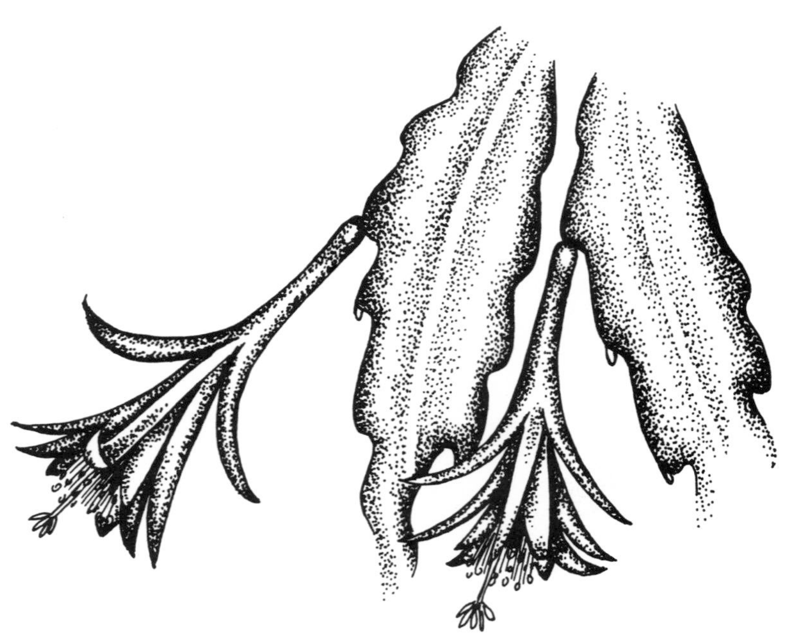

Disocactus eichlamii

Disocactus eichlamii

Common Name: None.
Size: Length 23 cm (9.2 in), width 30–40 cm (12–16 in).
Climate: Tropical.
Distribution: Honduras and Guatemala.
Flowering Time: Late spring and summer.
Description: This is a bushy, freely branching pendant species, with green shoots up to 23 cm (9.2 in) in length, and less than 5 cm (2 in) in width. The edges of the shoots with some forms are quite dentate between the areole positions. The tubular flowers are up to 7 cm (2.8 in) in length, in varying shades of red, and sometimes have a mauvy-purplish tube (as with the form illustrated). The small globular fruits are red when ripe.

Disocactus eichlamii

Disocactus nelsonii

Disocactus nelsonii

Common Name: None.
Size: Length 1.5 m (5 ft), width 4 cm (1.6 in).
Climate: Tropical.
Distribution: Southern Mexico.
Flowering Time: Late spring and summer.
Description: A free branching pendant species, it has fresh green flat stems, with slightly notched margins. The areoles bear no spines, and the 5 cm (2 in) bell-shaped flowers appear profusely near the ends of new stems. The flowers are varying shades of lilac pink. The fruits are spherical, smooth, very small, green becoming tinged with red as they ripen.

Dolichothele

(dŏl'-ĭ-kō-thē'-lē)

Dolichothele contains ten species, although if certain other smaller flowered plants that are in the genus *Mammillaria* (see page 116) are transferred here, this number is almost doubled. The generic name comes from the Gk meaning 'long nipple or tubercle'. The plants are dwarf in size, freely clustering, have long soft green tubercles, and possess a tuberous root system. The individual heads are 2.5–7.5 cm (1–3 in) in diameter. In between the tubercles there are quite woolly axil positions. On the tip of each tubercle is an areole bearing up to 10 radial spines, and up to 4 or 5 centrals, although in some species there are no centrals present. With certain species, one of the centrals can be hooked. The spines are whitish, yellowish or brownish in colour and very flexible, and are usually 1.25–2.5 cm (0.5–1 in) in length.

The sweetly scented flowers are 5–7.5 cm (2–3 in) in diameter, and are usually in varying shades of yellow. The fruits are 2.5 cm (1 in) or more in length, and are green to reddish-green when ripe.

Culture: *Dolichotheles* come from Mexico and just into south-western United States. They are very easy growing, free flowering plants, which can be grown from seed, or propagated by dividing up a cluster. When a cluster is divided, in some species many of the heads will already have some small roots that were formed above ground within the cluster. During the warmer months the plants can be watered quite freely, and some species grow best under light shade. In winter they will stand very cool conditions if kept dry.

Dolichothele longimamma

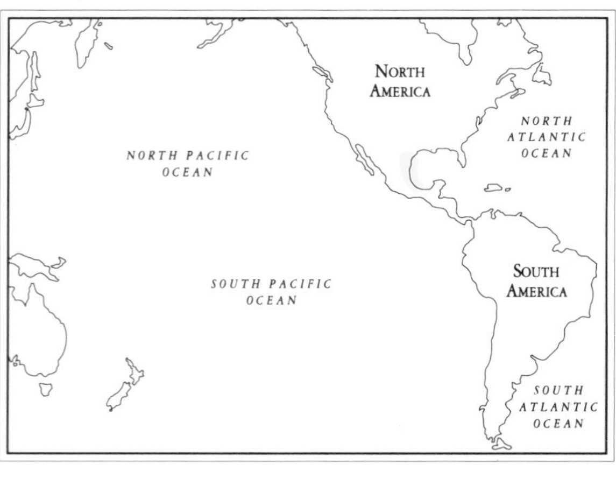

Dolichothele longimamma

Dolichothele longimamma

Common Name: Nipple Cactus.
Size: Height 7.5 cm (3 in), width 20 cm (8 in).
Climate: Medium elevation.
Distribution: Mexico.
Flowering Time: Summer.
Description: A sometimes solitary, but usually clustering, species with tubercles up to 7.5 cm (3 in) in length. The individual heads are usually 5-7.5 cm (2-3 in) in diameter. Each areole bears up to 10 radial spines, which are less than 2.5 cm (1 in) in length, plus a possible 3 centrals which are slightly longer than the radials. The yellowish spines usually have brownish tips. The yellow flowers are about 6 cm (2.4 in) in diameter, and the fruits are usually reddish-green when ripe.

ECHINOCACTUS

(ē-kī'-nō-kăk'-tŭs)

Echinocactus contains some ten species, and the generic name is derived from two Gk words meaning 'hedgehog' and 'prickly'. The plants are globular to cylindrical, solitary, or freely clustering, and the largest growing species can reach 1.8 m (6 ft) in height and 1 m (3 ft) in diameter. *Echinocacti* as young plants have a tubercled appearance but the tubercules eventually merge into a very prominent rib formation. There are 8–50 ribs depending on the species. The epidermis can be in varying shades of green to bluish, and is very tough. As a result mature plants can safely withstand the burning desert sun. The centres of the plants are invariably very woolly, ranging in colour from whitish to yellow. The hairy areoles are set fairly well apart, and are usually circular and bear 5–12 stout radial spines. These spines can be curved or straight, and radiating from the areoles or sometimes very appressed against the body of the plant. They can be up to 5 cm (2 in) in length. There are 1–4 central spines which are usually stouter than the radials are and 5–10 cm (2–4 in) in length, and stand out from the plant. The spines are quite variable in colour — from white, golden yellow and pinkish to nearly black.

The flowers appear from among the woolly centre, but away from the centre. This can be clearly seen in *E. grusonii* (see page 72). The larger species can form complete rings of flowers during a season. The flowers are in varying shades of yellow, with one exception, *E. horizonthalonious*, which has pink to purplish flowers. The flowers are usually around 6.25 cm (2.6 in) in diameter and the flower tube is woolly. Most flowers open wide, however some are prevented from doing so by numerous strong spines near the centre of a plant, eg *E. polycephalus*. The exterior of the fruits are very hairy or woolly, and of the same colour as that of the centre of the plant. The fruits are dry when ripe, and dehisce basally.

Culture: *Echinocacti* are native to central and northern Mexico, and south-western United States. They grow among bushes or in very arid rocky areas. The majority of species are quite easy to grow, are usually grown from seed, and develop quite rapidly. This is particularly true of the very well-known *E. grusonii* which, although now rare in habitat, it probably one of the most common plants in cultivation throughout the world. Species such as *E. horizonthalonius* (see page 72) and *E. polycephalus* are much slower to grow from seed, and the latter one can be classed as difficult to grow in cultivation. Most species, particularly when young, should be kept clear of frosts, but they are much tougher when mature, and will then safely withstand light frosts, provided they are kept dry.

Echinocactus horizonthalonius

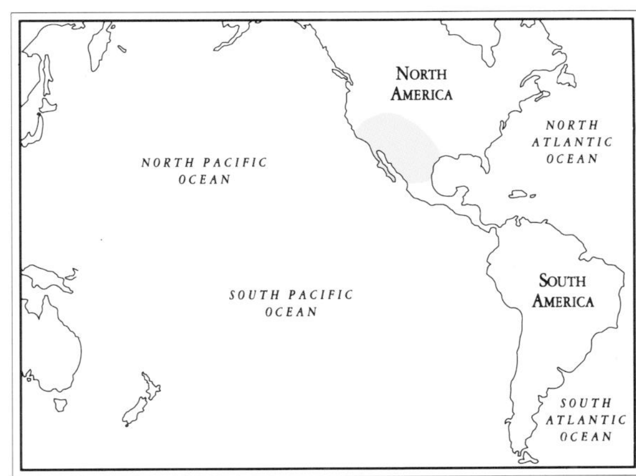

Echinocactus grusonii

Common Name: Golden Barrel Cactus (this is the most widely known common name).
Size: Height 1 m (3 ft), width 1 m (3 ft).
Climate: Medium elevation.
Distribution: Central Mexico.
Flowering Time: Late spring to autumn (fall).
Description: This is a large globular species, which usually remains solitary for 20 or 30 years, but can then sometimes cluster very freely. A single head normally reaches about 1 m (3 ft) in diameter. The 25–35 ribs are usually straight. The body of the plant is green, and has masses of white or creamy-yellow wool in its centre. The areoles bear up to 8 radial spines which are up to 3.5 cm (1.4 in) in length, and usually 4 centrals which are somewhat longer. The spines are yellow, but there is also a white spined form of this species, which is now becoming better known. The bell-shaped flowers are about 5 cm (2 in) in diameter. The fruit, which is covered with creamy-white wool, is about 2.5 cm (1 in) or less in length. The fruits are embedded in the woolly crown of the plant, and possess on their tops the dried brownish remains of the flowers.

Echinocactus grusonii

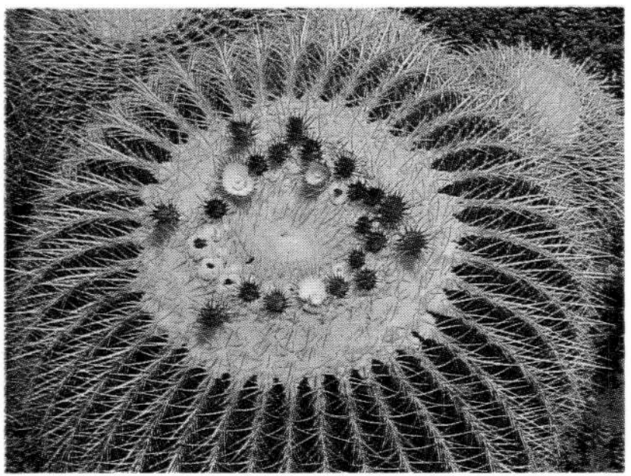
Echinocactus grusonii in flower

Echinocactus horizonthalonius

Echinocactus horizonthalonius

Common Name: Blue Barrel Cactus or Eagle's Claw Cactus.
Size: Height 25 cm (10 in), width 20 cm (8 in).
Climate: Medium elevation.
Distribution: South-western United States and northern Mexico.
Flowering Time: Late spring and summer.
Description: This is quite a variable species: some forms remain as flattened globular plants while others become columnar. The more common flattened globular variety can reach a diameter of about 20 cm (8 in). They can have up to 12 ribs which are rounded and sometimes slightly spiralling. The plant body varies in colour from bluish-green to bluish-grey and the areoles bear up to 10 fairly stout radial spines 2.5 cm (1 in) in length. They tend to be somewhat appressed against the plant. There can be up to 3 centrals, which are stouter and longer than the radial spines, and all the spines are somewhat flattened and grey in colour. The flowers usually exceed 5 cm (2 in) in diameter and range from pale pink to purplish-magenta. The fruit is just under 2.5 cm (1 in) in length, red when ripe, and covered with white wool.

ECHINOCEREUS

(ĕ-kī'-nō-sē'-rē-ŭs)

Echinocereus contains nearly one hundred species and many varieties, and the generic name comes from the Gk *echinus* (hedgehog or sea-urchin), and the Lat *cereus* (wax-candle). Some members of this genus are given the general common name of Hedgehog Cacti. This genus has some of the finest flowers within the family Cactaceae. *Echinocerei* are a very varied group of plants, with so many transitional forms that it is a very difficult genus to classify. They range from dwarf erect plants like *E. viridiflorus* (see page 77) which has small greenish flowers to *E. subinermis* (see page 77) which has quite large rotate yellow flowers from freely clustering, clambering types with soft fleshy stems and long tubed flowers such as with *E. gentryi* (see page 75) to erect, thicker stemmed types with beautiful pectinate spine formations such as *E. reichenbachii* (see page 76), and densely long spined species such as *E. longisetus* (see page 75), both of which have very similar large flowers; and finally to large erect clumping types which are strongly spined and have waxy flowers which stay open day and night, such as *E. triglochidiatus* (see page 77). The clambering species have stems with 4–6 ribs, whereas the erect pectinate spined types can have up to 24 ribs.

The flowers appear usually from the sides of the plants, although there are a few exceptions where the flowers come from near the areoles, bursting through the epidermis of the plant. In all species, with the exception of the small flowered species, the flowers open wide, and share the same type of spiny flower tube and fruit structure. The prominent pistil and stigma lobes visible in the centre of the flowers is quite a feature with this genus. The fruits are very spiny and fleshy, and when ripening the aroma from the fruits is similar to that of strawberries, then they carry the common name of Strawberry Hedgehog.

Echinocereus gentryi

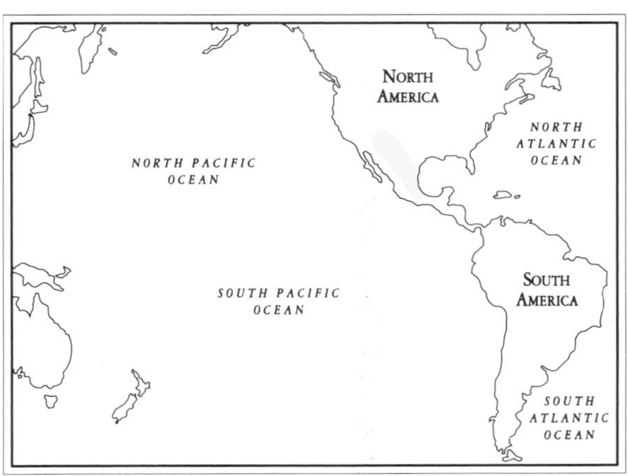

Culture: *Echinocerei* come from a wide area of south-western United States, and into northern and western Mexico. Some forms of *E. triglochidiatus* and *E. viridiflorus* come from higher altitudes a little further north in the United States where they experience snow and heavy frosts. The majority of species are quite easy to cultivate, and will flower very freely every year. They can be raised from seed without too much trouble, and almost without exception can be propagated vegetatively from cuttings — most of which will root within a few weeks. They like a sandy-humus soil, and most species can be watered freely from spring to autumn (fall), but in winter if the plants are kept dry, most species can withstand temperatures near freezing point.

Echinocereus chloranthus var. *russanthus*

Common Name: None.
Size: Height 20 cm (8 in), width 6.25 cm (2.5 in).
Climate: Medium elevation.
Distribution: South-western United States.
Flowering Time: Spring.
Description: This is a cylindrical stemmed species, which is usually solitary, with up to 18 slightly tuberculate ribs. The slightly oval areoles are fairly close together, with a little white wool. They bear up to 45 thin, flexible, radial spines, and up to 12 slightly stronger, spreading centrals. The radials are 0.5–1.5 cm (0.2–0.6 in) in length, while the centrals are 2–2.75 cm (0.8–1.1 in) in length. The spines vary in colour from white to brown to purplish-brown. The flowers are funnel-shaped, 2.5 cm (1 in) in length, but as they do not open wide, are no more than 1.25 cm (0.5 in) in diameter. The fruits are almost spherical, about 1.25 cm (0.5 in) in length and covered with short, white bristly spines.

Echinocereus chloranthus var. *russanthus*

Echinocereus engelmannii var. *nicholii*

Echinocereus engelmannii var. *nicholii*

Common Name: Nichol Hedgehog.
Size: Height 60 cm (2 ft), width 1 m (3 ft).
Climate: Medium elevation.
Distribution: South-western United States.
Flowering Time: Spring.
Description: This fine, fairly erect variety has 60 cm (2 ft) high stems, which have a diameter of about 7.5 cm (3 in). The green stems have up to 10 ribs, and the areoles bear up to 12 straight, fairly rigid, spreading radial spines, and 2–5 stronger centrals. The radial spines can be up to 2.5 cm (1 in) in length, and the centrals 5–6.25 cm (2–2.5 in). All the spines are golden yellow in colour. The funnel-shaped flowers are 7.5 cm (3 in) in diameter, and much the same in length, and pale magenta, in colour, but darker in the throat. The fruits are ovoid, 3.75 cm (1.5 in) in length, pinkish-red when ripe, with straw to golden yellow spines.

Echinocereus fendleri var. *bonkerae*

Common Name: Bonker Hedgehog.
Size: Height 20 cm (8 in), width 1 m (3 ft).
Climate: Medium elevation.
Distribution: South-western United States.
Flowering Time: Spring.
Description: This is another erect, freely clustering species with dark green or reddish-green stems, that can be up to 20 cm (8 in) high, and have a diameter of 6.25 cm (2.5 in). The stems have up to 16 ribs, and the areoles are set fairly close together, bearing up to 12 spreading radial spines, and usually only one central. The radial spines are white, up to 1 cm (0.4 in) in length, and the single central is slightly longer and white with a brown tip. The flowers are up to 8.75 cm (3.5 in) in diameter and dark magenta. The fruits are ovoid, up to 3.75 cm (1.5 in) in length and red when ripe, with whitish spines.

Echinocereus fendleri var. *bonkerae*

Echinocereus gentryi

Common Name: None.
Size: Height 15 cm (6 in), width 30 cm (12 in).
Climate: Mediterranean.
Distribution: Northern Mexico.
Flowering Time: Spring.
Description: This is a prostrate, freely branching species, with soft green stems up to 15 cm (6 in) in length and 2.5 cm (1 in) in diameter. The stems have 5-6 ribs, and the small, closely set white areoles bear up to 12 minute brownish, fine radial spines, and one similar central, which is slightly longer than the radial spines. The flowers are funnel-shaped, but with a longer, slender greenish tube, and are 8 cm (3.2 in) in length, and 5-6 cm (2-2.4 in) in diameter. The slightly ovoid-shaped fruits are about 2 cm (0.8 in) in length, greenish-red when ripe, and have a few tiny spines which are similar to those on the plant itself.

Echinocereus gentryi

Echinocereus longisetus

Common Name: None.
Size: Height 20 cm (8 in), width 60 cm (2 ft).
Climate: Medium elevation.
Distribution: Northern Mexico, close to Texas.
Flowering Time: Spring.
Description: A semi-erect species, usually branching from underground. Stems up to 20 cm (8 in) in height and 4-5 cm (1.6-2 in) in diameter, and have up to 14 ribs, with whitish areoles, bearing up to 25 radial spines and 7 centrals. Radial spines are 1.5 cm (0.6 in) in length; the centrals can reach 4-5 cm (1.6-2 in). Spines are bristly, strong and white with slightly darker tips. Funnel-shaped flowers are up to 7 cm (2.8 in) in diameter, have magenta pink petals and a green-tinged, off-white throat. Fruits are ovoid, pinkish-red when ripe with white bristly spines.

Echinocereus longisetus

Echinocereus melanocentrus

Echinocereus melanocentrus

Common Name: None.
Size: Height 15 cm (6 in), width 30 cm (12 in).
Climate: Medium elevation.
Distribution: A very localised species in Texas, United States.
Flowering Time: Spring.
Description: A cylindrical stemmed species, which will cluster to a certain extent. The stems rarely exceed 15 cm (6 in) in height and about 5 cm (2 in) in diameter. The stems are rather soft, with up to 13 ribs, and the areoles are set very close together. They bear up to 20 pectinate radial spines and one central which stands out and curves upwards from the plant. However, this is not always present, or is only present on quite old plants. The radial spines range from minute to about 1 cm (0.4 in) in length, and the central is up to 1 cm (0.4 in). The spines are quite variable in colour — from cream and brown to almost black. The funnel-shaped flowers are 5-7.5 cm (2-3 in) in diameter and in length. They are rose-pink to pale magenta with reddish centres, and sometimes have quite ragged tips to the petals. The exterior of the flower tube is greenish-brown with white or brownish spine clusters. The fruits are ovoid, about 3.75 cm (1.5 in) in length, reddish-green when ripe, and have white or brownish spine clusters. The fruits, although still fleshy when ripe, tend to split irregularly.

Echinocereus pectinatus var. *rigidissimus*

Echinocereus pectinatus var. *rigidissimus*

Common Name: Arizona Rainbow Hedgehog.
Size: Height 30 cm (12 in), width 10 cm (4 in).
Climate: Medium elevation.
Distribution: South-western United States and nearby parts of Mexico.
Flowering Time: Spring.
Description: This species is normally solitary and cylindrical stemmed. The areoles are set fairly close together and bear up to 18 pectinate radial spines. There are no central spines, and the radials are less than 1 cm (0.4 in) in length. The spines change their colour each season, varying from white to pink to reddish providing a rainbow effect, hence the species' common name. The flowers are 7–8 cm (2.8–3.2 in) in diameter, and magenta or pinkish magenta with a whitish throat. The exterior of the tube has small spine clusters. The fruits are slightly ovoid, reddish when ripe, and have whitish spine clusters.

Echinocereus pectinatus var. *rigidissimus*

Echinocereus reichenbachii

Echinocereus reichenbachii

Common Name: Lace Cactus.
Size: Height 20 cm (8 in), width 60 cm (24 in).
Climate: Medium elevation.
Distribution: South-western United States and nearby parts of Mexico.
Flowering Time: Spring.
Description: This is a solitary or freely clustering species. The single stemmed plants can reach 20 cm (8 in) in height, while the stems of the clustering forms rarely exceed 10 cm (4 in). The diameter of the stem is fairly constant between the two forms at 7–9 cm (2.8–3.6 in). The stems have up to 19 ribs, and the white areoles are set fairly close together and bear up to 30 pectinate radial spines. Central spines are usually absent, but there is only one when they are present. The spines are usually less than 1 cm (0.4 in) in length and are white, brownish, or tinged with red. The flowers are around 7 cm (2.8 in) in diameter and in length, and have white hair and bristly spines on their tube. They are varying shades of magenta-pink in colour, with a paler throat, but are reddish at their base. The fruits are ovoid and up to 5 cm (2 in) in length, and are reddish, with bristly spines.

Echinocereus subinermis

Echinocereus subinermis

Common Name: None.
Size: Height 10 cm (4 in), width 20 cm (8 in).
Climate: Medium elevation.
Distribution: North-eastern Mexico.
Flowering Time: Spring and summer.
Description: This is a solitary or sparingly clustering species. The stems rarely exceed 10 cm (4 in) in height and 5 cm (2 in) in diameter, and have 6–8 ribs. They are green in colour and are often tinged with red. The tiny areoles are set fairly well apart, bear up to 8 minute radial spines, and sometimes one central which is usually less than 0.5 cm (0.2 in) in length. Some forms are almost spineless. The bright yellow, funnel-shaped flowers often open very wide, and can be up to 9 cm (3.6 in) in diameter, and have a slender green tube with small, white bristly spine clusters. The fruits are also green tinged with red, and have small white bristly spines.

Echinocereus triglochidiatus

Common Name: Claret Cup.
Size: Height 15 cm (6 in), width 1.5 m (4.5 ft).
Climate: Medium to high elevation.
Distribution: South-western United States, over a wide area, and at great variations in altitude — up to 2600 m (8528 ft).
Flowering Time: Spring.
Description: This is a very variable species, and a number of varieties have been described. It is freely clustering, forming large mats up to 1.5 m (4.5 ft) in diameter. Individual stems rarely exceed 15 cm (6 in) and have 6–10 ribs. The areoles are set well apart on the green, somewhat creased stems, and bear 3–8 radial spines, and up to 5 centrals, although in some forms there are no centrals. The spines are angular, 2.5–3.75 cm (1–1.5 in) in length, and can be grey or brownish. The flowers are 5 cm (2 in) in diameter and 7.5 cm (3 in) in length, are in varying shades of red in colour, and have rather waxy petals. The fruits are somewhat ovoid, 2.5 cm (1 in) in length and reddish when ripe.

Echinocereus viridiflorus

Common Name: Green Hedgehog.
Size: Height 5 cm (2 in), width 15 cm (6 in).
Climate: Medium to high elevation.
Distribution: South-western United States, mainly at higher altitudes.
Flowering Time: Spring and early summer.
Description: An unusual, solitary or clustering dwarf species. Some varieties can reach 20 cm (8 in) in height. Greenish-brown stems have 12–16 ribs, and closely set areoles bear up to 16 fine radial spines and 4 slightly stouter centrals, although these can be absent. The radial spines are 0.75 cm (0.3 in) in length; centrals are fractionally longer. Spines are white or cream with reddish-brown tips. The green or greenish-brown flowers do not open very wide, and are 1.85 cm (0.7 in) in diameter and 2.5 cm (1 in) in length. Fruits are spherical, greenish-brown when ripe, 1.5 cm (0.6 in) in diameter, with a few whitish spine clusters.

Echinocereus viridiflorus

Echinocereus triglochidiatus

ECHINOFOSSULOCACTUS

(ē-kī'-nō-fŏs-ū-lō-kăk'-tŭs)

Echinofossulocactus contains some 30 species. The generic name is a mixture of Gk and Lat meaning 'hedgehog' and 'groove'. This genus was for a long time known as *Stenocactus*, and even today, because this name is so much shorter, many people still refer to them as *Stenocacti*. They are globular to slightly columnar plants, and some species will branch moderately freely from around the base. It is a very interesting, but difficult genus to classify, as there are many variable forms. All but a few have a wavy rib structure, with up to one hundred narrow ribs. In some species the spination is so dense that this very unusual rib structure is hardly visible (in others such as *E. lancifer*, see below, the rib structure can clearly be seen). The areoles are small, and can either be set very close together, or up to 4 cm (1.6 in) apart. There can be 4–20 radial spines and 1–4 centrals. The radials can be fine and needle-like, or much stouter as with *E. lancifer*, from very short and to 2.5 cm (1 in). Their colour ranges from white or yellow to brown. The centrals are usually much stouter than the radials and in many species are very flattened, and are brown, reddish-brown to black in colour. Their length is 2.5–7.5 cm (1–3 in) in length.

The flowers are small, 2.5–3.5 cm (1–1.4 in) in diameter, and range from almost white or cream to magenta, but the petals invariably have a darker median stripe. The fruits are small, less than 1.25 cm (0.5 in) in diameter, reddish-green or brownish when ripe, and usually split open allowing the seeds to disperse.

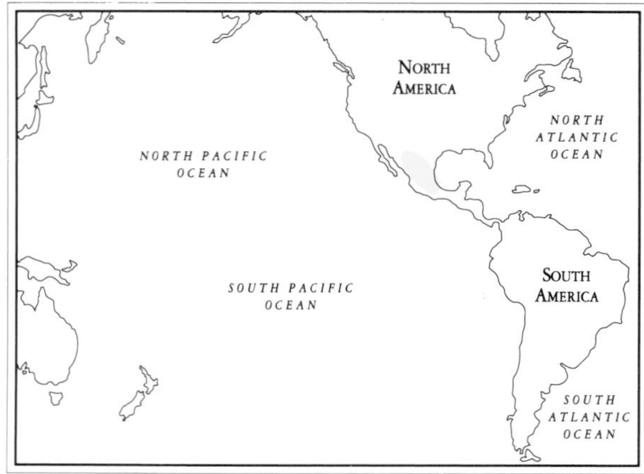

Culture: *Echinofossulocacti* come from central and northern Mexico, where they can be found in varying locations — from among grass to rocky fissures. They are usually raised from seed, and many species can flower in their second or third year. From late winter to early autumn (fall) they like a sunny situation, and plenty of water. In winter, if kept dry, they tolerate temperatures to within a few degrees of freezing.

Echinofossulocactus lancifer

Echinofossulocactus lancifer

Common Name: None.
Size: Height 15 cm (6 in), width 10 cm (4 in).
Climate: Medium elevation.
Distribution: Central Mexico.
Flowering Time: Late winter onwards.
Description: This is a globular species, which usually remains solitary, and has up to 35 narrow, wavy, green ribs. The areoles are set in excess of 2.5 cm (1 in) apart. The small areoles bear 4 small curved white radials, which point downwards, and 4 strong, but flexible, flattened centrals. The spines are off-white in colour, but often have brown tips, and are up to 5 cm (2 in) or more in length. The flowers are about 3.5 cm (1.6 in) in diameter, and are pinkish with a darker median stripe down each petal. The fruits are round, less than 1.25 cm (0.5 in) in diameter, and greenish-brown when ripe.

Echinofossulocactus lancifer

Echinofossulocactus violaciflorus

Common Name: None.
Size: Height 15 cm (6 in), width 10 cm (4 in).
Climate: Medium to high elevation.
Distribution: Central Mexico.
Flowering Time: Late winter onwards.
Description: A spherical species (usually solitary) which becomes slightly columnar as an old plant. The body of the plant is dark green to bluish-green, with up to 35 thin, well notched ribs. The areoles have whitish wool, greying with age, bearing four white terete radial spines, and three thicker yellowish centrals, which are often slightly flattened. The spines rarely exceed 1.25 cm (0.5 in) in length. The flowers are about 2.5 cm (1 in) in length and diameter, white with a purplish-violet centre and have similar coloured median stripes down the petals. The fruits are spherical, about 1 cm (0.4 in) in diameter, and brownish when ripe.

Echinofossulocactus violaciflorus

ECHINOPSIS

(ĕk-ĭ-nŏp'-sĭs)

Echinopsis contains some 60 species and many varieties. The generic name is derived from the Gk, meaning 'like a hedgehog'. They are globular to short and cylindrical in age, and can be solitary or cluster freely. A few species can have individual heads reaching 70 cm (28 in) in height and 35 cm (14 in) in diameter. There can be 8–30 ribs which are usually straight and are very prominent in larger species. The areoles are round, white, or grey to brown, and can be set very close together, or more than 2.5 cm (1 in) apart. There can be 5–30 radial spines per areole, and when present up to 4 centrals. The radials are straight or curved, spreading, and sometimes appressed against the plant, and the centrals invariably stand out very prominently from the plant. In the case of the very dwarf species, all the spines are fine and quite short, however, in the larger species, the radials are strong, and 1.25–5 cm (0.5–2 in) in length. The centrals can be longer — up to 7.5 cm (3 in). The spine colour varies from off-white or grey to brown and black.

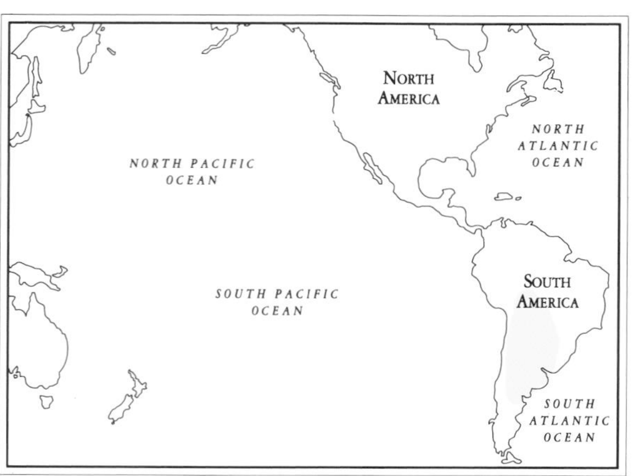

The feature of the flowers in this genus is their long trumpets. In some species the flowers can be 20 cm (8 in) in length, occasionally longer. The highly scented night flowering species are white or very pale pink, whereas the day flowering species can be in shades of yellow and red. There are usually some hairs on the exterior of the flower tube. The fruits are usually round, hairy, and sometimes have short spines, and are 1.25–5 cm (0.5–2 in) in diameter. When ripe they are greenish-brown to reddish-brown, and partially split open, allowing the seeds to disperse.

Culture: They come from northern Argentina, southern Brazil, Bolivia, Paraguay and Uruguay, growing in many very different locations, including some at quite high altitudes. They are very easy plants to grow from seed, and some species will flower within 2 or 3 years. In most species the offsets can be removed by just breaking them off, as the joint position is very narrow. When a plant is very densely clustered, these offsets can already have a few rudimentary roots. If so, it is only necessary to allow the cut to callus for a few days, and such offsets will root very rapidly. Most species appreciate plenty of water during spring to early autumn (fall), and growth is quite rapid. In winter the majority tolerate near freezing and lower termperatures.

Echinopsis spegazziniana

Echinopsis spegazziniana

Common Name: Queen of the Night (this is used for many white night flowering cacti, of many different genera).
Size: Height 30 cm (12 in), width 10 cm (4 in).
Climate: Medium elevation.
Distribution: North-western Argentina.
Flowering Time: Late spring and summer.
Description: This plant becomes cylindrical with age. It has a dark green body with 12 or more angular ribs, which bear off-white areoles. There can be up to 8 short, brown radial spines, and usually one curved central of the same colour which rarely exceeds 2.5 cm (1 in) in length. The tubular flower can reach nearly 20 cm (8 in) in length, and its petals are white or very pale pink. The exterior of the tube is pinkish-brown and it has some hairs of the same colour. The fruit is round, less than 2.5 cm (1 in) in diameter, slightly hairy, and pinkish-brown when ripe.

Echinopsis torrecillasensis

Echinopsis torrecillasensis

Common Name: None.
Size: Height 2 cm (0.8 in), width 10 cm (4 in).
Climate: High elevation.
Distribution: Bolivia.
Flowering Time: Summer.
Description: This is a wonderful miniature, clustering species. Its individual heads do not exceed 2.5 cm (1 in) in diameter, but below ground it is much larger with a carrot-like taproot 7.5–10 cm (3–4 in) in length. It can have up to 16 ribs, and the areoles are set close together and bear up to 7 radial spines and one central. The spines are less than 1 cm (0.4 in) in length, and are grey, often with a brown tip. The tubular flower is 7.5 cm (3 in) or more in length, and is in varying shades of orange-red to dark red. The exterior of the tube is light green and has some white hairs. The fruit is very small, and reddish-brown when ripe.

Echinopsis spegazziniana

ENCEPHALOCARPUS

(ēn-sĕf'-ă-lō-kăr'-pŭs)

This is another monotypic genus, and the generic name comes from *enkephale* meaning top, and *karpos* meaning fruit. It is a solitary spherical plant, with rather flat imbricate tubercles, so it looks rather like a greyish-green to slate coloured pine cone, hence its specific name of *strobiliformis*. It grows rather slowly and rarely exceeds 7.5 cm (3 in) in height and 5-6 cm (2-2.4 in) in diameter, with some white in the centre of the plant. It only has a few minute white bristly spines on the youngest areoles, otherwise it is virtually spineless.

The flowers appear from the centre, and they are 3 cm (1.2 in) in length and about 2-2.5 cm (0.8-1 in) in diameter. The flowers are a brilliant magenta-red, but the outer sepals are paler with darker median stripes.

The fruits are spherical, very small, almost buried in the white centre of the plant, and brownish when ripe.

Culture: *Encephalocarpus strobiliformis* is native to central Mexico, where it is found in very arid situations (but seeking shade between rocks). It is a slow growing plant, requiring a sandy/humus soil mixture and can only be watered freely during the hottest summer months. At other times water sparingly, and not at all during the winter months, unless you live in a climate where temperatures do not go very low. They can only be raised from seed, and this is a fairly slow process, particularly in the first two to three years.

Encephalocarpus strobiliformis

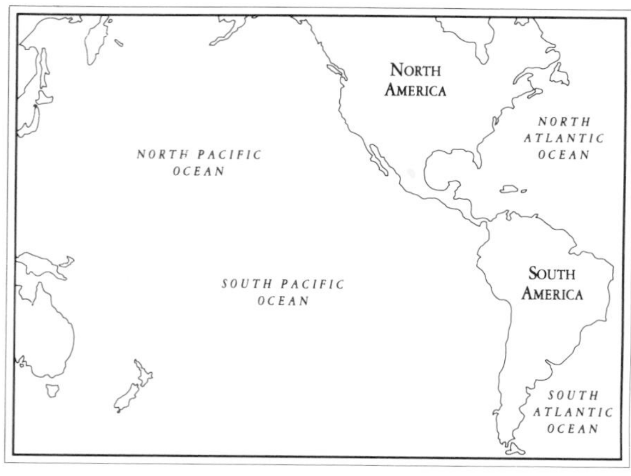

Encephalocarpus strobiliformis

Encephalocarpus strobiliformis

Common Name: None.
Size: Height 7.5 cm (3 in), width 5-6 cm (2-2.4 in).
Climate: Medium elevation.
Distribution: Central Mexico.
Flowering Time: Summer.
Description: As this genus has only one species see genus text above.

EPIPHYLLUM

(ĕp-ĭ-fĭl'-ŭm)

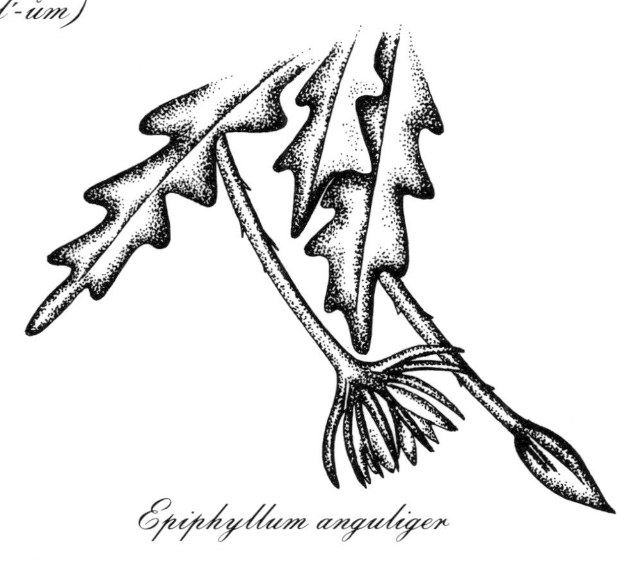

Epiphyllum anguliger

This genus contains some 25 species and a few varieties. The generic name is derived from the Greek, meaning 'upon a leaf'. This was based on an incorrect conclusion that the flowers appeared from leaves. They are bushy epiphytic plants, usually with long, thin flattened stems. The green stems are usually narrow at the base, up to 50 cm (18 in) or more in length, and from 5–12.5 cm (2–5 in) in width. The stem margins may be smooth, crenate or deeply dentate.

The nocturnal flowers can either have a short or long thin, glabrous tube. The flowers normally open widely from 5–15 cm (2–6 in) in diameter, white or yellowish in colour, and generally heavily scented.

The fruits are usually oblong, scaly, and sometimes rather angular. They are 5–9 cm (2–3.6 in) in length, and red or purple coloured when ripe.

Culture: *Epiphyllums* are native to southern Mexico, and southwards through central America to Bolivia, Brazil and Paraguay, with one species also being found in the West Indies on Trinidad and Tobago. Being epiphytic plants, they like a soil rich in humus, and some shade during the hottest weather, when they need plenty of overhead watering. In winter, some water is still required, but a minimum temperature of 10°C (50°F) is advisable. (Ideally this should be even higher for some species, so that unsightly blotches do not appear.) They are very easy plants to grow from seed or cuttings, and most species are very free flowering.

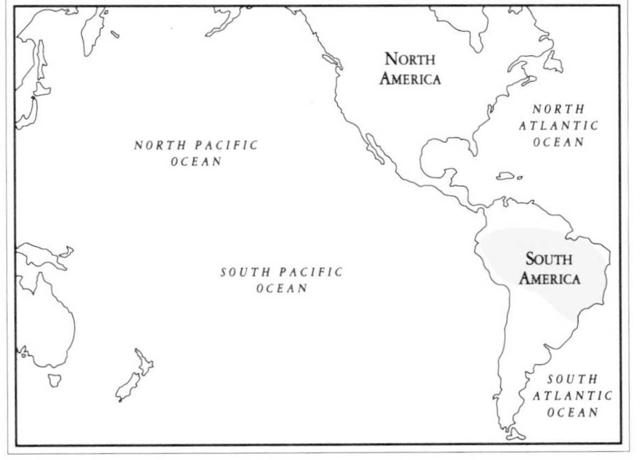

Epiphyllum anguliger

Epiphyllum anguliger

Common Name: Queen of the Night or Moon Cactus.
Size: Height 1 m (3 ft), width 2 m (6 ft) or more in diameter.
Climate: Tropical.
Distribution: Southern Mexico.
Flowering Time: Early summer onwards.
Description: Bushy, free branching species with flattened green stems up to 40 cm (16 in) in length, which are deeply dentate. The areoles sometimes bear a few bristles. The white flowers are around 8.5 cm (3.4 in) long, bearing yellowish to pale pink coloured sepals. The slightly elongated fruits are 5 cm (2 in) long, and red when ripe.

EPITHELANTHA

(ĕp′-ĭ-thē-lăn′-thă)

Epithelantha contains two species and a number of varieties and forms. The generic name is derived from the Gk meaning the flowers 'arise from a nipple or tubercle'. They are magnificently formed, but their real beauty cannot be appreciated without a magnifying glass. They are solitary or clustering, and some forms have a taproot. Individual heads are 2.5–5 cm (1–2 in) in diameter and covered with masses of minute tubercles, and even smaller areoles, which bear up to 40 very short, white, or brownish pectinate spines, that virtually hide the body of the plant. Often in the centre of a mature flowering head are numerous fractionally longer spines that stand more erect. But, as the plant grows, these usually disappear.

The flowers are off-white, cream to pale pink, and 0.6–1.25 cm (0.25–0.5 in) in diameter. The fruits are elongated, 1 cm (0.4 in) or less in length, bright red when ripe, and contain just a few black seeds.

Culture: *Epithelanthas* come from northern Mexico and south-western United States. They are to be found among grass in sandy or rocky locations where drainage is very good. In cultivation they can be grown from seed, but are relatively slow growing and it is unlikely that even with ideal growing conditions flowers can be expected in under 5 years. Offsets can be rooted up, or seedlings grafted and then in 2 years, after flowering size has been obtained, put back on to their own roots. They require well drained soil, and in temperate climates under glass full sun gives the best results.

Epithelantha micromeris

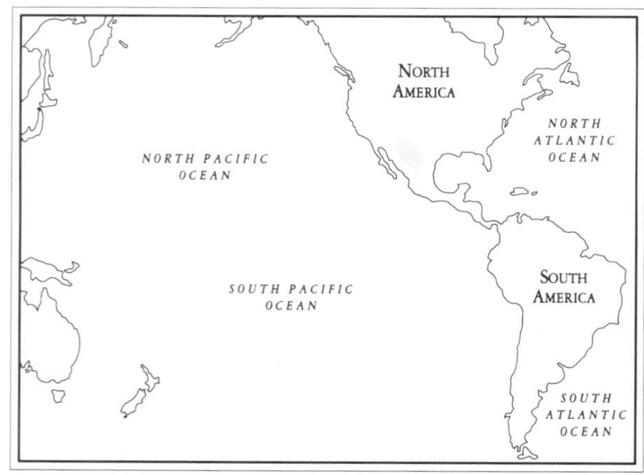

Epithelantha bokei

Common Name: Button Cactus.
Size: Height 5 cm (2 in), width 3.5 cm (1.4 in).
Climate: Medium elevation.
Distribution: Northern Mexico and south-western United States.
Flowering Time: Late spring.
Description: This species is solitary, or it has a few offsets, and individual heads are up to 5 cm (2 in) high and 3.5 cm (1.4 in) in diameter. The dense covering of 40 or more very short off-white to white pectinate spines totally obscures the body of the plant. The flowers are off-white to cream in colour and 1.25 cm (0.5 in) in diameter. The fruits are elongated, 0.7 cm (0.3 in) in length, and red when ripe.

Epithelantha bokei

Epithelantha micromeris in flower

Epithelantha micromeris

Epithelantha micromeris in habitat

Epithelantha micromeris

COMMON NAME: Button Cactus.
SIZE: Height 5 cm (2 in), width 25–30 cm (10–12 in).
CLIMATE: Medium elevation.
DISTRIBUTION: Northern Mexico and south-western United States.
FLOWERING TIME: Late spring and summer.
DESCRIPTION: This is a solitary or very freely clustering plant, with individual heads up to 5 cm (2 in) in diameter. The number of tubercles and the density of the spination are slightly less than that of *E. bokei* (see above). However, there can also be white wool as well as short spines in the centre of a flowering head. The spines can be very white, but some forms can have partially brown or black ones. The flowers are usually pale pink and no more than 0.6 m (0.2 in) in diameter. The elongated fruit is about 1 cm (0.4 in) or less in length, and is red when ripe.

ESCOBARIA

(ĕs-kō-bà'-rĭ-à)

Escobaria contains about 20 species, although some species have been considered to belong to the genus *Coryphantha*. The generic name honours two Mexican brothers, R. and N. Escobar. *Escobarias* are small, globular to short cylindrical plants, and can be solitary or, more often than not, clustering very freely. The species rarely exceed 5–7.5 cm (2–3 in) in height, but in some species, such as *E. tuberculosa*, an individual stem can occasionally reach 20 cm (8 in) in height. The diameter of the stems is 2.5–6 cm (1–2.4 in). Many species are so densely spined that the tubercles are hardly visible. The tubercle has a distinctive furrow on the top, behind the spine cluster. Areoles can bear 10–40 small radial spines, radiating in all directions, plus 10 or more centrals, which are slightly stronger and longer than the radial spines and are up to 2 cm (0.8 in) in length. In some forms there are no centrals, or it is very difficult to distinguish them from the radials. The spine colour varies from white and yellow through to pinkish or even nearly black.

The small flowers, which are often produced in profusion, arise from the centre of a head. The flowers rarely exceed 2.5 cm (1 in) in length, do not usually open widely, and some of them have ciliate edges to their petals. The flowers range from off-white, greenish-yellow, yellow through to pink. The fruits are small, red when ripe but sometimes pink or green, and are completely smooth on the outside.

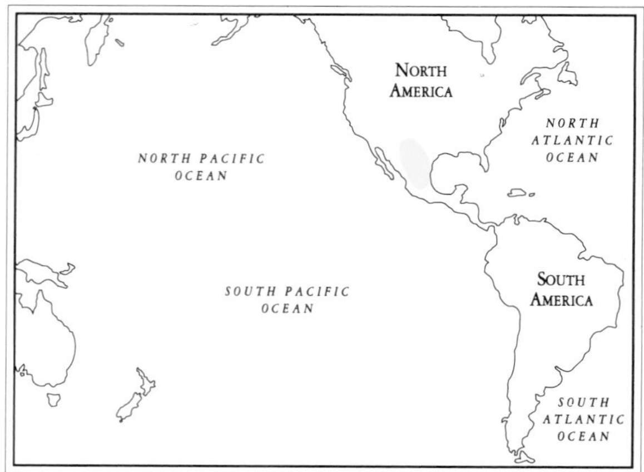

Culture: *Escobarias* are native to south-western United States and central and northern Mexico. The very small species, which are often less densely spined, are found where they receive some shade from other plants. Densely spined forms grow among rocks, in much more exposed positions. All species may be raised from seed, or by division of clumps, and like a reasonable amount of water from spring to autumn (fall). In winter, if kept dry, they can withstand temperatures close to freezing point — and below in a few cases.

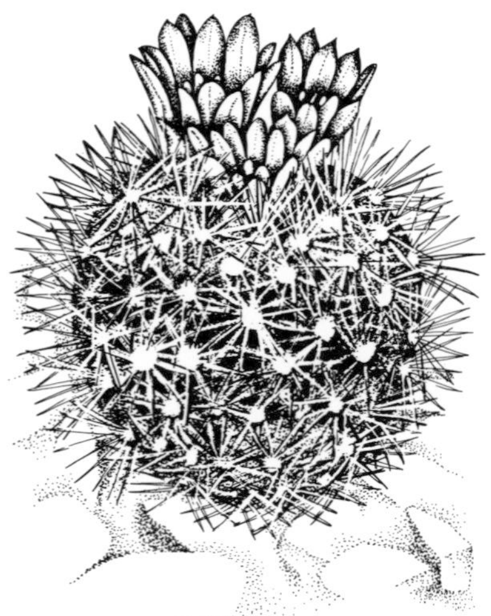

Escobaria roseana

Escobaria chaffeyi

Common Name: None.
Size: Height 12 cm (4.8 in), width 6 cm (2.4 in).
Climate: Medium elevation.
Distribution: Central and northern Mexico.
Flowering Time: Early summer.
Description: This is a solitary or sparingly branching species of columnar habit, which can reach 10-12 cm (4-4.8 in) in height. The well tubercled body is virtually obscured by the dense, mainly white spination. The pale green tubercles are quite short, and each areole bears from 15-20 spreading radial bristly spines, plus one or more centrals, which can have brown or black tips. The radial spines can reach 1.25 cm (0.5 in) in length, and the centrals are usually shorter. The flowers are 1.5 cm (0.6 in) in length, creamy-white with pronounced pinkish-brown median stripes down the petals. The elongated fruits are about 2 cm (0.8 in) long, and red when ripe.

Esobaria chaffeyi

Esobaria roseana

Escobaria roseana

Common Name: None.
Size: Height 4 cm (1.6 in), width 20 cm (8 in).
Climate: Medium elevation.
Distribution: Central Mexico.
Flowering Time: Late spring to summer.
Description: Individual heads of this very freely clustering species rarely exceed 4 cm (1.6 in) in height. The green body is covered with small tubercles, bearing yellowish areoles. The areoles have up to about 15 thin, acicular, creamy-yellow radial spines, which can reach 1.25 cm (0.5 in) in length. There are 5 or 6 slightly stouter and longer centrals, which are yellow in colour. The flowers open a little wider than is typical of the genus and have a brownish median stripe down each petal. The fruit is 1.25 cm (0.5 in) in length and green when ripe.

Escobaria runyonii

Common Name: None.
Size: Height 5 cm (2 in), width 60 cm (24 in).
Climate: Low elevation.
Distribution: Northern Mexico and south-western United States.
Flowering Time: Spring.
Description: This is a very freely clustering species, where clumps can consist of more than 100 heads. However, individual heads are small, up to 5 cm (2 in) in height, and are often much shorter. The tiny, well tubercled body is obscured by the dense, fine spination. There can be up to 30 very short, fine, spreading radial spines per areole, and between five and ten centrals. These also spread out from the centre of the areole, and are usually longer, up to 1.25 cm (0.5 in) in length. The spines are white, but the centrals can be more prominently tipped with brown or black. The flowers are about 2 cm (0.8 in) in diameter, off-white in colour, with median pinkish-brown stripes down the petals. The outer petals are often ciliate. The fruits are slightly egg-shaped, about 1 cm (0.4 in) in length, and red when ripe.

Esobaria runyonii

ESPOSTOA

(ĕs-pō´-stō-à)

Espostoa contains some eight species, and a few varieties. The generic name honours N. E. Esposto of Lima, Peru, from which most of the species originate. They are shrubby or tree-like plants and 2–7 m (6.5–23 ft) in height. Branches are 5–15 cm (2–6 in) in diameter. The green body is completely masked by the dense covering of white (or sometimes ginger) silky hair. There are 20–30 ribs, and the areoles are set quite close together, bearing 20–40 very short spreading radial spines, and sometimes one or two centrals 1–4 cm (0.4–1.6 m) in length. The radials are fine, white, yellow, or reddish in colour, and the centrals are usually a little stouter, and of a similar colour. They have pronounced lateral cephaliums, consisting of a dense mass of hair, from yellowish-green to brown or ginger in colour.

The white funnel-shaped nocturnal flowers are 4–8 cm (1.6–3.2 in) in length, appearing from the lateral cephalium. The slightly oblong fruits rarely exceed 4 cm (1.6 in) in length, are red when ripe, and have some hair.

Culture: *Espostoas* come mainly from northern Peru, and just into Ecuador. Moderately easy to grow raised from seed, they can be watered fairly freely in hot weather; they prefer well drained soil. In colder climates keep dry in winter; they can tolerate a temperature of 5°C (40°F) and light frosts.

Espostoa hylaea

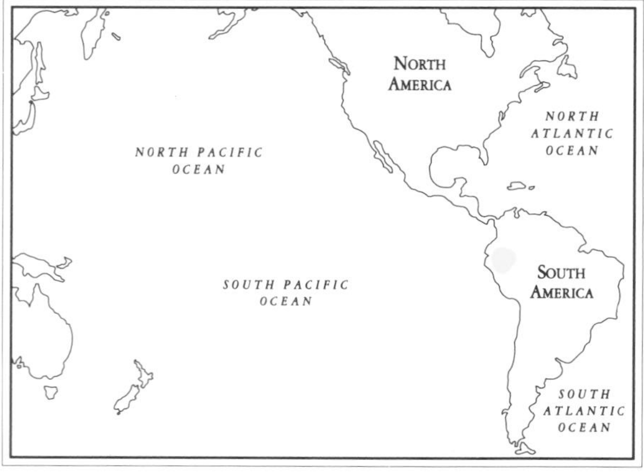

Espostoa hylaea

Espostoa hylaea

COMMON NAME: None.
SIZE: Height 3 m (10 ft).
CLIMATE: Medium elevation.
CLIMATE: Northern Peru.
FLOWERING TIME: Summer.
DESCRIPTION: This species branches at quite a young age, with branches no more than 5 cm (2 in) in diameter. The stems have 20–28 ribs, and the closely set areoles bear up to 40 very short, fine radial spines, and sometimes one central up to 1 cm (0.4 in) in length. The spines can be yellow or reddish-brown in colour. The dense white covering of silky hair can be 1–2 cm (0.4–0.8 in) in length. The lateral cephalium is pale brown, and bears white nocturnal flowers up to 5 cm (2 in) in length, and a little more in diameter. The oblong red fruits have some hair and are about 4 cm (1.6 in) in length.

EULYCHNIA

(ū-lĭk'-nĭ-ă)

Eulychnia contains about ten species, and the generic name is derived from the Gk, meaning 'a good lamp-stand'. They are either erect growing, freely branching and tree-like, or sprawling and slender stemmed. The tree-like species can reach 7 m (23 ft) in height, with a main trunk up to 25 cm (10 in) in diameter. The green or bluish-green branches rarely exceed 10 cm (4 in) in diameter. There are 10–17 ribs; the areoles are set well apart and are quite large, reaching 1 cm (0.4 in) in diameter and containing plenty of wool. There can be up to 15 radial spines, and up to 4 centrals. They are 2–15 cm (0.8–6 in) in length, and are off-white to brown and nearly black in colour.

The pink or white bell-shaped flowers are 5–7.5 cm (2–3 in) in both diameter and length and sweetly scented. The fruits are spherical or pear-shaped, 1–5 cm (0.4–2 in) in length; often hairy on the outside.

Culture: *Eulychnias* come mainly from the coastal areas of Chile; can be easily raised from seed and cuttings can be rooted quite successfully. They are very popular as young plants because the areoles of many species then possess a lot of white wool. They grow well in a variety of soils, but prefer a humus-enriched soil and require plenty of water from spring to autumn (fall). The plants should be kept dry in winter and they can withstand a temperature of 8°C (46°F), or where the atmospheric humidity is low in winter, even lower temperatures.

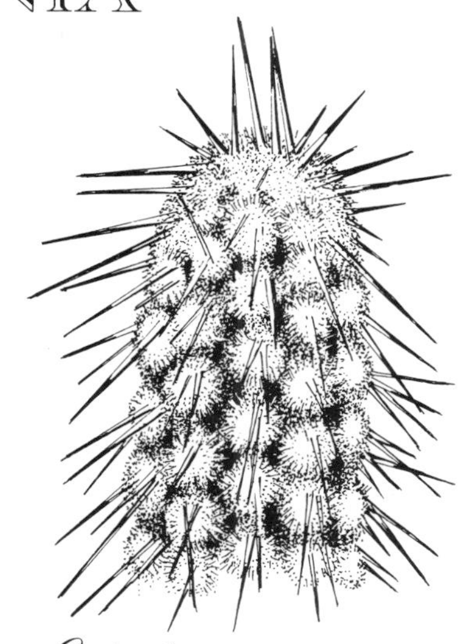

Eulychnia saint-pieana

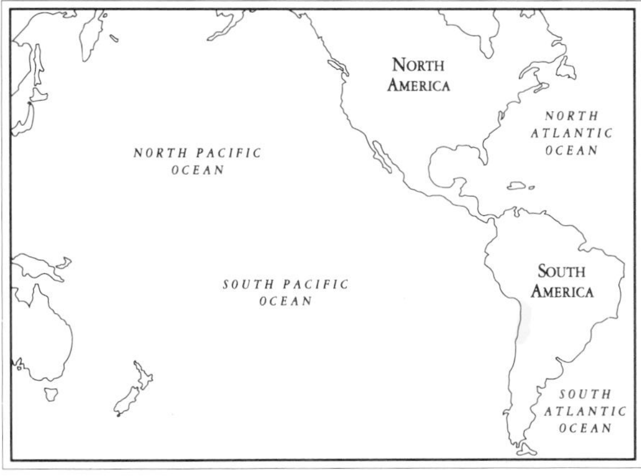

Eulychnia saint-pieana

Eulychnia saint-pieana

COMMON NAME: None.
SIZE: Height 4–5 m (13–16 ft).
CLIMATE: Mediterranean.
DISTRIBUTION: Northern Chile.
FLOWERING TIME: Spring.
DESCRIPTION: This species is erect and freely branching. The branches rarely exceed 7.5 cm (3 in) in diameter, and have 12–15 ribs. The areoles are set fairly close together, are circular, nearly 1 cm (0.4 in) in diameter, and full of white wool when on new stems or when young. The areoles bear up to 20 spines, one or two of which are much longer than is normal for the genus, from 5–10 cm (2–4 in). These are brown when young, but gradually change to grey with age. The flower can be up to 7.5 cm (3 in) in diameter and in length, and white with pink median stripes down the petals. The pear-shaped fruit is very small for this genus, no more than 1 cm (0.4 in) in length.

FEROCACTUS

(fĕ-rō-kăk'-tŭs)

Ferocactus contains some 40 species and varieties. The generic name refers to the very strong spines which the majority of the species possess. They are very variable in formation: there are small growing species, which can be globular or have a flattened globular habit, and others which can grow quite tall, about 3 m (10 ft) in height and have a diameter of up to 1 m (3 ft). The majority of species are solitary, but there are a few which can cluster freely, with 20 or 30 tall stems 3 m (10 ft) in height, eg *F. stainesii.* The stems have a prominent rib structure which in young plants appear as tubercles on the stems. As the plants approach maturity and start to flower, the raised tubercles merge into the rib formation. There can be 8–30 ribs on a stem, depending on the species, which can be straight or sometimes tending to spiral. The areoles are usually quite large and bear 10–20 radial spines which tend to be flattened against the body of the plant, and up to 4 centrals which stand out from the areole. The radials are quite strong, vary in shape from cylindrical to flattened in shape, and may reach 7.5 cm (3 in) in length. The centrals have colour banding, sometimes have hooked tips and are usually much stronger and longer than the radials, reaching 15 cm (6 in) in length.

The bell-shaped flowers form in rings around the centre of a stem, appearing from the newer areoles, usually 5–7.5 cm (2–3 in) in diameter, they vary in colour from greenish-yellow to orange, red and violet. The fruits are usually egg-shaped, up to 5 cm (2 in) in length, with parts of the dried remains of the flowers remaining attached; the outer part is scaly. When ripe the large black seeds run out from a basal pore.

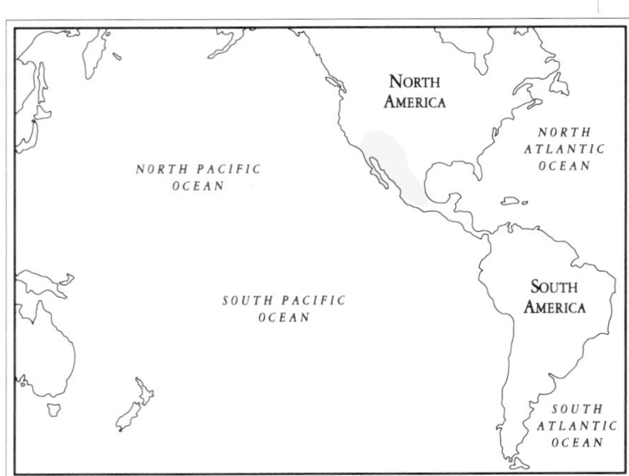

Culture: *Ferocacti* are native to south-western United States, many parts of Mexico, and islands in the Gulf of California. They are found in well drained, often rocky, locations, and the plants tend to be quite shallow rooted. *Ferocacti* are quite easy to grow, are usually raised from seed, but, depending on the species, take many years to reach flowering size. A well drained compost is required, and they can be watered quite freely from spring to autumn (fall). Most of the species from south-western United States can take a few degrees of frost if kept dry and if the atmospheric humidity is low, eg *F. acanthodes* and *F. wislizenii* (see pages 91, 92). Where winter atmospheric humidity is high, plants can develop unsightly blotches or orange spots, if the temperature drops close to freezing point. Young plants up to 5 or 10 years of age are particularly prone to this trouble.

Ferocactus wislizenii

Ferocactus acanthodes

COMMON NAME: Barrel Cactus or Compass Barrel.
SIZE: Height 2.2 m (7 ft), width 60 cm (24 in).
CLIMATE: Low to medium elevation.
DISTRIBUTION: South-western United States and northern Mexico.
FLOWERING TIME: Late spring to summer.
DESCRIPTION: This species has a solitary, cylindrical habit in age, with mature plants having up to 25 ribs, which are usually spiralling to a certain degree. The areoles are fairly close together, brown, and bear up to 12 spreading radial spines, and up to four centrals. The radials are somewhat bristly, whitish, and up to 3.75 cm (1.5 in) in length. The centrals are much stronger, yellowish, or reddish, and often twisted. Two of the centrals are somewhat flattened and up to 11.25 cm (4.5 in) in length. The flowers are up to 5 cm (2 in) in diameter, yellow in colour. The fruits are egg-shaped, 3 cm (1.2 in) long, yellowish-green when ripe.

Ferocactus histrix

Ferocactus acanthodes

Ferocactus histrix

COMMON NAME: None.
SIZE: Height 30 cm (12 in), width 75 cm (30 in).
CLIMATE: Low to medium elevation.
DISTRIBUTION: Central Mexico.
FLOWERING TIME: Spring to early summer.
DESCRIPTION: This species has a solitary, spherical habit, and a pale green to olive-green body with up to 24 ribs on a mature specimen. The elongated brownish areoles are set fairly well apart, and bear up to 12 spreading radial spines, and up to four centrals. The radial spines rarely exceed 4 cm (1.6 in) in length, however the longest central can reach 6 cm (2.4 in). All the spines are yellowish, and the centrals are somewhat stronger. The flowers are funnel-shaped, up to 3.5 cm (1.4 in) in diameter, yellow, sometimes with a slight reddish median stripe down the petals. The fruits are almost spherical, less than 2.5 cm (1 in) in diameter, and reddish coloured when ripe.

Ferocactus macrodiscus var. *multiflorus*

Ferocactus latispinus

COMMON NAME: None.
SIZE: Height 40 cm (16 in), width 40 cm (16 in).
CLIMATE: Low to medium elevation.
DISTRIBUTION: Central and western Mexico.
FLOWERING TIME: Summer.
DESCRIPTION: This species has a solitary, spherical, or somewhat flattened spherical habit, with up to 23 ribs on a mature specimen. The large white areoles bear up to 10 spreading thin radial spines, and four stronger centrals, one of which will be flattened and hooked. The radials are up to 2.5 cm (1 in) long, and white or pink. The longest central can reach 5 cm (2 in) in length and is of a similar colour. The flowers are bell-shaped, up to 4 cm (1.6 in) in diameter, but very variable in colour, ranging from whitish through to purple. The fruits are egg-shaped, 4 cm (1.6 in) long, and purplish when ripe.

Ferocactus latispinus

Ferocactus macrodiscus var. *multiflorus*

COMMON NAME: None.
SIZE: Height 15 cm (6 in), width 45 cm (18 in).
CLIMATE: Low to medium elevation.
DISTRIBUTION: Central Mexico.
FLOWERING TIME: Summer.
DESCRIPTION: This variety has a solitary, flattened spherical habit, and a green to bluish-green body with up to 21 ribs. The yellow areoles are set well apart, and bear up to eight spreading radial spines, and up to 4 centrals. The radials are up to 2 cm (0.8 in) in length and the centrals are somewhat stouter, but of a similar length. Both radials and centrals are yellowish. The flowers are funnel-shaped, up to 4 cm (1.6 in) in diameter, and pink with a darker median stripe down the petals. The fruits are almost spherical, 3 cm (1.2 in) in diameter, and purple when ripe.

Ferocactus stainesii

Ferocactus wislizenii

Common Name: Barrel Cactus or Fish-hook Barrel.
Size: Height 2.7 m (9 ft), width 60 cm (2 ft).
Climate: Medium elevation.
Distribution: South-western United States and north-western Mexico.
Flowering Time: Autumn (fall).
Description: This species has a solitary, cylindrical habit in age, with mature plants having 25 ribs, and brown areoles bearing 10–20 radial spines, some of which can be white and quite fine, and up to 4 centrals. One of these centrals is usually flattened with a strong hook and is up to 5 cm (2 in) in length. The flowers are over 5 cm (2 in) in diameter and variable in colour, ranging from yellow and orange through to red. The fruits are 5 cm (2 in) in length and are yellow when ripe.

Ferocactus viridescens

Ferocactus stainesii

Common Name: None.
Size: Height 3 m (nearly 10 ft), width 2 m (6 ft).
Climate: Medium elevation.
Distribution: Central Mexico.
Flowering Time: Summer.
Description: A cylindrical green bodied, freely clustering species, where individual stems reach 3 m (nearly 10 ft) in height, and have a diameter of 60 cm (24 in). It can have up to 18 ribs, and the areoles are set fairly closely together, bearing up to five spreading radial spines, and four centrals. The radials rarely exceed 3 cm (1.2 in) in length. However, the centrals (which are in a cruciform arrangement), are up to 4 cm (1.6 in) in length, much stronger, banded and flattened, and the longest upper one is curved. All the spines are reddish coloured. The flowers are about 4 cm (1.6 in) in diameter, and orange-red. The fruits are egg-shaped, up to 5 cm (2 in) long, and yellow when ripe.

Ferocactus wislizenii

Ferocactus viridescens

Common Name: None.
Size: Height 50 cm (20 in), width 35 cm (14 in).
Climate: Low elevation.
Distribution: South-western United States and Baja California, Mexico.
Flowering Time: Summer.
Description: This species is solitary, spherical, becoming cylindrical in age, and the green body is almost obscured by the dense spination. A mature specimen has up to 21, somewhat wavy acute ribs, and the areoles are set fairly closely together. These bear up to 20 spreading radial spines, and up to four much stronger, flattened centrals. The radial spines are whitish and up to 2 cm (0.8 in) in length, and the centrals are pinkish, and up to 4 cm (1.6 in) in length. The flowers are funnel-shaped, 4 cm (1.6 in) in diameter, and yellow or greenish-yellow. The fruits are egg-shaped, 2 cm (0.8 in) long, and reddish when ripe.

FRAILEA

(frī'-lē-ā)

Frailea contains some 40 species and numerous varieties. The generic name honours Manuel Fraile of Washington. The plants are small headed globular to short cylindrical, and can be solitary or very freely clustering. In the case of the short cylindrical species, the maximum height rarely exceeds 6 cm (2.4 in). The average diameter of an individual head is 2.5–3.5 cm (1–1.4 in). The rows of tubercles do form a rib structure, although in some cases it is not clearly defined. Where the ribs are visible, there are 12–20 in number. The body colour of the plants can range from light green, to reddish-brown or even violet-brown. The areoles are minute and bear 8–20 short, fine radial spines. When present there are up to 4 fine centrals which are usually less than 1 cm (0.4 in) in length. The spines range in colour from white and cream to brownish or black.

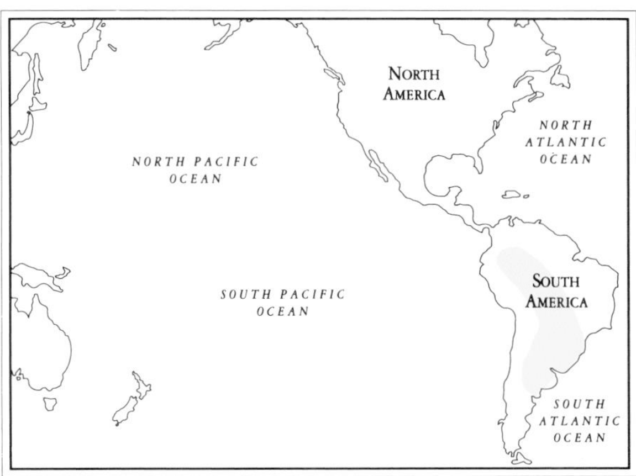

The flowers in this genus are cleistogamous, ie they can set seed without opening. However, when they do open, they are in varying shades of yellow, and from 2.5–4 cm (1–1.6 in) in diameter. The fruits are small, round, and often covered with whitish, yellow or brown wool, as are the flower buds, which may also have a few fine brown spines.

Culture: *Fraileas* have a widespread habitat in South America — from Bolivia and Uruguay, to Argentina, Paraguay and Colombia. They are mostly exceedingly easy plants to raise from seed, or by dividing clusters. Seedlings can flower in just over 12 months. In cultivation they do not like full sun, appreciate plenty of water from spring to autumn (fall), and like a soil containing plenty of humus. In winter they can be left dry, but should be kept clear of frosts.

Frailea pygmaea

Frailea pumila

Frailea pumila

Common Name: None.
Size: Height 2 cm (0.8 in), width 7.5 cm (3 in).
Climate: Mediterranean.
Distribution: Paraguay and nearby parts of Argentina.
Flowering Time: Late spring to autumn (fall).
Description: This globular, freely clustering species has individual heads usually less than 2.5 cm (1 in) in diameter. It can have up to 15 ribs, and the tiny areoles bear up to 14 very short, bristly radial spines, and one or two centrals of the same colour. The radial and central spines are usually the same length and are brown or golden brown in colour. The flower bud has plenty of white wool, and a few fine brown spines. The flowers are pale yellow, and no more than 2.5 cm (1 in) in diameter. The fruits are very small and are of the same colour as the flower buds.

Frailea pygmaea

Frailea pygmaea

Common Name: None.
Size: Height 3 cm (1.2 in), width 7.5 cm (3 in).
Climate: Mediterranean.
Distribution: Uruguay and nearby parts of Argentina.
Flowering Time: Summer and autumn (fall).
Description: The plant body of this species is very similar to that of *F. pumila* (see above), except that it often remains solitary and is a little larger, up to 3 cm (1.2 in) high and 2.5 cm (1 in) in width. The body of the plant is dark green, almost olive-green, and has up to 21 ribs. The tiny greyish areoles bear up to 9 whitish, bristly, very short spines, which are appressed against the body of the plant. It is very difficult to distinguish between the radial and the central spines. Although, as with other species, seeds will set without the flower opening, more often than not the flowers of this species do open. The flowers are variable in diameter and occasionally over 4 cm (1.6 in). The tiny fruits are covered with brownish wool, and a few short bristly spines.

GYMNOCALYCIUM

(jĭm'-nō-kă-lĭs'-ĭ-ŭm)

Gymnocalycium contains over 120 different species, and very nearly a similar number of varieties. The generic name originates from the Gk meaning 'naked bud' and is in reference to the exterior tube of the flower. It is a very varied and attractive genus, and virtually all the species are freely flowering and colourful. They range from miniatures such as *G. baldianum* which is less than 7.5 cm (3 in) in diameter, to *G. spegazzinii* (see page 97) which can exceed 20 cm (8 in) in diameter. Some of the smaller species are freely clustering, in contrast to the larger species, which tend to remain solitary. They can have 6–20 or so very prominent ribs, often with prominent chin-like tubercles. The colour of the plant body can vary from green to reddish-brown and slate-grey. The areoles are set close together in the smaller species, but are well separated in the larger species. They are round or oval, usually contain white or yellowish wool, and bear 2–12 radial spines. The spines may be appressed against the body or partially standing out from it. They can be minute, but are usually 1–6 cm (0.4–2.4 in) in length. The centrals when present are usually stronger and a little longer than the radials, and stand out more from the plant. The spines vary from fine and bristly to very rigid, and also vary in colour.

The flowers are very variable in size and formation: some are bell-shaped, others are funnel-shaped; and they are 2.5–7.5 cm (1–3 in) in height and in diameter. Their colour ranges from white or greenish, through to pink and varying shades of red. The naked scales of the exterior of the tube of the flower are clearly visible in the illustration of *G. spegazzinii* (see page 97). The exterior of the fruits is similar to the exterior of the flower tube, and the fruits are oval-shaped, up to 3.5 cm (1.4 in) in length, and when ripe can range from greenish-brown, reddish-brown, red, or even slate in colour.

Culture: *Gymnocalyciums* come from many parts of Argentina, and from Bolivia, Paraguay and Uruguay. They are to be found at altitudes of up to 3500 m (11 480 ft), among grass, rocks, and in sandy locations where many of the flat globular species are virtually covered by the sand during the hottest months. The plants are easy to grow and some of the smaller species will flower within 2 or 3 years, while others may take twice as long. They will cope with varied conditions, but most species like plenty of water during the warm growing season. In winter, if kept dry, they will tolerate very cool conditions, and some of the high altitude species can obviously withstand frosts.

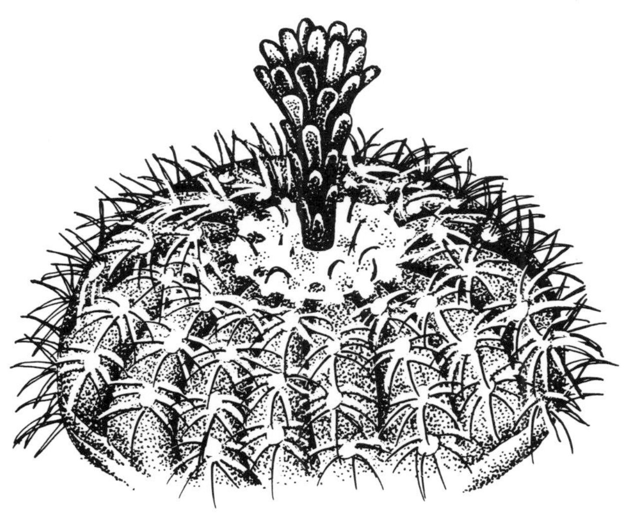

Gymnocalycium spegazzinii

Gymnocalycium asterium

Gymnocalycium moserianum

Gymnocalycium asterium

Common Name: None.
Size: Height 4 cm (1.6 in), width 15 cm (6 in).
Climate: Medium elevation.
Distribution: Argentina.
Flowering Time: Summer.
Description: This species has a very flattened habit, is usually grey or reddish-brown in colour, and up to 15 cm (6 in) in diameter. There can be up to 11 ribs, with quite a prominent chin between the areole positions. The areoles are small, have a little white wool, and bear 3-5 radial spines, which are appressed against the body of the plant and are off-white to grey. There are no centrals. The flowers are about 6.25 cm (2.5 in) high, white to pink in colour — darker in the flower tube. The fruit is oval, about 3 cm (1.2 in) in length, and slate in colour when ripe.

Gymnocalycium mihanovichii

Common Name: None.
Size: Height 3–4 cm (1.2–1.6 in), width 6 cm (2.4 in).
Climate: Tropical.
Distribution: Paraguay.
Flowering Time: Late spring and summer.
Description: This is a miniature globular species, greyish-green to brownish-green body, with up to eight slightly notched ribs, transversely marked with green and greyish-green. The small areoles bear up to six spreading grey spines, no more than 1 cm (0.4 in) in length. The flowers do not open very widely, are yellowish-green in colour with a narrow tube of the same colour, and about 4 cm (1.6 in) in height. The fruits are egg-shaped, up to 2 cm (0.8 in) long, and greenish-brown when ripe.

Gymnocalycium mihanovichii

Gymnocalycium moserianum

Common Name: None.
Size: Height 10 cm (4 in), width 15 cm (6 in).
Climate: Medium elevation.
Distribution: Northern Argentina.
Flowering Time: Summer.
Description: This species has a solitary, flattened globular habit, a bluish-green body, and up to 14 tuberculate ribs with transverse furrows. The new areoles have white wool, but this gradually disappears with age, and they bear up to five spreading grey to greyish-brown stiff spines, up to 2.5 cm (1 in) in length. The flowers are funnel-shaped, up to 5 cm (2 in) in diameter, with white petals and a red or greenish-red throat. The fruits are somewhat elongated, up to 4 cm (1.6 in) in length, and are bluish-grey to brown when ripe.

Gymnocalycium multiflorum

Gymnocalycium multiflorum

Common Name: None.
Size: Height 10 cm (4 in), width 12 cm (4.8 in).
Climate: Medium elevation.
Distribution: Argentina.
Flowering Time: Summer.
Description: This species has a globular habit; individual heads rarely exceed 10 cm (4 in) in height and 12 cm (4.8 in) in diameter. The body is a fresh green colour, and it has up to 15 tuberculate ribs. The areoles have a little white wool, are set well apart, and bear up to 10 somewhat flattened, spreading yellow radial spines, up to 3 cm (1.2 in) in length. They are quite strong, and there are no centrals. The flowers are bell-shaped, white to pale pink; 5 cm (2 in) in height and 7.5 cm (3 in) in diameter. The fruit is oval, 3.5 cm (1.4 in) in length and green or greenish-brown when ripe.

Gymnocalycium netrelianum

Common Name: None.
Size: Height 10 cm (4 in), width 25 cm (10 in).
Climate: Medium elevation.
Distribution: Argentina and Uruguay.
Flowering Time: Summer.
Description: A somewhat flattened globular species, which sometimes clusters a little in age, whose body is a fresh green colour. An individual head reaches 12.5 cm (5 in) in diameter, and has up to 14 tuberculate ribs. The areoles are set very close, have quite a lot of white wool, and bear up to 8 yellowish-brown bristly radial spines (mostly less than 1 cm (0.4 in) in length). There are no centrals. The greenish-yellow flowers do not open very wide, and are 5 cm (2 in) in height. The fruits are olive-green when ripe; 2.5 cm (1 in) in length.

Gymnocalycium valnicekianum

Gymnocalycium netrelianum

Gymnocalycium spegazzinii

Gymnocalycium spegazzinii

Common Name: None.
Size: Height 20 cm (8 in), width 15 cm (6 in).
Climate: Medium elevation.
Distribution: Argentina.
Flowering Time: Summer.
Description: A very variable species, it can be of a flattened globular habit or globular to slightly cylindrical. In the latter case it can reach 20 cm (8 in) in height and a little less in diameter. It can have up to 20 ribs, each with a prominent furrow between the areole positions. The body ranges from bluish-green to olive-green. The oval-shaped areoles are set well apart, have some white wool, and bear up to 7 curved, rigid radial spines, and sometimes one central. The grey or pinkish-grey spines are up to 6 cm (2.4 in) in length. The tubular-shaped flowers only open widely when temperatures are very high. They can be up to 7.5 cm (3 in) in length and off-white to pink in colour, with a smoky-purplish throat; the naked scales on the tube are clearly visible. The fruits are 3 cm (1.2 in) in length and greyish-red when ripe.

Gymnocalycium valnicekianum

Common Name: None.
Size: Height 30 cm (12 in), width 20 cm (8 in).
Climate: Medium elevation.
Distribution: Argentina.
Flowering Time: Summer.
Description: A globular to short and cylindrical species with a dark green body. It has up to 12 ribs, each with a swollen tuberculate structure and a distinct furrow between each areole position. The areoles are large, with white to grey wool and bear 8–15 radial spines of very varied length (up to 5 cm (2 in)), and up to 6 centrals. The white or very pale pink flowers are about 5 cm (2 in) in diameter, with a red or purplish-red throat. The fruits are 2.5 cm (1 in) in length and reddish-green when ripe.

HAAGEOCEREUS

(hä -gĕ-ō-sē'-rē-ŭs)

Haageocereus is quite a large genus with over 50 described species and many varieties. Curt Backeberg erected this genus, honouring Walther Haage, a fellow countryman who spent his working life growing and studying cacti. They are erect, or semi-erect columnar cacti, which branch freely from the base, and are 1–2 m (3–6.5 ft) in height. The stems average 4–6 cm (1.6–2.4 in) in diameter, with 15–25 straight ribs. The areoles are very varied in size, are usually set fairly close together, and bear 20–60 spreading spines which sometimes have hair. There can be one or two stouter centrals. The radial spines are 0.5–2 cm (0.2–0.8 in) in length, and the centrals are 2–5 cm (0.8–2 in). The spine colour is exceedingly variable — from creamy-yellow and golden yellow to reddish-brown, and sometimes have black tips. The spination in most species virtually masks the green stem colour. When grown under glass, the central spines tend not to develop.

The funnel-shaped nocturnal flowers are 4–10 cm (1.6–4 in) in length and 5–7 cm (2–2.8 in) in diameter. The flower colour ranges from greenish-white to pink and deep red. The fruits are spherical but slightly flattened, 2–6 cm (0.8–2.4 in) in diameter, slightly hairy, and red when ripe.

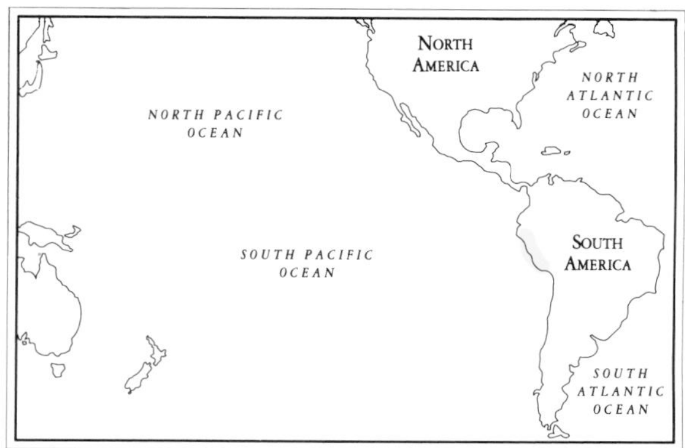

Culture: *Haageocerei* originate from the coastal regions of Peru, at altitudes from sea level to 2400 m (7872 ft). They are mostly very easy to cultivate, and grow quite quickly from seed, but may take many years to flower. However, their spine colouration makes them very attractive plants. They can be watered fairly freely from spring until the early autumn (fall). In winter, most species will tolerate near freezing temperatures if they are kept dry, and those from higher altitudes will withstand light frosts.

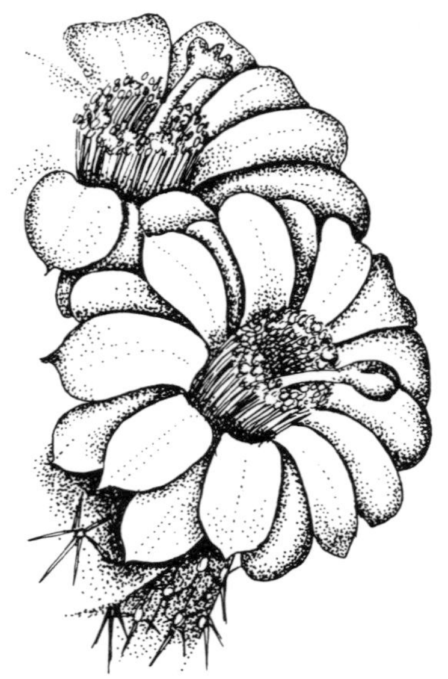

Haageocereus acranthus

Haageocereus acranthus

Common Name: None.
Size: Height 3 m (10 ft).
Climate: Medium elevation.
Distribution: Central Peru.
Flowering Time: Early summer.
Description: This is an erect plant initially, but it tends to become semi-erect before it reaches its maximum height. The dark green stems are up to 8 cm (3.2 in) in diameter and have up to 14 ribs. The yellowish areoles are quite large, about 1 cm (0.4 in) apart, and bear 20–30 radial spines, and usually one central. The radials are spreading, up to 1 cm (0.4 in) in length, and the central, which is much stouter, is up to 4 cm (1.6 in) in length. All the spines are usually yellowish-brown in colour. The nocturnal off-white or greenish-white flowers are 6–8 cm (2.4–3.2 in) in length and in diameter. The fruits are 4 cm (1.6 in) in diameter, have a little hair, and are greenish-red when ripe.

Haageocereus acranthus

Haageocereus laredensis

Haageocereus laredensis

Common Name: None.
Size: Height 1.3 m (4 ft), width 1 m (3 ft).
Climate: Medium elevation.
Distribution: Northern Peru.
Flowering Time: Summer.
Description: This is an erect, freely branching species, with stems up to 1.3 m (4 ft) in length, and a diameter of about 7 cm (2.8 in). The stems have up to 18 ribs, and the small brown areoles are set quite close together. These bear up to 45 radial spines, and one central. The radials are not much more than 1 cm (0.4 in) in length, and the central is about 2 cm (0.8 in). The spines on the top of a stem are dark brown — further down the stem they can be golden yellow or golden brown. The white nocturnal flowers are 5 cm (2 in) in length, and the fruits are similar to those of *H. acranthus* (see above).

HAMATOCACTUS

(hă-mā'-tō-kăk'-tŭs)

Hamatocactus contains about six species and a few varieties. The generic name is derived from the Lat meaning 'hooked cactus'. They are globular to short and cylindrical plants. The green to bluish green plant body is sometimes tinged with reddish-brown, and there are 12–14 prominent ribs. The areoles are not close together, bear 7–15 radial spines, are usually oval-shaped and have a fairly prominent gland, from which nectar exudes during the growing season. The radial spines are round or somewhat flattened, and less than 1.25–7.5 cm (0.5–3 in) in length, somewhat appressed against the plant, and are straight, curved, or even slightly hooked. There are 1–5 centrals, ranging from less than 1 cm (0.4 in) to as much as 12.5 cm (5 in) in length. The longest central is usually very hooked, and the general spine colour varies from off-white or yellowish, to brown and shades of red.

The flowers are funnel-shaped, some possess a slender tube, and all are 2.5–7.5 cm (1–3 in) in length. Some flowers have yellow petals and a red throat, others are fairly uniformly yellow or brownish-purple to purple. The fruits are round or egg-shaped, 2.5–5 cm (1–2 in) in length.

Culture: Native to south-western United States and northern Mexico, they can be raised from seed, and depending on the species, can be expected to flower within 1–5 years. They will grow successfully in varying types of soil, and like a reasonable amount of water during spring to early autumn (fall). Mature plants will take full sun. In winter, if kept dry, they will withstand cool conditions and light frosts.

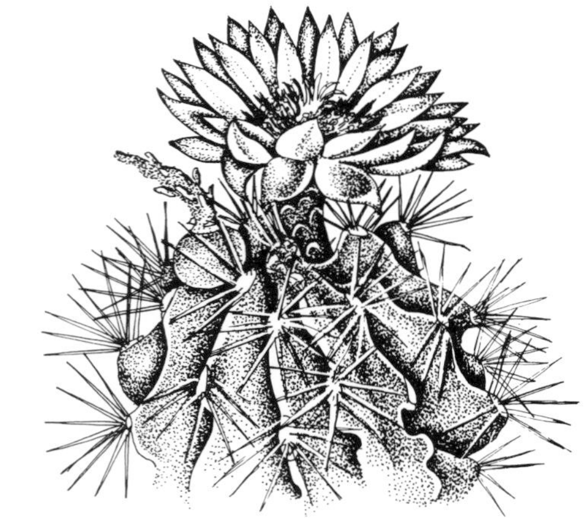

Hamatocactus setispinus

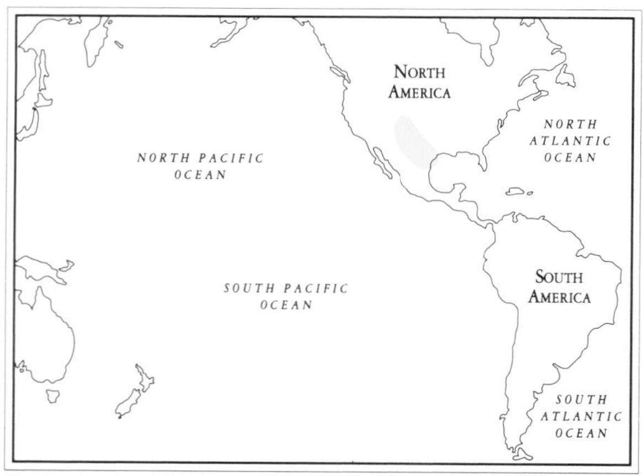

Hamatocactus setispinus

Hamatocactus setispinus

Common Name: Fish-hook Cactus.
Size: Height 15 cm (6 in), width 10 cm (4 in).
Climate: Mediterranean.
Distribution: Northern Mexico and south-western United States.
Flowering Time: Spring to autumn (fall).
Description: Usually a solitary species, it has a green body with up to 13 ribs, and the small white areoles bear up to 15 spreading subulate, radial spines, 0.5–4 cm (0.2–1.6 in) in length, and 1–3 hooked centrals. The upper radials are usually brown and the lower ones are white. The centrals are hooked, brown to dark-brown with a light tip and 3–5 cm (1.2–2 in) in length. The funnel-shaped flowers are up to 7 cm (2.8 in) in length and 5–6 cm (2–2.4 in) in diameter, and yellow with a red centre. The fruits are spherical, 1–1.5 cm (0.4–0.6 in) in diameter, and bright red when ripe.

Hamatocactus uncinatus

Hamatocactus uncinatus

Common Name: Texas Hedgehog or Fish-hook Cactus.
Size: Height 20 cm (8 in), width 11 cm (4.4 in).
Climate: Medium elevation.
Distribution: Northern Mexico and south-western United States.
Flowering Time: Spring to early summer.
Description: This species is solitary and short and cylindrical in shape, and has a bluish-green body with up to 14 narrow ribs. The oval-shaped areoles are quite large, and white or yellowish, with a very prominent gland. There can be up to 8 curved, radial spines, 2.5–5 cm (1–2 in) in length, and up to 4 centrals. These are usually hooked, and one of them can be 5 cm (2 in) in length. The spine colour is variable from plant to plant, ranging from off-white or cream to pink or reddish-brown. The flowers do not open very wide, and are about 2.5 cm (1 in) in length. They are brownish-purple in colour, with a distinct darker median stripe down each petal. The egg-shaped fruits are about 2.5 cm (1 in) in length and reddish when ripe.

Hamatocactus uncinatus

HARRISIA

(hă-rĭs'-ĭ-ă)

Harrisia contains some 24 species and a few varieties. The generic name honours William Harris, of the famous Hope Gardens in Jamaica. A clambering, freely branching species, the stems have 4–12 ribs varying in colour from green and bluish-green to grey with age. The white to brown areoles are slightly woolly, and bear 5–20 radial spines, which can be fine or quite stout, vary from minute to 5 cm (2 in) in length, and range in colour from white, yellow, and brown to reddish-black. There are 1–4 centrals, and they are of a similar length and colour to the radials.

The white or very pale pink flowers are nocturnal, up to 25 cm (10 in) in diameter, and funnel-shaped with a fairly long tube. The exterior of the tube is green or brownish, with brown or whitish hairs and a few very short, fine spines. The fruits are spherical or ovoid, up to 7.5 cm (3 in) in diameter, and yellow or various shades of red when ripe. They also carry hairs and tiny spines.

Culture: *Harrisias* are native to south-eastern United States, the Caribbean, and southwards into Paraguay, Uruguay, Brazil and Argentina. They are sometimes found in dense shade, or scrambling over rocks and cliff faces. Most species like a rich soil with plenty of nutriment, plenty of water from spring to autumn (fall)—their main growing season. In cultivation, most species should be kept well clear of frosts.

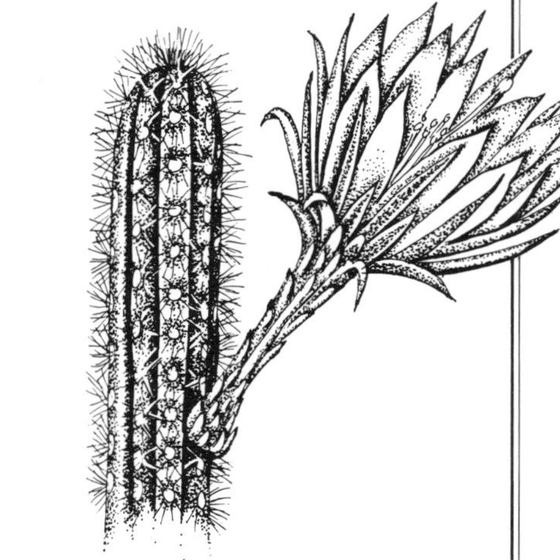

Harrisia simpsonii

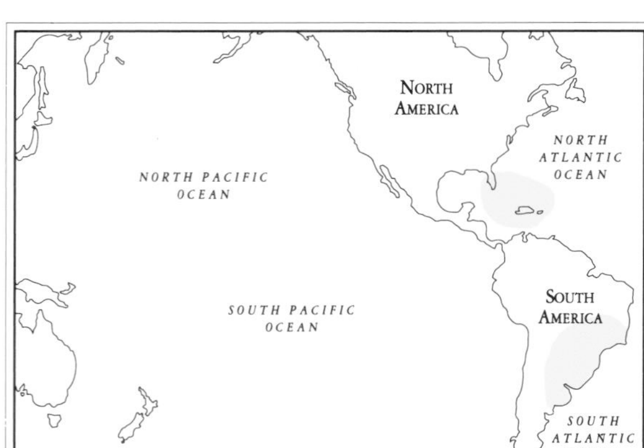

Harrisia simpsonii

Harrisia simpsonii

Common Name: Queen of the Night.
Size: Length up to 7 m (2 ft).
Climate: Mediterranean.
Distribution: South-eastern United States.
Flowering Time: Summer and autumn (fall).
Description: The stems of young plants are fairly rigid and erect, but can grow to 6–7 m (18–22 ft) in length and usually need some support as the plant grows. The stems have up to 10 rounded ribs, and the circular, white areoles are about 1 cm (0.4 in) apart. The areoles bear up to 15 spines, which are yellowish-brown when new, changing to white or grey later. It is not possible to clearly distinguish between the radials and the centrals, and they are fairly fine, rarely exceeding 2.5 cm (1 in) in length. In fact, in habit when growing in well shaded positions, most of the spines are half the normal maximum length. The white funnel-shaped flowers are 17.5 cm (7 in) in length, and have a long narrow tube. The exterior of the tube is reddish-brown, and there are a few hairs and tiny fine spines along its length. The spherical fruit is usually about 6 cm (2.4 in) in diameter, and orange-red when ripe.

HELIOCEREUS

(hĕl-ĭ-ō-sē'-rē-ŭs)

Heliocereus contains some four species and a few varieties. The generic name is derived from Gk and Lat, meaning 'sun' and 'wax-candle', which is in reference to their diurnal flowers. They are epiphytic freely branching plants, and are very similar vegetatively to *Epiphyllums* (see page 83), except that the clambering stems are normally 3 angled — occasionally 4 or 5. The green or reddish-green stems are up to 1 m (3 ft) in length and 2.5 cm (1 in) in diameter. The white areoles bear up to 10 bristly spines, 1–1.5 cm (0.4–0.6 in) in length, and white, yellowish, or brown in colour.

The flowers are up to 15 cm (6 in) in length, and some species open to 15 cm (6 in) in diameter. The base of the short tube is somewhat spiny, and the flowers are in varying shades of red or white. The fruits are egg-shaped, up to 5 cm (2 in) in length, spiny, and red when ripe.

Culture: *Heliocerei* come from Guatemala and Mexico, and are very easy plants to grow from seed or cuttings. They like a soil containing plenty of leaf mould or peat, lightly shaded conditions, and plenty of water. In winter watering should be reduced, but not stopped, and the plants should be protected from frosts, and will not withstand temperatures below 10°C (50°F).

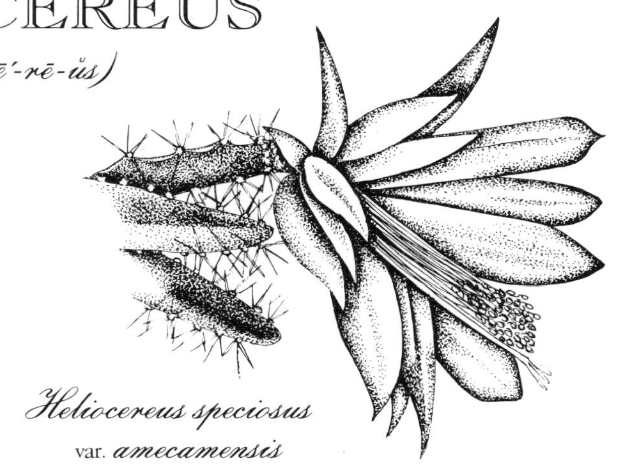

Heliocereus speciosus var. *amecamensis*

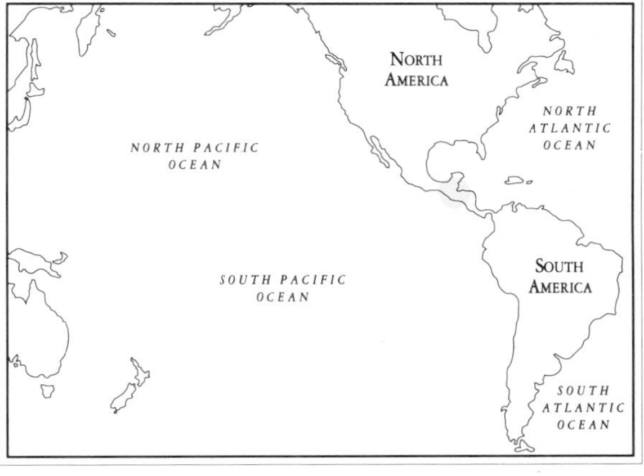

Heliocereus speciosus var. *amecamensis*

Heliocereus speciosus var. *amecamensis*

Common Name: None.
Size: Length up to 1 m (3 ft).
Climate: High elevation.
Distribution: Central Mexico.
Flowering Time: Summer.
Description: These are freely branching, clambering plants, which become pendant with age. The green to dark green stems can reach 1 m (3 ft) in length, and can be 3, 4, or 5 angled. The areoles are large, and bear up to 8 or more subulate spines (on old parts of a plant there can be twice as many spines), which can be up to 1.5 cm (0.6 in) in length, and vary in colour from yellow to brown. The white flowers are 15 cm (6 in) in length and 10 cm (4 in) in diameter. The fruits are egg-shaped, 5 cm (2 in) in length, spiny, red when ripe.

HILDEWINTERA

(hĭl'dē-wĭnt'-ēr-ȧ)

Hildewintera is a monotypic genus, and the generic names erected in 1966 honours Hilde Winter of Germany. It is a pendant growing plant which branches very freely from the base. The stems can grow up to 1.5 m (5 ft) in length, but are no more than 2.5 cm (1 in) in diameter. The green stems have up to 17 narrow ribs, which bear small light brown felted areoles set quite close together. The areoles bear up to 30 radial spines and 20 centrals. The radials are quite fine, radiate in all directions, are of variable length and do not exceed 1 cm (0.4 in). The centrals are a little stouter and slightly longer than the radials, and both the centrals and the radials are golden yellow in colour.

The flowers clearly separate this genus from any other, and are characterised by the apparent double corolla. It consists of an outer pinkish-orange whorl of petals, and a paler smaller whorl which surrounds the filaments. The flowers are up to 6 cm (2.4 in) in length and 5 cm (2 in) in diameter, and remain open day and night for a few days. The fruits are globular, a little over 1.25 cm (0.5 in) in diameter, and green with scales.

Culture: *Hildewintera* comes from Bolivia, where it is to be found on cliff faces, or scrambling over rocks. It is an easy plant to grow, whether raised from seed or cuttings — the latter method being the most common. The plants like plenty of water during the warmer months, and will flower over a long period. In the winter they can be left dry and should be protected from frosts. When cultivated in warmer climates where frosts are unknown the plants should be watered sporadically during the winter and they will flower for at least 9 months of the year.

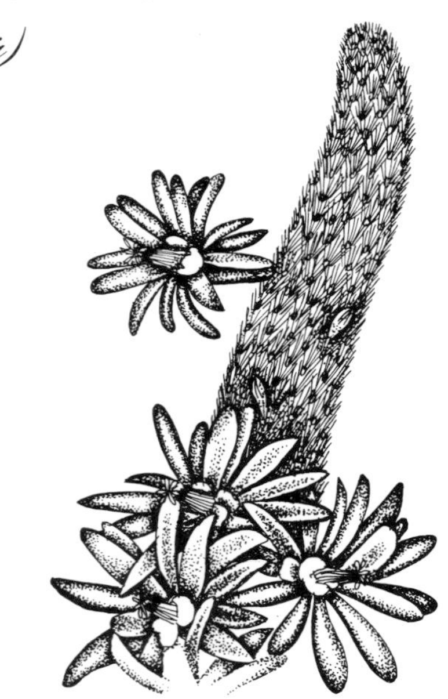

Hildewintera aureispina

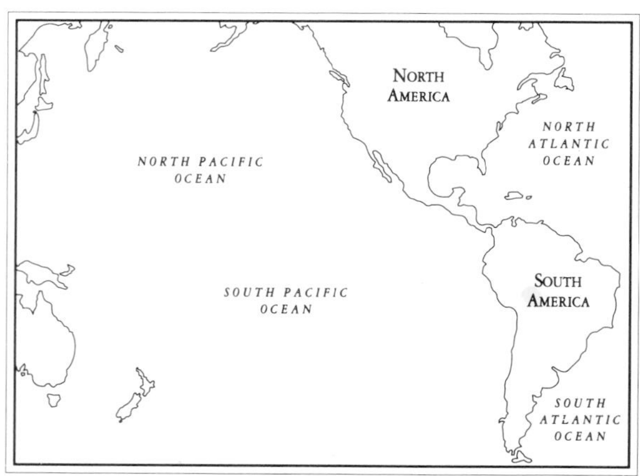

Hildewintera aureispina

Hildewintera aureispina

Common Name: None.
Size: Length up to 1.5 m (5 ft), width up to 60 cm (2 ft).
Climate: Medium elevation.
Distribution: As above.
Flowering Time: Spring to late autumn (fall).
Description: As there is only one species, this information is found above.

HYLOCEREUS

(hī-lō-sē'-rē-ŭs)

Hylocereus contains some 24 species. The generic name is derived from Gk and Lat, meaning 'forest cereus'. *Hylocerei* are clambering epiphytic cacti, usually with three angled stems, which also produce a profusion of aerial roots. The fresh green to dark green stems can grow up very high trees, forming a massive cluster. The stems sometimes have a horny margin, and can be 3–7.5 cm (1.2–3 in) in diameter. The areoles are usually set well apart, and bear few, if any, spines. When present, the spines are minute, and may be white, brown, or black in colour.

The nocturnal flowers are usually white, creamy-white, or pink and sometimes have a slightly greenish throat. They are funnel-shaped, scaly and glabrous on the outside of the tube, and are 15–35 cm (6–14 in) in diameter, occasionally larger. The fruits are oblong and up to 12.5 cm (5 in) in length, and in varying shades of red or purple when ripe.

Culture: *Hylocerei* are native to most parts of the Caribbean, Mexico, and southwards into northern areas of South America. It is very much a forest dweller, and although referred to as an epiphyte, it does sometimes take root on the ground. In cultivation it can be grown from seed, but it is usually easier and quicker to propagate from cuttings. Under free root-run conditions, some species can grow 1 m (3 ft) or more in a season. The plants like plenty of water and warm conditions, but in winter are liable to rot if temperatures fall below 10°C (50°F).

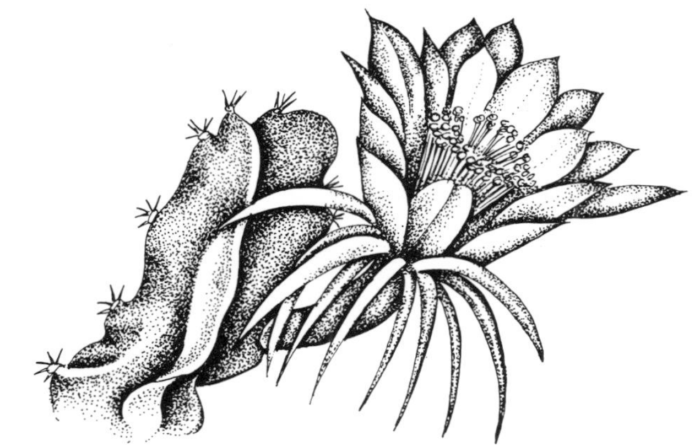

Hylocereus undatus

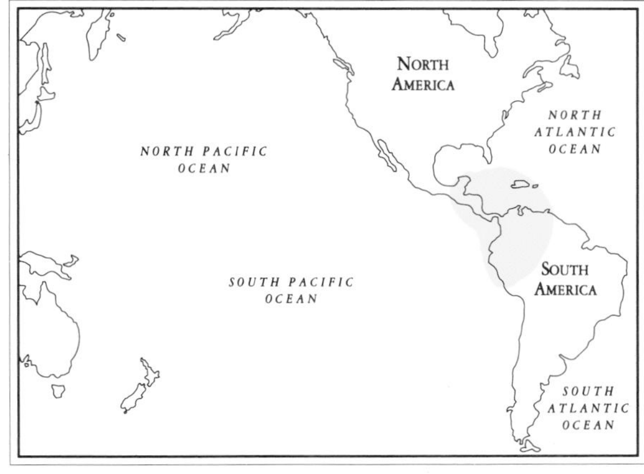

Hylocereus undatus

Hylocereus undatus

Common Name: Queen of the Night (this is possibly the most correct usage of this common name).
Size: Length 3–4 m (10–13 ft). Massive free branching habit.
Climate: Tropical.
Distribution: Origin unknown, but in cultivation in most tropical parts of the world.
Flowering Time: Late summer and autumn (fall).
Description: A very freely branching, robust, clambering species, with three dark green angled stems. Older stems have a horny margin, and are up to 7.5 cm (3 in) in diameter. The prominently jointed stems have areoles set well apart, and there are 1–3 spines which are minute and cream to brown in colour. The nocturnal funnel-shaped flowers open very widely, and are usually 30 cm (12 in) in diameter. The petals are white, and the exterior is yellowish-green. The oblong fruit is about 12.5 cm (5 in) in length, brilliant red when ripe, and contains many large black seeds.

ISLAYA

(ĭs-lā'-ă)

Islaya krainziana

Islaya contains about 12 species and a few varieties. It is named in honour of R. Islay who discovered the genus. They are usually solitary, globular to short, cylindrical plants, with the exception of *I. krainziana* (see below) which has longer stems and becomes prostrate, and have pale green or bluish-green bodies which tend to be quite densely felted in the crown of the plant. There are 8–24 ribs, and the areoles are quite large and felted with up to 24 radial spines and 8 centrals. The radial spines tend to be very fine and short and less than 1 cm (0.4 in) in length, while the centrals are usually stouter and can be up to 2 cm (0.8 in) in length. In a few species the radials and the centrals are indistinguishable. The spine colour varies from cream through to brown or almost black.

The flowers appear from near the centre of the plant, and are 1.5–4 cm (0.6–1.6 in) in diameter. The flower colour is generally varying shades of yellow, with the exception of *I. copiapoides* which has red flowers. The fruits are elongated, reddish, and have a covering of hairs and bristly spines.

Culture: *Islayas* come from southern Peru and northern Chile, and are to be found at altitudes of up to 1000 m (3280 ft). They are fairly slow growing plants, and are not easy to cultivate, requiring a very well drained compost and plenty of water during very hot weather. In winter they should be kept dry and protected from frosts.

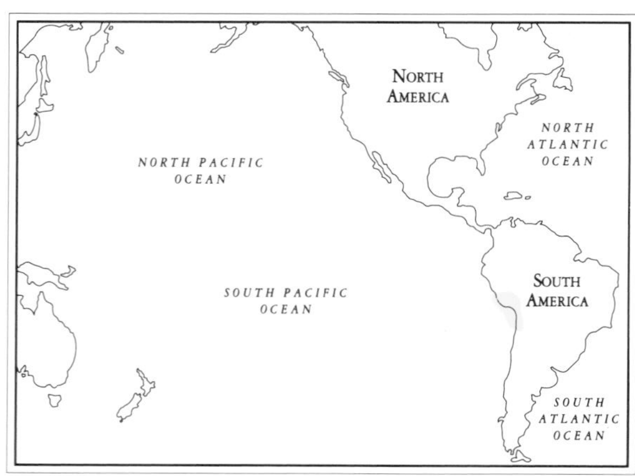

Islaya krainziana

COMMON NAME: None.
SIZE: Length up to 75 cm (2.5 ft), width 10 cm (4 in).
CLIMATE: Medium elevation.
DISTRIBUTION: Northern Chile.
FLOWERING TIME: Summer.
DESCRIPTION: Erect when young, but becoming prostrate and branching sparingly with age. It can have up to 23 ribs which have a somewhat tuberculate structure, and can bear quite large creamy-white areoles. On an old plant the areoles can be up to 1.5 cm (0.6 in) in length, and they bear up to 12 fine radial spines and up to 8 subulate centrals. The creamy-white radials are usually under 1 cm (0.4 in) in length and the longest central spine can reach 1.5 cm (0.6 in) and is usually dark brown. The flowers are about 3 cm (1.2 in) in diameter, varying in colour from lemon-yellow to golden yellow. The fruit is 3 cm (1.2 in) in length, purplish in colour with the same covering as the exterior of the flower tube.

Islaya krainziana

LEMAIREOCEREUS

(lĕ-mā'-rō-sē'-rē-ŭs)

Lemaireocereus contains about 20 species. The generic name honours Charles Lemaire, an early expert on cacti from France. Mostly erect growing, freely branching plants, the majority reach 4–20 m (13–65 ft) in height, though one or two species rarely exceed 1 m (3 ft). The smaller species have stems up to 12.5 cm (5 in) in diameter, whereas the larger species are 20–50 cm (8–20 in) in diameter. The stems vary in colour from green to bluish. There are 5–20 rounded or acute ribs. The areoles tend to be fairly large, whitish or brown, set fairly well apart, and bear 6–12 radial spines, and up to 3 centrals. The spines range in colour from off-white to brown or black, and are straight or curved. The radials are 1–3.5 cm (0.4–1.4 in) in length. The centrals tend to be somewhat stouter than the radials.

The flowers range from cylindrical to funnel-shaped, are white or pink, and up to 10 cm (4 in) in length. The green or bluish-green fruits are globular or egg-shaped, up to 7.5 cm (3 in) in length, and are sometimes covered with spines.

Culture: *Lemaireocerei* are native to Guatemala, Haiti, Honduras, the West Indies, Mexico and south-western United States. They are easy plants to grow from seed or cuttings, and most species develop quite rapidly. However, they need to be protected from frosts, although *L. thurberi* (see below), at the northern end of its range in habitat, does experience occasional frosts. This invariably damages the growing points on the stems and the plants are more freely branching.

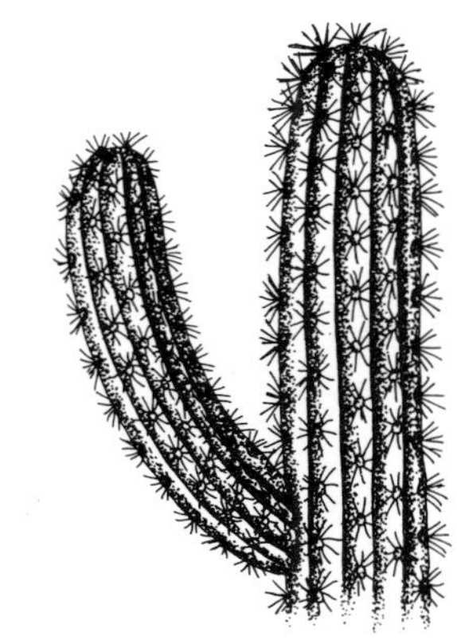

Lemaireocereus thurberi

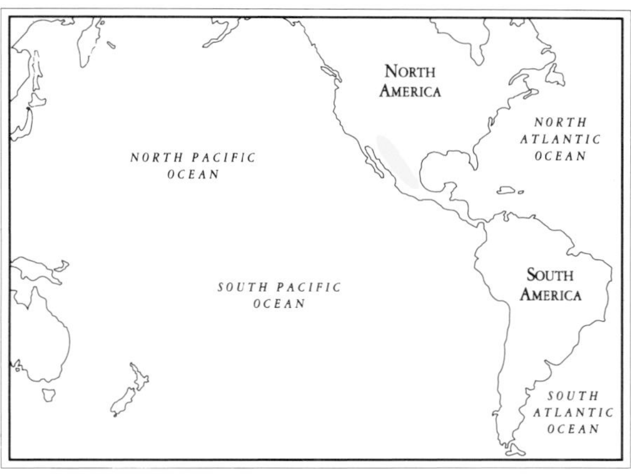

Lemaireocereus thurberi

Lemaireocereus thurberi

COMMON NAME: Organ Pipe Cactus.
SIZE: Height 13 m (42 ft), width 5–6 m (16.25–19.5 ft).
CLIMATE: Medium elevation.
DISTRIBUTION: Northern Mexico and south-western United States.
FLOWERING TIME: Early summer onwards.
DESCRIPTION: An erect growing, freely branching species, with many branches appearing from the base of the main stem. At the southern end of its range in habitat, specimens can reach a height of 13 m (42 ft). The branches can be up to 20 cm (8 in) in diameter, and have up to 18 rounded ribs. The brown felted areoles are set at least 2.5 cm (1 in) apart, and bear up to 10 fine acicular radial spines, and up to 3 stouter centrals. These are brown or black when young, but in age change to grey with dark tips. The radials are about 1 cm (0.4 in) in length, and the centrals can reach 5 cm (2 in). The white, nocturnal flowers are 7.5 cm (3 in) in length and 5 cm (2 in) or more in diameter. The globular fruits can be up to 7.5 cm (3 in) in diameter, are green and have a few short spines.

LEUCHTENBERGIA

(loŏk-tĕn-bĕrg'-ĭ-ă)

Leuchtenbergia is a monotypic genus, and the generic name honours the Duke of Leuchtenberg. It remains solitary for many years but it can eventually cluster and is a very distinctive plant with triangular tubercles 10 cm (4 in) or more in length. The actual plant can reach a height of 70 cm (28 in), with individual heads having a diameter of 30 cm (12 in) and it can develop a lengthy taproot. The tubercles are green, but in the sun often become somewhat reddish, eventually drying up and dropping off. The areoles on the ends of the tubercles have some greyish-yellow felt and up to 14 radial spines and 2 centrals. The radial spines can be 5 cm (2 in) in length, and the centrals can reach 10 cm (4 in). The spines are papery and straw coloured.

The flowers appear from the newest areoles in the centre of the plant, and can exceed 8 cm (3.2 in) in diameter. They are funnel-shaped and yellow with green or reddish-green sepals. The yellowish fruits are somewhat egg-shaped, and scaly and dry when ripe.

Culture: *Leuchtenbergia* comes from central and northern Mexico, and grows in rocky, sandy situations where the strong taproot can penetrate to 30 cm (12 in) or more on occasions. It is an easy plant to grow and it can be raised from seed, and it flowers readily. It likes a moderately well drained compost, and can be watered fairly freely during warm weather. In winter it can be left dry, and it tolerates a minimum temperature of 5°C (40°F). In warmer climates it should be given water throughout the year, although to a lesser degree in winter, to avoid too many of the tubercles shrivelling and drying up.

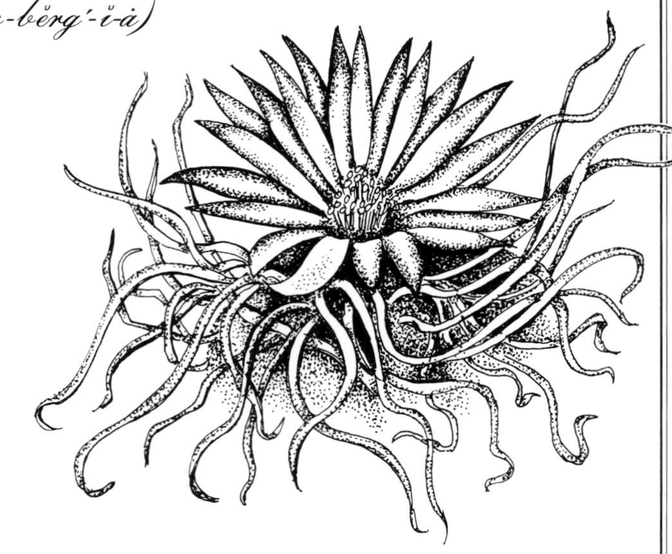

Leuchtenbergia principis

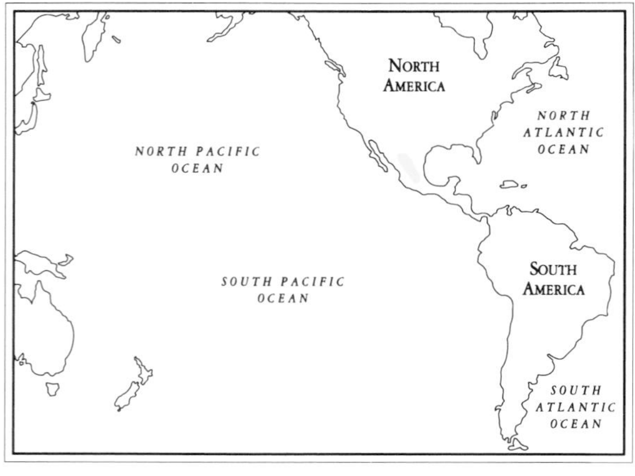

Leuchtenbergia principis

Leuchtenbergia principis

Common Name: None.
Size: Height 70 cm (28 in), width 65 cm (24 in).
Climate: Medium elevation.
Distribution: As above.
Flowering Time: Summer.
Description: As there is only one species, this information is found above.

LOBIVIA

(lō-bĭv'-ĭ-ă)

Lobivia is today considered to contain some 160 species, and a very large number of varieties and forms. The generic name is derived as an anagram of Bolivia, the country from which so many species originate. Today, as a result of including in *Lobivia* all those species previously in the genus *Helianthocereus, Lobivia* is now the most vegetatively varied genus of the family Cactaceae. They range from miniature clustering species which have individual heads no more than 2.5 cm (1 in) in diameter, to large columnar plants 10 m (32 ft) or more in height and possessing stems with a diameter of 35 cm (14 in). The vast majority of *Lobivias* are relatively dwarf globular to short cylindrical plants, and often fairly freely clustering. There are 10–30 ribs which bear usually woolly, white or brownish areoles. In the miniature species they are very close together; in the tall columnar species they are set well apart. The number of radial spines can be from 4 or 5 to as many as 50 or more. They can be very fine or rigid, and range in length from minute to 7.5 cm (3 in) or more. The centrals when present or when distinguishable from the radials are equally varied in form, but can be even longer. The spine colour ranges from white and cream, to brown and nearly black.

The funnel-shaped flowers of *Lobivias* are from 5–15 cm (2–6 in) in length and have a diameter of 5–10 cm (2–4 in). *Lobivias* are renowned for their beautiful flowers, which range from white to the most vivid red or magenta. Many species have a conspicuous hymen within the flower tube from which the stamens arise. The fruits are spherical or ovoid, 2.5–5 cm (1–2 in) in length, hairy, and usually whitish or brown.

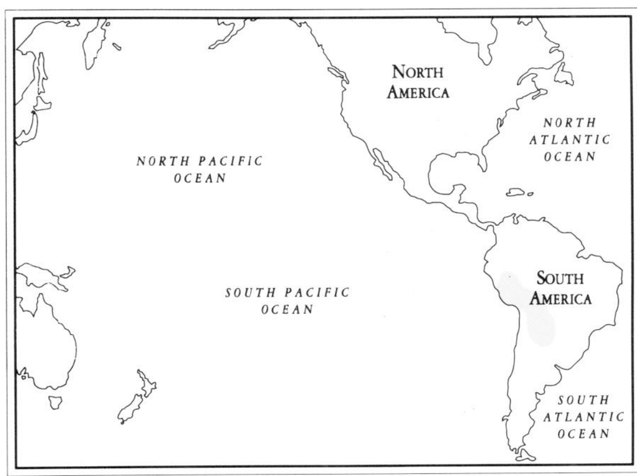

Culture: *Lobivias* are native to Bolivia, Argentina and Peru, and are to be found in many very differing locations, from rock crevices and steep mountain slopes, to an altitude of 3000 m (9840 ft) or more. They are very easy plants to grow from seed or by division of clusters. Some of the smaller species will flower within 2 years, while a few of the giant species can take 10 or 20 years or more to reach maturity. The majority of the species like plenty of water during the main growing period, which is spring and autumn (fall). In winter, if kept dry, most species will withstand near freezing temperatures and some will tolerate frost.

Lobivia acanthoplegma fa. *roseiflora*

Lobivia acanthoplegma fa. *roseiflora*

Lobivia culpinensis

Common Name: None.
Size: Height 20 cm (8 in), width 15 cm (6 in).
Climate: High elevation.
Distribution: Bolivia.
Flowering Time: Summer.
Description: Usually a solitary, globular to slightly cylindrical species. The plant body is usually dark green, with up to 30 or so narrow ribs. The small circular areoles have a little white wool, are fairly well separated, and bear up to 12 radial spines which are appressed against the body and are 1–5 cm (0.4–2 in) in length. There can be 1–6 centrals, which are usually slightly longer and stronger and stand out from the plant. The spine colour varies from off-white to nearly black. The funnel-shaped flowers are usually over 5 cm (2 in) in diameter, and range in colour from yellow to red. The fruits are spherical, no more than 1 cm (0.4 in) in diameter, hairy, and brownish when ripe.

Lobivia acanthoplegma fa. *roseiflora*

Common Name: None.
Size: Height 7.5 cm (3 in), width 10 cm (4 in).
Climate: Medium to high elevation.
Distribution: Bolivia.
Flowering Time: Late spring to summer.
Description: This species usually has a solitary, flattened globular habit, and a maximum diameter of 10 cm (4 in). It tends to have an almost tuberculate, rather than ribbed, body, which is dark green. The woolly, oval-shaped areoles and bear up to 12 off-white, horny radial spines, which are slightly curved and somewhat appressed against the body. These spines rarely exceed 2 cm (0.8 in) in length, and there are no centrals. The wide-opening flowers have a short tube, are pink with a paler throat, and have a diameter of about 5 cm (2 in). The fruit is slightly ovoid, 1 cm (0.4 in) in length and greenish-brown when ripe.

Lobivia culpinensis

Lobivia bruchii

Common Name: None.
Size: Height 30 cm (12 in), width 50 cm (20 in).
Climate: High elevation.
Distribution: Northern Argentina.
Flowering Time: Summer.
Description: Large, solitary occasionally clustering plants, with individual heads which can have a diameter of 50 cm (20 in). The plant illustrated has about 30 ribs, but an old plant can have 50 ribs. When young the plants have a fresh green body, but older plants tend to become rather corky, particularly around the base. The oval-shaped areoles have some creamy-white wool, and bear 7–14 curved radial spines, and up to 4 centrals. The spines are moderately stout, but are usually less than 5 cm (2 in) in length, and are off-white to pale brown in colour. The flowers open wide, sometimes exceed 5 cm (2 in) in diameter, possess a hairy tube, and range in colour from orange-red to dark red. The fruits are slightly ovoid, about 2.5 cm (1 in) in length, are covered with hairs, and greenish-brown when ripe.

Lobivia bruchii

Lobivia famatimensis

Lobivia famatimensis

Common Name: None.
Size: Height 5 cm (2 in), width 15 cm (6 in).
Climate: High elevation.
Distribution: Argentina.
Flowering Time: Summer.
Description: This is a very variable species, of which some 20 varieties have been described (although this number could be reduced to four or five). It can be solitary, but may also cluster very freely, with individual heads reaching 5 cm (2 in) in height, and a little less in diameter. The colour of the plant ranges from dark green to nearly black. It can have 15–25 narrow ribs, which bear tiny areoles set very close together. The spines tend to be pectinate, very short, and cream to brown in colour. The flowers are funnel-shaped, with a very prominent hymen in the tube and are usually 4–5 cm (1.6–2 in) in diameter. The flower colour is very variable from white through to crimson. The fruits are spherical and covered with dark brown hair.

Lobivia famatimensis

Lobivia huascha fa. *rubra*

Common Name: None.
Size: Height 65 cm (24 in), width 50 cm (20 in).
Climate: High elevation.
Distribution: Argentina.
Flowering Time: Late spring and summer.
Description: This is a columnar species, with stems up to 65 cm (24 in) in height and about 5 cm (2 in) in diameter, and it branches freely from the base. It can have 14–17 narrow straight ribs, which bear small areoles set fairly close together. These bear 12 or more spreading radial spines, up to 1.5 cm (0.6 in) in length, and off-white to brown in colour. There can be up to 2 somewhat stouter centrals 3.5 cm (1.4 in) in length and sometimes slightly darker than the radials in colour. The diurnal flowers are funnel-shaped, up to 10 cm (4 in) in length and 7.5 cm (3 in) in diameter. The exterior of the tube is very hairy. The spherical fruit is also hairy, and up to 3.75 cm (1.5 in) in diameter.

Lobivia huascha fa. *rubra*

Lobivia jajoiana

Common Name: None.
Size: Height 10 cm (4 in), width 7.5 cm (3 in).
Climate: Medium elevation.
Distribution: Northern Argentina.
Flowering Time: Summer.
Description: A solitary, spherical species, it has a fresh green body with up to 14 acute ribs. The white areoles are set well apart, and bear up to 10 spreading radial spines, and sometimes one central, particularly on older plants. The radial spines are up to 1 cm (0.4 in) in length and white to reddish in colour. The central (when present) is stouter than the radials, 2.5 cm (1 in) long, and black. The flowers are funnel-shaped, 5–6 cm (2–2.4 in) in diameter, from pink to wine-red in colour, with an almost black hymen in the throat. The fruits are spherical, about 1 cm (0.4 in) in diameter, and become olive-green (with blackish hairs) when ripe.

Lobivia jajoiana

Lobivia schreiteri

Lobivia schreiteri

Common Name: None.
Size: Height 3–5 cm (1.2–2 in), width 30 cm (12 in).
Climate: Medium elevation.
Distribution: Northern Argentina.
Flowering Time: Summer.
Description: This species is solitary for the first few years, but then clusters, with individual heads measuring 3–4 cm (1.2–1.6 in) in diameter. The green to grey-green bodies have up to 14 shallow ribs, and the small whitish areoles are set well apart. These bear up to eight, but often fewer, very short curved radial spines. Sometimes there are one or two centrals from 1–2 cm (0.4–0.8 in) long, but these are usually missing. The flowers are up to 4 cm (1.6 in) long, and purplish-red with a blackish throat. The fruits are spherical, small, and greenish-brown when ripe.

Lobivia maximiliana

Common Name: None.
Size: Height 5 cm (2 in), width 20 cm (8 in).
Climate: Medium to high elevation.
Distribution: North-western Bolivia and south-eastern Peru.
Flowering Time: Summer.
Description: A freely clustering species, it is dark green in colour, with flattened and globular heads up to 7.5 cm (3 in) in diameter; each head has up to 30 ribs. The areoles are oval, have a little wool, and bear up to 6 or 8 spreading radial spines, which can be 1.25–2.5 cm (0.5–1 in) in length. It usually has one or two stronger centrals, which exceed 6 cm (1.2 in) in length. The spine colour varies from off-white and yellow to brown. The red flowers are funnel-shaped, and have quite a long yellowish tube relative to their diameter. This tube is very hairy, and about 5 cm (2 in) in length. The hairy fruits are spherical, and no more than 1.25 cm (0.5 in) in diameter.

Lobivia maximiliana

LOPHOCEREUS

(lō-fō-sē'-rē-ŭs)

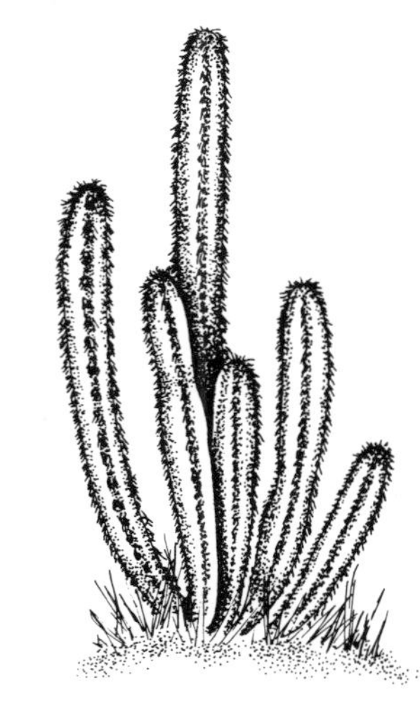

Lophocereus schottii

Lophocereus contains four species and two varieties. The generic name is derived from *lophos* (crested), referring to the plant's crest of bristly spines. The plants are columnar, freely branching *cerei*, which can reach 7 m (22 ft) in height. The light green stems have a diameter to 10 cm (4 in) and possess 5–15 straight ribs. The small round areoles on the non-flowering sections of the stems are up to 2.5 cm (1 in) apart. They bear 5–10 radial spines, 1–2 cm (0.4–0.8 in) in length, and 1–5 centrals, which are slightly longer. The areoles on the upper parts of flowering stems are larger and bear 25–50 bristly spines, of the same colour as the radials and the centrals, and can be 2.5–6 cm (1–2.4 in) in length.

The flowers are funnel-shaped, have a short, scaly tube, and the white or pink flowers rarely exceed 4 cm (1.6 in) in diameter. The fruits are spherical, less than 1.25 cm (0.5 in) in diameter and red when ripe.

Culture: *Lophocerei* come from north-eastern Mexico and south-western United States. They are invariably found on flat ground — sometimes in virtual sand — where temperatures are exceedingly high during the summer months. They are very easy to raise from seed, and non-flowering stems root very easily from cuttings. If grown from seed, plants are unlikely to flower under 6 or 7 years of age. They require a moderately well drained, humus enriched soil and plenty of water during the warmer months. In winter the plants should be kept dry, and protected from frosts.

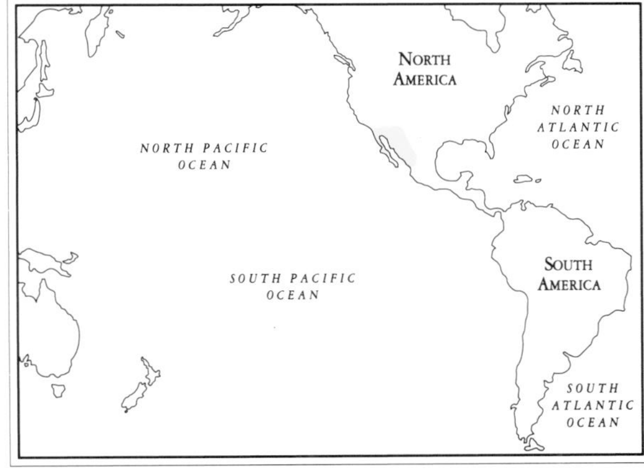

Lophocereus schottii

Lophocereus schottii

Common Name: Senita Cactus.
Size: Height 7 m (22 ft) width 3–4 m (9.5–13 ft)..
Climate: Mediterranean to medium elevation.
Distribution: North-western Mexico and south-western United States.
Flowering Time: Spring and summer.
Description: This is a columnar and freely branching species. The light green stems have 5–9 straight ribs, and the small areoles are set about 1.25 cm (0.5 in) apart on the non-flowering stems. They bear up to 5 very short, fine, off-white to greyish spines. On the flowering stems the areoles tend to be closer together, larger, and have up to 30 or so bristly spines of the same colour, but up to 2.5–4 cm (1–1.6 in) in length. The funnel-shaped flowers are pink, about 4 cm (1.6 in) in length and a little less in diameter. The fruits are spherical, smooth, about 1.25 cm (0.5 in) in diameter and red when ripe.

LOPHOPHORA

(lō-fof'-ō-rà)

Lophophora contains two species and a number of varieties, but there is considerable variation from plant to plant. The generic name is derived from the Gk, meaning 'crest-bearing'. They are simple or clustering, globular plants, with large fleshy roots, and the body of the plant is quite soft. The diameter of an individual head is 8–13 cm (3.2–5.2 in). Their body colour ranges from pale yellowish-green to bluish. There are 5–13 ribs, and the white woolly tufted areoles are usually set fairly well apart. In some species plants can have a more tubercled appearance. There are no spines on any variety in this genus.

The flowers appear from amidst the white wool in the centre of the plant, and they are 1.25–2.5 cm (0.5–1 in) in diameter. The flower colour ranges from white or creamy-yellow to pink, with usually a somewhat darker median line down each petal. The fruits are elongated, rather small, contain only a few seeds, and when ripe can be white, pink, or red.

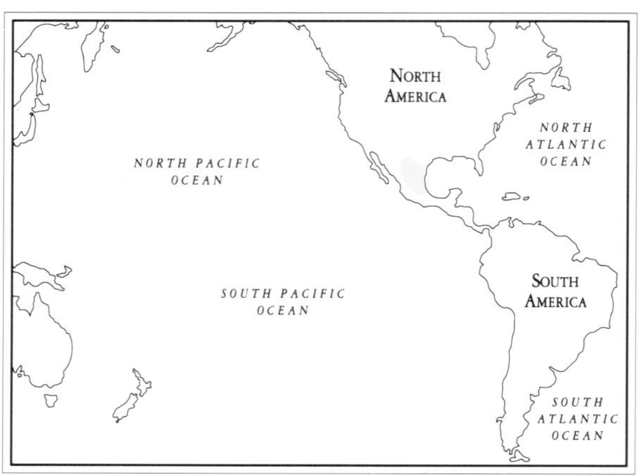

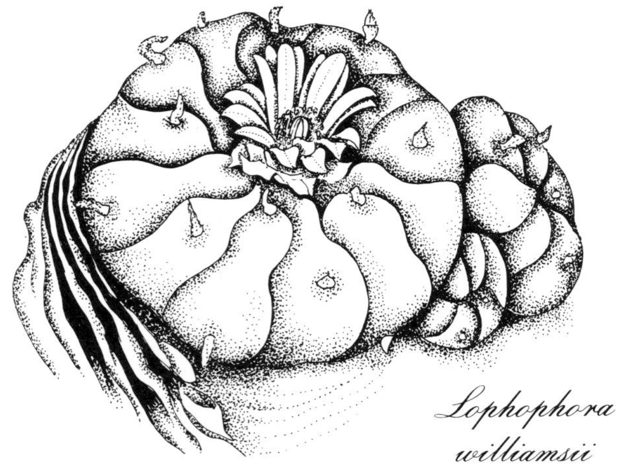

Lophophora williamsii

Culture: *Lophophoras* are to be found over quite a wide area of central Mexico, and just into Texas in south-eastern United States. They grow in sandy or clay soils, usually beneath other xerophytic shrubs. Although they are not fast growing plants, they are quite easy to raise from seed, and can flower within 5 or 6 years. They like a well drained soil, but can be watered freely during all hot weather, when they should be given a little shade. In winter they can be left dry, and tolerate a temperature of 5°C (40°F).

Lophophora williamsii

Lophophora williamsii

Common Name: Peyote Cactus.
Size: Height 4–5 cm (1.6–2 in), width 25 cm (10 in).
Climate: Medium elevation.
Distribution: Central Mexico to south-eastern United States.
Flowering Time: Summer onwards.
Description: This is a solitary or freely clustering species with up to 10 ribs per head, but sometimes having a more tubercled appearance. A mature head is usually 10 cm (4 in) in diameter, pale bluish-green in colour, and has prominent white woolly tufts at the areoles, and plenty of wool in the centre. The flowers are 1.25 cm (0.5 in) in diameter and off-white to pink with a darker median stripe down each petal. The elongated fruits are reddish in colour when ripe and less than 1 cm (0.4 in) in length.

Mamillopsis

(măm-ĭ-lŏp'-sĭs)

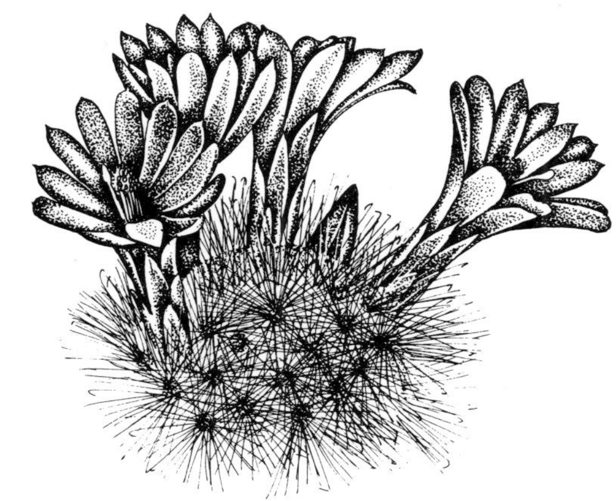

Mamillopsis senilis

Mamillopsis contains two species, and it resembles the genus *Mammillaria* (see page 116) hence its genus name. They are globular to short and cylindrical headed plants, which in age cluster freely, and a clump of 30 or more heads is not uncommon. Individual heads can be 15 cm (6 in) in height and the diameter is 7.5–25 cm (3–10 in). The green body, which is strongly tubercled, is completely masked by the dense spination — as is the spiral arrangement of the tubercles. The areoles are small and bear 25–40 radial spines, which are 1–2 cm (0.4–0.8 in) in length. There can be up to 6 centrals, which are slightly longer and stronger than the radials, and the lowest central is strongly hooked. The spine colour ranges from white to straw in colour.

The flowers are zygomorphic, 3–7 cm (1.2–2.8 in) in length, and 2–6 cm (0.8–2.4 in) in diameter. They are orange-red to dark red in colour. The fruits are spherical, about 1 cm (0.4 in) in diameter, and red when ripe.

Culture: Both species come from central and western Mexico, where they grow at fairly high altitudes — in winter, they can sometimes be covered with snow. However, they grow on rocky well drained slopes, and without these conditions in cultivation are prone to rotting. They are easily raised from seed and develop quite rapidly, preferring plenty of water during very hot weather and to be kept dry during the cool winter months, when high atmospheric humidity can cause problems.

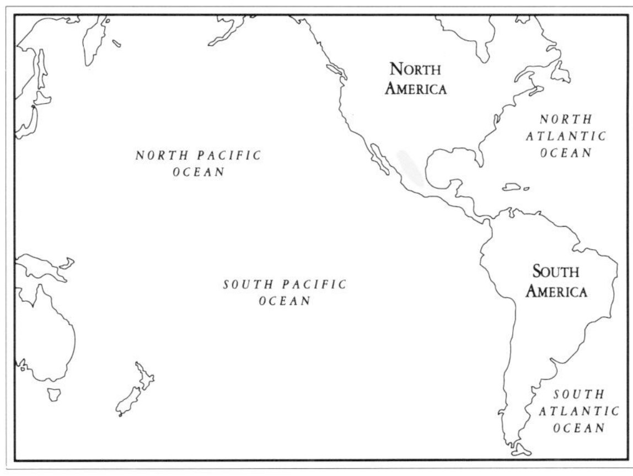

Mamillopsis senilis

Common Name: None.
Size: Height 15 cm (6 in), width 7.5 cm (3 in).
Climate: High elevation.
Distribution: Central and western Mexico.
Flowering Time: Summer.
Description: This species is globular and solitary when young. The stems become columnar, reaching 15 cm (6 in) in height and a diameter of up to 7.5 cm (3 in), with age. The body of the plant is a bright shiny green, and has its tubercles arranged in spirals of 8 and 15. The small areoles bear up to 40 or more spreading radial spines, and 5–6 centrals. They are white to straw-coloured, and about 1.25 cm (0.5 in) in length. The lower central is slightly stouter and strongly hooked. The zygomorphic flowers are about 7 cm (2.8 in) in length and 6 cm (2.4 in) in diameter and orange-red to bright red in colour. The fruits are spherical and 1 cm (0.4 in) in diameter.

Mamillopsis senilis

MAMMILLARIA

(măm-ĭ-lā'-rĭ-ȧ)

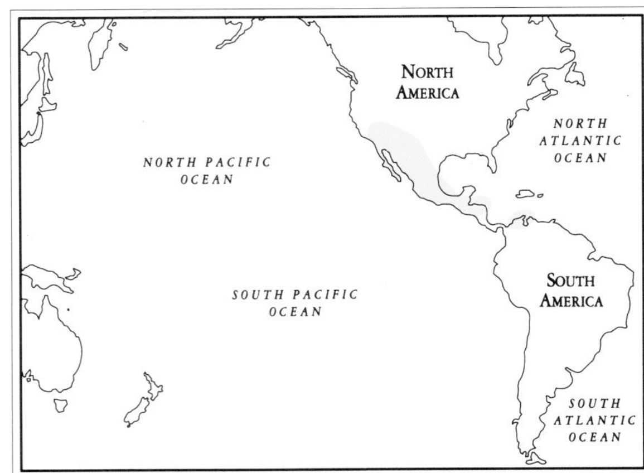

Mammillaria contains over 400 species and numerous varieties and forms. The generic name is derived from the Lat *mammilla* (nipple), which is in reference to the small tubercled structure of the plants. This genus was erected in 1812 by E. H. Haworth, an English botanist. There is a tremendous variety of plant shape and size in the genus — they may be spherical or short and cylindrical, solitary or freely clustering, and with or without milky sap. Their tubercled structure is in many shapes and sizes, and always has an intersecting spiral arrangement and there is often hair in the axils between the tubercles. The spines are varied in length and colour and can be hooked or covered with hair etc.

The flowers usually appear in rings away from the apex of the plant; vary in size and colour, but in the majority of species are fairly small. They can be bell-shaped or funnel-shaped, and most species have a very short tube, but a few such as *M. saboae* fa. *haudeana* (see page 122), have a much longer slender tube. The fruits which usually appear some months after flowering has finished are relatively small, ovoid or elongated and slender, are green, pink, or red when ripe, and are quite smooth without scales, hair, or spines. The illustration of *M. heyderi* var. *hemisphaerica* shows the most common type of fruit in this genus (see page 120).

Culture: The main home of this genus is in Mexico, but some species occur in south-western United States, the West Indies and just into South America. The majority of species are very easy to cultivate and flower readily — particularly those from higher altitudes which are well suited to conditions of low temperature and high humidity. The desert species, however, require a well drained soil, and can only be watered freely during very hot weather. However, even these species can tolerate a temperature of 5°C (40°F), if they are kept dry in winter, and there is good air circulation. During the spring to autumn (fall) growing season, when temperatures are very high, the less densely spined species may need a little light shade.

Mammillaria microcarpa

Mammillaria albilanata

Mammillaria albilanata

Common Name: None.
Size: Height 15 cm (6 in), width 8 cm (3.2 in).
Climate: Medium elevation.
Distribution: Central Mexico.
Flowering Time: Late spring onwards.
Description: This species is usually solitary, and initially globular and up to 8 cm (3.2 in) in diameter, but eventually reaches 15 cm (6 in) in height. The green body has small tubercles with white hair in the axils, and a lot of white hair around the crown. The areoles bear up to 20 very short, appressed radial spines, and 2–4 centrals. The spines are 0.4 cm (0.16 in) in length. The radials are white, and the centrals, which are not always present on young plants, are white or cream with a slightly brownish tip. The flowers are small, 0.7 cm (0.28 in) in length and pale to dark carmine. The fruits are elongated, less than 1 cm (0.4 in) in length and bright red when ripe.

Mammillaria boolii

Mammillaria boolii

Common Name: None.
Size: Height 3.5 cm (1.4 in), width 3.5 cm (1.4 in).
Climate: Low elevation.
Distribution: North-western Mexico.
Flowering Time: Summer.
Description: A dwarf spherical species, which can remain solitary or cluster, with a bluish-green tubercled body. Individual heads rarely exceed 3.5 cm (1.4 in) in height and diameter, and are often smaller. It has circular white woolly areoles which bear up to 20 acicular radial spines, and one subulate, hooked central. The white radial spines are up to 1.5 cm (0.6 in) in length, and the central can reach 2 cm (0.8 in), and is yellowish or slightly grey. The flowers are funnel-shaped, open widely, and are pink to pale magenta in colour, with a darker median stripe down the petals. The fruits are elongated, up to 3 cm (1.4 in) long, and orange when ripe.

Mammillaria camptotricha

Common Name: None.
Size: Height 5 cm (2 in), width 25 cm (10 in).
Climate: Low elevation.
Distribution: Western Mexico.
Flowering Time: Summer through to autumn (fall).
Description: A densely clustering species, which forms low mounds, but the individual tubercled heads are up to 7.5 cm (3 in) in diameter. The plant body is bright green, with soft conical tubercles up to 2 cm (0.8 in) in length. The axils between the tubercles possess yellowish wool. The areoles are small, and bear up to eight fine, spreading contorted spines, but there are no centrals. These spines are up to 3 cm (1.2 in) long, cream coloured when new, but changing to yellow. The white flowers are small, do not open widely, and are up to 1.25 cm (0.5 in) in length, with median greenish stripes down the petals. The fruits are elongated and very slender, up to 2 cm (0.8 in) in length, and are green tinged with red.

Mammillaria candida

Mammillaria camptotricha

Mammillaria candida

Common Name: None.
Size: Height 5–10 cm (2–4 in), width 30 cm (12 in).
Climate: Medium elevation.
Distribution: Central Mexico.
Flowering Time: Late spring to early summer.
Description: A spherical to slightly elongated, solitary or clustering species, with a bluish-green tubercled body virtually masked by the very dense spination. The tubercles are spirally arranged, with some white wool in the axils between them. The circular white woolly areoles bear up to 50 fine acicular spreading radial spines, and up to 12 similar, but stronger centrals. The radial spines are up to 1 cm (0.4 in) long, and white, but the centrals tend to be slightly shorter, and are white with brown tips (which are sometimes very pale). The flowers are up to 1.5 cm (0.6 in) in diameter, and off-white with reddish-brown stripes down the petals. Fruits are elongated, to 2 cm (0.6 in) long, and pink when ripe.

Mammillaria carmenae

Mammillaria carmenae

Common Name: None.
Size: Height 3–5 cm (1.2–2 in), width 15 cm (6 in).
Climate: Low to medium elevation.
Distribution: Central Mexico.
Flowering Time: Spring and early summer.
Description: Usually a clustering species, with a green tubercled body completely masked by the dense plumose spination. The individual tubercled heads are spherical to slightly elongated, and are up to 7.5 cm (3 in) in diameter. There is white wool in the axils between the conical tubercles. The circular brownish areoles bear up to 100 or more very short white or yellowish soft plumose spines, which are flattened against the plant. The flowers open widely, are about 1 cm (0.4 in) in diameter, and white or pale pink. The fruits are slim and elongated, no more than 0.6 cm (0.2 in) in length, and greenish-white when ripe.

Mammillaria couperae

Common Name: None.
Size: Height 12 cm (4.8 in), width 10 cm (4 in).
Climate: Medium to high elevation.
Distribution: Central Mexico.
Flowering Time: Late spring to early summer.
Description: A solitary, spherical to slightly elongated species, with a tubercled dark green body. The brownish areoles are almost circular, and bear up to 50 very fine acicular radial spines (but fewer spines on young plants), and up to 10 stronger centrals, of which one or more will be hooked. The white radial spines are up to 1 cm (0.4 in) long, and the centrals are up to 2 cm (0.8 in) in length, and are creamy-yellow or brownish coloured. The flowers are bell-shaped, up to 1.5 cm (0.6 in) in diameter, and are white or very pale pink, with slightly darker median pink stripes on the petals. The fruits are elongated, up to 1 cm (0.4 in) in length, and are whitish to pale green when ripe.

Mammillaria couperae

Mammillaria guelzowiana

Mammillaria guelzowiana

Common Name: None.
Size: Height 7 cm (2.8 in), width 25 cm (10 in).
Climate: Medium elevation.
Distribution: Western Mexico.
Flowering Time: Summer.
Description: This magnificent species has a solitary, flattened globular habit when young, but clusters from around the base with age. An individual head can be 6 cm (2.4 in) in diameter. The axils between the tubercles are naked, but the areoles bear up to 80 hairlike radial spines and 1–4 hooked centrals. The radials and the centrals are up to 1.5 cm (0.6 in) in length and the radials are white, while the centrals are yellowish or reddish in colour. The flowers are 5 cm (2 in) in length and 6 cm (2.4 in) in diameter, and pinkish-magenta. The fruits are slightly ovoid, less than 1 cm (0.4 in) in length, and yellowish or reddish when ripe — matching the colour of the central spines.

Mammillaria heyderi var. *hemisphaerica*

Common Name: None.
Size: Height 2.5-7.5 cm (1-3 in), width 30 cm (12 in).
Climate: Medium elevation.
Distribution: North-eastern Mexico and south-western United States.
Flowering Time: Spring and early summer.
Description: This is a flattened globular species, which is usually solitary, but occasionally multi-headed. A single head rarely exceeds 12.5 cm (5 in) in diameter, and the axils between the tubercles are naked. The areoles bear up to 13 straight, spreading radial spines, and one central. The spines are usually less than 1 cm (0.4 in) in length and vary in colour from grey to brown with dark tips. The flowers are up to 2 cm (0.8 in) in diameter and off-white to cream with a slightly darker median stripe down each petal. The fruits are elongated, slightly swollen at the tips, up to 2.5 cm (1 in) in length, and bright red when ripe.

Mammillaria heyderi var. *hemisphaerica*

Mammillaria longiflora

Mammillaria longiflora

Common Name: None.
Size: Height 6 cm (2.2 in), width 15 cm (6 in).
Climate: High elevation.
Distribution: Western Mexico.
Flowering Time: Summer.
Description: A solitary or sparingly clustering species, with individual heads up to 6 cm (2.2 in) in height, and 5 cm (2 in) in diameter. The fresh green tubercled body has circular white areoles, bearing up to 30 fine spreading radial spines, and up to four centrals, one of which is hooked. The radial spines are up to 1.25 cm (0.5 in) in length, and are white. The straight centrals are of a similar length, but the hooked one can be up to 3 cm (1.2 in) or more in length. The centrals range in colour from pale yellow to reddish-brown. The flowers open widely, but possess quite a long tube, so the flowers measure up to 5 cm (2 in) in length, and around 4 cm (1.6 in) in diameter. The fruits are egg-shaped, up to 1 cm (0.4 in) in length, and brownish when ripe.

Mammillaria louisae

Common Name: None.
Size: Height 4-5 cm (1.6-2 in), width 3 cm (1.2 in).
Climate: Low elevation.
Distribution: North-western Mexico.
Flowering Time: Summer.
Description: Normally a solitary miniature species, possessing a dark green tubercled body, prominently spirally arranged. The small circular areoles have some white wool when new, but this disappears with age. They bear up to 11 spreading radial spines, and usually four centrals, of which the lower one is hooked. The radial spines are very short, and white with dark brown or black tips, but the centrals are up to 1 cm (0.4 in) long, and brown with darker tips. The flowers do not open very wide, and are up to 3.5 cm (1.4 in) in length. They are white or very pale pink with median brown or pinkish-brown stripes down the petals, although in some cases this feature is not very prominent. The fruits are slightly elongated, up to 2 cm (0.8 in) long, and red when ripe.

Mammillaria louisae

Mammillaria mammillaris

Mammillaria mammillaris

Common Name: None.
Size: Height 20 cm (8 in), width 6 cm (2.4 in).
Climate: Medium elevation.
Distribution: Curacao and Venezuela.
Flowering Time: Late spring and summer.
Description: A solitary, globular plant when young, and up to 6 cm (2.4 in) in diameter, it eventually becomes short and cylindrical and up to 20 cm (8 in) in height, and freely branching. The dark green body becomes sometimes tinged with red in the sun, and there is a little white wool in the axils between the tubercles. The areoles also have a little wool, and bear up to 16 radial spines and up to 5 centrals. The spines are less than 1 cm (0.4 in) in length and reddish when new, changing to grey with age. The flowers are 1 cm (0.4 in) in length, creamy-yellow, with greenish-brown tips to the petals. The fruits are slender and elongated, just under 1 cm (0.4 in) in length, and brilliant carmine.

Mammillaria microcarpa

Mammillaria microcarpa

Common Name: Arizona Fishhook.
Size: Height 15 cm (6 in), width 20 cm (8 in).
Climate: Medium elevation.
Distribution: South-western United States and nearby parts of Mexico.
Flowering Time: Summer.
Description: This is a globular plant when young, with a diameter of about 5 cm (2 in), and it tends to become slightly cylindrical and up to 15 cm (6 in) in height with age. It is solitary or clustering, strongly tubercled, and the axils are naked. The areoles bear up to 30 thin needle-like radial spines, and 1–3 hooked centrals. The radials are usually around 1 cm (0.4 in) in length and usually white with dark brown or black tips, and the centrals can be up to 2 cm (0.8 in) in length and entirely dark brown or black. The flowers are 3–4 cm (1.2–1.6 in) in diameter, pink to pinkish-magenta and sometimes have a darker median stripe down each petal. The fruits are elongated, slightly swollen at the tips, about 1.5 cm (0.6 in) in length and red when ripe.

Mammillaria pennispinosa

Mammillaria pennispinosa

Common Name: None.
Size: Height 2.5 cm (1 in), width 15 cm (6 in).
Climate: Medium elevation.
Distribution: Western Mexico.
Flowering Time: Spring.
Description: This is a globular, solitary or clustering species about 4 cm (1.6 in) in diameter, with a little short hair in the axils between the tubercles. The areoles bear up to 20 thin radial, pubescent spines, and 1–3 centrals, one of which is hooked. The radial spines are less than 1 cm (0.4 in) in length, and the central spines are yellow at the base and reddish-brown towards the tips. The flowers are 1.5 cm (0.6 in) in length and whitish with a pinkish-brown median stripe on each petal. The fruits are elongated, 1.5–2 cm (0.6–0.8 in) in length and red when ripe.

Mammillaria saboae fa. *haudeana*

Common Name: None.
Size: Height 3–4 cm (1.2–1.6 in), width 15 cm (6 in).
Climate: Medium elevation.
Distribution: North-western Mexico.
Flowering Time: Spring.
Description: This is a very miniature, freely clustering species, and the slightly elongated heads are 2 cm (0.8 in) in diameter, and 3–4 cm (1.2–1.6 in) in height. The green body is often tinged with red at the base, and the axils between the tubercles are naked. The areoles have up to 27 thin and slightly recurved radial spines that are no more than 0.6 cm (0.24 in) in length, and are white. There are no central spines. The flowers are up to 6.5 cm (2.6 in) in diameter, and 4.5 cm (1.8 in) in length, with a thin reddish tube. They are in varying shades of lilac pink. The fruits remain within the body of the plant, with sometimes a slightly reddish tip visible.

Mammillaria saboae fa. *haudeana*

Mammillaria sempervivi

Mammillaria sempervivi

Common Name: None.
Size: Height 3–4 cm (1.2–1.6 in), width 7.5 cm (3 in).
Climate: Low to medium elevation.
Distribution: Central Mexico.
Flowering Time: Late spring to early summer.
Description: A solitary species, it can cluster sparingly, but is normally seen as a solitary plant. It has a dark green tubercled body, spirally arranged, with masses of white wool in the axils between the tubercles, particularly near the centre where the rings of flowers appear. The areoles bear up to seven minute acicular radial spines and up to four stouter subulate centrals. The radial spines are pure white, but the centrals rarely exceed 0.6 cm (0.2 in), and vary in colour from off-white to brown or black. The flowers are up to 1 cm (0.4 in) long, whitish with olive-green or dirty pink in the centres. The fruits are elongated, and under 1 cm (0.4 in) in length, and red when ripe.

Mammillaria theresae

Common Name: None.
Size: Height 5 cm (2 in), width 10 cm (4 in).
Climate: Medium to high elevation.
Distribution: Western Mexico.
Flowering Time: Early spring.
Description: A dwarf growing species, cylindrical, with an olive-green to reddish-green tubercled body. The small circular woolly areoles bear up to 30 minute, translucent white plumose radial spines. The flowers are funnel-shaped, open widely, and are up to 3 cm (1.2 in) in diameter, with a slender tube up to 4.5 cm (1.8 in) in length. The flowers range from dark pink to violet purple, and the exterior of the tube is a dull pink to purple colour. The fruits are small, but remain embedded within the body of the plant.

Mammillaria theresae

Mammillaria zeilmanniana

Mammillaria zeilmanniana

Common Name: None.
Size: Height 7 cm (2.6 in), width 20 cm (8 in).
Climate: Medium elevation.
Distribution: Central Mexico.
Flowering Time: Spring.
Description: This is a globular to very short, cylindrical, freely clustering species, with a slightly bluish-green body. Individual heads are about 5 cm (2 in) in diameter and slightly more in height, and the axils between the tubercles are naked. The areoles bear up to 18 bristle-like radial spines, and up to 4 slightly stronger centrals, one of which is hooked. The radial spines are up to 1 cm (0.4 in) in length, and the hooked central which is slightly longer. The flowers, which are produced very freely in many complete rings, are 2 cm (0.8 in) in length. They are in many shades of magenta and pink, and there is a white form. The fruits are elongated, less than 1 cm (0.4 in) in length and pink when ripe, but partially hidden by the dense spination.

MATUCANA

(mä-tōō-kä'-nä)

Matucana contains some 20 species and a number of varieties. The generic name is derived from the name of a village in Peru near where the first species was discovered. The plants are flattened, globular to short and cylindrical, and can be solitary or clustering. The body diameter is 10–15 cm (4–6 in), and a few species can reach a height of 50 cm (20 in). They are green bodied plants, although in some species the body colour is almost obscured by the dense spination. The rib structure can be straight or slightly spiralled, and there are 25–50 ribs. The areoles are usually set fairly close together, are circular or oval, and have some white or pale brown wool. They bear up to 30 or so radial spines, and up to 3 centrals, but in some species it is not possible to distinguish between radials and the centrals. The radial spines can be pectinate or spreading, are usually somewhat bristly and are up to 2 cm (0.8 in) in length. The centrals can be bristly or very stout, and 2.5–7.5 cm (1–3 in) in length. The spine colour is very variable, ranging from white to brown or even black.

The flowers are zygomorphic, diurnal, up to 7.5 cm (3 in) in length, and range in colour from yellow and orange to red or even violet. The fruits are very small — less than 1 cm (0.4 in) in diameter — naked or slightly hairy, and greenish or reddish-brown when ripe.

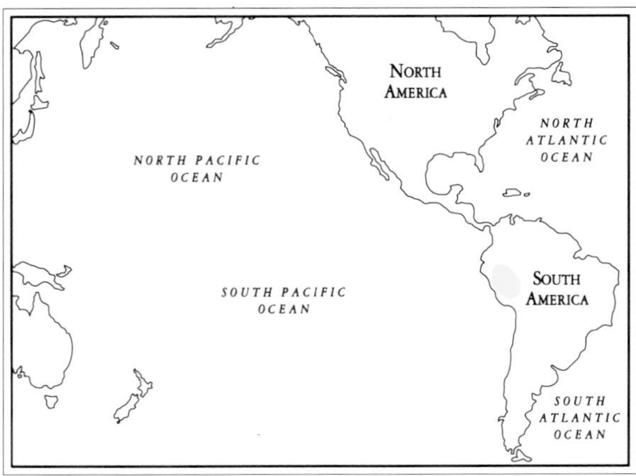

Culture: *Matucanas* are found in differing parts of Peru, and occur in quite varied locations, from well drained rocky habitats to grass areas. They are relatively easy plants to raise from seed, which is the normal method of propagation. Depending on the species, plants can reach flowering size in 3–5 years. They require a moderately well drained soil mixture, full sun, and reasonable amounts of water from spring to early autumn (fall). In winter, if kept dry, most species can tolerate temperatures to within a few degrees of freezing, some below freezing.

Matucana intertexta

Matucana crinifera

Common Name: None.
Size: Height 30 cm (12 in), width 40 cm (16 in).
Climate: High elevation.
Distribution: Peru.
Flowering Time: Summer to early autumn (fall).
Description: This species is solitary or clustering in age, when stems can reach 30 cm (12 in) in height and have a diameter of up to 10 cm (4 in). It can have up to 26 ribs, which are notched and adjacent to the areole positions. They are brownish, and bear up to 25 bristly spines, up to 5 cm (2 in) in length. The spines can vary from white and yellowish to brown with blackish tips. The zygomorphic tubular flower can be up to 5 cm (2 in) in length and yellowish-orange, with red to crimson tips to the petals. The fruits are spherical, 0.8 cm (0.24 in) in diameter and greenish-brown when ripe.

Matucana crinifera

Matucana intertexta

Common Name: None.
Size: Height 36 cm (15 in), width 18 cm (7 in).
Climate: Medium elevation.
Distribution: Peru.
Flowering Time: Summer.
Description: This species has a solitary, flattened globular habit for some years, eventually reaching 36 cm (15 in) in height and a diameter of up to 18 cm (7 in). It has a green body with up to 25 notched ribs. The large elongated areoles are not set close together, and they bear up to 12 radial spines and 2 centrals. The radial spines are 1–2 cm (0.4–0.8 in) in length, and the centrals can reach 3.5 cm (1.4 in). The radials are brown, and the centrals are brown with dark tips. The flowers are slightly zygomorphic, up to 10 cm (4 in) in length and golden-yellow to orange. The fruits are spherical, less than 1 cm (0.4 in) in diameter and greyish-brown when ripe.

Matucana intertexta

MELOCACTUS

(mĕl-ō-kăk'-tŭs)

Melocactus contains some 60 species, although many more species have been described in recent years. However, individual species vary considerably, and therefore many of the newer species are probably only differing forms of previously described species. The generic name is derived from the Gk *melos* (melon), in reference to the shape of the plant. They are globular to short and cylindrical plants, and are solitary or occasionally clustering. With maturity they produce an apical cephalium, from which the small flowers appear. The height of the plant, including the cephalium, is 0.15–1 m (.5–3 ft). The diameter of the main body of the plant is 10–20 cm (4–8 in). The body of the plant has 9–20 ribs. These are usually fairly straight, with oval-shaped areoles up to 2.5 cm (1 in) apart which bear 8–15 radial spines. The spines are often curved and appressed against the body of the plant, and can be 1.25–7.5 cm (0.5–3 in) in length. There can be 1–9 centrals which stand out from the plant and are 2–9 cm (0.8–3.6 in) in length. The spines are usually stout — except in the shorter spined species when the spines are fine — and are sometimes slightly bulbous at the base. The spine colour ranges from off-white to dark reddish-brown and almost to black. The cephalium when it appears consists of white or coloured hair, and masses of fine bristly spines in many different colours.

The flowers appear in rings and are usually virtually submerged in the cephalium. The flowers can be 1.25–3.75 cm (0.5–1.5 in) in length, but most of their length is concealed within the cephalium. The flowers are usually in varying shades of magenta. The fruits, which are elongated or slightly club-shaped, can be up to 2.5 cm (1 in) in length, and range from pink to brilliant red when ripe. The fruits emerge brightly coloured from the cephalium many weeks, months, or even a year after the cephalium appears.

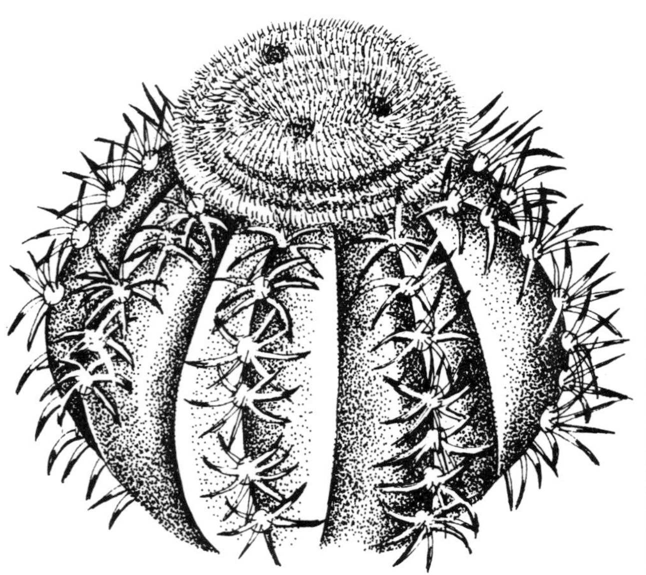

Melocactus violaceus

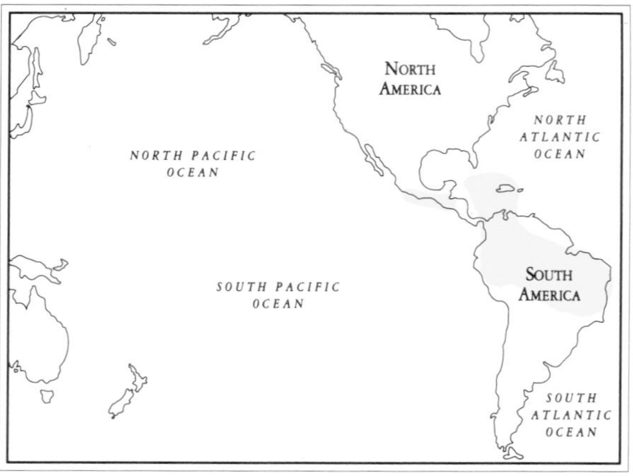

Culture: *Melocacti* are to be found on the majority of the islands in the West Indies, southern Mexico, and southwards into South America, and a lot of species come from Brazil. They are easy plants to raise from seed, but with the exception of some of the dwarf species, take many years to reach maturity, and to produce the cephalium. The species discussed can be expected to produce their cephaliums within from five to 10 years, if not less. They can be found growing in varied terrain — from almost pure sand to pure leaf mould. During warm weather, they can be watered freely from spring to early autumn (fall). In winter, in countries where cold weather is accompanied by high atmospheric humidity, they cannot withstand temperatures below 10°C (50°F).

Melocactus azureus

Common Name: Turk's Cap.
Size: Height 25 cm (10 in), width 14 cm (5.4 in).
Climate: Tropical.
Distribution: Eastern Brazil.
Flowering Time: Spring to late autumn (fall).
(NB: Given sufficient light and warmth during the winter, it can flower continuously all the year round.)
Description: This species is solitary, and short and cylindrical in habit, and has a bright blue body. It has up to 10 acute ribs which bear oval areoles with a lot of white wool. The areoles have up to 7 spreading, fairly rigid, curved radial spines, of very variable length — the longest is up to 4 cm (1.6 in). There can be 1-3 centrals, which are usually shorter than the longest radials. All the spines are off-white in colour, with brownish tips. The cephalium consists of a mass of white wool and fine bristly, reddish-brown to ginger spines. The small tubular flowers are dark red to carmine, and the elongated fruits can be 1.25 cm (0.5 in) in length and are red when ripe.

Melocactus azureus

Melocactus violaceus

Common Name: Turk's Cap.
Size: Height 10 cm (4 in), width 12.5 cm (5 in).
Climate: Tropical.
Distribution: Eastern Brazil.
Flowering Time: Spring to late autumn (fall).
Description: This species is solitary and flattened and globular, rarely exceeding 10 cm (4 in) in diameter. The light green body has up to 10 ribs, and the small circular areoles have no wool and are set fairly close together. They bear up to 7 curved radial spines, which are 0.5-1.5 cm (0.2-0.6 in) in length, and sometimes one central of a similar length. The spines are slightly curved and reddish-violet when new, becoming greyish with darkish tips. The cephalium is about 7 cm (2.8 in) in diameter, and consists of white wool and a mass of short fine ginger spines. The tiny tubular flowers are in varying shades of pink, and the slender fruit is slightly club-shaped and red when ripe.

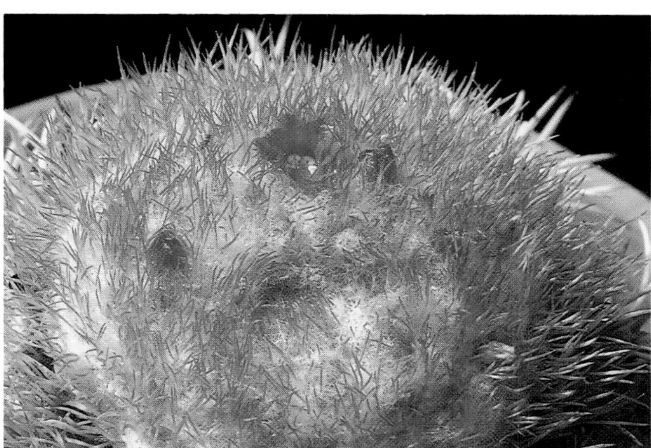

Melocactus matanzanus

Melocactus matanzanus

Common Name: Turk's Cap.
Size: Height 10 cm (4 in), width 12.5 cm (5 in).
Climate: Tropical.
Distribution: Eastern Brazil.
Flowering Time: Spring to late autumn (fall).
Description: This species has a solitary, flattened globular habit, and rarely exceeds 12.5 cm (5 in) in diameter. The green body has up to 10 somewhat rounded ribs, and the sunken areoles have no hair or wool and are set well apart. They bear up to 8 spreading, rigid off-white to grey spines with brownish tips. Some specimens have uniformly brown spines. It is difficult to differentiate between the centrals and the radials, and they can be up to 2.5 cm (1 in) in length. The cephalium consists of white wool and masses of fine ginger spines, from which a profusion of tiny pink to pale magenta flowers appear. The elongated fruits are up to 1.25 cm (0.5 in) in length and are red when ripe.

Melocactus violaceus

Mila

(mī'-lă)

Mila contains some 12 species and a few varieties. The generic name is an anagram of Lima, the capital of Peru, from where several species originate. They are dwarf, freely clustering plants, and are rather soft bodied with a distinct rib structure. The individual stems are 7.5–30 cm (3–12 in) in length and have a diameter of 2.5–5 cm (1–2 in). The shorter stemmed species hold their stems fairly erect, but the longer stemmed species are somewhat sprawling in their habit. The stems have 10–15 shallow ribs, with small areoles set close together which sometimes possess a little brownish or white wool. There can be 8–40 fine, spreading radial spines, 0.5–1 cm (0.2–0.4 in) in length, and 3–7 centrals, 1–3 cm (0.4–1.2 in) in length. The centrals tend to stand out from the stems further and are usually somewhat stronger than the radials. The spine colour ranges from off-white, grey and yellowish to brown, with some species having distinctly darker tipped spines.

The yellow or cream coloured flowers are funnel-shaped, have a short tube, appear from near the tops of the stems, and are 1.5–2 cm (0.6–0.8 in) in diameter. The fruits are small naked berries; yellow to reddish-brown when ripe.

Culture: *Milas* are native to central Peru, and grow in rock fissures and among grass. They are very easy plants to grow, and can be grown from seed or cuttings. From spring to autumn (fall) they can be watered freely, and appreciate a sunny position. In winter, if kept dry, they can tolerate very cool conditions and light frosts.

Mila caespitosa

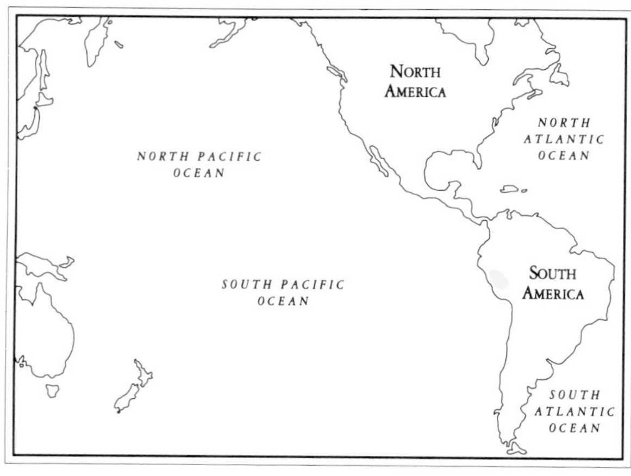

Mila caespitosa

Mila caespitosa

Common Name: None.
Size: Height 15 cm (6 in), width 30 cm (12 in).
Climate: High elevation.
Distribution: Central Peru.
Flowering Time: Summer.
Description: Clumps of 50 or more stems are not uncommon. Individual stems can reach 15 cm (6 in) in length and up to 3 cm (1.2 in) in diameter, and have a semi-prostrate habit. The pale green stems have up to 10 ribs bearing small areoles, with initially brownish wool, changing to white or grey with age. There are about 20 fine, spreading radial spines, 0.5–1 cm (0.2–0.4 in) in length, and 3–6 stouter centrals, some of which can be 3 cm (1.2 in) in length. The spines can be yellowish-brown changing to grey or off-white with age. The yellow, funnel-shaped flowers are 1.5 cm (0.6 in) in diameter, and the exterior of the tube is greenish. The tiny berry-like fruits are greenish-brown when ripe.

Myrtillocactus

(mûr-tĭl'-ō-kăk'-tŭs)

Myrtillocactus contains four species, and the generic name originates from the resemblance of the flowers to those of the Myrtle (*Lagerstroemia*). They are columnar, freely branching plants. The stems have 5–8 ribs, which are bluish, bluish-green or green in colour. The areoles are set well apart, and have 5–8 spreading radial spines, which are rigid and up to 2.5 cm (1 in) in length. There is usually only one central spine, which stands straight out from the areole, and is 4–7 cm (1.6–2.8 in) in length. The spines vary in colour from grey and brown, to black.

The flowers usually appear in groups from an areole, which is uncommon in the family Cactaceae. The funnel-shaped flowers are 2.5–3.5 cm (1–1.4 in) in diameter, and creamy-white, greenish, or pink in colour. The fruits are spherical, glabrous, reddish to purplish-black and similar to black currants when ripe, and are edible.

Culture: *Myrtillocacti* are native to central and western Mexico, and to Guatemala, and are to be found in many differing types of locations with varied soils and rainfall. They are very easy plants to grow from seed or cuttings, and develop quite rapidly. In cultivation they can be watered freely from spring to autumn (fall), but should be kept dry in winter. In warmer climates the plants will tolerate water during the winter, and as a result all the species are superb for landscaping. However, the plants can form orange blotches if the temperature drops too much below 10°C (50°F).

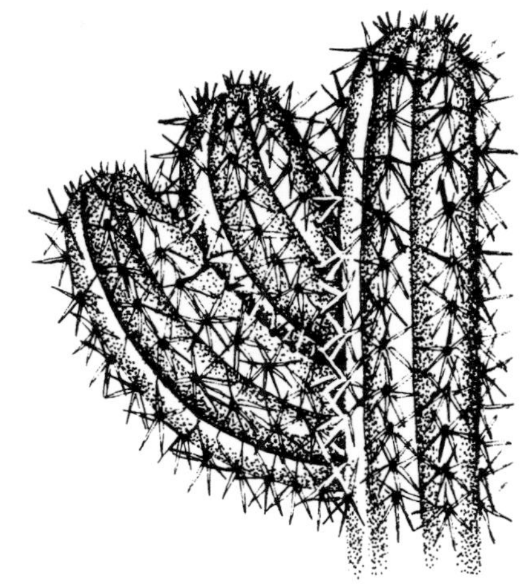

Myrtillocactus geometrizans

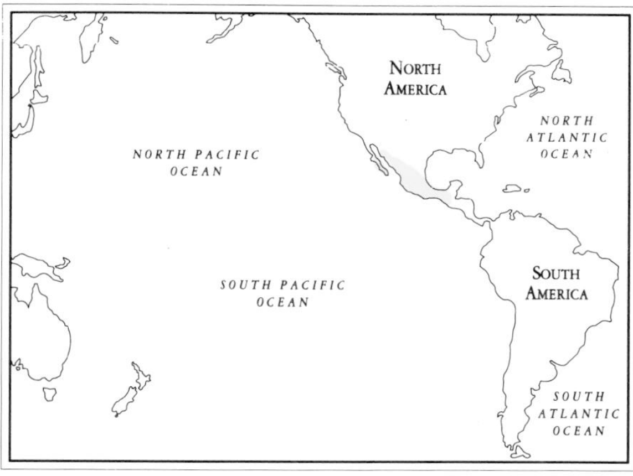

Myrtillocactus geometrizans

Myrtillocactus geometrizans

Common Name: None.
Size: Height 4 m (13 ft) width 3 m (9.5 ft).
Climate: Medium elevation.
Distribution: Central Mexico.
Flowering Time: Spring to early summer.
Description: This freely branching species has a tree-like habit and a basal trunk. The mature branches can be up to 10 cm (4 in) in diameter and are chalky-blue to bright blue in colour. The stems have 5–6 ribs, and the areoles are set well apart and bear 5 or more spreading radial spines which are up to 2 cm (0.8 in) in length, and one central up to 7 cm (2.8 in) in length. The spines are angular and very stout, and grey to black in colour. The funnel-shaped flowers can be up to 3 cm (1.2 in) in diameter and are greenish-white in colour. The tiny berry-like fruits are bluish-purple when ripe.

NEOBESSEYA

(nē-ō-bĕs'-ē-ȧ)

Neobesseya contains some seven species. The generic name honours Dr C. E. Bessey (1845–1915) of the University of Nebraska, United States. They are small, solitary or, more often than not, freely clustering plants and are very soft bodied. The prominent tubercles each have a furrow as with the genus *Coryphantha* (see page 63) and are 0.5–2.5 cm (0.2–1 in) in length. The heads are usually 2.5–7.5 cm (1–3 in) in diameter, but the freely clustering species can produce a clump 30 cm (12 in) in diameter. The areoles are usually quite prominent, have white wool, and bear 7–20 radial spines and 1–3 centrals — although they are sometimes absent. The fine spines rarely exceed 1.25 cm (0.5 in) in length.

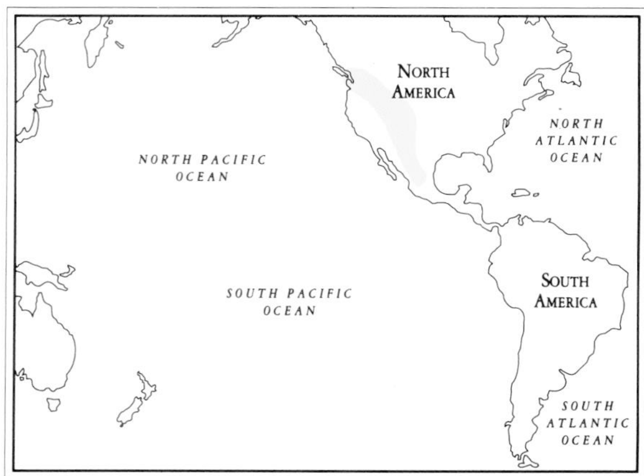

The flowers appear from near the centre of each head, are 2.5–5 cm (1–2 in) in diameter, and range from greenish-yellow to pink in colour. The fruits are globular to egg-shaped, 1–2 cm (0.4–0.8 in) in diameter, and are usually red when fully ripe. They contain a small number of very hard black seeds.

Culture: With the exception of *N. asperispina* from Mexico, the Neobesseyas from central, south-western and north-western United States are very frost resistant. They are invariably found growing among grass, and during the hotter months the smaller species become almost invisible. With the approach of winter, the plants tend to shrivel considerably in order to safely withstand severe frosts and snow. *Neobesseyas* are easily raised from seed, and will often flower within two years. They are ideal subjects for a hardy cactus rockery in colder climates, provided they have exceptionally good drainage. When grown in a greenhouse they require some shade during the heat of summer, and should be kept cool during the winter months.

Neobesseya similis

Neobesseya asperispina

Common Name: None.
Size: Height 2 cm (0.8 in), width 6 cm (2.4 in).
Climate: Medium elevation.
Distribution: Northern Mexico.
Flowering Time: Early summer.
Description: This is usually a solitary, flattened globular plant, not more than 6 cm (2.4 in) in diameter. It consists of acute conical tubercles which are dark bluish-green in colour. The areoles contain quite a lot of white wool, and bear up to 10 radial spines and sometimes one central. The subulate radials are quite thin, up to 1 cm (0.4 in) in length and off-white to grey in colour. The central spine when present, is similar in colour, and slightly stouter. The flowers are up to 3 cm (1.2 in) in diameter and off-white to pale greenish-yellow in colour. The fruits are spherical, about 1.5 cm (0.6 in) in diameter and reddish-green when ripe.

Neobesseya asperispina

Neobesseya missouriensis

Neobesseya missouriensis

Common Name: Missouri Pincushion.
Size: Height 2-3 cm (0.8-1.2 in), width 15 cm (6 in).
Climate: Medium to high elevation.
Distribution: Central and south-western United States.
Flowering Time: Early summer.
Description: A dwarf growing, solitary or clustering species, with individual heads from 5-7.5 cm (2-3 in) in diameter. The dark green heads are strongly tubercled, and the areoles have a little white wool. Each areole bears from 10-20 radial spines, and sometimes one central. The spines are up to 1.25 cm (0.5 in) in length, are off-white to grey in colour (usually with brown tips), acicular and slightly curved. The flowers are about 2.5 cm (1 in) in diameter, yellowish-green but with somewhat darker median stripes down the petals. The fruits are spherical, 1 cm (0.4 in) in diameter, and bright red when ripe.

Neobesseya similis

Neobesseya similis

Common Name: None.
Size: Height 15 cm (6 in), width 30 cm (12 in).
Climate: Medium elevation.
Distribution: Eastern Texas, United States.
Flowering Time: Early summer.
Description: A freely clustering species with individual heads that can reach 7.5 cm (3 in) in diameter, and have tubercles up to 2 cm (0.8 in) in length. Each tubercle has a prominent furrow and plenty of white wool at each areole. There are up to 15 radial spines which are white with slightly brown tips. The central spines, when present, are similar but slightly stouter. The pale yellow or greenish-yellow flowers are about 5 cm (2 in) in diameter. The slightly egg-shaped fruits are about 2 cm (0.8 in) in length and bright red when ripe.

NEOCHILENIA

(nē-ō-chĭl'-ĕn-ĭ-ă)

Neochilenia contains over 50 species and a few varieties. The generic name is derived partly from the Gk prefix *neo* (new), and the country name Chile, from which all of the species originate. The genus name was erected by Curt Backeberg and were previously included in the genus *Neoporteria* (see page 137). *Neochilenias* are mostly spherical or elongated, and in some species are very dwarf — these species usually have a swollen taproot. The rib structure can be very distinct, or tuberculate in appearance, and the body colour ranges from green and reddish hues, to almost slate black. The areoles tend to be oval, have hair, and can be quite large relative to the size of the plant. They bear 5–20 radial spines and 1–10 centrals. The radials can be minute, but in a few species are up to 3 cm (1.2 in) in length, and the centrals, which are not always present, are usually longer. The radials are often appressed and quite fine, as with *N. reichii*, while some species, such as *N. hankeana*, have much longer, curved spines which stand out from the plant.

The funnel-shaped flowers generally are 3–5 cm (1.2–2 in) in diameter, and the colour varies from almost white or yellowish to different shades of red. The exterior of the short tube is often very hairy. The fruits are slightly elongated, up to 2 cm (0.8 in) in length, hollow and various colours when ripe. The seeds are dispersed by a basal pore.

Culture: *Neochilenias* come from many, often very different, parts of Chile. The majority of species flower within a few years from seed, and then do so very freely and regularly each year. They are usually grown from seed, and require a soil that drains moderately well. From spring to autumn (fall), they can be watered fairly freely, and if kept dry in winter they can tolerate a minimum temperature of 5°C (40°F). Many of the species will withstand light frosts.

Neochilenia reichii

Neochilenia hankeana

Common Name: None.
Size: Height 15 cm (6 in), width 10 cm (4 in).
Climate: Medium elevation.
Distribution: Northern Chile.
Flowering Time: Late spring.
Description: This species is initially globular with a diameter of 10 cm (4 in), and elongates slightly to a height of 15 cm (6 in) with age. The body of the plant is green, and it has up to 13 ribs which have very prominent chins above each areole. The areoles contain some white wool, and bear up to 7 radial spines and 1-4 centrals. The general spine length is 1.5-3 cm (0.6-1.2 in). They are black when young but pale with age. The funnel-shaped flowers are up to 4 cm (1.6 in) in diameter, and are creamy-white with a green tint in the throat. The slightly elongated fruits are 1.5 cm (0.6 in) in length, have some blackish hair, and are reddish-green when ripe.

Neochilenia hankeana

Neochilenia reichii

Neochilenia reichii

Common Name: None.
Size: Height 8-9 cm (3.2-3.6 in).
Climate: Medium elevation.
Distribution: Northern Chile.
Flowering Time: Summer.
Description: This is a slow growing, dwarf species, no more than 3.5 cm (1.4 in) in diameter, and eventually reaching 8-9 cm (3.2-3.6 in) in height. The crown of the plant is somewhat sunken and contains matted hair, and the olive-green to brownish body is almost obscured by the minute, appressed, interlacing spine structure. This species has a very dense tuberculate rib structure, and the whitish hairy areoles bear up to 9 white or grey spines. The yellowish flowers are 3-4 cm (1.2-1.6 in) in length and in diameter, and have greyish hair on the exterior of the short tube. The reddish fruits are 1.25 cm (0.5 in) in length, also have greyish hair and dehisce by a basal pore when ripe.

NEOGOMESIA

(nē-ō-gŏm'- ēes-ĭ-ă)

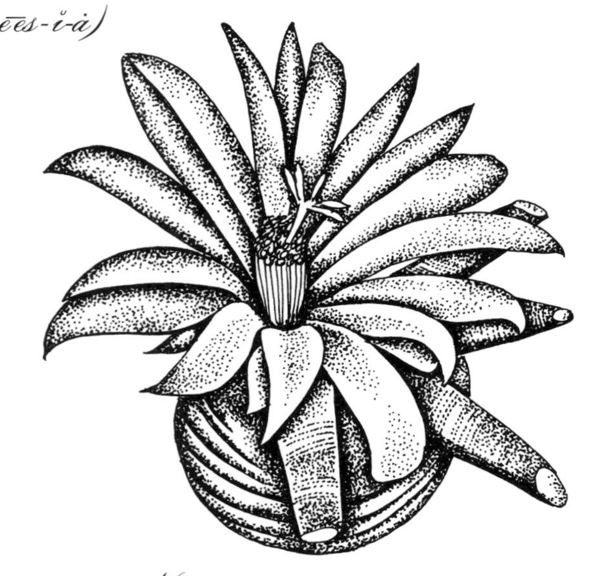

Neogomesia agavioides

Neogomesia is a monotypic genus, and the generic name honours engineer M. Gomez, the governor of the State of Taumalipas, Mexico, where the genus was discovered. It was first described in 1941. Although some authorities consider that this plant belongs within the genus *Ariocarpus* (see page 37), it is very distinctive in many ways — even as regards its cultural requirements. It is a dwarf solitary plant with a very succulent taproot, and it possesses elongated tubercles which have very woolly areoles set back from the tips. The plants rarely exceed 8 cm (3.2 in) in diameter, and the tubercles reach about 4 cm (1.6 in) in length. They are dark green to bluish green in colour, with a slightly roughened surface.

The flowers are funnel-shaped and have 2 cm (0.8 in) long tubes, giving the flowers a total length of about 5 cm (2 in). The flowers, which normally only stay open for one day, range from pink to pale magenta. The fruits are slightly club-shaped, up to 2.5 cm (1 in) in length and are red when ripe.

Culture: This plant comes from central Mexico, where it grows on limestone hills. It is not as slow growing as most species of *Ariocarpus*, and it can be raised from seed quite easily, and grows to flowering size within five years. It likes a well drained soil, but can be watered quite freely during spring to early autumn (fall). However, in cultivation when temperatures exceed 37°C (100°F), the plants prefer a little shade, otherwise some of the tubercles can shrivel and die back. In winter plants should be dry, and can withstand temperatures to within a few degrees of freezing.

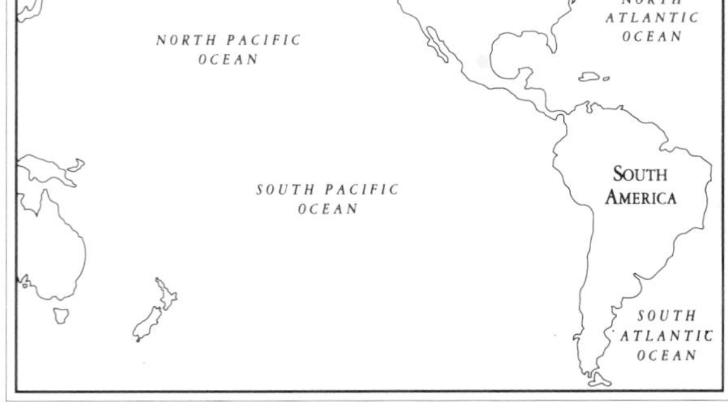

Neogomesia agavioides

Neogomesia agavioides

COMMON NAME: None.
SIZE: Height 3 cm (1.2 in), width 8 cm (3.2 in).
CLIMATE: Medium elevation.
DISTRIBUTION: Central Mexico.
FLOWERING TIME: Late autumn (fall) to early winter.
DESCRIPTION: As there is only one species, this information is found above.

NEOLLOYDIA

(nē-ō-loi'-dĭ-ă)

Neolloydia contains some 10 species, and the generic name honours Prof. Frances E. Lloyd. They are usually freely clustering plants, which branch from the base and have short, cylindrical stems 10–20 cm (4–8 in) in height. The Texas form of *N. conoidea* (page 136), is usually solitary. The green to bluish-green stems are prominently tubercled, and have a furrow behind the areole position. Between the tubercles there is usually a lot of white wool (see the illustration of *N. conoidea* below). The areoles bear 6–25 spreading radial spines, 0.4–1 cm (0.16–0.4 in) in length. The 1–5 centrals, when present, are usually stouter and stand out further from the plant, and can be up to 2.5 cm (1 in) in length. The centrals can be hooked, and the colour of the radials and the centrals varies considerably from white to brown or black.

The flowers are funnel-shaped, 1.5–6 cm (0.6–2.4 in) in diameter, and range in colour from greenish-yellow to yellow, and purple or magenta. The fruits possess a few scales, are green or brown, and become dry and papery when ripe.

Culture: These plants are to be found in central and northern Mexico, south-western United States, and Cuba, in many differing types of location and soil, but usually require well drained positions. They are mostly easy plants to grow from seed or from cuttings of individual heads, and can be watered moderately freely from spring to early autumn (fall). If kept dry in winter all but the Cuban species can withstand temperatures near freezing. Plants of *N. conoidea* in Texas endure frosts and snow.

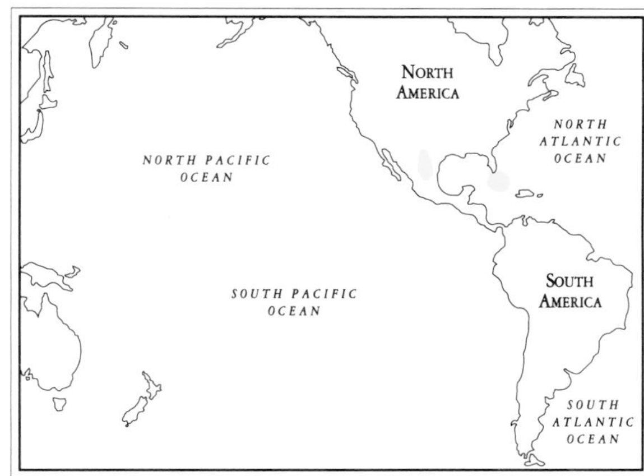

Neolloydia conoidea

Neolloydia conoidea

Common Name: None.
Size: Height 10 cm (4 in), width 20 cm (8 in).
Climate: Medium elevation.
Distribution: Central and northern Mexico, and south-western United States.
Flowering Time: Spring and early summer.
Description: This is a solitary or clustering species, with prominently tubercled stems up to 10 cm (4 in) in height, and 5 cm (2 in) in diameter. There is a lot of white wool between the tubercles, and the areoles bear up to 16 thin white radial spines, which are somewhat appressed against the plant. There are usually 4-5 centrals, which are much stronger, stand out from the plant, are up to 3 cm (1.2 in) in length and are black in colour. The funnel-shaped flowers are 5-6 cm (2-2.4 in) in diameter and are various shades of purple or magenta. The fruits are very small and are brownish-black until they dry up.

Neolloydia conoidea

Neolloydia conoidea in habitat

Neolloydia grandiflora

Common Name: None.
Size: Height 10 cm (4 in), width 4-5 cm (1.6-2 in).
Climate: Medium elevation.
Distribution: Central Mexico.
Description: Normally a solitary, cylindrical species, with a dark green body, tubercled, with a lot of white wool in the axils between the tubercles. The white areoles bear up to 25 white, very short radial spines. There can be one or two centrals, slightly longer and stronger, white with black tips. The flowers open very widely, and are 5 cm (2 in) or more in diameter, and appear in varying shades of purple. The fruits are spherical, very small, with a few scales, and are dark green when ripe.

Neolloydia grandiflora

NEOPORTERIA

(nē'-ō-pōr-tĕr'-ĭ-ȧ)

Neoporteria contains over 24 species and many varieties. The generic name honours Carlos Porter, who was a Chilean entomologist. It is a very variable genus with some fairly small globular species no more than 10 cm (4 in) in diameter, and other large cylindrical species up to 1.5 m (5 ft) high. Most species have a strong rib structure, with 10–25 ribs, which are sometimes notched into chins at the areole positions. The areoles are oval and up to 1.5 cm (0.6 in) in length. The spination is also very varied: from quite stout spines (as with *Neoporteria subgibbosa* page 138), to bristly, twisted, and interlacing spines. There are 10–50 radials and up to 6 centrals per areole, and the longest spine rarely exceeds 3.5 cm (1.4 in). They range in colour from almost white to golden yellow, brown and nearly black.

The flowers do not open widely and consist of narrow petals, rarely exceeding 5 cm (2 in) in length (usually much less). Produced from near the centre of the plant, they are usually carmine-pink in colour. The fruits are small, oblong, and range in colour from yellow to red when ripe.

Culture: *Neoporterias* come from central and northern Chile, and are found in very different habitats, from near sea level, to high altitudes. They are mostly easy to grow, and can be raised from seed. They require a moderately well drained soil and can be watered freely from spring to early autumn (fall), and if kept dry in winter will withstand temperatures close to freezing point. Many species flower in early spring and again in autumn (fall), and the smaller species produce an abundance of flowers.

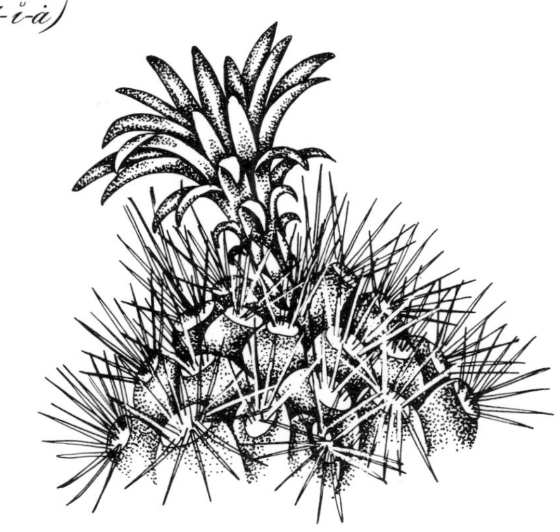

Neoporteria subgibbosa

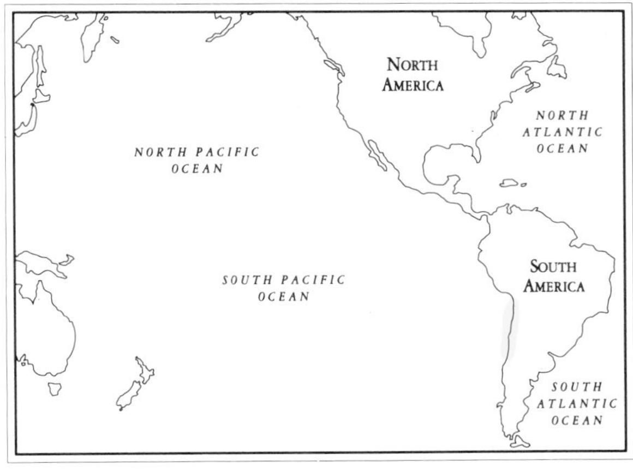

Neoporteria cephalophora

Neoporteria cephalophora

Common Name: None.
Size: Height 15 cm (6 in), width 7.5 cm (3 in).
Climate: Low elevation.
Distribution: Northern Chile.
Flowering Time: Early spring and again in the autumn (fall).
Description: This species is solitary, becoming slightly cylindrical in age, has a dark green to olive-green body with up to 20 ribs, and these are sometimes slightly spiralled. The areoles are oval, with some whitish hair, and are set quite closely together, and bear up to 20 or so fine, almost hair like spines, from 1–2.5 cm (0.4–1 in) in length. The spine colour varies from off-white to almost golden-brown. The flowers are about 2 cm (0.8 in) in length, yellowish in the throat, but with rose-pink to cerise petals. Fruits are almost spherical, very small, and olive-green when ripe.

Neoporteria subgibbosa

Common Name: None.
Size: Height 1 m (3 ft), width 10 cm (4 in).
Climate: Mediterranean.
Distribution: Coastal regions of central Chile.
Flowering Time: Spring and again in the autumn (fall).
Description: This is a short cylindrical species. It has up to 20 ribs, which are somewhat tuberculate in structure and have large oval-shaped areoles. The areoles contain a lot of white wool when new and bear up to 24 stout spreading radial spines, and up to 4 even stouter, subulate centrals. The spines are golden-brown in colour, tending to be slightly paler lower down. The flowers are 4 cm (1.6 in) in length, carmine-pink in colour, with a yellowish tinge towards the base of the short tube. The fruits are oblong, 1.25 cm (0.5 in) in length, pink, and dehisce by a means of a basal pore.

Neoporteria subgibbosa

Neoporteria nigrihorrida

Neoporteria nigrihorrida

Common Name: None.
Size: Height 7.5 cm (3 in), width 10–12.5 cm (4–5 in).
Climate: Low elevation.
Distribution: Central Chile.
Flowering Time: Twice, spring and autumn (fall).
Description: A solitary or sparingly clustering species, it is globular, with individual heads rarely exceeding 7.5 cm (3 in) in height and diameter. The body of the plant is greyish-green to slate coloured, with up to 18 ribs. The circular off-white areoles bear up to 16 interlacing radial spines, and up to 7 subulate centrals. The radial spines are spreading, fairly stiff, off-white to yellowish, and up to 1.5 cm (0.6 in) in length. The centrals are stouter, slightly curved, and stand out from the plant. These central spines are black when new, but quickly change to silvery-grey. The flowers are 4 cm (1.6 in) long, creamy-white in the centre, with pink to carmine petals, particularly the upper parts of the petals. The fruits are spherical, very small, and reddish-green when ripe.

Neoporteria villosa

Common Name: None.
Size: Height 15 cm (6 in), width 7.5 cm (3 in).
Climate: Low elevation.
Distribution: Northern Chile.
Flowering Time: Spring and again in the autumn (fall).
Description: Solitary, becoming slightly columnar in age, this species has a grey-green to slate coloured body. It has up to 15 ribs, with chin-like protuberances by the areoles. These are circular, with white wool, and bear up to 30 or more fine spreading radial spines, and up to three or four centrals. The radial spines are up to 1.25 cm (0.5 in) in length, and off-white to brown; the centrals are stouter, slightly longer, and usually blackish. The flowers are about 2 cm (0.8 in) in diameter, ranging in colour from white with pink or cerise petals, to almost completely cerise coloured. The fruits are spherical, very small, and brownish when ripe.

Neoporteria villosa

NOTOCACTUS

(nō-tō-kăk'-tŭs)

Notocactus contains over 35 species and numerous varieties. The generic name is derived from the Gk meaning 'southern cactus'. *Notocacti* vary from dwarf globular or flattened globular species no more than 7.5–10 cm (3–4 in) in diameter, to columnar forms up to 1 m (3 ft) in height. The body colour ranges from pale green to dark green, sometimes tinged with reddish-brown. They can be solitary or clustering, with a clear rib structure with 10–30 ribs. The ribs are often notched into low warts, on which the areoles are positioned. The areoles vary in size, are set very closely together in some species, are usually circular and have some white, yellowish, or brownish wool. There can be up to 20 bristle-like radial spines, which are often appressed against the plant and are 0.6–2.5 cm (0.24–1 in) in length, and up to 6 centrals. They are curved or straight, stand out further from the plant, and are occasionally slightly stouter and up to twice the length of the radials. The spine colour varies from white, yellow and gold, to reddish-brown.

The flowers which come from near the centre of the plant tend to be funnel-shaped, and usually have a short tube. With the exception of the smaller flowered species, they are fairly widely opening, and are 1.25–7.5 cm (0.5–3 in) in diameter. The exterior of the flower tube has scales and bristly spines, which are the same colour as the spines on the plant. The flower colour varies from yellow to red and deep magenta. The fruits are small, up to 1.25 cm (0.5 in) in diameter, and covered with short bristles.

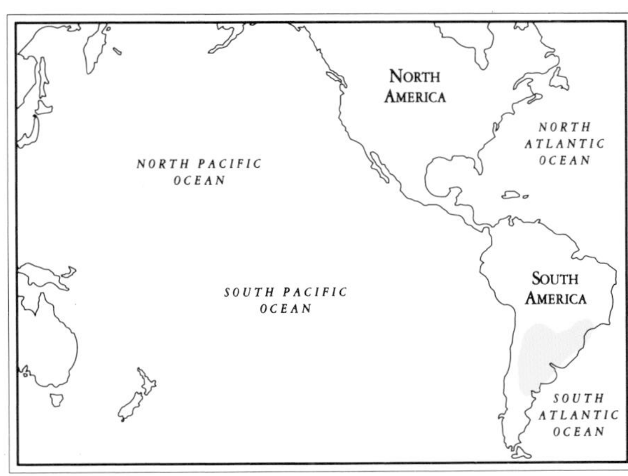

Culture: *Notocacti* come from Brazil, northern Argentina, Paraguay and Uruguay. They are found in moderately well drained situations, in rock crevices, sand and even grass, and are all easy plants to grow from seed, and the clustering species can be divided. The less densely spined species prefer to be grown in little light shade, but all are exceedingly freely flowering plants, and like a reasonable amount of water from spring to autumn (fall). In winter, if kept dry, all species can tolerate temperatures to within a few degrees of freezing.

Notocactus uebelmannianus

Notocactus crassigibbus

Common Name: None.
Size: Height 8 cm (3.2 in), diameter 15 cm (6 in).
Climate: Medium elevation.
Distribution: Southern Brazil.
Flowering Time: Late spring and summer.
Description: Usually has a solitary, flattened globular habit, and a dark green body which is sometimes tinged with reddish-brown — often from too much sun. It has up to 15 very rounded, tuberculate ribs which bear quite hairy areoles. These bear up to 10 twisted spines which are appressed against the plant and up to 2.5 cm (1 in) in length. There is usually one downwards-pointing central, which is slightly longer than the radials. The spines are usually pale yellow, as are the funnel-shaped flowers, which have a somewhat longer tube than many of the species in this genus. The fruits are less than 1.25 cm (0.5 in) in length, and green, with short white and yellow spines.

Notocactus crassigibbus

Notocactus uebelmannianus

Notocactus leninghausii

Common Name: None.
Size: Height 1 m (3 ft), width 30 cm (12 in).
Climate: Medium elevation.
Distribution: Southern Brazil.
Flowering Time: Late spring, summer; occasionally early autumn (fall).
Description: This is eventually a columnar species, grows up to 1 m (3 ft) in height, and clusters freely from the base in maturity. Individual stems rarely exceed 8 cm (3.2 in) in diameter. The crown of the plant, particularly in older plants, is usually obliquely angled. It has a pale green body with up to 30 fine ribs, and the small areoles are set very closely together and bear up to 15 short, fine, whitish-yellow to yellow radial spines. There can be up to 4 centrals, which are more bristly, curved, up to 4 cm (1.6 in) in length, and are more golden-yellow than the radials. The flowers which appear from the crown of the plant are funnel-shaped, yellow, open very wide, and have a diameter of about 5 cm (2 in). The exterior of the base of the tube is densely covered with fine, bristly golden spines. The 1.25 cm (0.5 in) diameter fruits are of a similar colour.

Notocactus leninghausii

Notocactus uebelmannianus

Common Name: None.
Size: Height 8 cm (3.2 in), width 17 cm (7 in).
Climate: Medium elevation.
Distribution: Brazil.
Flowering Time: Summer.
Description: A solitary, somewhat flattened globular species, 17 cm (7 in) in diameter. The dark green body can have up to 16 rounded, tubercled ribs, with a groove beneath each areole position. The slightly white areoles are fairly close together and bear up to 6 appressed radial spines. There are no centrals. The greyish-white spines are 1–3 cm (0.4–1.2 in) in length. The funnel-shaped flowers are up to 5 cm (2 in) in diameter, wine-red to deep magenta; the fruits are spherical, small, and red when ripe.

OBREGONIA

(ō-brĕ-gō'-nĭ-ă)

Obregonia is a monotypic genus erected in 1925, and the generic name honours the then President of Mexico. It is an unusual, solitary globular plant which can grow up to 15 cm (6 in) in diameter. It consists entirely of thick tubercles which appear as green angular scales, with their upper part curving outwards. They are up to 2.5 cm (1 in) across at their base, and keeled on their underside. The areoles at their tips have some white wool, from which up to 4 weak spines appear. These can be up to 1.5 cm (0.6 in) in length, but soon drop off.

The flowers appear from the white woolly centre of the plant, and are up to 2.5 cm (1 in) in diameter. They are usually white, but pale pink forms are not unknown. The fruits are very small white or pale pink berries, which usually dry up completely, and dehisce irregularly, scattering the seeds in the woolly crown of the plant.

Culture: This plant is found over a rather limited area of north-east Mexico, often seeking protection from the sun by growing in rocky positions under other xerophytic shrubs. It is quite slow growing although not as slow growing as for example most species of *Ariocarpus* (see page 37), and it requires a well drained soil. During hot weather it can be watered freely and it requires light shade, otherwise the plant reddens and stops growing. It is not unduly difficult to grow from seed, and flowering plants can be produced in 5–10 years. In winter it should be kept dry, and will tolerate a minimum temperature of 5°C (40°F).

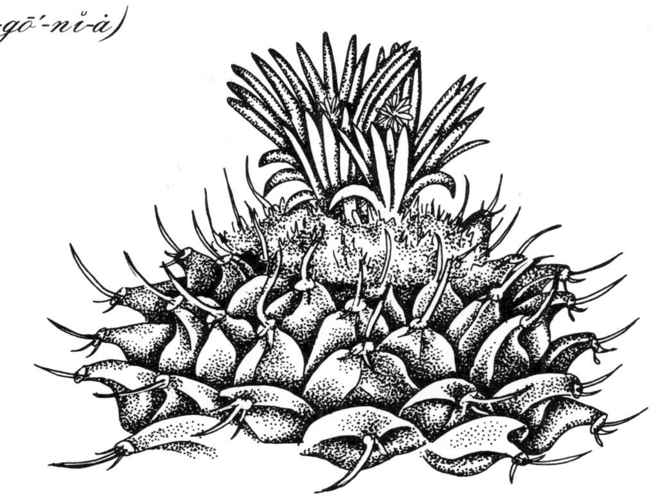

Obregonia denegrii

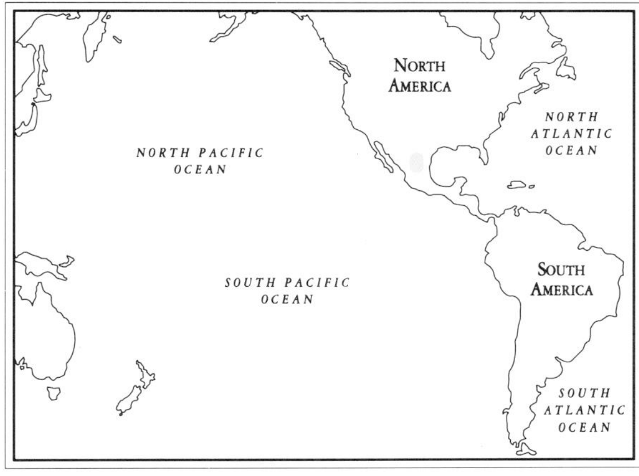

Obregonia denegrii

Obregonia denegrii

Common Name: None.
Size: Height 4 cm (1.4 in), width 15 cm (6 in).
Climate: Medium elevation.
Distribution: As above.
Flowering Time: Summer.
Description: As there is only one species, this information is found above.

OPUNTIA

(ō-pŭn'-shĭ-à)

Opuntia is a large and very varied genus, with nearly 400 species and a large number of varieties. The genus is named for Opuntia, a town in Greece where some cactus-like plants were said to have grown. *Opuntias* range from miniatures with small spherical joints, to larger species 2 m (6.5 ft) in height with cylindrical joints or stems, and flat padded species. They may be sprawling plants, erect bushes, or tall trees — sometimes with a basal cylindrical trunk. However, they all have many small barbed glochids at the areole positions, and usually have long stout spines which can be sheathed and viciously barbed, as with *O. bigelovii* (see page 144), or flat, harmless and papery, as with *O. platyacantha* (see page 145).

The flowers are very uniform in their general appearance, do not have a tube, but usually have a large swollen ovary, which also possesses areoles full of glochids. There is also a tremendous range in flower colour from white or yellow, to orange, red and magenta. The fruits are spherical to ovoid, but the upper surface where the petals originate is usually concave to some degree. They are 2.5–7.5 cm (1–3 in) in length and yellow to red in colour when ripe. In quite a number of species, particularly those similar to *O. fulgida*, the fruits are sterile, and the flowers appear year after year from the previous sterile fruits. These sterile fruits can also drop off and take root. Perhaps it is no wonder, given the many differing methods *Opuntia* have of perpetuating themselves, that this genus is so prolific.

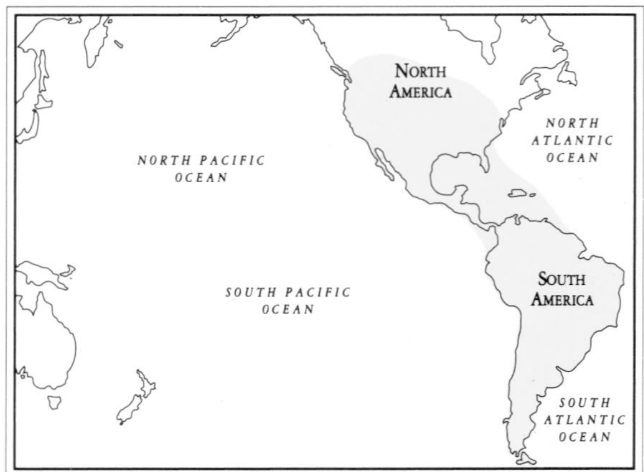

Culture: *Opuntias* have the widest distribution of any genus within the family Cactaceae, from as far north as parts of Canada, southwards through the United States, Mexico, Central America, the West Indies, Galapagos Islands, all of South America, to as far south as Tierra del Fuego in Patagonia. They can be found at sea level to altitudes of 3700 m (about 12 136 ft). Most species are exceedingly easy to grow and do well in a variety of soils, appreciating plenty of water from spring to autumn (fall). Some of the West Indian species however cannot withstand temperatures approaching freezing during the winter, while many species can cope with temperatures to –18°C (0°F), or even lower. A list of frost hardy species which will flower very freely each year can be found on page 29. *Opuntias* in general are superb flowering plants, particularly when they can be given a free root run. *Opuntia microdasys* fa. *alba* is one of the smaller species (50 cm (20 in) in diameter and 30 cm (12 in) in height), which is a prolific flowerer, producing over 200 flowers in late spring.

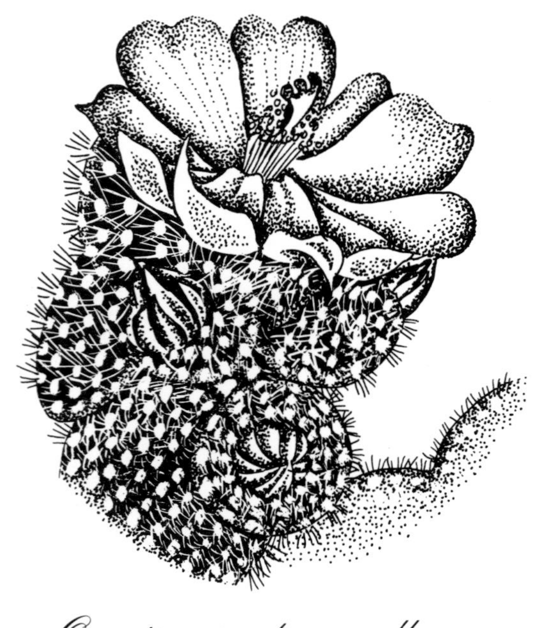

Opuntia microdasys fa. *alba*

Opuntia acanthocarpa var. *thornberi*

Common Name: Thornber Cholla.
Size: Height 1.6 m (5 ft), width 1 m (3 ft).
Climate: Medium elevation.
Distribution: South-western United States.
Flowering Time: Early summer.
Description: This is a cylindrically jointed species, which branches freely. The individual green joints, which are often tinged with red, are 30–50 cm (12–20 in) in length and up to 2 cm (0.8 in) in diameter. The joints are tuberculate, and the areoles bear yellow glochids and up to 10 brownish spines, measuring 2–3 cm (0.8–1.2 in) in length. The flowers are around 3 cm (1.2 in) in diameter, and nearly 4 cm (1.6 in) in length. They tend to be cupped, rather than open completely flat, and are a lovely dusky orange colour. The fruits are up to 2 cm (0.8 in) in length, with masses of short needle-like spines.

Opuntia acanthocarpa var. *thornberi*

Opuntia ammophila

Opuntia ammophila

Common Name: None.
Size: Height 2 m (6 ft), width 1 m (3 ft).
Climate: Mediterranean.
Distribution: South-eastern United States.
Flowering Time: Spring and early summer.
Description: This is an erect growing, flat padded species. Mature specimens have a cylindrical trunk up to 25 cm (10 in) in diameter. The green oval-shaped pads are 15–20 cm (6–8 in) in length. The areoles are set well apart, and bear cream glochids, and spines 1–6 cm (0.4–2.4 in) in length. The spines are more prominent when grown in the open air than when grown under glass, and range in colour from yellowish to reddish-brown. The flowers are 6–8 cm (1.2–3.2 in) in diameter and are bright yellow. The fruits are ovoid, 3 cm (1.2 in) in length, have many glochids, and are purple when ripe.

Opuntia basilaris

Common Name: Beavertail Prickly Pear.
Size: Height 20 cm (8 in), width 1 m (3 ft).
Climate: Medium to high elevation.
Distribution: South-western United States.
Flowering Time: Late spring to early summer.
Description: This is a low growing, flat padded species, which branches freely from the base. The pads are 12–20 cm (4.8–8 in) in length, bluish-green to grey and often tinged with red around the areoles, which bear reddish-brown glochids, but no spines. The flowers are about 5 cm (2 in) in diameter and pinkish-purple. The fruits are up to 3.75 cm (1.5 in) in length, and 2.5 cm (1 in) in diameter, are velvety, greyish-brown, and dry when ripe.

Opuntia basilaris in habitat

Opuntia bigelovii

Opuntia bigelovii

COMMON NAME: Teddy Bear Cholla.
SIZE: Height 2 m (6 ft), width 1 m (3 ft).
CLIMATE: Medium elevation.
DISTRIBUTION: South-western United States and Mexico.
DESCRIPTION: A very beautiful but vicious, erect growing, freely branching species. It has a blackish cylindrical trunk, and a fine head of short, cylindrical, pale golden yellow, spined joints. These can be 7.5–25 cm (3–10 in) in length and 3.75–5 cm (1.5–2 in) in diameter. The areoles are set quite close together, bear creamy-white glochids, and up to 8 viciously barbed spines up to 2.5 cm (1 in) in length. It is very densely spined, despite its common name, the Teddy Bear Cholla. The flowers appear from the apical joints, are 3.5 cm (1.4 in) in diameter, slightly cupped, and off-white to greenish-yellow in colour. The fruits are strongly tuberculate, yellowish when ripe, 2 cm (0.8 in) in length, with short spines.

Opuntia macrocentra

COMMON NAME: Black Spined Prickly Pear.
SIZE: Height 60 cm (2 ft), width 2–3 m (6.5–9.6 ft).
CLIMATE: Medium elevation.
DISTRIBUTION: South-western United States.
FLOWERING TIME: Late spring to early summer.
DESCRIPTION: This is a low growing, clumping, flat padded species. The pads are nearly circular, are light blue tinged with pink or purple, and are 15–20 cm (6–8 in) in diameter. The areoles are well scattered, bear brown or blackish glochids, and 1–2 porrect spines which are 7.5–15 cm (3–6 in) in length, and of a similar colour to the glochids. The flowers, which open fairly wide, are up to 6.25 cm (2.5 in) in diameter, and are yellow with a red centre. The fruits are about 6.25 cm (2.5 in) in length, have no spines and are purple when ripe.

Opuntia macrocentra

Opuntia microdasys fa. *alba*

COMMON NAME: Angel's Wings (an unusual form where the glochids are not barbed).
SIZE: Height 60 cm (2 ft), width 1 m (3 ft).
CLIMATE: Medium elevation.
DISTRIBUTION: Central and northern Mexico.
FLOWERING TIME: Late spring and early summer.
DESCRIPTION: This is a quite densely branching, erect growing species, with oval-shaped pads 10–12.5 cm (4–5 in) in length. The areoles are set quite close together, bear masses of short white glochids, which are usually barbed, but have no spines. The flowers are 4–5 cm (1.6–2 in) in diameter, are very pale yellow and slightly veined. The fruits are 2.5–4.5 cm (1–1.8 in) in length, purple when ripe, and very densely covered with the white glochids.

Opuntia platyacantha

Opuntia phaeacantha

COMMON NAME: Purple Fruited Prickly Pear.
SIZE: Height 1.5 m (4.5 ft), width 2.5 m (8 ft).
CLIMATE: Medium to high elevation.
DISTRIBUTION: South-western United States up to 2500 m (8200 ft).
FLOWERING TIME: Late spring.
DESCRIPTION: This is a low growing, erect or sprawling species, which branches quite freely and can reach 1.5 m (4.5 ft) in height. Clumps can attain a diameter of 2.5 m (8 ft). The more northerly and higher altitude forms tend to be smaller and more resistant to frost. The oval-shaped, dark green pads are up to 15 cm (6 in) in length and up to 10 cm (4 in) in width. The areoles are set moderately well apart, are full of dark reddish-brown glochids, and have up to 5 spines, which point downwards. The spines can be up to 5 cm (2 in) in length and are light brown to reddish-brown in colour. The flowers are 5–7.5 cm (2–3 in) in diameter and are yellow and reddish at the base of the petals. The fruits are up to 6.25 cm (2.5 in) in length, yellow when ripe, but have plenty of reddish-brown glochids.

Opuntia microdasys fa. *alba*

Opuntia platyacantha

COMMON NAME: None.
SIZE: Height 30 cm (12 in), width 20 cm (8 in).
CLIMATE: Medium elevation.
DISTRIBUTION: Argentina.
FLOWERING TIME: Late spring and early summer.
DESCRIPTION: This is a low clumping species, which consists of spherical, pale green joints, 3–4 cm (1.2–1.6 in) in length. The areoles are set quite well apart, bear greyish glochids and 3–4 flexible, almost papery spines of the same colour. These can be 4–6 cm (1.6–2.4 in) in length. The flowers are to 5 cm (2 in) in diameter and are pale yellow. Fruits are not known.

Opuntia phaeacantha

OREOCEREUS

(ō'-rē-ō-sē'-rē-ŭs)

Oreocereus contains some eight species and a few varieties. The generic name is derived from Gk and Lat, meaning 'mountain cereus'. They are mostly erect columnar plants, some of which branch very freely from the base, and are 0.6–3 m (2–10 ft) in height, and their stem diameter is 8–20 cm (3.2–8 in). There are 8–25 ribs and usually large oval-shaped areoles, from which a lot of coarse or fine curly hair and spines appear. In some species the white or pale brownish hair is so dense and long (to 7.5 cm (3 in)), that the green stem colour is completely obscured. There can be 8–16 radial spines and 1–4 centrals per areole. The radials are curved or straight, spread out from the plant, are fairly rigid, and are 1.5–5 cm (0.6–2 in) in length. The centrals, when distinguishable from the radials, are stouter, and 4–15 cm (1.6–6 in) in length. The spine colour varies from white and brown to almost blood-red.

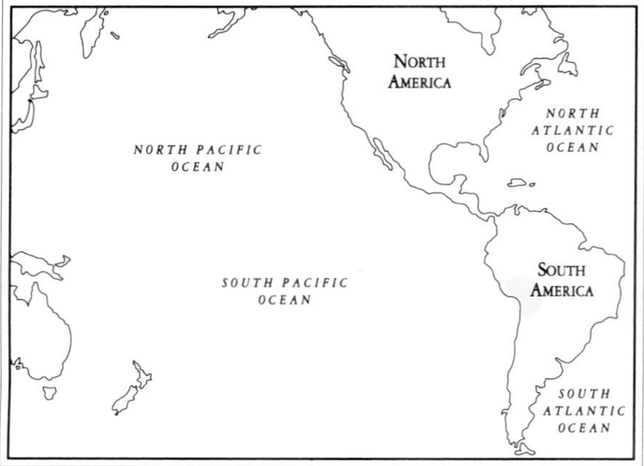

The flowers are tubular, zygomorphic, 5–9 cm (2–3.6 in) in length, and appear from the apical part of the stem. They vary in colour from pink to various shades of red, to almost violet. The exterior of the flower tube has scales and some hairs, which may or may not match the colour of the hair on the plant itself. The fruits are spherical, yellowish-green or green, and are hollow, dehiscing basally. They are 5 cm (2 in) or more in diameter.

Culture: These plants come from northern Argentina, Bolivia, northern Chile and southern Peru. They grow on the slopes of the Andes mountains, and some species can endure frost as well as snow. In cultivation, they are easily raised from seed, although most species will take many years to reach flowering size. A species such as *O. doelzianus* (see below) can also be grown from cuttings, and will flower within 2 or 3 years. They tolerate different soils, but like plenty of water from spring to autumn (fall). In winter, if kept dry, they can withstand near freezing temperatures, and the very hairy species will tolerate even lower temperatures.

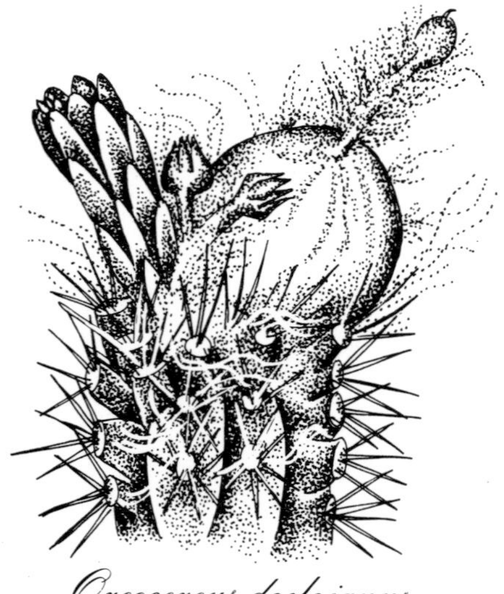

Oreocereus doelzianus

Oreocereus doelzianus

Common Name: Old Man of the Andes, but more applicable to the very hairy species.
Size: Height 1 m (3 ft), width 2 m (6.5 ft).
Climate: High elevation.
Distribution: Central Peru.
Flowering Time: Summer.
Description: This is somewhat quicker growing than any of the other species in the genus. It branches very freely from the base into very large semi-erect clumps. The green stems have about 11 ribs, and upon reaching maturity become slightly swollen at the apex. The white woolly, oval-shaped areoles are set fairly well apart, bear some curly white hairs and up to 20 radial spines, which are no more than 3 cm (1.2 in) in length, and a maximum of 4 centrals, which are slightly longer. The spines are fairly strong, yellowish to reddish-brown, and greying with age. The flowers appear, often many at one time, from an apical cephalium which has a little more hair than the areoles. They are tubular and zygomorphic, 10 cm (4 in) in length and dark rose to red in colour. The spherical, yellowish-green, hollow fruit is 5 cm (2 in) in diameter, and has a few white hairs on its exterior.

Oreocereus doelzianus

Oreocereus hendriksenianus var. *densilanatus*

Oreocereus hendriksenianus var. *densilanatus*

Common Name: Old Man of the Andes.
Size: Height 1 m (3 ft), width 2 m (6.5 ft).
Climate: High elevation.
Distribution: Southern Peru.
Flowering Time: Summer.
Description: This is a clustering, erect species, with stems up to 10 cm (4 in) in diameter. The green stems have up to 10 ribs, with a transverse furrow, which is completely obscured by the dense white mass of hairs between the areoles. There can be up to 10 fine radial spines, which are no more than 1 cm (0.4 in) in length, and sometimes 4 yellowish centrals, which are a little stronger, but are no more than 5 cm (2 in) in length. The pink to carmine, tubular, zygomorphic flowers are up to 7.5 cm (3 in) in length and have mainly brown hairs on the exterior of the tube. The green spherical fruits are up to 3.75 cm (1.5 in) in diameter, and have some white and brown hairs.

Oroya

(ō-rō'-yà)

Oroya contains some six species and a few varieties. The generic name is the name of the village in Peru near which the first species was discovered. The plants are globular, usually solitary, and up to 25 cm (10 in) in diameter. The plant body ranges from green to bluish-green, and they have 20–35 ribs, which bear very elongated areoles usually containing some white to yellowish wool. There are 10–30 fine, pectinate radial spines, 1–1.5 cm (0.4–0.6 in) in length, and sometimes 1–4 centrals. When present, the centrals are up to 2.5 cm (1 in) in length, and are usually a little stouter than the radials. The spines vary in colour from golden yellow to reddish-brown.

The flowers appear in one or more rings, away from the growing point, and are only 2–2.5 cm (0.8–1 in) in diameter.

Oroya peruviana

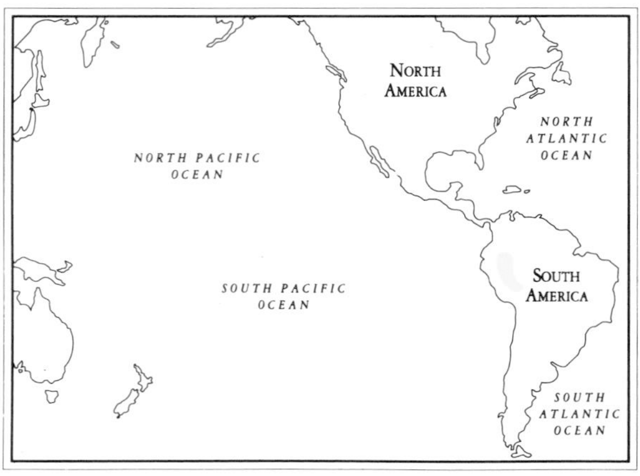

They do not open wide, and range in colour from pale yellow to red. The fruits are spherical, hollow, yellowish-green to green, usually less than 2.5 cm (1 in) in diameter, and virtually glabrous on the outside.

Culture: *Oroyas* are found in central and northern Peru, growing in arid conditions at altitudes above 3500 m (11 480 ft), where they endure heavy frosts and snow. They are not difficult to grow from seed, but will take 5–6 years to reach maturity — some species take even longer. From spring to autumn (fall) they like a reasonable amount of water, and they like full sun. In winter if kept dry, they will endure many degrees of frost provided the atmospheric humidity is fairly low.

Oroya peruviana

Oroya peruviana

COMMON NAME: None.
SIZE: Height 10 cm (4 in), width 25 cm (10 in).
CLIMATE: High elevation.
DISTRIBUTION: Central Peru.
FLOWERING TIME: Late spring and summer.
DESCRIPTION: This species has a solitary, slightly flattened globular habit, and a green to bluish-green body. It has up to 21 rather tuberculate ribs, which bear very elongated, white woolly areoles. The areoles bear up to 16 pectinate radial spines, and a maximum of 5 centrals. The spines are 1.5–2 cm (0.6–0.8 in) in length and pale yellow to reddish-brown in colour, changing to black with age. The flowers are just over 2 cm (0.8 in) in diameter, have pale carmine petals, and are pale yellow within their very short tube. The small fruits are glabrous and green.

Pachycereus

(păk-ĭ-sē'-rē-ŭs)

Pachycereus contains about 20 species, and the generic name is derived from the Gk, meaning 'thick cereus'. They are a large tree-like species, up to 16 m (52 ft) in height, or even taller (eg the specimen of *P. grandis* illustrated on page 150). Some species branch very densely and have 10–20 straight ribs, which can be 1–2.5 cm (0.4–1 in) in height. The stems can be green or bluish-green in colour, and the areoles on old plants are sometimes set fairly well apart. They bear up to 20 or more stout radial spines and up to 4 centrals. The radials can be 2–7 cm (0.8–2.8 in) in length, and the centrals are 2–10 cm (0.8–4 in) in length. All the spines tend to be greyish in colour and sometimes have black tips.

The nocturnal flowers are bell-shaped or funnel-shaped, and 4–10 cm (1.6–4 in) in length. The flower colour is variable — from white, yellowish-white to greenish-brown. The exterior of the flower tube is scaly, and the base is quite hairy and has bristly spines. The fruits are somewhat oblong, up to 7.5 cm (3 in) in length, and densely covered with reddish or golden yellow spines.

Culture: *Pachycerei* are native to quite a wide area of Mexico, excluding the most southerly jungle areas, but do occur in Baja California. They are easy plants to grow and develop fairly rapidly from seed and will tolerate differing soils. From spring to early autumn (fall) they can be watered freely but should be kept dry in winter, unless the climate is warm in which case some water can be provided. The more northerly species such as *P. pringlei*, will tolerate a temperature of 5°C (40°F). However, some species prefer a higher temperature, particularly when the plants are more tender.

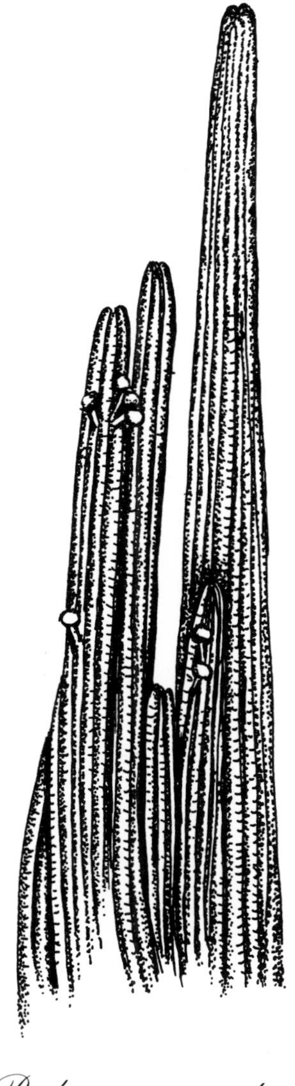

Pachycereus grandis

Pachycereus grandis

Common Name: None.
Size: Height 15 m (49 ft), width 6 m (19.5 ft).
Climate: Mediterranean to medium elevation.
Distribution: Central and western Mexico.
Flowering Time: Spring and early summer.
Description: This is a densely branching, tree-like species, with average size specimens reaching 10–15 m (32.5–49 ft) in height. The specimen illustrated has a trunk over 1 m (3 ft) in diameter and is estimated to be in excess of 25 m (82 ft) in height (see opposite). The stems are pale green and have whitish stripes and up to 11 ribs. The areoles are set well apart and bear up to 10 radial spines and 3 centrals. The spines tend to be somewhat flattened, and the longest spines reach 6 cm (2.4 in) and are white or grey in colour and have black tips. When plants reach flowering size, that area of the plant has many more bristly spines. The whitish flowers are only 4 cm (1.6 in) in length. The fruits are densely covered with yellow bristly spines and are about 7.5 cm (3 in) in diameter.

Pachycereus pringlei

Pachycereus grandis

Pachycereus pringlei

Common Name: None.
Size: Height 11 m (34 ft), width 5 m (16.3 ft).
Climate: Mediterranean to medium elevation.
Distribution: North-western Mexico, including Baja California and some of the nearby islands.
Flowering Time: Summer.
Description: This is another tree-like species, but not so densely branched as the previous species. The trunk is, however, much bigger, up to 2 m (6.5 ft) in diameter. The stems have up to 13 ribs, and are chalky-blue when young. The areoles are large, and tend to be joined together, felted, and bear up to 20 spines which are 2–12 cm (0.8–4.8 in) in length. They are white with black tips, and it is not possible to distinguish between the radials and the centrals. The bell-shaped to funnel-shaped flowers are white and about 8 cm (3.2 in) in length. The fruits are slightly oblong, about 7 cm (2.8 in) in length, and are slightly felted with golden brown spines.

PARODIA

(pă-rō-dĭ-ă)

Parodia contains over one hundred species and numerous varieties. The generic name honours Dr Domingo Parodi, who was one of the first people to make a study of the flora of Paraguay. The plants are flattened, globular to short, cylindrical plants, which usually remain solitary. They can have 12–25 ribs, which are often spirally formed, and bear areoles usually containing some wool. The spination is exceedingly variable — the spines can be straight, curved, or hooked. Each areole can bear 10–40 radial spines and 1–10 centrals. The radial spines are usually fairly fine, and the centrals can be somewhat stouter. The spine colour can range from white or yellow, to reddish-brown.

The flowers have a very short, somewhat funnel-shaped tube, and in some species they open irregularly and very wide. The exterior of the flower has scales, hair and sometimes bristly spines. There is a tremendous range of flower colour, from yellow to the most vivid shades of orange and red. The cream or pale brown fruits are spherical or slightly elongated, and are rather small with bristly spines, and dry up completely when ripe.

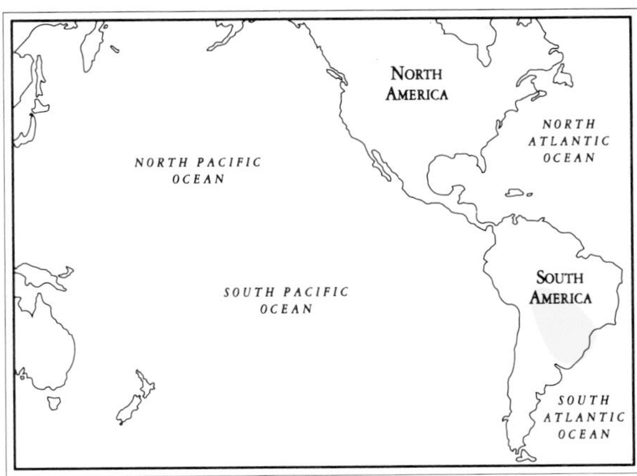

Culture: *Parodias* have quite a wide range in habitat, from Bolivia and northern Argentina, to Paraguay and parts of Brazil. The plants are freely flowering, and relatively easy to cultivate, but most species grow slowly from seed for the first 18 months. They need a light, moderately well drained soil, and can be watered freely from spring until the early autumn (fall). In winter they should be kept dry, and they can tolerate a minimum temperature of 5°C (40°F). *Parodia penicillata* (page 153) is a hardy species which can withstand a few degrees of frost in habitat.

Parodia aureispina

Parodia aureispina

Parodia aureispina

Common Name: None.
Size: Height 4 cm (1.6 in), width 6.5 cm (2.4 in).
Climate: Medium elevation.
Distribution: Northern Argentina.
Flowering Time: Summer.
Description: The fresh green spherical body tends to be slightly flattened, and has up to 16 spirally arranged tuberculate ribs. The crown of the plant contains quite a lot of white wool, as do the areoles which bear up to 40 fine, white radial spines and 4–6 centrals. At least one of the centrals, usually the lowest one, is hooked and golden brown. The remaining centrals are whitish. The golden-yellow flowers are about 3 cm (1.2 in) in diameter, and the fruits are less than 1 cm (0.4 in) in diameter, are brownish, and have hair and bristles.

Parodia chrysacanthion

Common Name: None.
Size: Height 4 cm (1.6 in), width 10 cm (4 in).
Climate: Medium elevation.
Distribution: Northern Argentina.
Flowering Time: Spring.
Description: This species has a very flattened globular habit, and up to 24 tuberculate ribs in a spiral formation. Once a plant starts to flower the crown tends to produce more wool. The white areoles bear 10–20 fine spreading spines, and 4–6 slightly stronger, straight centrals. The radials rarely exceed 1 cm (0.4 in), but some of the centrals may be twice that length. The spines range in colour from creamy-white to brilliant golden yellow, the latter being the most common colour. The yellow flowers are less than 1.25 cm (0.5 in) in diameter. The fruit is cream in colour when ripe, and covered with short fine, off-white or yellowish spines.

Parodia laui

Parodia laui

Common Name: None.
Size: Height 7.25 cm (3 in), width 10 cm (4 in).
Climate: High elevation.
Distribution: Bolivia.
Flowering Time: Summer to early autumn (fall).
Description: Has a solitary, flattened globular habit, and a dull green body with up to 13 spirally arranged ribs. The circular areoles have a lot of white wool when young, which becomes less prominent. The areoles bear up to 20 thin spreading radial spines, and up to 6 centrals, of which 1–3 are hooked. The radial spines are up to 1.5 cm (0.6 in) long, and whitish coloured, whereas the slightly stronger centrals are off-white to pale brown. On young plants the number of spines per areole is far less than when mature. The flowers are funnel-shaped, up to 4 cm (1.6 in) in diameter, and salmon-pink through to red. The fruits are spherical, very small, spiny and brown when ripe.

Parodia gracilis

Parodia chrysacanthion

Parodia gracilis

Common Name: None.
Size: Height 12.5 cm (5 in), width 10 cm (4 in).
Climate: High elevation.
Distribution: Bolivia.
Flowering Time: Summer.
Description: This species is solitary and spherical, but older plants become slightly elongated. The dark green body has up to 19 tuberculate ribs, usually spirally arranged. The oval areoles have white wool, and bear up to 22 fine but stiff radial spines, and from 4–10 centrals, which are slightly stronger. Occasionally there can be 1 slightly hooked central. The radial spines are up to 1.25 cm (0.5 in) in length, and off-white to pale brown in colour, whereas the centrals are browner and a little longer. The flowers are 2.5 cm (1 in) in length, deep yellow, but because of the spination do not open wide. The fruits are spherical, very small, spiny and brownish when ripe.

Parodia mutabilis

Parodia mutabilis

Common Name: None.
Size: Height 8 cm (3.2 in), width 8 cm (3.2 in).
Climate: Medium elevation.
Distribution: Northern Argentina.
Flowering Time: Summer.
Description: This species is solitary, spherical and has a fresh green body with up to 14 very spiralled ribs. The circular areoles have some white wool, and bear up to 50 fine radial spines (on an old plant), and up to 4 stouter centrals, one of which is hooked. The radial spines are very short, and white in colour, whereas the centrals can reach 1.25 cm (0.5 in) in length. The flowers are funnel-shaped, opening very wide, from 3–4 cm (1.2–1.6 in) in diameter, ranging in colour from pale yellow to a deep golden-yellow. The fruits are spherical, very small, spiny, brownish when ripe.

Parodia mairanana

Common Name: None.
Size: Height 6 cm (2.4 in), width 15 cm (6 in).
Climate: Medium elevation.
Distribution: Bolivia.
Flowering Time: Summer.
Description: Initially solitary, but then starting to cluster after 3 or 4 years of age. Individual heads are up to 6 cm (2.4 in) in height and diameter, with up to 14 very slightly spiralled dull green ribs. The areoles have a little whitish wool, and bear up to 14 fine spreading radial spines, and from 1–3 stronger curved and hooked centrals. The radial spines barely exceed 1 cm (0.4 in) in length, and are off white to slightly yellowish. The centrals are up to 2 cm (0.8 in) long and rather browner. The flowers are funnel-shaped, but vary in colour, from golden-yellow through to red. The fruits are spherical, very small, spiny, brownish when ripe.

Parodia mairanana

Parodia pencillata

Parodia penicillata

Common Name: None.
Size: Height 70 cm (28 in), width 12.5 cm (5 in).
Climate: Medium elevation.
Distribution: Northern Argentina.
Flowering Time: Summer.
Description: This is a magnificent species, globular when young, but eventually becoming cylindrical and up to 70 cm (28 in) in height, with a diameter of about 12.5 cm (5 in). The fresh green body has about 17 spirally arranged tuberculate ribs, which bear woolly areoles. The areoles bear up to 40 fine radial spines, some of which are appressed, and up to 20 slightly stronger centrals. The radial spines are 1–2 cm (0.4–0.8 in) in length, and some of the centrals can reach 5 cm (2 in) in length. The flowers are in varying shades of red and are up to 3 cm (1.2 in) in diameter. The small fruits are brown and have bristly spines.

Parodia thionantha

Parodia thionantha

Common Name: None.
Size: Height 15 cm (6 in), width 7.5–10 cm (3–4 in).
Climate: High elevation.
Distribution: Northern Argentina.
Flowering Time: Summer.
Description: A solitary, slightly columnar species, with a bluish-green body, although it is somewhat masked by the spination, and has up to 21 spiralled, tuberculate ribs. The circular areoles are very close together, and possess a lot of white wool, even on the sides of an old plant. The areoles bear up to 10 fine radial spines, and usually 4 centrals, of which one is slightly stouter, longer and hooked. The radial spines rarely exceed 0.6 cm (0.2 in) in length, and are white, whilst the longest central can reach 1.5 cm (0.6 in) dark pink to carmine coloured. The flowers are funnel-shaped, opening very wide, up to 6 cm (2.4 in) in diameter, and usually pale yellow coloured. The fruits are spherical, small, spiny, and brown when ripe.

PEDIOCACTUS

(pĕd'-ĭ-ō-kăk-tŭs)

Pediocactus contains four species and a few varieties or forms. The generic name is derived from the Gk, meaning 'plains cactus'. They are solitary or clustering, globular plants — some of which are very dwarf — are pale green to dark green in colour and are about 2.5–15 cm (1–6 in) in diameter. The tubercles are usually spirally arranged, and the plants sometimes have a woolly apex. The areoles bear 4–30 radial spines which are often appressed against the body and are 0.2–1 cm (0.1–0.4 in) in length. The centrals, when present, can be up to 2 cm (0.8 in) in length. The spines can be fine and rigid, or of a corky spongy texture, and their colour can range from off-white to brown.

Pediocactus knowltonii

The flowers are funnel-shaped and have a short tube which usually has naked scales on its exterior. The flowers rarely exceed 2.5 cm (1 in), and in most species are much less, and they vary in colour from off-white or cream to pink. The fruits are spherical, 0.4–0.7 cm (0.16–0.28 in) in diameter, and green or brownish when ripe. They split open irregularly when ripe.

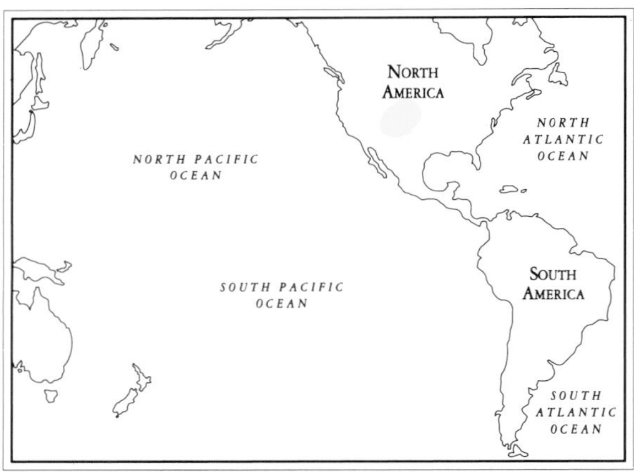

Culture: These plants come from south-western United States and are to be found usually at altitudes of 1300–2800 m (4264–9184 ft). They grow among rocks or barren slopes, and they pull themselves into the soil for protection from the elements. In cultivation, although they can be raised from seed, they are not easy to cultivate — particularly in temperate climates where there is high humidity in winter. They require a well drained soil, full sun and modest amounts of water during spring to autumn (fall). All species will withstand frosts (some more than others) when atmospheric humidity levels are low.

Pediocactus knowltonii

Common Name: Thimble Plains Cactus.
Size: Height 3.5 cm (1.4 in), width 8 cm (3.2 in).
Climate: Medium elevation.
Distribution: South-western United States, but in a limited habitat area.
Flowering Time: Late spring to early summer.
Description: Solitary or clustering in habit and light green in colour, the individual heads of this species rarely exceed 2.5 cm (1 in) in diameter and up to 3.5 cm (1.4 in) in height. The tubercles are small and have tiny areoles, which bear 18–24 minute, whitish pectinate radial spines. There are no centrals. The small funnel-shaped flowers are 1.5 cm (0.6 in) in diameter and pale pink in colour. The fruits are about 0.6 cm (0.25 in) in diameter, and are grey-green or tinged with pink when ripe.

Pediocactus knowltonii

Pelecyphora

(pĕl-ē-sĭf'-ō-rȧ)

Pelecyphora contains just three species and a variety, and the generic name is derived from the Gk, meaning 'hatchet bearer' and is in reference to the shape of the tubercles. The plants are solitary or clustering, dwarf with elongated heads, 5–10 cm (2–4 in) in height and 2–6 cm (0.8–2.4 in) in diameter. The heads are densely covered with hatchet-shaped tubercles which are spirally arranged. The tubercles bear the areoles which have very distinctive pectinate spine formations. The very short spines are united at their bases, and are off-white or cream to grey in colour.

The flowers are 2–3 cm (0.8–1.2 in) in diameter, white, pink or magenta in colour, and sometimes have dark median stripes down the petals. The fruits are very small and are dark green to greyish-green when ripe.

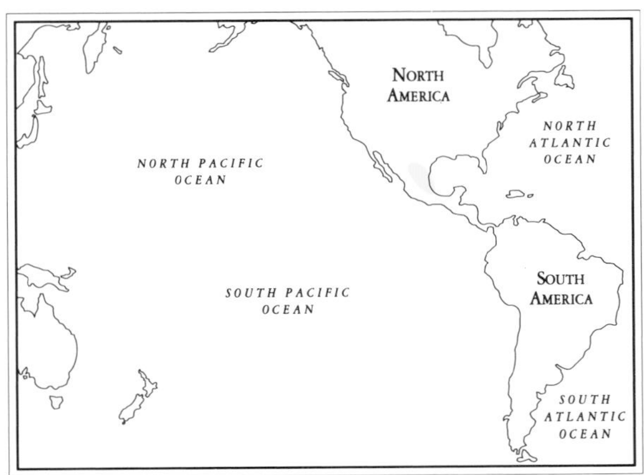

Pelecyphora pseudopectinata

Culture: *Pelecyphoras* come from central and northern Mexico, and usually grow in very dry rocky locations. Although they are slow growing plants, they are not unduly difficult to grow from seed — provided you have patience. They are very freely flowering plants, which require a well drained soil, and can only be watered freely during the hottest weather. In winter they should be kept dry, and they can withstand a temperature down to 5°C (40°F).

Pelecyphora aselliformis

Pelecyphora aselliformis

Common Name: None.
Size: Height 10 cm (4 in), width 20 cm (8 in).
Climate: Medium elevation.
Distribution: Central Mexico.
Flowering Time: Summer.
Description: This species clusters quite freely in age, relative to its slow growth rate. The elongated heads can be up to 10 cm (4 in) in height and 5 cm (2 in) in diameter. The body of the plant is bluish-green, but its colour is almost obscured by the fairly dense tubercle formation. The flat topped tubercles bear whitish pectinate spines. The funnel-shaped flowers are 3 cm (1.2 in) in diameter, and magenta in colour. The fruits are very small and are greyish-green when ripe.

Pelecyphora aselliformis

Pelecyphora pseudopectinata

Common Name: None.
Size: Height 6 cm (2.4 in), width 4.5 cm (1.8 in).
Climate: Medium elevation.
Distribution: Northern Mexico.
Flowering Time: Summer.
Description: Unlike the previous species, *P. pseudopectinata* is solitary. The body of the plant is bluish-green, and has closely set tubercles, which are four sided beneath and flattened above. The tubercles bear very short, whitish pectinate spines. The funnel-shaped flowers are 2–3 cm (0.8–1.2 in) in diameter, whitish pink in colour, and have a darker median stripe down each petal. The fruits are very small and are dark green when ripe.

Pelecyphora pseudopectinata

PERESKIA

(pĕr-ĕs'-kĭ-ă)

This genus contains some 25 species, and a few varieties. The generic name honours N.C.F. de Pieresc (1580-1637). The Type species was first introduced into Europe during the latter part of the 16th century, and was originally described by Linnaeus in 1753 as *Cactus pereskia*. Today it is known as *Pereskia aculeata*, and is described in detail below. Pereskias are very different in general appearance to most other cacti. They can be slightly succulent shrubs, climbing plants and trees, with flattish, deciduous leaves, but possessing prominent spiny areoles. The small shrub-like species may not exceed 1 m (3 ft) in height, but the climbing or tree-like species range from 5–20 m (15–65 ft) in height.

The flowers are produced singly or in clusters, each one in general appearance being similar to a single rose, and are from 1–5 cm (0.4–2 in) in diameter. Their colour ranges from white or lemon through to magenta or wine-red.

The fruits are usually spherical, from 2–5 cm (0.8–2 in) in diameter, and yellowish to wine-red in colour when ripe.

Culture: *Pereskias* are native to the West Indies, Central America, and southwards to northern Argentina, Paraguay and Peru. Being basically tropical plants, they like warmth, and plenty of water. Most species will grow rapidly, and flower very freely in these conditions. A few species, despite their tropical origin, can be kept in a dormant state during the winter months at temperatures well below anything they are likely to endure in their native habitat. They are easily raised from seed or cuttings.

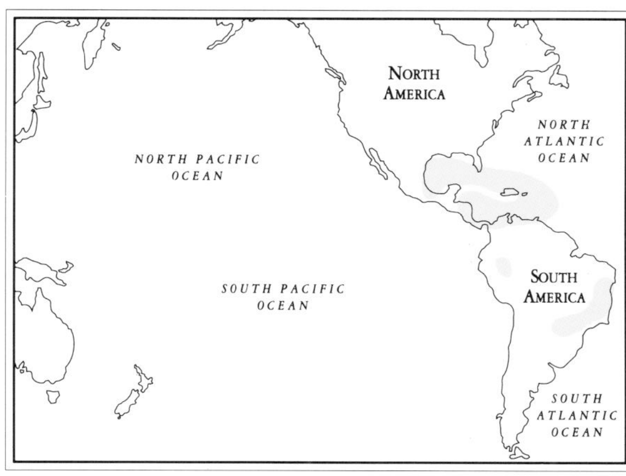

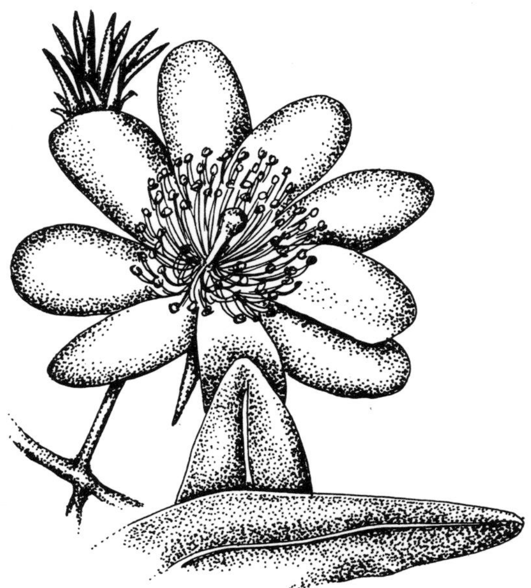

Pereskia aculeata

Pereskia bleo

Pereskia aculeata

Common Name: None.
Size: Height 5–10 m (15–32 ft), width 4–5 m (12–15 ft)
Climate: Tropical.
Distribution: Venezuela.
Flowering Time: Autumn (fall).
Description: A scrambling species which needs some support, it has slim green stems when young, which become woody with age. The areoles bear from one to three brown or black coloured spines. The leaves range from lanceolate to ovate, are green and up to 7.5 cm (3 in) in length. The flowers are just under 5 cm (2 in) in diameter, and off-white, or yellowish to pink coloured. The spherical fruits are small, no more than 2 cm (0.8 in) in diameter, light yellow when ripe.

Pereskia bleo

Common Name: None.
Size: Height 7 m (21 ft), width 4–5 m (12–15 ft).
Climate: Low elevation.
Distribution: Colombia.
Flowering Time: Autumn (fall).
Description: A tree-like species, with a trunk up to 10 cm (4 in) in diameter. The young branches are red coloured, and the areoles bear up to six spines, usually black in colour, and the longest ones can exceed 2.5 cm (1 in) in length. The leaves are large, up to 20 cm (8 in) in length, and 5 cm (2 in) in width. The flowers usually appear in twos or fours, with up to 15 petals, and are 3.5 cm (1.4 in) in length, and pinkish-red coloured. The fruits are very different in shape to most of the species, being truncate, up to 6 cm (2.4 in) long, and yellow when ripe.

Pereskia aculeata

PFEIFFERA

(pfi'-fer-à)

Pfeiffera contains some seven species, although some of the newer species may eventually be considered to be varieties or forms of previously described species. The generic name honours Dr Ludwig Pfeiffer. They are small erect growing or hanging cacti, which branch sparingly, and may grow on the ground or in trees as epiphytes (however, they do not possess areial roots). The stems can be 25–50 cm (10–20 in) in length and 2 cm (0.8 in) in diameter, are green to reddish-green in colour, and have 4–7 ribs. The round areoles are set fairly close together, usually possess some white wool, and bear 8–16 fine bristly spines. The spines are 0.2–1 cm (0.1–0.4 in) in length, and may be off-white, yellowish or brown in colour.

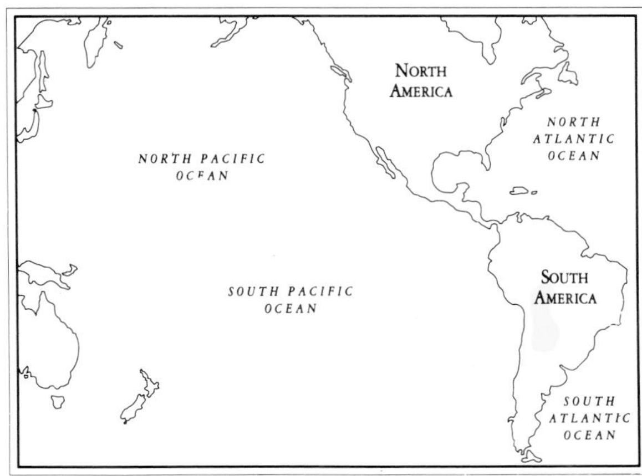

The flowers appear from around the tips of the stems, are diurnal, and not particularly wide opening. They are about 2 cm (0.8 in) in length and 1.5 cm (0.6 in) in diameter. The fruits are spherical, translucent, spiny, about 1 cm (0.4 in) in diameter, and purplish-brown when ripe.

Culture: *Pfeifferas* come from Bolivia and northern Argentina, and grow in areas of reasonable rainfall. They are very easy plants to raise from seed or from cuttings, and develop quite rapidly, appreciating a humus enriched soil and plenty of water from spring to autumn (fall). In winter they can be kept dry and can withstand a minimum temperature above 5°C (40°F). They grow best under light shade.

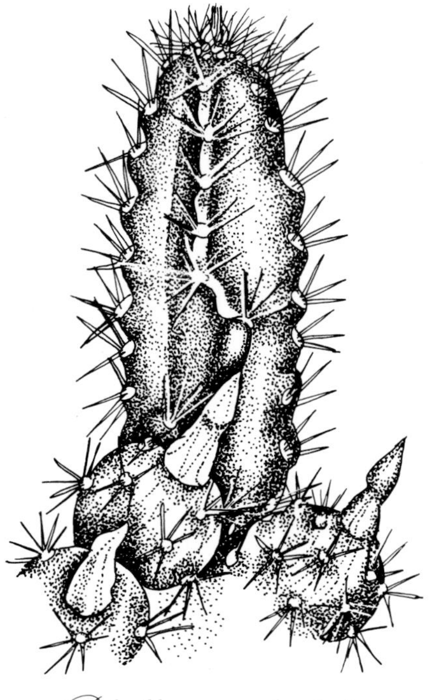

Pfeiffera ianthothele

Pfeiffera ianthothele

Pfeiffera ianthothele

Common Name: None.
Size: Length 50 cm (20 in), width 10–15 cm (4–6 in).
Climate: Medium elevation.
Distribution: Bolivia to northern Argentina.
Flowering Time: Late spring through to autumn (fall).
Description: This species is erect growing when young, but becomes pendant when the stems branch and grow towards their maximum length of 50 cm (20 in). The usually four angled stems are 2 cm (0.8 in) in diameter, and green or reddish-green. The small woolly areoles bear up to 7 yellowish spines, 0.5 cm (0.2 in) in length. The creamy-white flowers are 1.5 cm (0.6 in) in diameter, and the spiny spherical fruits are translucent, and pale purple in colour.

Pfeiffera tarijensis

Common Name: None.
Size: Length 30 cm (12 in), width 10–15 cm (4–6 in).
Climate: Medium elevation.
Distribution: Bolivia and northern Argentina.
Flowering Time: Summer to early autumn (fall).
Description: This species also has an erect habit initially, but it branches only sparingly. The olive-green to reddish stems grow to 30 cm (12 in) in length, but are only about 1.5 cm (0.6 in) in diameter. The white woolly areoles are more pronounced than in *P. ianthothele* (opposite), and bear up to 8 or 9 stiffer, spreading yellowish-brown spines. The longest of the spines can be 1 cm (0.4 in). The flowers are creamy-white, and not much more than 1.25 cm (0.5 in) in diameter. The spherical fruits are of the same size as *P. ianthothele*, but having rather stronger spines.

Pfeiffera tarijensis

PILOSOCEREUS

(pī'-lōs-ō-sē'-rē-ŭs)

Pilosocereus contains over 50 species, and the generic name is derived from the Lat meaning 'hairy cereus'. They are mostly erect plants, are moderately free branching, and are 1–10 m (3–32 ft) in height. The pale green to glaucous stems are 3–10 cm (1.2–4 in) in diameter, and have 6–14 ribs. The areoles are usually quite hairy, and they bear 5–25 radial spines, and up to 8 centrals. The radials are 1–2 cm (0.4–0.8 in) in length, and the centrals in some species can reach 10 cm (4 in). In some species the radials and centrals are virtually indistinguishable. They vary in colour from white or yellow to brown. The flowers appear on the upper sections of stems, where there tends to be more somewhat finer spines per areole, and usually considerably more hair (see, *P. palmeri*, page 162). This does not form a cephalium, unlike *Cephalocereus* (see page 52) which has a true 'cephalium', rather, this increase in spines and hair is often referred to as 'pseudocephalium'.

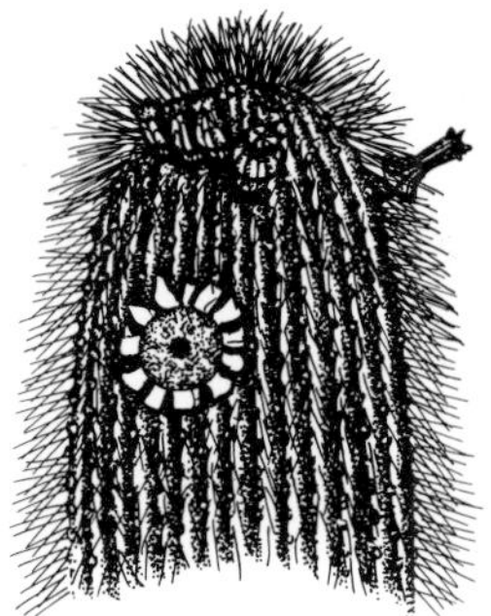

Pilosocereus polylophus

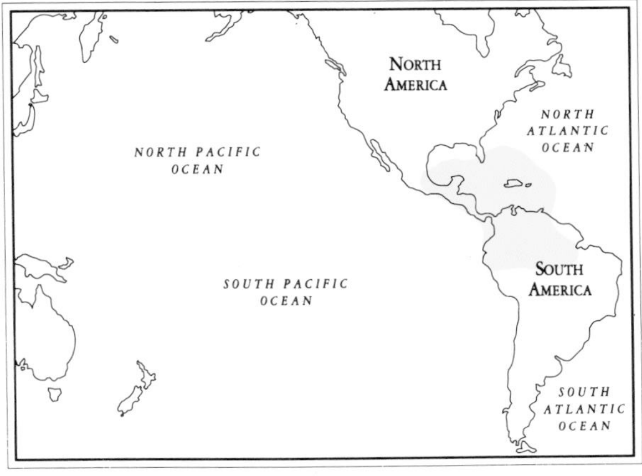

The flowers are usually funnel-shaped, 4–7.5 cm (1.6–3 in) in length, up to 7.5 cm (3 in) in diameter, and white or greenish-white to pink or purple. The fruits are usually globular, glabrous, about 5 cm (2 in) in diameter, and have persistent floral remains.

Culture: *Pilosocerei* come from the Bahamas, Brazil, Cuba, Mexico, south-eastern United States and the West Indies. They are mostly easy plants to grow from seed or cuttings and many of them grow moderately rapidly. During the warmer months they enjoy plenty of water. In winter, most species will not withstand frosts and a minimum temperature of 10°C (50°F) is recommended.

Pilosocereus glaucochrous

Common Name: None.
Size: Height 4 m (13 ft), width 1 m (3 ft).
Climate: Tropical.
Distribution: Eastern Brazil.
Flowering Time: Summer onwards.
Description: This is quite a freely branching species. The beautiful light blue stems are usually less than 7.5 cm (3 in) in diameter and have up to 9 ribs. There is a distinct horizontal furrow between each areole position on the ribs. The areoles contain a lot of white wool and long hairs, which darken with age. There are up to 12 radial spines and 4 centrals, all of which are straw coloured. The radials can be up to 2 cm (0.8 in) in length, and the centrals, which are somewhat stouter, can reach 5 cm (2 in). The flowers, which are produced in abundance, do not open very wide, and barely exceed 5 cm (2 in) in length. The flowers of the plant illustrated are plum coloured, but some forms can be much paler. The fruits are globular, 5 cm (2 in) in diameter and reddish-green when ripe.

Pilosocereus glaucochrous

Pilosocereus palmeri

Pilosocereus palmeri

Common Name: None.
Size: Height 6 m (19.5 ft).
Climate: Mediterranean.
Distribution: Eastern Mexico.
Flowering Time: Summer and autumn (fall).
Description: This is an erect growing, freely branching species. The bluish-green to chalky-blue stems rarely exceed 7.5 cm (3 in) in diameter, and have up to 9 ribs. The areoles are full of long white hair, and have up to 12 thin radial spines and usually one stouter central. They are brown in colour, greying with age, and about 2.5 cm (1 in) in length. The flowering areas of stems become very hairy, as can be seen in the accompanying illustration. The bell-shaped flowers can be up to 7.5 cm (3 in) in diameter and are in varying shades of pink. The fruits are globular, 5 cm (2 in) or more in diameter and bluish-red when ripe.

Pilosocereus polylophus

Pilosocereus polylophus

Common Name: None.
Size: Height 13 m (42.5 ft), width 30 cm (12 in).
Climate: Medium elevation.
Distribution: Central Mexico.
Flowering Time: Summer.
Description: This species only branches if the growing point is damaged. They grow up to 13 m (42.5 ft) in height, and have a stem diameter often exceeding 30 cm (12 in). The stems have up to 50 or so narrow ribs, and the areoles are set fairly close together. The areoles contain a lot of white wool when new, and they bear up to 8 radial spines and one central. The spines are up to 2 cm (0.8 in) in length and are golden brown in colour. The nocturnal flowers are 4–7 cm (1.6–2.8 in) in diameter, and vary in colour from pink to dark red. The spherical fruits are spiny and about 4 cm (1.6 in) in diameter.

PTEROCACTUS

(tĕr-ō-kăk'-tŭs)

Pterocactus contains about seven species. The generic name is derived from the Gk meaning 'wing cactus' and is in reference to the unusual winged seeds. They are small plants with thick taproots, and they have either spherical or thin cylindrical stems. The spherical stemmed species can have joints up to 10 cm (4 in) in length and a diameter of 1-3 cm (0.4-1.2 in). The cylindrical stemmed species have stems up to 36 cm (14 in) or more in length and usually less than 1 cm (0.4 in) in diameter. The stems are greenish-brown or purplish-brown. The areoles are usually small, slightly felted, and bear up to 15 radial spines and rarely more than 4 centrals. In some species the spines are minute, but in a few species they can reach 3 cm (1.2 in) in length and have flattened centrals.

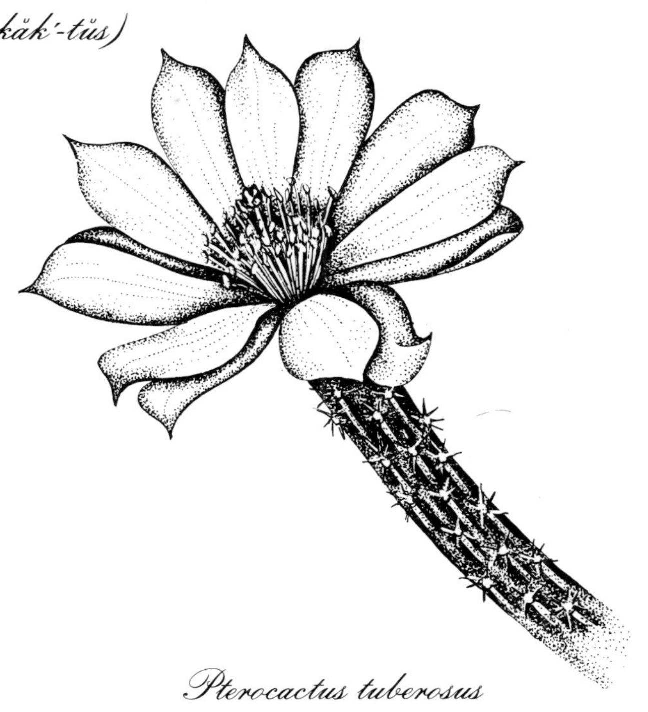

Pterocactus tuberosus

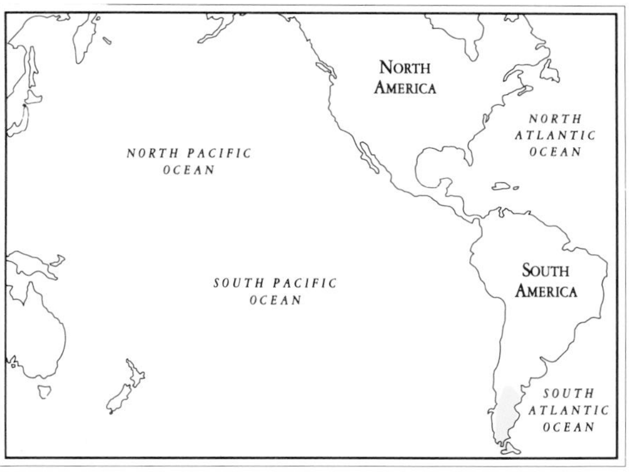

The flowers open wide, are 3-6 cm (1.2-2.4 in) in diameter and are in varying shades of yellow. The fruits are small, dry, and no more than 0.5 cm (0.2 in) in diameter.

Culture: *Pterocacti* come from western and southern Argentina, and are very easy plants to grow from seed or cuttings. A small tuber will form from a cutting within 12-18 months. They like plenty of water during the warmer months, and the slender stemmed species do not grow or flower well if in full sun. In winter, if kept dry, most species can withstand light frosts.

Pterocactus tuberosus

Common Name: None.
Size: Length 15 cm (6 in).
Climate: Mediterranean.
Distribution: Western Argentina.
Flowering Time: Summer.
Description: This species has very slender stems, which appear from a tuberous root. The root on an old plant can be 12 cm (5 in) or more in length and 7.5 cm (3 in) in diameter. The brownish-purple stems are no more than 1 cm (0.4 in) in diameter — usually much less — and bear minute areoles. These bear equally minute, appressed fine spines. The pale yellow flowers are about 3 cm (1.2 in) in diameter, and appear from the tips of the stems. The fruits are 0.4 cm (0.16 in) in diameter, and dry.

Pterocactus tuberosus

RATHBUNIA

(răth-bŭn'-ĭ-à)

Rathbunia contains just four species, and is named in honour of Dr Robert Rathbun. They are freely branching plants, erect or of a semi-sprawling habit, and 2–3 m (6.5–9.8 ft) high. The green to purplish-green stems have 4–8 ribs. The areoles are set fairly well apart, are white or brownish, and bear up to 18 radial spines and 1–4 centrals. The radials are spreading, up to 2.5 cm (1 in) in length, the centrals are usually porrect, slightly stouter, and the longest centrals can reach 5 cm (2 in). The spines are usually off-white to grey in colour.

The flowers are diurnal, tubular and red in colour. The flowers of *R. kerberi* (see below) are distinctly zygomorphic. The fruits are globular, about 1 cm (0.4 in) in diameter, spiny, and red when ripe.

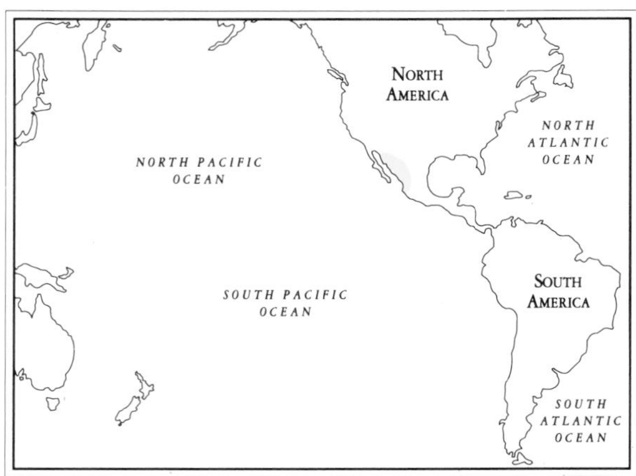

Culture: *Rathbunias* come from north-western Mexico, and are all exceedingly easy plants to grow from seed or cuttings. They like plenty of water during the warmer months, and they should be kept dry and protected from frosts in winter.

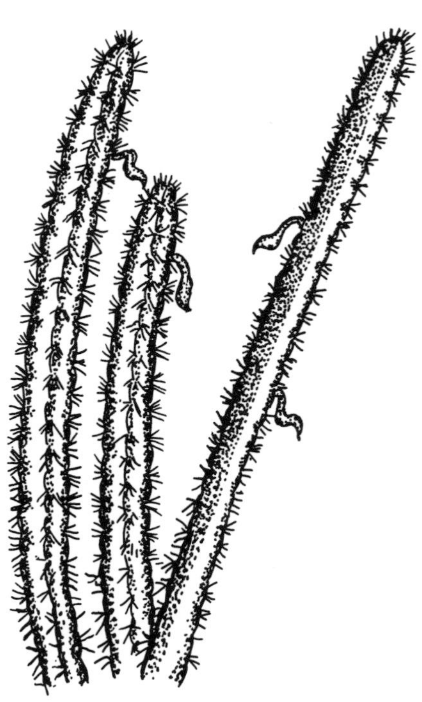

Rathbunia kerberi

Rathbunia alamosensis

COMMON NAME: None.
SIZE: Height 2 m (6.5 ft), width 6–10 m (19.5–32.5 ft).
CLIMATE: Mediterranean.
DISTRIBUTION: North-western Mexico.
FLOWERING TIME: Early summer onwards.
DESCRIPTION: This is a shrubby, somewhat clambering species, and its branches tend to go in all directions — even curving downwards. In habitat they form virtually inpenetrable clumps, with numerous branches curving over and rerooting. The branches can be up to 7.5 cm (3 in) in diameter and have up to 8 obtuse ribs. The circular areoles are off-white, and bear up to 18 spreading radial spines and up to 4 centrals. The radial spines are all fairly rigid and up to 2.5 cm (1 in) in length, while the lowest central can be up to 3.5 cm (1.4 in) in length. The spines are whitish or can be greyish-brown with age. The flowers are tubular, up to 4 cm (1.6 in) in length and are bright red. The fruits are spherical, no more than 1.25 cm (0.5 in) in diameter, and are reddish-green when ripe.

Rathbunia alamosensis

Rathbunia kerberi

Rathbunia kerberi

COMMON NAME: None.
SIZE: Height 2 m (6.5 ft), width 60 cm (2 ft).
CLIMATE: Mediterranean.
DISTRIBUTION: Western Mexico.
FLOWERING TIME: Summer to early autumn (fall).
DESCRIPTION: This is a shrubby, but much more erect plant, which has green to purplish-green stems and only 4 ribs. The areoles, which are set fairly well apart, are greyish-brown, and bear up to 12 subulate radial spines and 4 porrect centrals. The radials rarely exceed 2.5 cm (1 in) in length, while the centrals can reach 5 cm (2 in). The spines range in colour from off-white to greyish-brown. The flowers are distinctly zygomorphic, about 12.5 cm (5 in) in length and bright red in colour. The fruits are spherical and about 1.25 cm (0.5 in) in diameter.

REBUTIA

(rĕ-bōōt'-ĭ-ă)

Rebutia contains over 70 species and a large number of varieties. The generic name honours P. Rebut, who was a cactus dealer in 1895. They are a group of small, freely clustering plants with globular heads. The heads may be depressed, eg *R. senilis* var. *sieperdaiana* (see below), or slightly cylindrical, eg *R. costata* (see page 167). They are soft bodied plants, and have a tubercled structure, although those similar to *R. costata* have a tuberculate rib structure. The areoles are very small, and they bear short fine acicular spines, or in some species rather bristly ones. The spines may be appressed or radiate out from the areoles, and they range in colour from white or yellowish to brown.

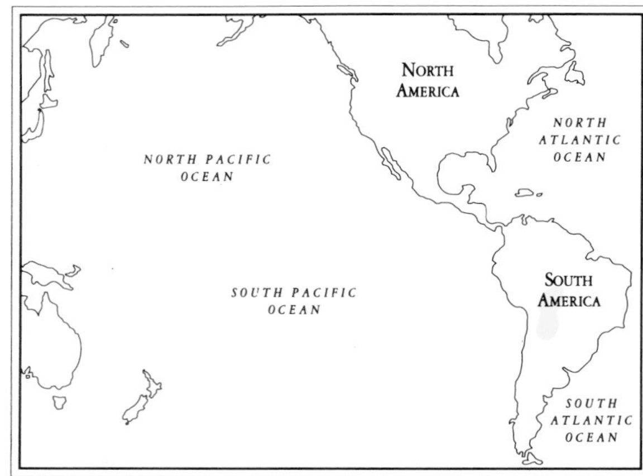

The funnel-shaped flowers come from around the sides of the heads and, in many species, from near soil level. The flowers rarely exceed 3 cm (1.2 in) in diameter, and can be in any colour except blue. The fruits are spherical, very small, and yellowish, brown, or reddish when ripe, and have a few bristly spines.

Culture: *Rebutias* come from the mountainous areas of Bolivia and northern Argentina, at altitudes of up to 3600 m (11 800 ft), where they experience snow and heavy frosts, but low atmospheric humidity. They are among the best species for anyone new to cacti to start growing as they take up very little room, and unless the climate is hot and the temperature stays well above 5°C (40°F) in winter, they will flower very freely. A soil mixture containing at least 30 per cent humus will produce the best results. The less densely spined species can burn if not given light shade during the hottest months, and all species should be watered freely from spring to autumn (fall). In winter if kept dry the plants can withstand temperatures at around freezing, even in a damp climate.

Rebutia senilis var. *sieperdaiana*

Rebutia costata

Common Name: None.
Size: Height 4 cm (1.6 in), width 15 cm (6 in).
Climate: High elevation.
Distribution: Northern Argentina.
Flowering Time: Spring.
Description: This species has a dwarf habit, is freely clustering, and the individual heads reach 2.5–4 cm (1–1.6 in) in height. They have up to 9 slightly tuberculate ribs, and the small areoles bear up to 12 bristly, yellowish-brown radial spines, which rarely exceed 1 cm (0.4 in) in length — often much less. The flowers are 3 cm (1.2 in) in diameter and are orange-red in colour. The exterior of the very short tube has scales, some brownish hair and a few bristly spines which are also brownish. The fruits are very small, dry when ripe, and have a few short bristly spines.

Rebutia costata

Rebutia fiebrigii

Common Name: None.
Size: Height 5 cm (2 in), width 30 cm (12 in).
Climate: High elevation.
Distribution: Bolivia.
Flowering Time: Late spring.
Description: This species is freely clustering, has a dwarf habit, spherical to slightly elongated individual heads, and a glossy green body. The tubercles are usually in 18 rows, with very prominent white areoles, which bear up to 40 fine but quite stiff spines, up to 1 cm (0.4 in) long. These are glassy white with a dark brown tip. The flowers are funnel-shaped, 3.5 cm (1.4 in) long with a short narrow tube. The flowers are usually a brilliant dark red colour, and the exterior of the tube is purplish-brown. The fruits are spherical, very small, spiny, and dark red when ripe.

Rebutia fiebrigii

Rebutia muscula

Common Name: None.
Size: Height 4 cm (1.6 in), width 20 cm (8 in).
Climate: High elevation.
Distribution: Northern Argentina.
Flowering Time: Spring and summer.
Description: This species is also freely clustering, has a dwarf habit, and the flattened heads are so densely spined that the green body colour is completely obscured. It has a tuberculate body structure, and the tiny areoles bear 30–40 very fine spines, ranging from minute to some which can attain a length of 1 cm (0.4 in). The spines are white with the exception of 3 or 4 which are slightly yellowish-brown, and are also slightly stouter. The orange flowers are 2 cm (0.8 in) in diameter and the fruits are very small, brownish when ripe, and covered with tiny white bristly spines.

Rebutia minuscula fa. *violaciflora*

Common Name: None.
Size: Height 4–5 cm (1.6–2 in), width 10 cm (4 in).
Climate: Medium to high elevation.
Distribution: Northern Argentina.
Flowering Time: Spring.
Description: This species has a dwarf habit, is freely clustering, the individual heads are fresh green in colour, and 3–4 cm (1.2–1.4 in) in diameter. The areoles are whitish, bearing up to 20 fine, but stiff, off-white to brownish radial spines, up to 2.5 cm (1 in) in length, and one slightly longer and stronger central of the same colour. The flowers are funnel-shaped, up to 3 cm (1.2 in) in diameter in varying shades of violet-pink. The fruits are spherical, very small, spiny, reddish-green when ripe.

Rebutia minuscula fa. *violaciflora*

Rebutia muscula

Rebutia pulvinosa

Common Name: None.
Size: Height 4 cm (1.6 in), width 7 cm (2.4 in).
Climate: High elevation.
Distribution: Bolivia.
Flowering Time: Spring to early summer.
Description: This species has a very dwarf habit, is freely clustering, the individual heads are pale green, and 2-3 cm (0.8-1.2 in) in diameter. It is densely covered with small tubercles, with off-white areoles bearing up to 22 fine and minute radial spines, and up to six brownish centrals, which are slightly stouter and longer. The flowers are funnel-shaped with a slender tube, up to 2 cm (0.8 in) long, and slightly less in diameter, and orange-yellow in colour. The fruits are spherical, very small, spiny, brownish when ripe.

Rebutia pulvinosa

Rebutia senilis var. *sieperdaiana*

Rebutia spegazziniana var. *atroviridis*

Rebutia senilis var. *sieperdaiana*

Common Name: None.
Size: Height 4 cm (1.6 in), width 15-20 cm (6-8 in).
Climate: High elevation.
Distribution: Northern Argentina.
Flowering Time: Spring.
Description: This species has a flattened globular habit, and is freely clustering once the heads have reached their mature size of about 7.5 cm (3 in) in diameter. The dark green body is also tubercled in a spiral formation, and the small white areoles bear up to 25 white spines which range in length from less than 1 cm (0.4 in) to as much as 3 cm (1.2 in) in old plants. The funnel-shaped flowers are 3.5 cm (1.4 in) in diameter and have a slender tube. They are yellow, and the exterior of the tube is yellow with reddish scales. The flower buds are red when they appear, and the upper surface of the petals are yellow (in the illustration a few petals have a little red on them towards their tips). The tiny fruits are red when ripe and have a few bristly spines.

Rebutia spegazziniana var. *atroviridis*

Common Name: None.
Size: Height 5 cm (2 in), width 10 cm (4 in).
Climate: High elevation.
Distribution: Northern Argentina.
Flowering Time: Spring.
Description: This is a very dwarf species, which clusters with age, and has very short, cylindrical heads. The green body is up to 5 cm (2 in) high, with a diameter of 2.5 cm (1 in) and has a tubercled structure with tiny felted areoles which bear up to 10 fine radial spines, and usually 2 slightly stouter centrals. The radials are very short, but the centrals are 1-2 cm (0.4-0.8 in) in length, and all the spines are greyish in colour. The flowers are 4 cm (1.6 in) in diameter and are dark red, and note how the stamens spread out over the petals (see below), which is very typical of this variety. The fruits are very small, brownish, and covered with tiny greyish spines.

Rhipsalidopsis

(rĭp-să-lĭ-dŏp'-sĭs)

Rhipsalidopsis is a monotypic genus, but there are in fact numerous cultivars, which have been produced by hybridising this genus with *Schlumbergera* and *Zygocactus* (see page 193). The generic name means 'similar in appearance to *Rhipsalis*' (see page 170). It is a small growing, very freely branching, epiphytic plant, which has initially 4–5 angled segments or shoots and tiny yellowish-white bristles. With age these segments become flattened, green or purplish-green in colour, and up to 3.5 cm (1.4 in) in length and about 1 cm (0.4 in) in width. The margins of these segments are usually purplish-red.

The flowers are rotate, pink, have a short tube, and are about 3.5 cm (1.4 in) in diameter. The fruits are four angled, depressed, 1 cm (0.4 in) in length, and yellowish when ripe.

Rhipsalidopsis rosea

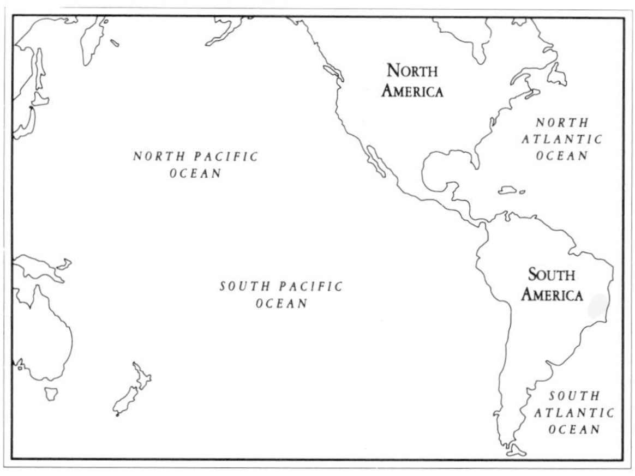

Culture: This genus comes from southern Brazil, and as with many of the other smaller epiphytic cacti has been very popular as a house plant. It can be grown quite easily from seed, but is normally propagated from cuttings which will invariably produce many flowers within a year. From spring to autumn (fall) it should be grown under light shade, and watered freely and it likes a soil incorporating plenty of humus. In winter the watering should be reduced, but not stopped, and to keep a perfect plant it should be protected from frosts and at a minimum temperature of 10°C (50°F).

Rhipsalidopsis rosea

Rhipsalidopsis rosea

Common Name: Easter Cactus.
Size: Height 15–20 cm (6–8 in), width 50 cm (20 in).
Climate: Tropical to Mediterranean.
Distribution: Southern Brazil.
Flowering Time: Spring.
Description: As there is only one species, this information is found above.

RHIPSALIS

(rĭp'-să-lĭs)

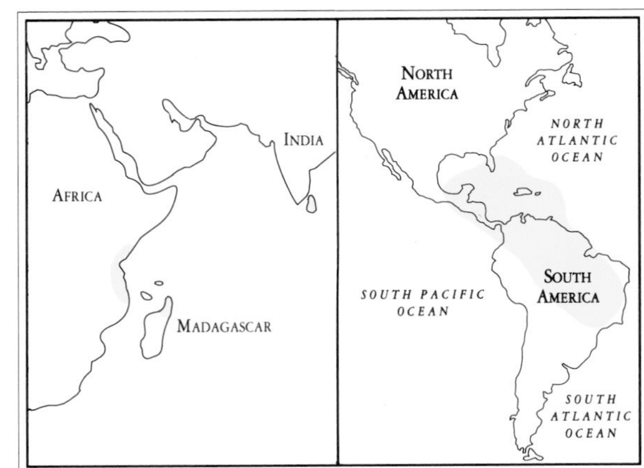

Rhipsalis contains over 60 species and many varieties. The generic name is derived from the Gk, meaning 'wicker-work' which is in reference to the thin, pliable branches which are typical of many species. They are epiphytic, freely branching, and usually pendant plants 0.3–2 m (1–6.5 ft) in length. The stems are usually fairly thin, and come in many shapes. They can be flattened or cylindrical, and are sometimes somewhat angular. The stems vary from yellowish-green to dark green, and sometimes have reddish tinges near the areole positions. The areoles are small and can be with or without spines, which, when present, are hairy or bristly.

The flowers are small, appear from the areole — and sometimes a number appear from one areole position. The flower colour ranges from white or yellowish, to pink or purple. The fruits are similar to small berries, and equally varied in colour when ripe, ranging from white through to purple.

Culture: *Rhipsalis* are native mainly to Mexico, the West Indies and various parts of South America. One species extends into Florida, United States but in contrast to other genus in the family Cactaceae, a few species have been found in East Africa, Madagascar and Sri Lanka. Even today there is still controversy as to whether these species are native, or whether migrating birds introduced them in seed form. A few species have been given the common name Mistletoe Cactus. Most species of *Rhipsalis* are very easy to grow, and as with other epiphytic cacti, like a soil with a high humus content. In cultivation they can be watered throughout the year, and enjoy a humid atmosphere, so overhead spraying is most important. They prefer some shade, particularly during the hottest months. All species need protection from frosts.

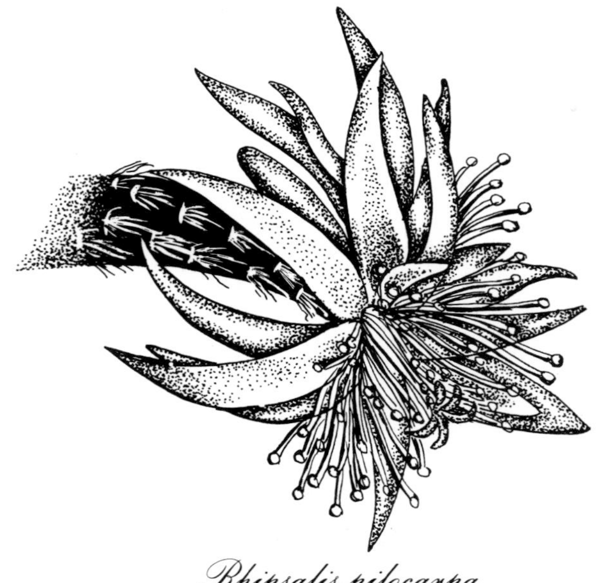

Rhipsalis pilocarpa

Rhipsalis houlletiana

Rhipsalis houlletiana

Common Name: None.
Size: Length 2 m (6.5 ft), width 50 cm (20 in).
Climate: Tropical to Mediterranean.
Distribution: Eastern Brazil.
Flowering Time: Summer.
Description: This freely branching species can grow up to 2 m (6.5 ft) in length. The branches are cylindrical, but become flattened, and develop serrated margins with age. The fresh green to dark green stems can reach 40 cm (16 in) in length, and up to 5 cm (2 in) in width. The small areoles are slightly felted, but do not possess any spines. The flowers are up to 2 cm (0.8 in) in length and are creamy-yellow in colour. The spherical fruits are very small and are carmine when ripe.

Rhipsalis pilocarpa

Common Name: None.
Size: Length 60 cm (2 ft), width 30 cm (12 in).
Climate: Tropical to Mediterranean.
Distribution: Eastern Brazil.
Flowering Time: Summer.
Description: This is another pendant species, which can reach 60 cm (2 ft) or more in length. The thin cylindrical stems can have up to 10 ribs, but it is often very difficult to distinguish them. The thin greyish-green stems can reach 12–15 cm (4.8–6 in) in length, and the areoles bear up to 10 short, white, hairy or bristle-like spines. The flowers appear singly or in pairs, and they are 2.5 cm (1 in) in diameter, creamy-ivory in colour, with a pinkish tinge in the centre. The fruits are spherical, up to 1.25 cm (0.5 in) in diameter and yellow when ripe.

Rhipsalis pilocarpa

SCLEROCACTUS

(sklĕr-ō-kăk'-tŭs)

Sclerocactus contains four species and a number of varieties. The name is derived from the Gk, meaning 'hard or dry cactus'. They are globular to short, cylindrical plants, and are up to 45 cm (18 in) high, and up to 10 cm (4 in) in diameter. The plant body ranges from green to bluish-green, and mature specimens have up to 17 ribs. Most species have a somewhat interlacing spine structure, and although some of the spines are flattened, they are also hooked. The areoles can bear up to 20 radial spines, and 3–7 centrals. The radials radiate from the areole, and in some cases are appressed against the body of the plant, but they rarely exceed 2.5 cm (1 in) in length. The centrals may be straight or flattened, rigid or flexible, and in some cases very variable as regards their direction, hence the interlacing effect of the spine structure. Their length is exceedingly variable — 3–12.5 cm (1.2–5 in). The spine colour is equally varied, ranging from white to brown, black or reddish.

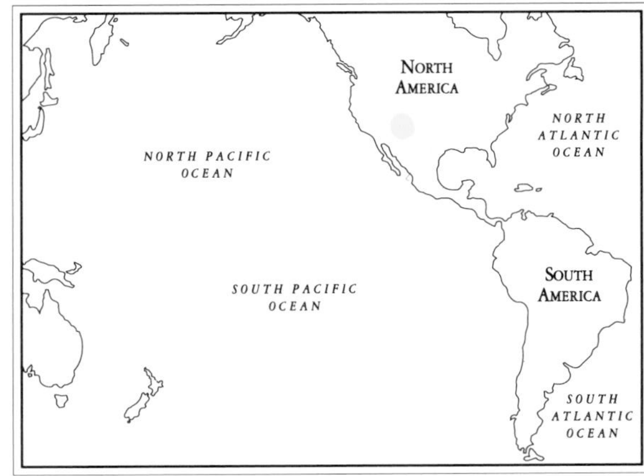

The diurnal, funnel-shaped flowers are 2.5–8 cm (1–3.2 in) in length and 2–5 cm (0.8–2 in) in diameter. The flower colour is very variable — from white, and pink to purple. The fruits are somewhat oblong, 1.5–4 cm (0.6 –1.6 in) in length, purple or brown, and tend to dry out. In some species, the fruit dehisces by a basal pore.

Culture: *Sclerocacti* come from south-western United States, but are not easy plants to grow, and long-term cultural success is usually only possible in a climate where the atmospheric humidity is very low in winter. Most of the species tolerate frosts in conditions of low humidity. They can be raised from seed, which is best achieved by either scarifying them, or freezing them for a few hours, and require a very porous medium for growth, and once well beyond the seedling stage they need full sun. During very hot weather they can be watered fairly freely, but at other times they should be watered only sparingly, and in winter not at all.

Sclerocactus polyancistrus

Sclerocactus polyancistrus

Sclerocactus whipplei var. *roseus*

COMMON NAME: Rose Devil Claw.
SIZE: Height 22.5 cm (9 in), width 10 cm (4 in).
CLIMATE: Medium elevation to Mediterranean.
DISTRIBUTION: South-western United States.
FLOWERING TIME: Spring.
DESCRIPTION: This species has a globular to short, cylindrical habit, and is up to 22.5 cm (9 in) high, and no more than 10 cm (4 in) in diameter. It has up to 15 spiral ribs, which are somewhat tuberculate, and the circular white areoles bear up to 12 spreading radial spines and 4 centrals. The radials rarely exceed 2 cm (0.8 in) in length, while the flattened centrals can reach 6 cm (2.4 in). The centrals range from pink to red in colour, and the lower centrals are usually hooked. The plant illustrated is flowering for the first time and so its spination is juvenile. On a mature plant, the density of the spination is comparable with that of *S. polyancistrus* (above). The flowers are up to 2.5 cm (1 in) in length and in diameter. The fruits are oblong, about 2 cm (0.8 in) in length and reddish-green, and release their seeds from a split near their base.

Sclerocactus polyancistrus

COMMON NAME: Devil Claw.
SIZE: Height 30 cm (12 in), width 12.5 cm (5 in).
CLIMATE: Mediterranean to medium elevation.
DISTRIBUTION: South-western United States.
FLOWERING TIME: Spring.
DESCRIPTION: This species has a simple, cylindrical habit, and the body of the plant is obscured by the interlacing spine formation. They have up to 17 ribs which are up to 1.5 cm (0.6 in) high, and wavy. Each areole has up to 20 flattened radial spines and up to 5 centrals. The radials are spreading, white, flattened, and up to 2.5 cm (1 in) in length. The centrals are porrect, spreading, and 2 or 3 of them are hooked and up to 13 cm (5.2 in) in length. They can be whitish or even brown. The flowers are up to 7.5 cm (3 in) in length, and about 6 cm (2.4 in) in diameter, and vary in colour from magenta to purple. The fruits are oblong, about 4 cm (1.6 in) in length, purple when ripe, partially dry, and dehisce by a basal pore.

Sclerocactus whipplei var. *roseus*

SELENICEREUS

(sē-lē'-nĭ-sē'-rē-ŭs)

Selenicerus contains some 24 species and a few varieties. The generic name is derived from the Gk, meaning 'moon cereus' which is in reference to the nocturnal flowers. They are slender stemmed, clambering plants which produce numerous aerial roots. The green stems branch freely, are exceedingly long, and normally have 4–5 angled stems which are 1.25–2.5 cm (0.5–1 in) in diameter. The small areoles bear 0–15 spines, and in a few species it is possible to differentiate between the radials and the centrals. Where this is possible there may be 1–4 centrals. The spines are fine and stiff in most species, and rarely exceed 1.25 cm (0.5 in) in length (and are generally much less). The spine colour usually ranges from white or straw in colour to brown.

The nocturnal funnel-shaped flowers can appear anywhere along the stems, although usually appearing from the upper part of the stem. They are exceedingly fragrant, can be up to 40 cm (16 in) in length, and have a long tube. The exterior of the tube can have hairs, bristles, or spines. The inner petals are fairly broad, and white, while the interior of the flower contains a large number of stamens, which are usually in two series. The fruits are usually spherical, up to 10 cm (4 in) in diameter, and covered either with hairs, bristles, or spines. When ripe, the fruits can be green, yellow, or in varying shades of red or purple.

Culture: *Selenicerei* come from northern parts of South America, Central America, many parts of the West Indies, and just into south-eastern United States. They are mostly quick growing plants, and can be easily raised from seed or propagated from cuttings. During spring to autumn (fall) they like plenty of water and if temperatures are high and watering is continued they will grow throughout the year. Very few species will withstand even light frosts, and all prefer a minimum temperature of 10°C (50°F). Cuttings can be used as grafting stock for seedlings of other slow growing rarities. Although they are clambering, fast growing plants, they are very free flowering.

NORTH AMERICA
NORTH PACIFIC OCEAN
NORTH ATLANTIC OCEAN
SOUTH PACIFIC OCEAN
SOUTH AMERICA
SOUTH ATLANTIC OCEAN

Selenicereus urbanianus

Selenicereus grandiflorus var. *ophites*

Common Name: Queen of the Night.
Size: Length 4 or 5 m (13–16.25 ft).
Climate: Low to medium elevation.
Distribution: Eastern Mexico.
Flowering Time: Summer onwards.
Description: A free branching species, with six to eight dark green angled stems, up to 2.5 cm (1 in) in diameter. The tips of new stems are strongly tinged with red. The areoles are set fairly well apart, bearing up to ten fairly rigid, acicular brown spines, usually less than 0.5 cm (0.2 in) in length. The nocturnal flowers are up to 30 cm (12 in) in diameter, heavily scented, and white, but the outer petals and sepals are tinged with green. The spherical fruits are up to 5 cm (2 in) or more in diameter, changing from green to purplish as they ripen, and possessing a few clusters of short, but quite strong spines.

Selenicereus grandiflorus var. *ophites*

Selenicereus hamatus

Selenicereus urbanianus

Common Name: Queen of the Night.
Size: Length 4–5 m (13–16.3 ft).
Climate: Mediterranean to tropical.
Distribution: Cuba and Haiti.
Flowering Time: Late spring onwards.
Description: This species is freely branching, and 4–6 angled green stems which are sometimes tinged with red. On old parts of a plant the stems can be up to 5 cm (2 in) in diameter. Younger stems have a diameter well below 2.5 cm (1 in). The small white areoles bear up to 6 or 7 fine acicular spines which are up to 1 cm (0.4 in) in length and usually straw or brown in colour. The flowers are 20–30 cm (8–12 in) in length and the petals are white on the upper parts and slightly yellowish below. The sepals are green, but, as with the stems, tinged with red. The fruits are spherical, spiny, 5 cm (2 in) in diameter and reddish-green when ripe.

Selenicereus hamatus

Common Name: Queen of the Night.
Size: Length 4–5 m (13–16.3 ft).
Climate: Tropical to mediterranean.
Distribution: Eastern Mexico.
Flowering Time: Late spring onwards.
Description: This is a freely branching, light green, stemmed species, which barely exceed 2 cm (0.8 in) in diameter. It has 4 angled stems, which are distinctly notched at the areole positions. The areoles bear up to 6 white to brownish bristly spines — 2 or 3 of the spines are slightly stouter than the others. The flowers are up to 40 cm (16 in) in length, have white petals, and reddish to reddish-green sepals. The fruits are spherical, 5 cm (2 in) in diameter, reddish-green when ripe, and have numerous bristles.

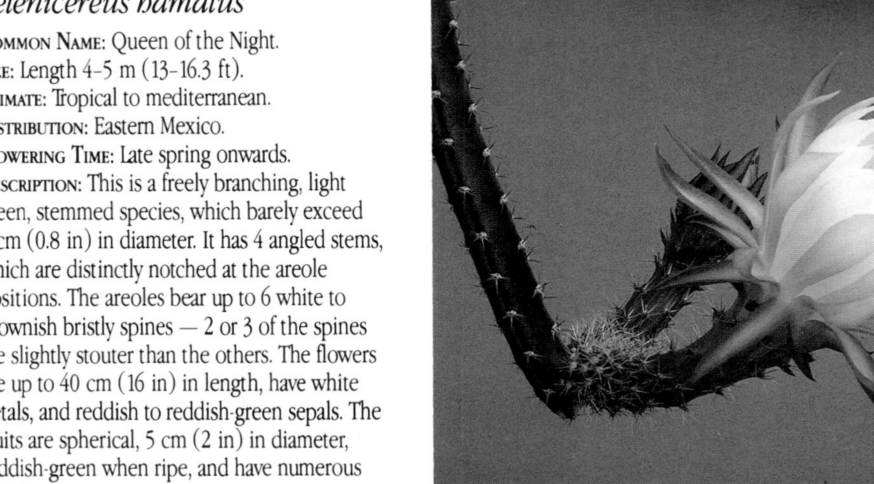

Selenicereus urbanianus

Stetsonia

(stĕt-sō'-nĭ-ă)

Stetsonia is a monotypic genus, and the generic name honours Francis Lynde Stetson of New York. It is a freely branching columnar plant, which can reach a height of 8 m (26 ft), and it has a basal trunk which has a diameter of 40 cm (16 in). Old specimens have been seen with more than 100 branches. The stems have 8–9 obtuse ribs, which are bluish-green to green in colour, and the white areoles are set well apart. The areoles bear up to 9 stout porrect spines, which tend to be thickened towards the lower parts. The spines are 3–5 cm (1.2–2 in) in length, yellowish-brown when young, and off-white with black tips when older.

The white nocturnal flowers are about 15 cm (6 in) in length and are glabrous and slightly curved and have a narrow tube. The fruits are almost spherical, and are densely covered with overlapping scales. They are greenish-red in colour when ripe.

Culture: It is a very striking plant, and is a dominant feature of the high plains of northern Argentina and adjacent parts of Bolivia. *Stetsonias* are very easy to raise from seed, and mature within a few years to the stoutly spined plant illustrated (see below). The plants can be rooted from cuttings quite easily, but they are rarely available to amateurs in this form — unlike many other columnar cerei. If the atmospheric humidity is low it can withstand light frosts, but young plants can be scarred by frosts in damp winter conditions. It enjoys a fairly rich soil, with plenty of water during the warmer growing months.

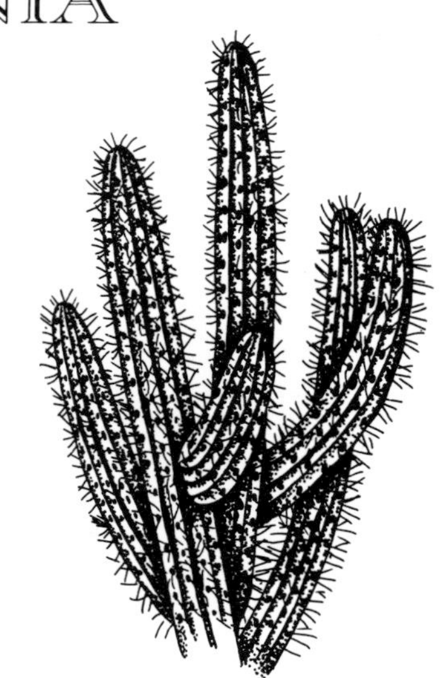

Stetsonia coryne

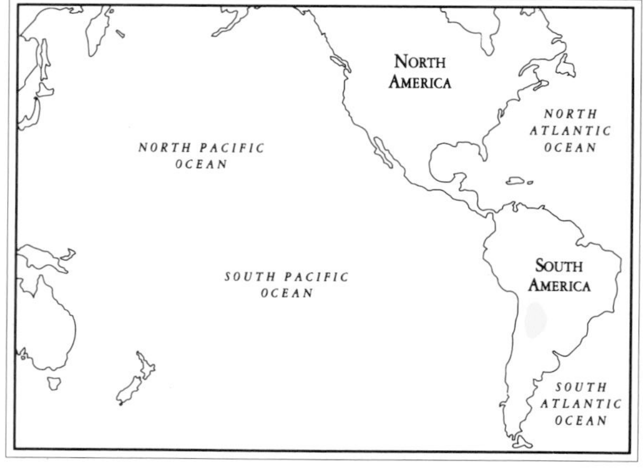

Stetsonia coryne

Stetsonia coryne

Common Name: None.
Size: Height 8 m (26 ft), width 3-4 m (9.7-13 ft).
Climate: High elevation.
Distribution: As above.
Flowering Time: Late spring onwards.
Description: As there is only one species, this information is found above.

STROMBOCACTUS

(strŏm-bō-kăk'-tŭs)

Strombocactus is a monotypic genus, and the generic name is derived from the Gk, meaning 'top-shaped cactus'. It is of a flattened, globular habit, is simple, and has a stout taproot. The body is bluish-green to grey, up to 15 cm (6 in) in diameter, and has up to 13 ribs, which are normally in a spiral formation. There is a little wool in the centre of the plant, but the areoles soon become glabrous and bear up to 5 short bristly spines, but are usually only present in the centre of the plant, and soon disappear.

The flowers are up to 4 cm (1.6 in) in diameter, are white, but are sometimes slightly tinged with yellow. The fruits are no more than 0.7 cm (0.3 in) in length, brownish, papery skinned, and scatter the dust-like seeds around the centre of the plant.

Culture: It comes from central Mexico, and has been much sought after by collectors. It can only be raised from seed and, as with genera such as *Ariocarpus* (see page 37), it takes many years to produce a flowering plant. If the minute seedlings survive the first 18 months they should grow to maturity. Mature plants need a well drained growing medium, and should only be watered freely during very hot weather. At other times they should be watered with care. During the winter, keep the plants dry and they will withstand quite cool conditions even when the atmospheric humidity is not low.

Strombocactus disciformis

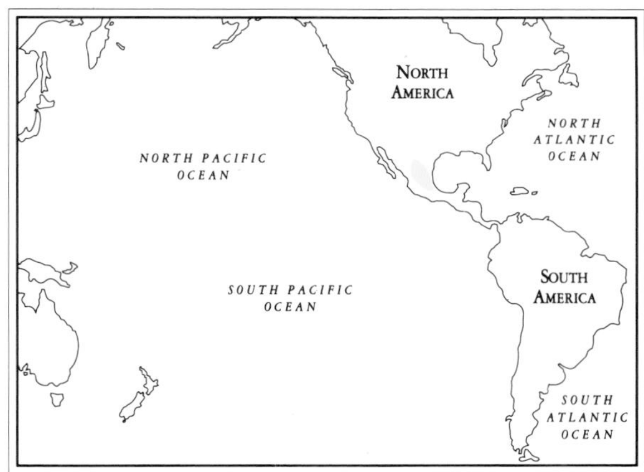

Strombocactus disciformis

COMMON NAME: None.
SIZE: Height 5 cm (2 in), width 15 cm (6 in).
CLIMATE: Medium elevation.
DISTRIBUTION: As above.
FLOWERING TIME: Late spring onwards.
DESCRIPTION: As there is only one species, this information is found above.

Strombocactus disciformis

SULCOREBUTIA

(sŭl'-kō-rĕ-bōōt'-ĭ-ă)

Sulcorebutia contains over 40 described species, and many varieties, although many of these species are very similar. The generic name is derived from the Lat *sulcus* (groove or furrow), and their similarity to the genus *Rebutia* (see page 166). The areoles however are narrow and elongated, unlike the small circular areoles on *Rebutias*. *Sulcorebutias* can be solitary or freely clustering, have globular heads, which are sometimes depressed, and they usually have substantial taproots, and rather stronger spination than the *Rebutias*. Many species have a true pectinate spine formation (invariably with no central spines). They are also much harder bodied plants than the *Rebutias* and usually have a distinct rib structure. The plant body can be green, reddish, or even slate black in colour.

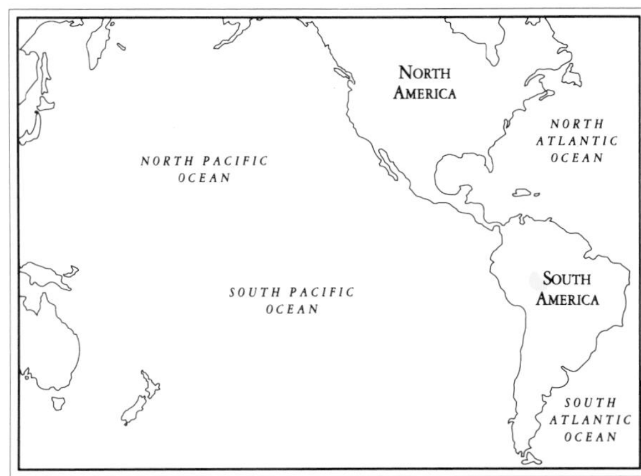

The flowers, like the *Rebutias*, appear quite low on the plant. However, unlike the *Rebutias*, in many species the petals are quite waxy, and there is an even greater range of colour and even some bi-coloured species. The fruits can be oblong or spherical, and smooth or have a few scales.

Culture: *Sulcorebutias* come from Bolivia, where they are found in mountainous habitats up to 3000 m (9840 ft). The genus was erected by Curt Backeberg in 1951, and it is only since 1970 that a wide range of species have become available to the amateur enthusiast. They are exceedingly popular in Europe, because of their freely flowering habit, ease of culture, and resistance to many degrees of frost if kept dry in winter. If temperatures are too warm in winter their flowering qualities will be adversely affected. Like the *Rebutias* they prefer a soil containing humus, and they should be watered freely from spring to autumn (fall).

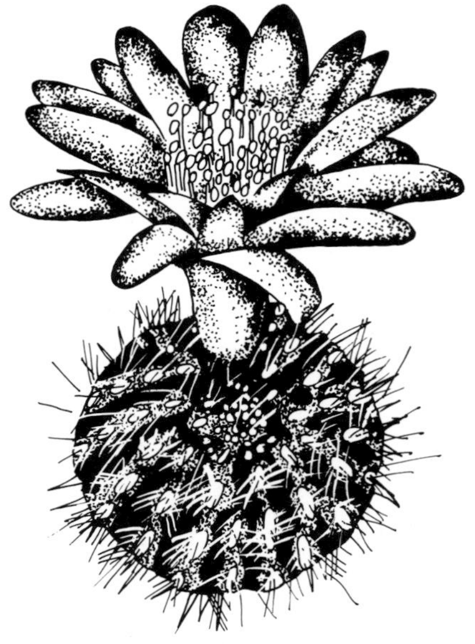

Sulcorebutia tiraquensis

Sulcorebutia hoffmanniana

COMMON NAME: None.
SIZE: Height 4 cm (1.6 in), width 20 cm (8 in).
CLIMATE: High elevation.
DISTRIBUTION: Bolivia.
FLOWERING TIME: Spring.
DESCRIPTION: This is a very variable species, but all forms are freely clustering, and have individual heads reaching a height and diameter of 4 cm (1.6 in). In colour the heads can be dark green to brownish-green, and they have a tubercled rib structure. The elongated areoles are white, bear 10–20 radial spines, and up to 3 longer, stouter centrals. The centrals can reach 1.5 cm (0.6 in) in length. The radial spines can be yellow, pink, or brown, while the centrals are often a dark reddish-brown colour. This species is a very variable one as regards its vegetative structure. The flowers are 3 cm (1.2 in) in diameter, bi-coloured — either red and yellow, or magenta and yellow. The fruits are very small, reddish-brown in colour and have a few pale brown scales.

Sulcorebutia hoffmanniana

Sulcorebutia tiraquensis

Sulcorebutia tiraquensis

COMMON NAME: None.
SIZE: Height 5 cm (2 in), width 20 cm (8 in).
CLIMATE: High elevation.
DISTRIBUTION: Bolivia.
FLOWERING TIME: Spring.
DESCRIPTION: This is a very variable, globular, clustering species, and individual heads can reach a diameter of 5 cm (2 in) or more. It has a dark green or bluish-green body, and up to 26 spirally arranged ribs. The oval areoles are quite large and have white or yellowish-brown wool. They bear up to 30 fine, radial spines on old mature plants, and 2 stronger centrals. The radials are 0.5–3 cm (0.2–1.2 in) in length, and the centrals are even longer. The general spine colour varies from straw yellow and brown to dark reddish-brown. The magenta flowers are 3–5 cm (1.25–2 in) in length and in diameter. The small fruits are violet-pink when ripe.

THELOCACTUS

(thē'-lō-kăk'-tŭs)

Thelocactus contains some 25 species and a number of varieties. The generic name is derived from the Gk, meaning 'nipple cactus'. The plants can be solitary or clustering, globular to elongated, and have a very tuberculate rib structure. They can be up to 25 cm (10 in) in height, and 20 cm (8 in) in diameter, and have up to 20 ribs. The body colour varies from shades of green to almost slate-grey. The areoles are fairly prominent, circular or oval, and often have some white or cream wool. They can bear up to 25 radial spines and 1–4 centrals. The radial spines can be very fine or moderately stout, spreading or appressed, and up to 3 cm (1.2 in) in length. The centrals are usually stronger, occasionally very stout, can be straight, curved or even flattened, and stand out from the plant. The spine colour varies from white and yellow, to reddish or black.

The flowers are generally wide opening, 4–7 cm (1.6–2.8 in) in diameter, and in a very wide range of colours — from white to vivid shades of red and magenta. The fruits are spherical or slightly egg-shaped, rarely more than 1 cm (0.4 in) in diameter and when ripe they are dry and split irregularly allowing the seeds to spill out and can be in any one of a variety of colours.

Culture: *Thelocacti* come from the mainland area of Mexico, and south-western United States. They are easy plants to raise from seed, although clustering species can be propagated vegetatively. They are not fast growing plants, but they are easy to cultivate, and need a moderately well drained soil, and can be watered freely during all hot weather. In winter they should be kept dry and they can withstand temperatures near freezing point. They are very rewarding plants, as most species are very freely flowering — often over a period of 2 or 3 months.

Thelocactus bicolor var. *bolansis*

Thelocactus bicolor var. *bolansis*

Thelocactus conothele fa. *argenteus*

Common Name: None.
Size: Height 10 cm (4 in), width 10 cm (4 in).
Climate: Medium elevation.
Distribution: Central Mexico.
Flowering Time: Early summer.
Description: This species is solitary and globular, and has 15–18 tuberculate ribs in a slight spiral. The green body colour is almost masked by the dense spination. The circular areoles are quite large, have up to 16 radial spines appressed against the body, and 1–3 centrals. The radials are slightly flexible, up to 3 cm (1.2 in) in length, and the longest centrals can exceed 5 cm (2 in) in length. The spines are white when young and grey a little with age. The flowers are about 4 cm (1.6 in) in diameter, have golden yellow petals, and a reddish tinge at their bases. The fruit is spherical, under 1 cm (0.4 in) in diameter, and greyish-green when ripe.

Thelocactus bicolor var. *bolansis*

Common Name: Nipple Cactus.
Size: Height 20 cm (8 in), width 10 cm (4 in).
Climate: Medium elevation.
Distribution: Mexico.
Flowering Time: Early summer onwards.
Description: This species is usually solitary and has a tapering upright habit in age. The usually pale green body has up to 13 ribs, which are sometimes slightly spiralled, and have oval, creamy-yellow areoles. These bear up to 25 thin spreading radial spines and up to 3 thicker centrals, which tend to be flattened. The radials can be up to 3 cm (1.2 in) in length, and the centrals can be up to 5 cm (2 in) — occasionally even longer. All the spines are off-white to cream in colour. The flowers are up to 7.25 cm (3 in) in diameter and are purplish-pink to pale magenta in colour. The fruits are 1 cm (0.4 in) in diameter and are greyish-green when ripe.

Thelocactus conothele fa. *argenteus*

Thelocactus saussieri

Thelocactus saussieri

Common Name: None.
Size: Height 7.5 cm (3 in), width 20 cm (8 in).
Climate: Medium elevation.
Distribution: Central Mexico.
Flowering Time: Summer.
Description: This is a solitary, globular species with a dark green body which is not masked by dense spination. The plants can reach a diameter of 20 cm (8 in), and the rib structure is barely visible. It is a very distinctive species and it has very prominent oblong tubercles, and smaller areoles, which bear 7–11 spreading fine radial spines, and 1–4 stouter centrals. The radials rarely exceed 1.25 cm (0.5 in) in length, but the straight or slightly curved centrals can reach 4 cm. The spines are off-white to brown in colour. The flowers are about 4 cm (1.6 in) in diameter, and are purple to pale magenta in colour. The fruits are almost identical to those of *T. conothele* var. *argenteus* (see above).

TOUMEYA

(too-mē-a)

Toumeya contains some 11 species, and it is named in honour of D. J. W. Toumey. They are small spherical plants, solitary or sparingly clustering, and 3–5 cm (1.2–2 in) in height and in diameter — with the exception of *T. papyracantha* which can grow up to 10 cm (4 in) high, with a diameter of 2.5 cm (1 in). In only a few species is there a distinct rib formation, and then it is in the form of spirally arranged tubercles. In the remaining species there are numerous very prominent tubercles. The areoles in some species have a lot of white wool, particularly around the apex of the plant. The areoles can bear 1–12 spines, and in only three species are there distinct centrals. In these species, the centrals are much longer than the radials, 1–5 cm (0.4–2 in). In *T. papyracantha* all the spines are very papery and somewhat flattened. However, with the others, the spines are usually flexible, bristly, or have a slightly corky appearance. The spine colour varies from white or varying shades of brown to black.

The small funnel-shaped flowers are 1.5–3.5 cm (0.6–1.4 in) in length and 2–4 cm (0.8–1.6 in) in diameter. Their colour ranges from off-white to pink or pale violet, and the petals sometimes have a darker median stripe. The very small fruits may be naked or have scales on their exterior. They are green or greenish-brown when young and dry up completely, splitting in different ways, so that the seeds are dispersed.

Culture: *Toumeyas* mainly come from central Mexico, whereas *T. papyracantha* comes from south-western United States. They are all easily raised from seed and relatively slow growing, but most species can be expected to reach flowering size within five years. *T. papyracantha* needs a very well drained soil, as it can easily rot at the neck (which is why it is so often seen in collections as grafted specimens). The other species can be watered fairly freely during hot weather, but should be kept dry and protected from frosts during the colder months.

Toumeya pseudomacrochele

Toumeya klinkerianus

Common Name: None.
Size: Height 3 cm (1.2 in), width 4 cm (1.6 in).
Climate: Medium elevation.
Distribution: Central Mexico.
Flowering Time: Early summer.
Description: These are solitary plants, with a light green to brownish-green body, and white wool in the centre. They do not have a distinct rib structure, but have spirally arranged tubercles. The areoles bear 1–3 short greyish spines, but in habitat the spines are gradually lost. The white flowers are about 1.5 cm (0.6 in) in height and in diameter. Each petal has a darker median stripe on the lower surface. The fruits are 0.5 cm (0.2 in) in diameter, green when young, and turning to grey as they dry up and split.

Toumeya klinkerianus

Toumeya pseudomacrochele

Common Name: None.
Size: Height 5 cm (2 in), width 4 cm (1.6 in).
Climate: Medium elevation.
Distribution: Central Mexico.
Flowering Time: Summer.
Description: This species has a solitary, flattened globular habit, but in cultivation (as illustrated) tends to grow slightly taller. It grows up to 4 cm (1.6 in) in diameter, has an olive-green body, and plenty of white wool on the top of the plant. The prominent tubercles have very white woolly areoles which bear up to 8 bristly, flexible yellowish to brownish spines. They are up to 1.25 cm (0.5 in) in length and tend to interlace with one another. The flowers are 3.5 cm (1.4 in) in diameter, and are white or pale pink, with a darker median stripe down each petal. The fruits are very small and olive-brown, turning to grey as they dry up and split.

Toumeya pseudomacrochele

TRICHOCEREUS

(trĭk-ō-sē´-rē-ŭs)

Trichocereus contains some 70 species and many varieties. The generic name is derived from two Gk words meaning, 'hair' and 'cereus'. They can be low growing, freely branching plants with either slim or thick stems, or erect, robust stemmed plants up to 10 m (32.8 ft) high. These tall growing species can have a stem diameter of 35 cm (14 in) or more. The stem colour ranges from pale green to bluish-green or chalky blue, with 6–25, usually straight, distinct ribs. The areoles are quite prominent, fairly well separated, and usually contain some wool, which is white, grey, or yellowish-brown. The spine count varies from five to more than 50 per areole. The spines can be short and fine, or as with the larger species, stout, and up to 15 cm (6 in) in length. The colour is equally variable — from white to brown and black.

The flowers can be nocturnal, diurnal or, as with the Chilean species, remain open for a few days. These variations, and the fact that not all the species have white flowers have been used by some authorities to place some species into other genera. However, the basic structure of all *Trichocereus* flowers is very similar. They are mostly funnel-shaped flowers with long tubes, 6–25 cm (2.4–10 in) in length and 7.5–30 cm (3–12 in) in diameter. The exterior of the tube usually has some hairs and fine spines, particularly towards the base and around the ovary area. The fruits are spherical to egg-shaped, green, bluish-green, or reddish when ripe, and are 4–7.5 cm (1.6–3 in) in diameter.

Culture: These plants come from Argentina, Bolivia, Chile and Ecuador. They are all easily raised from seed, and only a few species can be termed slow growing. Many of them are quite rapid growers, requiring a rich soil and plenty of water during spring to autumn (fall). The majority of species can also be easily propagated from cuttings, producing a flowering plant within 12 months. If kept completely dry in winter most species will tolerate cool conditions and even light frosts. Some species come from altitudes of up to 3000 m (9840 ft), where they endure very low temperatures, including snow. However, atmospheric humidity which is harmful to the plants is generally low.

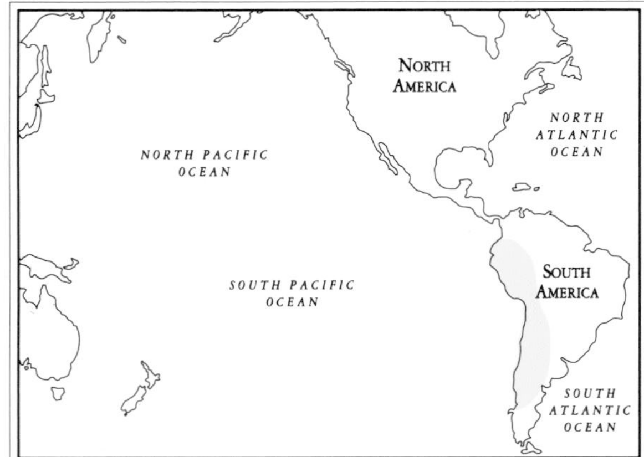

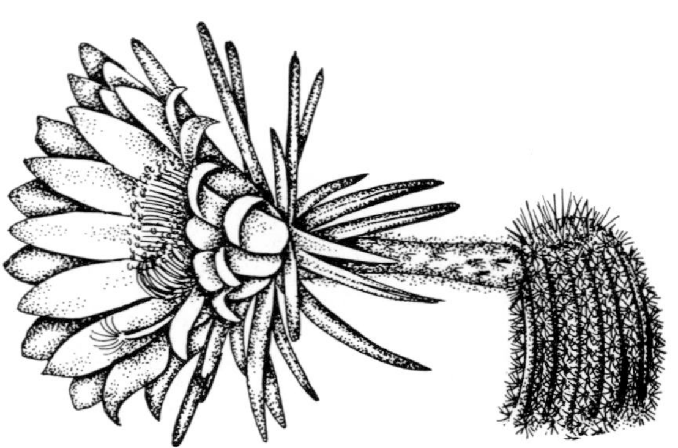

Trichocereus fabrisii

Trichocereus fabrisii

Common Name: None.
Size: Length 1.5 m (4.5 ft), width 8 cm (3.2 in).
Climate: High elevation.
Distribution: Argentina.
Flowering Time: Summer.
Description: This is a fairly robust, green stemmed species, which tends to be semi-prostrate. The apical ends of the stems, from which the large flowers appear, are lifted. The stems can grow to 1–1.5 m (3–4.5 ft) in length and to 8 cm (3.2 in) in diameter. There are up to 17 or 18 shallow ribs, and the small areoles have some wool, which is straw in colour. They bear up to 12 thin acicular, white to straw spines. These radiate out, but the longest ones are porrect, and up to 1.5 cm (0.6 in) in length. The funnel-shaped white flowers are 25 cm (10 in) in length and 20 cm (8 in) in diameter. The interior of the flower contains numerous stamens in two whorls. The exterior of the flower tube towards its base is covered with white hair and some fine bristly spines. The fruits are spherical, about 5 cm (2 in) in diameter, creamy-green when ripe, and covered with white hair and bristly spines.

Trichocereus fabrisii

Trichocereus poco fa. *albiflorus*

Trichocereus shaferi

Trichocereus poco fa. *albiflorus*

Common Name: None.
Size: Height 4.5 m (14 ft), width 20–25 cm (8–10 in).
Climate: High elevation.
Distribution: Bolivia.
Flowering Time: Summer.
Description: This is an erect, stout columnar species, which only branches sparingly when quite large. There are up to 25 straight ribs, which have quite large, oval grey areoles. These bear up to 20 reddish-brown spines, which can be up to 8 cm (3.2 in) in length. On the upper part of the plant the spines are shorter and they are quite flexible. Lower down the stem, the longest spines are quite stout. The white flowers are about 14 cm (5.6 in) in length and 10 cm (4 in) in diameter. The fruits are spherical, 5 cm (2 in) in diameter, and light green in colour.

Trichocereus shaferi

Common Name: None.
Size: Height 50 cm (18 in), width 12.5 cm (5 in).
Climate: Medium elevation.
Distribution: Argentina.
Flowering Time: Summer and autumn (fall).
Description: A robust stemmed species, clustering from the base, with individual stems attaining a height of 50 cm (18 in). The stems are pale green, possessing up to 14 ribs, which are about 1.25 cm (0.5 in) high. The white areoles bear up to ten somewhat flexible yellowish to yellowish-brown spines, of variable length, but rarely exceeding 1.25 cm (0.5 in). The central and radial spines are indistinguishable. The funnel-shaped white flowers are 18–20 cm (7–8 in) in length, with brown hairs on the exterior of the tube. The fruits are egg-shaped, up to 4 cm (1.6 in) in length, and green with brownish hairs.

WEINGARTIA

(wīn'-gā-tĭ-ă)

Weingartia contains over 24 species and a number of varieties. The generic name honours Wilhelm Weingart, although the first species were described under the generic name *Spegazzinia* (after Dr Carlos Spegazzini, an Argentinian botanist who was one of the first to make a study of the plants of his country). This was later found to be a homonym and thus invalid. The plants are simple or clustering, and have mainly globular heads, sometimes with a very narrow neck between the base of the head and the taproot. They can have up to 21 ribs, although in some species the rib structure is indistinct and the plants have a tubercled appearance. The oval areoles can be quite large, up to 1.25 cm (0.5 in) in length, and are usually filled with white wool. The areoles bear up to 16 spreading radial spines, 0.5–3 cm (0.2–1.2 in) in length, and 3–15 centrals 1–5 cm (0.4–2 in) in length. The radial spines are generally curved or appressed against the plant, whereas the centrals, although curved, stand out further. Their colour ranges from off-white and yellowish to brown, sometimes with darker tips.

The flowers are produced freely, usually in rings away from the centre of the plant, and are rarely more than 3 cm (1.2 in) in diameter. Their colour ranges from yellow and orange to purple. In some species more than one flower will come from a single areole. The fruits are slightly egg-shaped, up to 1 cm (0.4 in) in length, yellowish-green to reddish-green when ripe.

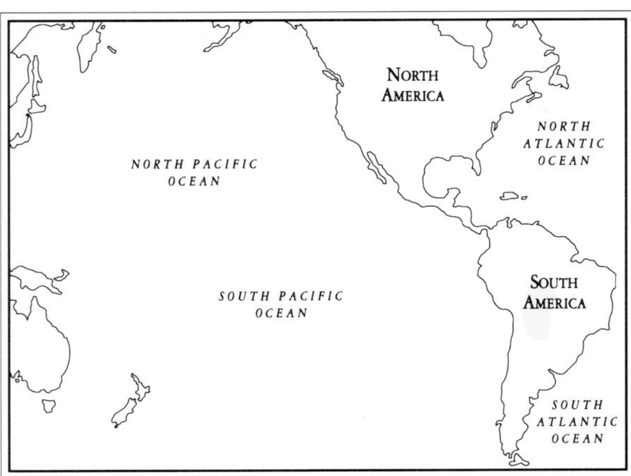

Culture: *Weingartias* come from eastern Bolivia, northern Argentina, and just into Chile. Few species present any cultural problems and they are easy plants to raise from seed, reaching maturity in a few years. They like a fairly well drained soil, but appreciate plenty of water during the hotter months. In winter they should be kept dry, and they can withstand quite cool conditions. A few species can endure a few degrees of frost in habitat.

Weingartia riograndensis

Weingartia neumanniana

Weingartia neumanniana

Common Name: None.
Size: Height 7 cm (2.8 in), width 5 cm (2 in).
Climate: Low elevation.
Distribution: Northern Argentina.
Flowering Time: Early summer onwards.
Description: This species is initially globular, but becomes slightly elongated, and it possesses a carrot-like tuberous root. The body of the plant varies in colour, from grey-green to almost black. The circular areoles have quite a lot of white wool, and bear up to six radial spines and one central. These are all quite stiff, standing out from the plant body. The central is slightly longer, up to 2.5 cm (1 in) in length, and the spines range in colour from reddish-brown to nearly black. The flowers are about 2.5 cm (1 in) in diameter, and range from yellow to almost orange. The fruits are slightly egg-shaped, about 0.5 cm (0.2 in) in length, and dark brown when ripe, with greenish scales.
Note: This species is very similar to *W. fidaiana*, and has been confused with it in the past.

Weingartia riograndensis

Weingartia riograndensis

Common Name: None.
Size: Height 12.5 cm (5 in), width 15–20 cm (6–8 in).
Climate: Medium elevation.
Distribution: Bolivia.
Flowering Time: Early summer onwards.
Description: This species is globular to slightly elongated, particularly in cultivation, and it branches sparingly with age. Individual heads are up to 10 cm (4 in) in diameter. It has a fresh green body and a tubercled rather than a ribbed structure. The areoles are nearly 1 cm (0.4 in) in length and have plenty of white wool. They bear up to 10 radial spines and 6 centrals. The spines are spreading, up to 2 cm (0.8 in) in length, off-white to greyish-brown, and often have darker tips. The golden-yellow flowers are 3 cm (1.2 in) in length and slightly less in diameter. The fruits are slightly egg-shaped, 1 cm (0.4 in) in length and yellowish-green when ripe.

WIGGINSIA

(wĭg´-ĭn-sĭ-ă)

Wigginsia contains some 15 species and a number of varieties. For over one hundred years the generic name used for this group of plants was *Malacocarpus*, but in 1964 this name was discontinued as it was a homonym, and D. M. Porter replaced it with *Wigginsia*. The plants are spherical to short and cylindrical, are usually solitary, and rarely exceed 25 cm (10 in) in height and 15 cm (6 in) in diameter. They have green to dark blue-green bodies, and up to 30 ribs, which are undulating or tuberculate in formation. The crowns of the plants are generally filled with white wool, as are the areoles which bear up to 12 radial spines, and if a central is present there is rarely more than one. The spine length is 0.5–2 cm (0.2–0.8 in) and they may be flexible or rigid, are sometimes appressed, and are white, grey, or brown in colour.

The flowers are 3–5 cm (1.2–2 in) in diameter, are in varying shades of yellow, and have short wool-covered tubes. The fruits are oblong, up to 6 cm (2.4 in) in length, are yellowish or reddish when ripe, and have wool attached to their base.

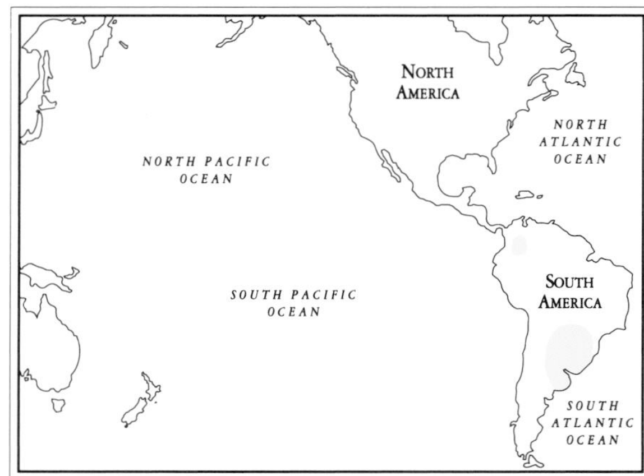

Culture: *Wigginsias* come from Argentina, Brazil, Colombia and Uruguay. They can be raised quite easily from seed, and plants can be expected to flower within three to five years. During spring to early autumn (fall) they can be watered fairly freely but should be kept dry and protected from frosts during the coldest months.

Wigginsia sessiliflora

Wigginsia corynodes

Common Name: None.
Size: Height 25 cm (10 in), width 15 cm (6 in).
Climate: Mediterranean.
Distribution: Argentina, southern Brazil and Uruguay.
Flowering Time: Summer.
Description: This is a spherical, but in age short and cylindrical. The body of the plant is a dark blue-green and has a very white woolly centre and up to 16 ribs which have transverse indentations. The areoles also contain a lot of white wool, and bear 12 radial spines and sometimes one central. The spines are rigid and brown to grey in colour, and the lower radials are the longest — up to 2 cm (0.8 in). The flowers are up to 5 cm (2 in) in length and in diameter, and are deep yellow with brown wool around the bases of the tubes. The fruits are oblong, about 4 cm (1.6 in) in length and reddish when ripe.

Wigginsia corynodes

Wigginsia sessiliflora

Common Name: None.
Size: Height 8 cm (3.2 in), width 15 cm (6 in).
Climate: Mediterranean.
Distribution: Argentina and Uruguay.
Flowering Time: Summer.
Description: This species has a flattened globular habit, a dark green body, a lot of white wool in its crown, and up to 30 ribs, which are rather tuberculate and swollen beneath the areoles. These bear up to 4 or 5 radial spines, and sometimes one central. The spines are appressed, up to 2 cm (0.8 in) in length and off-white to cream in colour. The flowers are no more than 2.5 cm (1 in) in diameter and are a pale yellow to golden-yellow colour. As with *W. corynodes* (see above) there is a lot of brown wool around the very short tubes of the flowers. The fruits are oblong, rarely more than 2 cm (0.8 in) in length and creamy-yellow when ripe.

Wigginsia sessiliflora

Wilcoxia

(wĭl-cŏk'-sĭ-ă)

Wilcoxia contains some ten species, and the generic name honours T. E. Wilcox, an American General. The plants are dwarf, shrubby, have slender multi-ribbed stems, and tuberous root systems. The stems are 15–60 cm (6–24 in) in length, and in cultivation tend to require some support. They are mostly flexible — some are rather soft and fleshy — and have minute areoles. These bear equally minute spines, fine white hair or fine bristly spines. In a few species it is possible to distinguish between the radial and the central spines, and in *W. poselgeri* the centrals can reach 1 cm (0.4 in) in length.

The flowers are funnel-shaped, 2–7 cm (0.8–2.8 in) in diameter, and appear from the upper parts of stems. Some species have a long slender tube. Their colour ranges from white and pink, to red and purple. The fruits are usually spherical, 1–2 cm (0.4–0.8 in) in diameter, and covered either with hair or bristly spines.

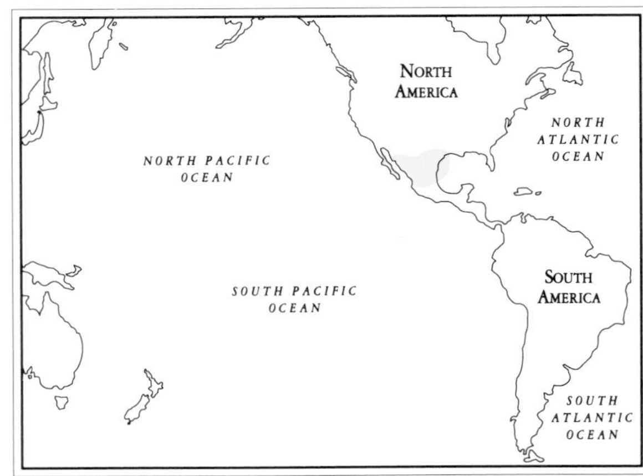

Culture: *Wilcoxias* are native to central and western Mexico, and just into south-western United States. They are easy plants to raise from seed or cuttings, and should be watered freely only during very hot weather. At other times they should be watered more carefully, and in winter should be kept dry. Most species can withstand cool conditions.

Wilcoxia schmollii

Wilcoxia schmollii

Wilcoxia schmollii

Common Name: None.
Size: Height 10 cm (4 in).
Climate: Medium elevation.
Distribution: Central Mexico.
Flowering Time: Early summer onwards.
Description: This is a rather weakly stemmed species, which is sometimes no more than 10 cm (4 in) in length, unless the plant is grafted. It is somewhat slower growing than most of the other species. The stems have up to 10 fine tuberculate ribs, and they are covered with white or blackish hair. The flowers are 4 cm (1.6 in) in diameter and pink to purplish-pink in colour. The fruits are very small, covered with hair less dense but the same colour as that on the stems.

Wilcoxia albiflora

Common Name: None.
Size: Height 15 cm (6 in), width 10 cm (4 in).
Climate: Medium elevation.
Distribution: Central Mexico.
Flowering Time: Late spring onwards.
Description: This is a freely branching species, which has mainly erect stems, up to 15 cm (6 in) in length, but rarely more than 0.6 cm (0.2 in) in diameter. The light green stems have minute areoles, which bear up to 12 equally minute spines appressed against the stem. The flowers are often produced apically, are 2.5 cm (1 in) in diameter, and are white or very pale pink. The fruits are very small and have a few spines.

Wilcoxia albiflora

WITTIA

(wĭt'-ĭ-ă)

Wittia is a monotypic genus (as *W. panamensis* is synonymous with *W. amazonica*), and the generic name honours N. H. Witt. They are small epiphytic shrubby plants, freely branching, have thin green flat shoots, and the mid-rib on each shoot shows up prominently. These shoots can be 15–45 cm (6–18 in) in length and 4–7 cm (1.6–2.8 in) wide. The edges of the shoots are distinctly notched between the areole positions, which do not bear any spines.

Wittia amazonica

The flowers are cylindrical in shape, do not open very wide, and are rarely more than 2.5 cm (1 in) in length. They are wine-red or purple, and have a slight bluish tinge. The fruit is small, tuberculate, rather angular with 3 angled scales, and greenish-red or red when ripe.

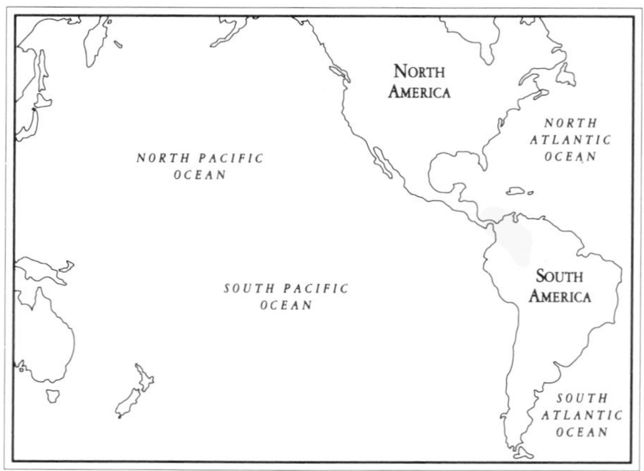

Culture: *Wittias* are native to Colombia, Panama and northern Peru, and are very popular in cultivation because the plants are usually massed with flowers. They are fairly easy plants to grow from seed or cuttings, and as with other epiphytic cacti need a soil rich in humus. A warm humid atmosphere is particularly important for these plants, otherwise shoots can die back very easily. They like plenty of water from spring to autumn (fall), light shade and in winter prefer a minimum temperature of 10°C (50°F), and some water.

Wittia amazonica

Wittia amazonica

Common Name: None.
Size: Length 45 cm (18 in), width 45 cm (18 in).
Climate: Tropical.
Distribution: As above.
Flowering Time: Spring to autumn (fall).
Description: As there is only one species, this information is found above.

ZYGOCACTUS

(zī-gō-kăk'-tŭs)

Zygocactus contains just one species, three varieties, and numerous colourful cultivars. The generic name is derived from the Gk, meaning 'yoke cactus'. They are epiphytic plants, which when young are erect bushes, but as the segmented stems get longer, become pendant. These segments, or leaf-like joints, come from a basal trunk, which becomes quite woody with age. The green leaf-like joints are up to 4.5 cm (1.8 in) in length and 2.5 cm (1 in) wide and have up to 4 acute teeth along the margins. The areoles are slightly felted, and can possess up to 3 very short fine bristles.

The zygomorphic flowers appear singly or in pairs from the apex of a joint, and are 5–7.5 cm (2–3 in) in length. The flower colour, particularly in the new cultivars, is exceedingly varied, ranging from white tinged with pink, to yellow, orange-red, and red to almost violet. The stigma and stamens appear from the end of the flower and are curved. The fruits are pear-shaped, about 1 cm (0.4 in) in length when ripe, and slightly translucent.

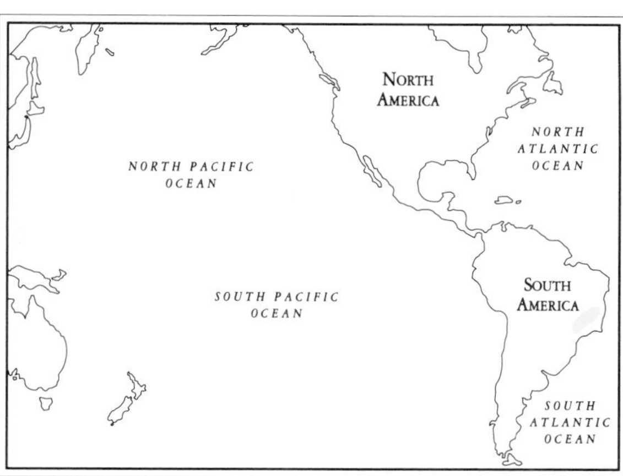

Culture: *Zygocacti* come from eastern Brazil, where they grow in the mountains. They are exceedingly popular house plants — particularly as they flower around Christmas time, hence their common name, Christmas Cactus — and are exceedingly easy plants to grow from seed or cuttings, although the latter method is the quickest. Cuttings rooted in the early part of the year will produce a few flowers by the following Christmas. As they are epiphytic plants, they enjoy a soil which consists mainly of leaf mould or peat. They prefer light shade and should be watered very freely during hot weather, and watering should be reduced only a little as temperatures fall. If kept dry when dormant they will withstand cool conditions, but prefer a minimum temperature of 10°C (50°F). They appreciate humid conditions, and like to receive overhead mist spraying.

Zygocactus truncatus

Zygocactus truncatus

Zygocactus truncatus

Common Name: Christmas Cactus.
Size: Length 60 cm (2 ft), width 45 cm (18 in).
Climate: Mediterranean to medium elevation.
Distribution: Eastern Brazil.
Flowering Time: Winter to early spring.
Description: See genus description page 193.

Zygocactus 'Snowflake'

Zygocactus truncatus var. *delicatus*

Zygocactus truncatus var. *delicatus*

Common Name: Christmas Cactus.
Size: Length 30 or 40 cm (12–16 in).
Climate: Low elevation.
Distribution: Eastern Brazil.
Flowering Time: Winter to early spring.
Description: As for *Zygocactus truncatus* (see genus description page 193), except that the stems and joints are not quite so strong. The flowers have protuberances at the base of the tube, and the flower colour varies, depending on the growing conditions. If grown in shade it is almost pure white, with only pink in the throat, but when grown in a sunnier situation, the pink colour is much more pronounced. *Zygocactus* 'Snowflake' is a selected cultivar commonly available, and is very similar to *Z. truncatus* var. *delicatus*.

Pests and Diseases

We are really very fortunate that cacti are not prone to attack from such a wide range of pests and diseases as many other types of plants. For one thing, in a greenhouse it is possible to control the environment far better than in the outside garden, although sometimes you may have in your garden useful natural predators. The majority of cacti have a tough epidermis, compared with many delicately leaved foliage plants, which reduces the number of pests and diseases that can cause serious trouble to your plants. There are some genera where the stem surface is so tough that sucking insects such as Mealy Bug cannot penetrate it, once the plant in question is well beyond the seedling stage. They might be troubled by such pests within their root system, but that is all.

The main pests are Mealy Bug, Red Spider Mite and Scale Insect. To a lesser degree Sciara Fly can be a nuisance for seedlings or during seed raising; they rarely trouble very mature plants.

Mealy Bugs are usually initially spotted by the appearance on the plant of little bits of fluffy white cotton, beneath which there will be small insects. In hot weather you can sometimes see them slowly moving. You can also find them in the roots of plants even though they are not visible on the plant itself. Plants that are overdue for potting on are more likely to be affected in this way. When you knock the plant out of its pot, you invariably find them on the surface of the root ball and on the interior of the pot itself. Mealy bugs can be easily removed from plants with the aid of a small artist's brush and a little alcohol. Having done this the plant must be shaded from direct sun for the rest of the day and sprayed with water prior to removing the shading on the day following. This method is perfectly satisfactory when you only have a few plants or for plants in the home. It is not a practical solution if you have more than around 50 plants. A dilute soap solution will kill off the adult pests but not the eggs.

Red Spider Mites are almost invisible to the naked eye but can be clearly observed scurrying around with the aid of a small magnifying glass. This pest can do more damage in a short space of time than any of the others. Most people usually first observe the tips of shoots or new growth going grey or pale brown. Invariably Red Spider Mite is the cause of the trouble. This pest thrives under hot dry conditions so regular overhead spraying of your plants reduces the chance of it occurring on your plants. Plants such as *Chamaecereus silvestri* and many *Coryphantha*, particularly young ones, are very prone to attack as their stem surfaces are not very tough. It is possible to use fumigants as recommended for many foliage plants, but the treatment needs repeating at least twice or even three times, at intervals of two to three weeks. The reason for this is that a fumigant only kills off the insects, not the eggs.

Scale Insects are usually very small limpet-like creatures that adhere to the body surface of cacti. They breed rapidly and if no action is taken will quickly cover a plant in a matter of months, to the point where the actual life of the plant is in danger. In the early stages before there are too many it is possible to remove them with a brush dipped in alcohol or even liquid soap, such as one of the household washing-up liquids. Again, as with this type of treatment for Mealy Bug, it is essential to shade the plant for a day and spray it with water before putting it back in the sun 24 hours later.

Sciara Flies or their grubs will quickly devour tiny cacti seedlings and they seem to breed well in peat-based soils. The warmth necessary for seed raising encourages them to breed rapidly. It is not advisable to use the stronger insecticides that are used on mature plants as it will kill the seedlings off as well as the Sciara Flies. I have found that they can be controlled quite satisfactorily in a seed-raising environment by means of a natural substance called pyrethrum. It can also be used against the other pests already referred to, but the results are not so long lasting compared with, for instance, systemic insecticides. In the case of cacti seedlings, we have found the aerosol form very useful at two or three day intervals, **but please be careful not to inhale it**. Spray the seedlings at a distance of about 30 cm (12 in) for a few seconds **only**, in the cool of evening and just prior to leaving the greenhouse.

Mealy Bugs, Red Spider Mites and Scale Insects can either be controlled in a greenhouse environment by the use of insecticides or by introducing the correct natural predators. I used in the United Kingdom, in rotation, three chemically different substances: one contact type and two systemics. The systemic insecticides are absorbed into the sap of the plant, whereby even a few weeks later it is still sufficiently active within the plant to kill off more 'sucking insects'. A range of insecticides invariably containing such chemicals as 'diazinon', 'dimethoate', 'formothion' and 'malathion' are obtainable under differing trade names in different countries. I suggest that you use types that are recommended for most house plants or general foliage plants. These will be perfectly safe to use on your cacti. I cannot over-emphasise the need to use three chemically different insecticides in rotation, so that you avoid problems later if these insect pests becoming resistant to them. If you use the same kind over and over again, this will happen. Do not think that a different brand name is sufficient, the insecticides must be chemically different. I prefer to dilute the insecticide with water according to the instructions and use it as an overhead drench. In other words use a watering can with a coarse rose on it.

It is always best to carry out the treatment in the cool of the evening, before locking up your greenhouse. The following morning and for the next few days your greenhouse should be well ventilated. Wire netting should be placed over the door if left open and over ventilators, otherwise you may adversely affect the health of any animal or bird that manages to get into your greenhouse. It is not advisable to remain in the greenhouse for more than a few moments for the next few days. Invariably this is not often mentioned on cans of insecticides, but one should never take chances with such lethal substances. When you apply the diluted insecticide always use long rubber gloves and rubber boots to avoid it coming into contact with your skin. If even more preventative clothing is required, this is usually stated on the can. If any of it does come in contact with your skin, wash it off immediately with hot soapy water. I do not consider any of the modern insecticides safe to use on plants inside the home.

In the United Kingdom and some other parts of the world, the use of predators is becoming more popular, and it does work very well when plants are grown on a commercial scale. However, when amateurs with a small collection of cacti use this method of control, the predators die off after they have completed their task. This means that when the pests appear again in the greenhouse or garden more predators must be purchased to do the job all over again. If you are interested in this healthier and safer method of pest control, I would strongly recommend that you buy or borrow a copy of *Biological Pest Control — The Glasshouse Experience* by N. W. Hussey and N. Scopes. It was originally published by Blandford Press in the United Kingdom in 1985, and was also distributed by Sterling Publishing Co., in the United States. It is a very detailed and easy-to-read book and actually lists the names and addresses of commercial producers of predators in Australia, Canada, Finland, France, Holland, Israel, Norway, Sweden, United Kingdom and the United States.

Freak Forms for the Collector

As with all hobbies, if something is rare or unusual enthusiasts want it, and that does not mean just rare species or varieties, but freak vegetative forms as well. These come basically in three ways — monstrous, crested and variegated.

A monstrous plant is basically one where a stem has produced multiple growing points, instead of just one at the end or apex of the stem. A crested (fasciated) plant is one where a head or stem has initially fanned out, whereby new cells continue to form along a continuous undulating line along the fan. In maturity they become very contorted like the internal structure of one's brain, and can become quite large. In fact, in some cases the fasciated form is so unusual it is almost impossible to relate it to the normal form of that species. Where a species is normally solitary, crests will continue growing for a very long time, without you having to do anything special to it, to ensure its survival. However, with a species that normally branches quite freely, crests can sometimes die out because many of them tend to produce normal shoots. If these normal shoots are not removed on a regular basis the crested section of the plant invariably disappears. The illustrations on pages 198 and 199 of *Opuntia vestita* and *Echinocereus melanocentrus* show normal shoots appearing. Once you can be certain that there is no sign of fasciation occurring, just cut them off with a sharp knife. These cuttings can always be dried off for a few days and rooted up. Sometimes these same normal shoots may at a later date produce a further fasciated branch. These monstrous and cristate forms are usually mutations, which can either appear as a seedling or as a branch on an otherwise normal plant.

A variegation is caused by an absence of chlorophyll on part or the entire surface of a plant. As a result, the plant has cream, pink, red, or even purplish markings amidst the normal part of the plant which is green because of the chlorophyll. If only part of a plant is affected it can survive as it is. However, if the entire plant is variegated it cannot survive. In these cases grafting is necessary in order to perpetuate it.

Monstrous, crested and variegated plants can still flower, and sometimes you even get fasciated flowers. Some of these freak forms are quite attractive, and if you like unusual things, are worth growing. The totally red variegated form of *Gymnocalycium mihanovichii* var. *friedrichiae* cv. 'Hibotan' is propagated on a vast scale in Europe and the Far East; it is usually grafted on to *Hylocereus* stock. Unfortunately this stock is very temperature sensitive and many thousands must be lost by purchasers when temperatures drop below 10° C (50° F). If *Opuntia*, *Cereus*, or *Trichocereus* stock is used this problem does not occur. As with monstrous and crested plants, any normal green shoots should be removed from your variegated plant. Otherwise the shoots will take over and your precious variegated plant may well disappear. These variegations can appear as minute seedlings or as a new part on a normal mature plant. Completely variegated seedlings will die out within a few days unless they are grafted. However, minute seedlings are difficult to graft — you almost require the skills of a surgeon — as they are very delicate to touch and cut at that size.

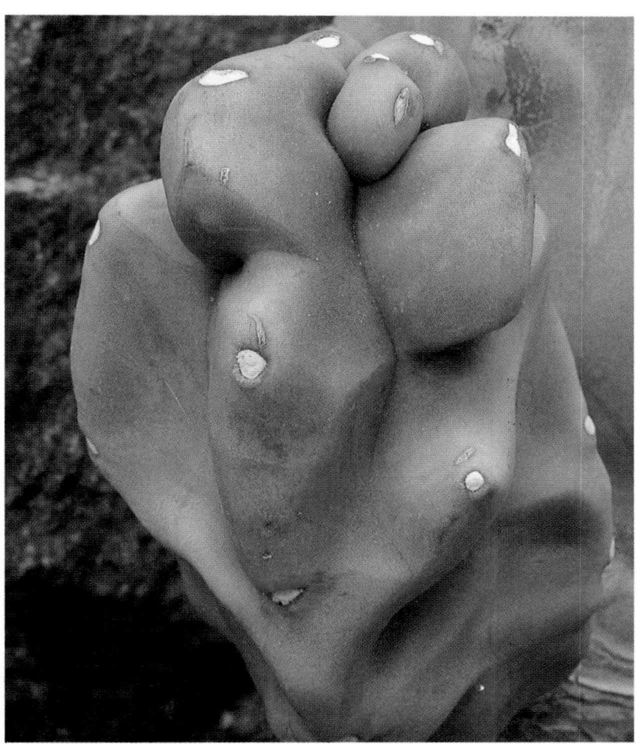

Lophocereus schottii *fa.* monstrosus *is a very well-known monstrous form that will grow to a comparable height to the normal plant. It is often called the Totem Pole Cactus and is ideal for landscaping in the right climate.*

Cereus peruvianus *fa.* monstrosus — *A monstrous stem of this species producing a perfectly normal flower.*

Cephalocereus senilis *fa.* cristata. *This will just grow into a mound of fasciated stems and is somewhat less hairy than the normal plant. The crest grows quite easily on its own roots and is propagated very easily.*

Opuntia vestita *fa.* cristata. *This is a very well-known crested species, which is commonly in cultivation grown on its own roots. As you can see normal stems are visible and they should be removed immediately.*

Rebutia haagei *fa.* variegata. *This is a plant I originally grew from seed and about six years later it started to produce a few variegated shoots.*

Echinocereus melanocentrus *fa.* cristata. *This fine fan-shaped crest appeared after a few years from one of the normal stems. However, in habitat at one particular location crested plants are far from uncommon.*

Gymnocalycium mihanovichii *var.* friedrichiae *cv. 'Hibotan'. This red variegated form is very well-known and being completely variegated it has to be grafted.*

A group of differing variegations of Gymnocalycium mihanovichii *var.* friedrichiae, *all grown as grafted plants.*

Gymnocalycium mihanovichii *var.* friedrichiae *cv.* 'Hibotan'. *Here is a scene of just part of one greenhouse bench in a Dutch nursery where up to 50 000 are propagated by grafting each year.*

Conservation and National Parks

People are more aware of the problems that arise when trying to ensure the survival of everything in this world for future generations than ever before. Animals and birds tend to get a lot of publicity in the media if a certain species faces extinction, particularly whales. Sadly plant life, with the exception of the rainforests, receives very little public attention. The cactus family, despite the laws on conservation, receives only sporadic publicity. These laws on exporting and importing plants have been in my opinion rather badly thought out, whereby at this point in time they are aiding the extinction of some species. At present good commercial nurseries, who produce seed and raise thousands of seedlings each year, are not being encouraged to propagate the really endangered species, as having done so it is virtually impossible to sell some of them afterwards. Nurseries are involved in so much red tape that the costs and delays from government departments makes the propagation of endangered species uneconomical. A way has to be found to make life easier and quicker for bona fide growers.

It is impossible to preserve all the native habitats for the future, and as it is thousands of species of plants are already extinct. In some ways cacti have been very fortunate as regards their habitats being destroyed by land being required for development purposes. As cacti in the main come from more arid areas, the habitats that have disappeared have been due to land being cleared for agricultural purposes, species that come from rocky and mountainous areas are largely unaffected. The only exceptions have been the miniature species; they are more popular with collectors, and are being stripped in their thousands by unscrupulous people. These have tended to be a number of the very slow growing species, which are difficult and time consuming to propagate commercially. These include genera such as *Ariocarpus, Aztekium, Pelecyphora* and *Sclerocactus.*

Although it is possible for large tracts of land to be put aside as National Parks, this will still only protect a limited number of species. At present these are mainly to be found in North America, where they are doing a marvellous job bringing to the notice of tourists from around the world the need for conservation.

In addition to this limited form of conservation, it is important that botanical gardens throughout the world should have accurately documented collections of plants, whereby they can share material, whether it be in seed or plant form. It would also help (if staffing allows) to sell documented seeds and plants to the general public, because the amateur enthusiasts around the world are a very important link for conservation. I personally feel that for the future, it is the interest of amateurs that will ensure no further species will become extinct. Once someone has been collecting cacti for three or four years it usually becomes a hobby for the rest of their life; the more these rare species of cacti are propagated and purchased by amateurs, the better.

It is imperative that plants are correctly labelled and that the label carries an accession number. An accession book should be kept, whereby each new plant added to your collection is given an accession number. Put in all the information you have on the plant in question; where it came from, date, whether purchased as a plant or grown from seed, and hopefully original habitat data, if this information was made available to you. When you pass on propagated spares to friends, this same information should go with them, and whether the spares have been produced vegetatively or from seed. This is why I would like to see botanical gardens making rare plants more generally available, once they have adequately distributed seeds and plants to other botanical gardens, and other well-known private collections of note. It is only by sharing spare material that we can try to ensure the survival of these wonderful plants for future generations.

It is equally important for the future that the species are kept true. When plants are propagated vegetatively there is no problem, but unfortunately a lot of seed that is produced for sale and exchange is often hybridised through carelessness. When plants are grown in the open air, this can be a real problem with some genera, whereas in a greenhouse it is possible to use fine screens to avoid accidental pollination by insects. The main requirement for pollinating cacti flowers are artists' brushes of differing sizes, to enable you to transfer pollen from the anthers to the stigma of another flower. If the same brush is to be used on a differing species within a few hours or days, it should be dipped in surgical spirit and left to dry, before using it again. The success of hand pollinating will depend on a number of factors. Invariably with many of the commoner species, seed can be produced by pollination between flowers on the same plant. However, with the less common species, it is necessary to pollinate between flowers on differing plants of the same species, and in some instances between different clones, otherwise you will not be successful.

Carnegiea gigantea *(Saguaro) in the Tucson Mountain section.*

The dead remains of a large Saguaro showing its internal structure.

Saguaro National Monument

The Saguaro National Monument is in two sections near Tucson, Arizona, in part of the Sonoran Desert that extends northwards from Mexico into the United States. In the late 1920s Homer Shantz, the then President of the University of Arizona, encouraged the state of Arizona to purchase a large reserve on the east side of the Tucson Basin, where dense stands of *Carnegiea gigantea* (Saguaro) occurred. When the Great Depression came, Arizona could not afford the payments for it, but fortunately the federal government stepped in financially and set up the monument in 1933. The Rincon Mountain section, east of Tucson, consists of 256 sq. km (99 sq. miles), whereas the Tucson Mountain section, 19 km (12 miles) west of the city, has an area of 62 sq. km (24 sq. miles). This latter section, if time is limited, is the best one to visit, as there are some very dense stands of Saguaro. In addition to these cacti, there are many other genera to be seen, including *Opuntia, Ferocacti, Echinocerei* and *Mammillaria.*

Both sections of the Saguaro National Monument have visitor or information centres, which are well stocked with a wide range of natural history books, displays, and dioramas with audio programmes. In addition you can obtain up to date information from the park rangers of plants in flower and where to look for them. Alternatively small groups of visitors can, if they wish, be taken on conducted tours and learn even more from the very knowledgeable park rangers.

A group of flowering-sized specimens of Mammillaria microcarpa *at the base of a large Saguaro.*

A dried cross-section of a Saguaro stem at the information centre.

Organ Pipe Cactus National Monument

The Organ Pipe Cactus National Monument is situated on the Arizona/Mexico border some 209 km (130 miles) south-west of Tucson and covers an area of about 1035 sq. km (400 sq. miles). Its eastern boundary is the Ajo range of mountains, where Mount Ajo attains a height of 1466 m (4808 ft). It is another part of the Sonoran Desert. Twenty-nine different species of cacti are to be found there, including the Saguaro. However, two cacti are particularly featured there, as few specimens are to be found outside the confines of the monument; they are *Lemaireocereus thurberi* (Organ Pipe Cactus) and *Lophocereus schottii* (Sonoita). These species are to be found growing in vast numbers in neighbouring parts of Mexico, but this is the most northern part of their range in habitat.

This monument is an outstanding natural preserve, where one of the earth's major ecosystems survives almost unspoiled. Recognising its significance, the United Nations in 1976 designated the monument as an International Biosphere Reserve, for conservation and research on protecting the life of the desert.

There is a visitor centre where literature can be purchased and information obtained, including advice from park rangers on where to go and where to camp.

The Big Bend National Park

The Big Bend National Park is situated in south-west Texas and borders the Rio Grande on its southerly flank, which is in fact the border with Mexico. This is where the vast Chihuahuan Desert extends northwards from Mexico, and on into parts of Texas and New Mexico. The proposal for a Big Bend National Park surfaced in 1935, but it was not

Opuntia bigelovii *(Teddy Bear Cholla) in the foreground, and in the background single stemmed Saguaro and branched Organ Pipe Cactus.*

A fine stand of Opuntia fulgida *(Chain-fruit Cholla).*

A 1 m (3 ft) diameter clump of Echinocereus stramineus *(Strawberry Hedgehog Cactus).*

until 1944 that Texas deeded 286 474 ha (707 894 acres) of the Big Bend country to the federal government. Mount Emery in the Chisos Mountains is the highest point within the park at 2388 m (7835 ft). The landscape and the vegetation is exceedingly varied and dramatic; with canyons on the Rio Grande, such as the Santa Elena Canyon, where the walls of it attain a height of about 500 m (1500 ft).

The visitor centre and park headquarters are at Panther Junction. It is also possible for visitors to stay in accommodation right in the middle of this vast park. You can also hire horses for trekking right up into the Chisos mountains, where *Echinocereus chisoensis* occurs. Alternatively, from just outside the park at Lajitas, raft trips can be made through the canyons, which involves shooting the rapids, and is yet another way to see a vast array of plant and animal life. Some of the finest specimens of *Hamatocactus hamatacanthus* can only be seen by this method, as they grow out of fissures on the vertical walls of the canyons, on both sides of the Rio Grande.

A 20 cm (8 in) high specimen of Echinocereus chloranthus *var.* russanthus.

To see a wide range of cacti in flower, April, May and June are very good months to do so. Because of the range of altitude within the park, the same species are to be seen in flower over quite a long period. Ask at the park headquarters, when you arrive, where to go to see the different species in bloom.

SYNONYMS

I have used in this book the most common generic and specific names. Listed below are other generic and specific names that have been applied to these same plants.

Botanical Name used in this book	Alternative Generic Name (SYNONYMS)	Alternative Specific Name (SYNONYMS)
Acanthocalycium thionanthum	*Lobivia*	—
Aporocactus flagelliformis	—	—
Ariocarpus kotschoubeyanus	*Roseocactus*	—
A. trigonus	—	—
Arrojadoa sp. *nova*	—	—
A. penicillata	*Cephalocereus*	
Astrophytum asterias	—	—
A. capricorne	—	—
A. myriostigma var. *coahuilensis*	—	—
Aztekium ritteri	—	—
Bergerocactus emoryi	*Cereus*	—
Blossfeldia liliputana	—	—
Borzicactus websterianus	—	—
Buiningia brevicylindrica	*Cephalocereus*	—
B. purpurea	*Cephalocereus*	—
Carnegiea gigantea	*Cereus* *Pilosocereus*	— —
Cephalocereus senilis	—	—
Cephalocleistocactus ritteri	*Cleistocactus* *Seticleistocactus*	—
Cereus hexagonus	—	—
C. peruvianus fa. *monstrosus*	—	—
Chamaecereus silvestrii	*Lobivia*	—
Cleistocactus dependens	*Seticleistocactus*	—
C. jujuyensis	—	—

Botanical Name used in this book	Alternative Generic Name (SYNONYMS)	Alternative Specific Name (SYNONYMS)
C. strausii	—	—
Coloradoa mesae-verde	*Echinocactus* *Sclerocactus*	—
Copiapoa haseltoniana	—	—
C. hypogaea	—	—
Corryocactus ayopayanus	*Erdisia*	—
Coryphantha echinus	—	*pectinata*
C. hesteri	*Escobaria* *Mammillaria*	—
C. minima	—	*nelliae*
C. sulcata	*Mammillaria*	—
C. vivipara var. *arizonica*	— *Mammillaria*	*arizonica* *arizonica*
C. vivipara var. *rosea*		*rosea*
Denmoza erythrocephala	—	—
Discocactus horstii	—	—
Disocactus eichlamii	*Chiapasia*	—
D. nelsonii	*Chiapasia*	—
Dolichothele longimamma	*Mammillaria*	—
Echinocactus grusonii	—	—
E. horizonthalonius	—	—
Echinocereus engelmannii var. *nicholii*	—	—
E. fendleri var. *bonkerae*	—	*fasciculatus* var. *bonkerae*
E. gentryi	—	—
E longisetus	—	—
E. melanocentrus	—	—
E. pectinatus var. *rigidissimus*	—	*rigidissimus*

SYNONYMS

Botanical Name used in this book	Alternative Generic Name	Alternative Specific Name
E. reichenbachii	—	*caespitosus*
E. stramineus	—	—
E. triglochidiatus	—	*paucispinus*
Echinofossulocactus lancifer	*Stenocactus*	—
E. violaciflorus	*Stenocactus*	—
Echinopsis spegazziniana	—	—
E. torrecillasensis	*Pseudolobivia*	—
Encephalocarpus strobiliformis	*Pelecyphora*	—
Epiphyllum anguliger	—	—
Epithelantha bokei	—	—
E. micromeris	—	—
Escobaria chaffeyi	*Gymnocactus*	—
E. roseana	*Gymnocactus*	—
E. runyonii	*Coryphantha* *Mammillaria*	—
Espostoa hylaea	—	—
Eulychnia saint-pieana	—	—
Ferocactus acanthodes	*Echinocactus*	—
F. emoryi	*Echinocactus*	—
F. histrix	— *Echinocactus*	*melocactiformis* *histrix*
F. latispinus	*Echinocactus*	—
F. macrodiscus var. *multiflorus*	*Echinocactus*	—
F. stainsii	*Echinocactus*	—
F. viridescens	*Echinocactus*	—
F. wislizenii	*Echinocactus*	—
Frailea pumila	—	—
F. pygmaea	—	—
Gymnocalycium asterium	—	*stellatum*
G. baldianum	—	*venturianum*
G. mihanovichii	—	—
G. moserianum	—	—
G. multiflorum	—	—
G. netrelianum	—	—
G. spegazzinii	—	—
G. valnicekianum	—	—
Haageocereus acranthus	—	—
H. laredensis	—	—

SYNONYMS

Botanical Name used in this book	Alternative Generic Name	Alternative Specific Name
Hamatocactus setispinus	*Glandulicactus* *Thelocactus*	—
H. uncinatus	*Glandulicactus* *Thelocactus*	— —
Harrisia simpsonii	*Eriocereus*	—
Heliocereus speciosus var. *amecamensis*	—	*amecamensis*
Hildewinteria aureispina	*Borzicactus* *Winteria* *Winterocereus*	—
Hylocereus undatus	—	—
Islaya krainziana	*Neoporteria*	—
Lemaireocereus thurberi	*Cereus* *Marshallocereus*	—
Leuchtenbergia principis	—	—
Lobivia acanthoplegma var. *roseiflora*	*Pseudolobivia*	—
L. bruchii	*Soehrensia*	—
L. culpinensis	—	—
L. famatimensis	*Hymenorebutia* *Reicheocactus*	—
L. huascha fa. *rubra*	*Helianthocereus*	—
L. jajoiana	*Hymenorebutia*	—
L. maximiliana	—	—
L. schreiteri	—	—
Lophocereus schottii	—	—
L. schottii fa. *monstrosus*	—	—
Lophophora williamsii	—	—
Mamillopsis senilis	*Mammillaria*	—
Mammillaria albilanata	—	*fuauxiana*
M. boolii	—	—
M. camptotricha	*Dolichothele*	—
M. candida	—	—
M. carmenae	—	—
M. couperae	—	—
M. guelzowiana	*Krainzia*	—
M. heyderi var. *hemisphaerica*	—	*hemisphaerica*
M. longiflora	*Krainzia*	—

SYNONYMS

Botanical Name used in this book	Alternative Generic Name	Alternative Specific Name
M. louisae	—	—
M. mammillaris	—	*simplex*
M. microcarpa	—	—
M. pennispinosa	—	—
M. saboae fa. *haudeana*	—	*haudeana*
M. sempervivi	—	—
M. theresae	—	—
M. zeilmanniana	—	—
Matucana crinifera	*Borzicactus*	—
M. intertexta	*Borzicactus* *Submatucana*	—
Melocactus azureus	—	—
M. matanzanus	—	—
M. violacea	—	—
Mila caespitosa	—	—
Myrtillocactus geometrizans	—	—
Neobesseya asperispina	*Escobaria* or *Coryphantha*	—
N. missouriensis	*Coryphantha* *Escobaria*	—
N. similis	*Escobaria*	—
Neochilenia hankeana	*Neoporteria*	—
N. reichii	*Neoporteria*	—
Neogomesia agavioides	*Ariocarpus*	—
Neolloydia conoidea	—	—
N. grandiflora	—	—
Neoporteria cephalophora	—	—
N. nigrihorrida	—	—
N. subgibbosa		
N. villosa	—	—
Notocactus crassigibbus	—	—
N. leninghausii	*Eriocactus*	—
N. uebelmannianus	—	—
Obregonia denegrii	*Strombocactus*	—
Opuntia acanthocarpa var. *thornberi*	*Cylindropuntia*	—

SYNONYMS

Botanical Name used in this book	Alternative Generic Name	Alternative Specific Name
O. ammophila	*Platyopuntia*	—
O. basilaris	*Platyopuntia*	—
O. bigelovii	*Cylindropuntia*	—
O. fulgida	*Cylindropuntia*	—
O. macrocentra	*Platyopuntia*	—
O. microdasys fa. *alba*	*Platyopuntia*	—
O. phaeacantha	*Platyopuntia*	—
O. platyacantha	*Tephrocactus*	—
Oreocereus doelzianus	*Morawetzia*	—
O. hendriksenianus var. *densilanatus*	—	*ritteri*
Oroya peruviana	—	—
Pachycereus grandis	—	—
P. pringlei	—	—
Parodia aureispina	—	—
P. chrysacanthion	—	—
P. gracilis	—	—
P. laui	—	—
P. mairanana	—	—
P. mutabilis	—	—
P. penicillata	—	—
P. thionantha	—	—
Pediocactus knowltonii	—	—
Pelecyphora aselliformis	—	—
P. pseudopectinata	—	—
Pereskia aculeata	—	—
P. bleo	—	—
Pfeiffera ianthothele	*Rhipsalis*	—
P. tarijensis	*Rhipsalis*	—
Pilosocereus glaucochrous	*Cephalocereus* *Pilocereus*	—
P. keyensis	*Cephalocereus* *Pilocereus*	—
P. palmeri	*Cephalocereus* *Pilocereus* *Carnegiea*	—
P. polylophus	*Cephalocereus* *Neobuxbaumia* *Pilocereus*	—
Pterocactus tuberosus	—	—

SYNONYMS

Botanical Name used in this book	Alternative Generic Name	Alternative Specific Name
Rathbunia alamosensis	—	—
R. kerberi	—	—
Rebutia costata	*Mediolobivia*	—
R. fiebrigii	*Aylostera*	—
R. minuscula fa. *violaciflora*	—	*violaciflora*
R. muscula	—	—
R. pulvinosa	*Aylostera*	—
R. senilis var. *sieperdaiana*	—	—
R. spegazziniana var. *atroviridis*	*Aylostera*	—
Rhipsalidopsis rosea (hybrid)	*Rhipsalis*	—
Rhipsalis houlletiana	—	—
R. pilocarpus	*Erythrorhipsalis*	—
Sclerocactus polyancistrus	*Thelocactus*	—
S. wrightii var. *roseus*	*Thelocactus*	—
Selenicereus grandiflorus var. *ophites*	—	—
S. hamatus	—	—
S. urbanianus	—	—
Stetsonia coryne	—	—
Strombocactus disciformis	—	—
Sulcorebutia hoffmanniana	*Lobivia*	—

SYNONYMS

Botanical Name used in this book	Alternative Generic Name	Alternative Specific Name
S. tiraquensis	*Rebutia*	—
Thelocactus bicolor var. *bolansis*	—	—
T. conothele var. *argenteus*	—	—
T. saussieri	—	—
Toumeya klinkerianus	*Turbinicarpus*	—
T. pseudo-macrochele	*Turbinicarpus*	—
Trichocereus fabrisii	*Helianthocereus*	—
T. shaferi	—	—
T. poco var. *albiflorus*	*Helianthocereus*	—
Weingartia neumanniana	—	—
W. riograndensis	—	*lanata* subsp. *riograndensis*
Wigginsia corynodes	*Malacocarpus*	—
W. sessiliflora	*Malacocarpus*	—
Wilcoxia albiflora	—	—
W. schmollii	—	—
Wittia amazonica	*Disocactus*	—
Zygocactus truncatus	*Schlumbergera*	—
Z. truncatus var. *delicatus*	*Schlumbergera*	—

Glossary

A

Acicular Needle-shaped.

Actinomorphic Radially symmetrical.

Aerial roots Roots forming on stems above ground level.

Apex/Apical Tip or upper part of a stem.

Appressed Lying flat against another surface.

Areole The area or organ from which spines, flowers, or new branches appear.

B

Banded Marked with stripes.

Basal pore Aperture at or near the bottom of a fruit from which seeds are discharged.

C

Centrals Stronger spines in the middle of a cluster of spines.

Cephalium A lateral or terminal head of hair and bristly spines on certain cacti from which flowers appear.

Ciliate Fringed or edged with hairs.

Cleistogamous In reference to flowers that can set seed without actually opening.

Corolla The interior part (perianth) of a flower that consists of petals.

Crest/Crested/Cristate A fasciated or malformed section of a plant, often in the form of an undulating fan.

Cultivar A plant that has become established in cultivation with its true habitat origin unknown. Such plants must have a 'Fancy Name' rather than a latinised one.

D

Dehisce The opening of a ripe fruit in order to discharge the seeds.

Dentate Leaves that have a toothlike margin.

Diurnal In reference to flowers that only open in the daytime.

E

Epidermis The surface skin of a plant.

Epiphyte/Epiphytic In reference to plants growing on other plants, which do not gain direct nourishment by so doing; in contrast to parasitic plants that do.

F

Fasciated Abnormally flattened stems or branches.

Felt/Felted An area of short fine hairs matted together.

Flower tube The narrow basal part of a flower which is joined together.

Form/Forma (fa.) Subdivision of a variety, which for taxonomic purposes has the smallest degree of differentiation to qualify for a name.

Funnel-form In respect of how many flowers widen out in an upwards direction from the actual flower tube.

Furrow Creased or longitudinal channel.

G

Genus Subdivision of a family, containing related species, and commencing with a capital letter.

Glabrous With a smooth surface.

Gland A secretory organ.

Glaucous Usually a bluish-grey waxy surface, similar to that found on certain fruits, such as grapes and plums.

H

Homonym A specific or generic name that has been used for two or more different organisms.

Hybrid The resulting progeny from seeds produced by transferring pollen from the flower of one plant to the stigma of another plant. This could be between different species, varieties, or even genera.

Hymen An inner tube or membrane formed within a flowering by filaments of the stamens uniting.

K

Keeled Possessing a projecting ridge.

L

Lax Loose, not tightly together.

M

Mealy White markings or spots.

Monotypic It can either mean a family containing only one genus, or as referred to in this book, a genus containing only one species.

Monstrous A malformation, usually with multiple growing points.

N

Nocturnal In reference to flowers that are open mainly at night.

O

Ovary The organ or female part of a flower, within which seeds form.

Ovoid Egg-shaped.

P

Pectinate In reference to spines formed or shaped like a comb.

Pendant Hanging down.

Perianth The floral envelope, consisting of calyx and corolla, which within the family CACTACEAE are virtually indistinguishable.

Petal Usually the inner part of the corolla; often brightly coloured.

Pistil The female reproductive part of a flower.
Porrect Spines extending horizontally from the plant.
Prostrate Lying along the ground.
Pseudocephalium Formation of some extra hair or spines, often as a sign of maturity, in the area from which flowers appear, but not possessing the same dense structure.

R
Radials Spines located on the outside of a cluster of spines.
Rib In cacti this refers to the raised ridges on the stems from which the areoles and spines appear.
Rotate Wheel-shaped.

S
Scales A modified overlapping leaf formation on the ovary and tube of a cactus flower.
Sepal The modified leaves forming the outer part of a flower.
Species A subdivision of a genus, which has greater importance than a variety.
Spine A leaf modified to become a sharp pointed structure.
Stigma The tip of the pistil, normally in the centre of a flower, which receives the pollen.
Subulate Awl-shaped.
Synonym (syn.) A name given to a genus or species that has already been validly named.

T
Taproot The main anchoring root of a plant.
Translucent Transmitting light, but not transparent.
Tubercle A conical protuberance.
Tuberculate Possessing tubercles.
Tuberous Thick, fleshy type of root.

V
Variety (var.) Subdivision of a species, and of lesser importance.

W
Whorl A ring or complete circle of organs, as with the arrangement or formation of the stamens in certain flowers.

X
Xerophyte/Xerophytic A plant that has adapted itself to survive on a very limited supply of water.

Z
Zygomorphic In reference to certain flowers that can only be divided into two symmetrical halves by a single longitudinal plane.

Bibliography

Anderson, E. F. *Peyote—The Divine Cactus*, University of Arizona Press, Tucson, 1980.

Backeberg, C. *Cactaceae*, Blandford Press, Dorset, 1977.

Barthlott, *Cacti*, Stanley Thornes Ltd, Cheltenham, 1982.

Benson, L. *The Native Cacti of California*, Stamford University Press, Stamford, 1969.

Britton, N. L. & Rose J. N. *The Cactaceae*, Carnegie Institution, Washington, 1931.

Craig, R. T. *The Mammillaria Handbook*, Abbey Garden Press, Pasadena, 1945.

Earle, W. H. *Cacti of the Southwest* (color edition), W. H. Earle, Phoenix, 1980.

Hussey, N. W. & Scopes, N. *Biological Pest Control—The Glasshouse Experience*, Blandford Press, Dorset, 1985.

Lamb, E. & Lamb, B. M. *The Illustrated Reference on Cacti & other Succulents* Volumes 1–5, Blanford Press, Dorset, 1955–1975.

Lamb, E. & Lamb, B. M. *Colourful Cacti of the Deserts*, Blandford Press, Dorset, 1975.

Lamb, E. & Lamb, B. M. *The Pocket Encyclopaedia of Cacti in Colour*, Blandford Press, Dorset, 1969.

Lamb, E. & Lamb, B. M. *Popular Exotic Cacti in Colour*, Blandford Press, Dorset, 1975.

Lamb, E. *The Exotic Collection* (monthly magazine), Sussex, 1947–1956.

Marshall, W. T. *Cactaceae*, Abbey Garden Press, Pasadena, 1941.

Marshall, W. T. & Woods, R. S. *Glossary of Succulent Plant Terms*, Abbey Garden Press, Pasadena, 1945.

Philip, G. *Concise Atlas of the World*, George Philip & Son Ltd, London, 1988.

Pilbeam, J. *Mammillaria—A Collector's Guide*, B. T. Batsford, London, 1981.

Rauh, W. *Kakteen an ihren Standorten*, Paul Parrey, Berlin, 1979.

Rausch, W. *Lobivia* (Volumes 1–3), Rudolf Herzig, Vienna, 1975.

Rowley, G. D. *The Illustrated Encyclopaedia of Succulents*, Salamander Books, London, 1978.

Rowley, G. D. *Name that Succulent*, Stanley Thornes Ltd, Cheltenham, 1980.

Warnock, B. H. *Wildflowers of the Big Bend Country, Texas*, Sul Ross State University, Alpine, 1970.

Weniger, D. *Cacti of the South-west*, University of Texas Press, Austin, 1977.

Further Reading

USEFUL PUBLICATIONS PRODUCED BY THE NATIONAL PARK SERVICE, UNITED STATES DEPARTMENT OF THE INTERIOR

Saguaro—Napier Shelton, based on the earlier work by Natt Dodge. 98 page, soft back book, mainly illustrated in colour.

Saguaro—A View of Saguaro National Monument and the Tucson Basin—by Gary Paul Nabham. 72 page, soft back book, mainly illustrated in colour.

Organ Pipe Cactus—Ajo Mountain Drive—16 page booklet in black and white.

Organ Pipe Cactus—Puerto Blanco Drive—16 page booklet in black and white.

The Big Bend—A History of the Last Texas Frontier—Ronnie C. Tyler. 288 pages, soft back book, well illustrated, but mainly in black and white.

Index of Common Names

Index of Botanical Names